Seven Deadly Sins

Seven Deadly Sins

Constitutional Rights and the Criminal Justice System

SECOND EDITION

Mark Denniston

Bruce Bayley

Molly Sween

David R. Lynch

CAROLINA ACADEMIC PRESS

Durham, North Carolina

Library of Congress Cataloging-in-Publication Data

Names: Denniston, Mark W., 1975- author. | Bayley, Bruce, author. | Sween,
Molly, author. | Lynch, David R. (David Richard), author.
Title: Seven deadly sins : constitutional rights and the criminal justice
system / by Mark Denniston, Bruce Bayley, Molly Sween, David R. Lynch.
Description: Second edition. | Durham, North Carolina : Carolina Academic
Press, LLC, [2021] | Includes bibliographical references and index.
Identifiers: LCCN 2021023817 (print) | LCCN 2021023818 (ebook) | ISBN
9781531018726 (paperback) | ISBN 9781531018733 (ebook)
Subjects: LCSH: Criminal justice, Administration of--United States. | Law
enforcement--United States. | Law enforcement--United States. | LCGFT:
Textbooks
Classification: LCC KF9223 .L96 2016 (print) | LCC KF9223 (ebook) | DDC
364.973--dc23
LC record available at https://lccn.loc.gov/2021023817
LC ebook record available at https://lccn.loc.gov/2021023818

Carolina Academic Press
700 Kent Street
Durham, North Carolina 27701
(919) 489-7486
www.cap-press.com

Mark Denniston
Thank you to my wife Christie and son Anders, and thank you also to students Cooper Maher and Hannah Olsen for research and editing assistance.

Bruce Bayley
To my beautiful wife Heather and my amazing boys, Erik and Logan—thank you for your love and support.

Molly Sween
Thank you to my family and friends for your love and support.

David Lynch
With much thanks as always from Dave to his best friend, Kathy.

All royalties from this textbook will go into the Raechale Elton Memorial Scholarship fund which was created by the family and friends of Ms. Elton to memorialize the life, vitality, and optimism of Raechale. She was pursuing her degree in criminal justice from Weber State University and was set to graduate in the Spring of 2006 before her life was tragically cut short. She chose this profession because she wanted to help troubled individuals and to make an impact on the world. This scholarship provides a lasting way for Raechale to continue doing good deeds in that it benefits future generations of criminal justice students who, like Raechale, plan to use their degree to make the world a better place.

Contents

Intolerance was a vice that the drafters of the Constitution could not "tolerate." Hence, in the very first amendment, they quickly provided protections for unpopular speech, minority religions, unpopular assemblies, and disliked media. Legislators sometimes try to make criminal acts of ideas or groupings which they and their constituents find to be highly offensive. Such statutory prohibitions are almost always constitutionally taboo.

The Constitution generally requires criminal justice actors to act with transparency. Officials are generally expected to avoid concealment, deception, evasion, and non-accountability. They are expected to refrain from subterfuge. This value finds expression in such practices as the recitation of Miranda *warnings, the "articulable facts" doctrine regarding police justification for stops, improper use of trickery to obtain confessions, mandated toleration of inmates acting as "jail-house lawyers" on behalf of others, and judicial hostility to attempts to cut off inmate communication with lawyers and others in the outside world.*

The Constitution conveys concerns regarding governmental intrusiveness when it prohibits unreasonable searches and seizures, the criminalization of elective abortions, and the outlawing of gay sex. Sources of constitutional resistance to governmental intrusiveness are located in the Fourth Amendment, as well as in the ever-controversial "general right to privacy" found in the shadow of the Bill of Rights.

Chapter Six • Intrusiveness in Law Enforcement and Corrections   151
Stories from the Field

Chapter Seven • Craftiness   181

We may want our criminal justice officials to play hard, but we also want them to play fairly. We want them to be smart but not too crafty, sly, clever, or cunning in getting the job done. The Constitution teaches us that abusive tactics like entrapment, suggestive line-ups, selective prosecution, double jeopardy, inflaming juror passions, or taking advantage of children as defendants are not to be tolerated. Fairness is an age-old ethical value.

The Constitution teaches us the value of avoiding cruelty by prohibiting modes of punishment that are barbaric, sentences that are disproportionately long, conditions of confinement that are too substandard, and executions that are unnecessarily torturous. This area of law teaches us the necessity of humaneness in our pursuit of justice.

The Drafters of the Constitution had a healthy dislike of authority. Subservience to the government was seen more as a vice than as a virtue. This reaction against subservience can be seen in constitutional guarantees to legal counsel [including even free counsel], trial by one's peers, jury nullification of unpopular laws, and the heavy burden of proof beyond a reasonable doubt. Some would even argue that the right to bear arms includes elements of this desire to avoid having to become too subservient.

Lessons in constitutional principles come not only from cases supposedly de-
cided correctly but also from cases in the past that now clearly constitute bad
decisions. The Supreme Court normally seems to do a good job at protecting
American constitutional values, but it has not always gotten its ethics right.

Introduction

Imagine legislators who create criminal statutes that go too far in suppressing vulgar and offensive expressions. Imagine a judge who secretly meets with a prosecutor to discuss a case. Or consider a police officer who is by nature very intrusive. Consider a jailer who is cruel. Picture a juror that is racist or a cunning prosecutor who gets a conviction by fighting dirty. Imagine a juror that is subservient to authority figures. These negative attributes—intolerance, subterfuge, intrusiveness, cruelty, favoritism, craftiness, and subservience to authority— are what could be termed "the seven deadly sins" of the American criminal justice system.

On the other hand, imagine a criminal justice professional who believes in always being humane and tolerant and knows that he or she must act with transparency. Imagine further that this same person values privacy rights, fair play, and equality. Further imagine that this person is sensitive to the corrupting nature of power, though she and her system colleagues are given extraordinary powers over life, liberty, and property. The person just mentioned could be described as adhering successfully to American constitutional criminal justice values.

Constitutional rights constitute a set of values to which nearly everyone in our society can agree. If America has a "civic religion," its doctrine would be found in the Constitution. There may be some in our society who do not like the protections provided by broad constitutional principles (specific and debatable interpretations aside), but such people seem to be exceedingly rare. In any event, the Constitution does not constitute a set of suggestions for those who work in the domain of criminal justice, but rather constitutes a set of mandates.

Properly approached, the study of constitutional rights can be ethically enlightening because it involves much more than the mere mechanical memorization of a body of black-letter rules and definitions. The careful examination of U.S. Supreme Court and other appellate opinions reveals not only the courts' final rulings on various matters, but provides in detail the (often moral) reasoning behind the courts' decisions. In explicating their rationales, judicial opinion writers typically address the opposite point of view before going on to explain why they sided the way they did. In the process of examining such decisions, students discover a court's ethical reasoning behind its ruling. Such cases make for excellent class discussion, and students often wind up teaching one another while making moral sense of the case with the instructor.

Seven core values in all will be examined in the chapters that follow. These virtues will be introduced via their mirror opposites, which we call the "seven deadly constitutional sins" of the criminal justice system. Once again, these negative attributes or "sins" are intolerance, subterfuge, intrusiveness, craftiness, favoritism, cruelty, and subservience to authority.

Each of these values shall span two chapters. One chapter per value shall be devoted to case law that will help to identify and illustrate the value in a constitutional sense. Then, a companion chapter shall provide a series of practical examples of the value played out in the real world of police and corrections.

Before we plunge into our book-length journey of examining many core values housed in the U.S. Constitution, we should pause to examine the role of the Supreme Court in this process of articulating our constitutional rights. The Court has the luxury of largely selecting the cases it wants to hear. It does not see itself as a court of error focused merely upon fixing legal (or factual) mistakes. Rather the Supreme Court largely sees its role as resolving disputes between lower courts. It is problematic when courts in one jurisdiction (e.g., state courts in New York) disagree on the meaning of the Constitution with courts in other parts of the country (e.g., the Tenth Circuit U.S. Court of Appeals, with jurisdiction over the states of Colorado, Oklahoma, Utah, etc.). When courts across the country disagree about the meaning of the Constitution (or other laws), the U.S. Supreme Court is more likely to agree to hear a further appeal by granting a request for a **writ of certiorari** (an order to hear an appeal). Granting a request for a writ of certiorari, or sometimes more simply referred to as "granting cert." is the mechanism the Court uses to agree to hear an appeal from a lower federal or state court. It takes four of the nine justices on the Supreme Court to agree to issue a writ of certiorari. For some perspective, the Court typically receives over 8,000 certiorari petitions annually, but agrees to hear fewer than 80 cases, so less than 1% of the requests it receives. In short, the Court is not trying to fix mistakes in these cases, but rather to bring uniformity and consistency to the law, across the entire country, especially regarding interpretation of the Constitution.

When the Supreme Court interprets the Constitution, such as when it considers whether to strike down a federal or state statute (or even the legality of a search by a local police officer), it is using the power of **judicial review** (the power to strike down a law or an act of a government official as unconstitutional). While the authority of the Court to use its power of judicial review to declare a law unconstitutional has been long established, the Court did not always see its role in using judicial review as it is now understood in the twenty-first century. Particularly, the Court did not interpret the Bill of Rights as applying against state and local governments for most of American history. You may be surprised to learn that this current understanding of the Constitution, which we take for granted today, is only approximately 60 years old.

Despite the Bill of Rights dating back to 1791 (when the first ten amendments to the Constitution were ratified by the states), a series of crucial changes in the understanding of these ten amendments drastically shifted the scope and application of these values. The three essential ingredients contributing to the shift in understanding of the Constitution are (1) the Bill of Rights, (2) the Fourteenth Amendment to the Constitution, and (3) the Due Process Revolution of the 1960s.

First, many values which we hold as particularly relevant to the criminal justice system (such as freedom of speech, the free exercise of religion, protection against unlawful searches and seizures, the right against self-incrimination, and rights to speedy trials, impartial juries, and protections against cruel and unusual punishments) were articulated in the Bill of Rights. However, originally these rights did not apply in the sense that we have come to understand over the past sixty years. Closer examination of the text of the First Amendment shows why:

> Congress shall make no law respecting an establishment of religion, or prohibiting the free exercise thereof; or abridging the freedom of speech, or of the press; or the right of the people peaceably to assemble, and to petition the Government for a redress of grievances.

The first word of the First Amendment is "Congress." The rights articulated in the First Amendment then are literally shielded only against violations by "Congress" (and the federal statutes and federal agents Congress might authorize). State actors, such as state legislatures, governors, local prosecutors, police, and corrections officials had no obligation to ensure the provisions of the Bill of Rights. In the case of *Barron v. Baltimore*, 34 U.S. 243 (1833) the Supreme Court held that the Bill of Rights and its protections did not apply to state and local governments. This was due in part to the states each having their own individual state constitutions, most of which include similar rights as contained in the Bill of Rights. State actors were thus not lawless; rather it was originally understood that state and local officials had to follow the similar rights as articulated in state constitutions and interpreted by state courts. There were similarities in constitutional rights across states, much as there is today in criminal law, but also significant variations too since states were not bound to follow constitutional precedents in other states or federal courts. The sculpting of fundamental national constitutional rights (as we have come to understand them), afforded to all persons, would not occur until 170 years after the adoption of the Constitution during the Due Process Revolution.

A second critical element necessary before that could happen, however, was the ratification of the Fourteenth Amendment following the Civil War. One of its most critical provisions, the Due Process Clause, reads "nor shall any state deprive any person of life, liberty, or property, without due process of law." Key are the words "any state," making clear that state governments, not just Congress, are also required to provide due process of law. The Due Process Clause encompasses protections against arbitrary and vague laws and provides "any person" in our country with both procedural and substantive due process—including the strict adherence to fair trial procedures and protection of fundamental rights (such as those in the Bill of Rights). The Fourteenth Amendment's Due Process Clause served as the vehicle by which **incorporation** (the process of applying to the states most, but not all, of the provisions in the Bill of Rights) was later achieved during the Due Process Revolution.

The third and final element in our current understanding of the Constitution is the **Due Process Revolution**. Generally considered to have begun in the early 1960s, the Due Process Revolution occurred when the Warren Court (the Supreme Court during the era in which Earl Warren served as Chief Justice of the Supreme Court) used the power of judicial review to begin applying the Bill of Rights to the states, expanded the scope of those constitutional rights, and crafted remedies to enforce those rights. The Due Process Revolution empowered the Court to oversee criminal justice processes in the states and review the actions of state and local government officials.

Today most of the protections of the Bill of Rights are applicable to all persons at all levels of government, regardless of the state in which one resides. In addition to incorporating most of the provisions of the Bill of Rights into the Due Process Clause, and thus making them applicable to states, the Warren Court also took steps to ensure these rights were enforced through effective deterrents against unconstitutional behavior. The Warren Court crafted specific consequences should an individual's rights be violated, such as the exclusionary rule, which bars unlawfully obtained evidence from being admissible in criminal court proceedings.

While the Warren Court receives the bulk of the credit for expanding constitutional rights and remedies during the Due Process Revolution, this is not a process that ended decades ago. Rather, the Court continues to expand the interpretation of constitutional rights. For instance, as recently as 2019 in *Timbs v. Indiana*, 586 U.S. ___, 139 S. Ct. 682, the Supreme Court clarified that the Excessive Fines Clause in the Eighth Amendment was incorporated and thus applied to and constrained state and local governments. The Court reasoned that the right against excessive fines has historically been central to the fundamental scheme of ordered liberty within the United States and is deeply rooted in the nation's history and tradition. As such the state of Indiana was not free to ignore the Court's precedents interpreting the Excessive Fines Clause, as the Supreme Court of Indiana had maintained.

So what types of interpretive approaches guide the Supreme Court in its decisions regarding constitutional rights? Two perspectives predominate: **originalism** and **living constitution** approaches. Adherents of an originalist approach believe the Supreme Court's authority comes directly from the amendment ratification process — language going through Congress and then the several state legislatures pursuant to Article V of the Constitution. The originalist perspective favors textual and historical analysis of constitutional language and emphasizes the original public meaning of provisions in the Constitution. Functionally, criminal justice reforms should occur through drafting of legislation, or even new constitutional amendments, as opposed to expanding the scope of implied rights via judicial interpretation. This perspective often coincides with the goals of crime control and tends toward prosecution-oriented outcomes.

An alternative living Constitution approach is informed by the recognition that the Framers of the Constitution intentionally employed vague and expansive language. Implicit in the broad wording of the Constitution is the understanding the Court should adopt evolving and adaptive interpretations of constitutional rights. This perspective believes in flexible principles informed by cultural and political changes in society leading to a dynamic and evolving understandings of constitutional rights. The Supreme Court should act as guardian of political minorities, protecting those such as criminal defendants unable to effectively resort to the elected political branches for redress of violations of human dignity. It is appropriate for courts to consciously implement needed criminal justice reforms either through expansion of old constitutional rights or recognition of new implied rights.

As you can see from the above discussion, the function and scope of the Constitution has been open to debate. Its meaning has been substantially revised throughout American history. Central to discussions of justice and what constitutes fair and equitable behavior are questions of how the courts generally, and the Supreme Court in particular, interpret and enforce constitutional rights.

This second edition of *Seven Deadly Sins: Constitutional Rights and the Criminal Justice System* includes updates to all outstanding cases that had yet to be decided when the first edition of this textbook was published. Additionally, several new cases (primarily in odd chapters) and vignettes (primarily in even chapters) have been added to the second edition of this textbook:

- Chapter 1 updates free exercise litigation concerning polygamy, expands the discussion of RFRA and RLUIPA, and features a new case, *Holt v. Hobbs*, discussing the application of RLUIPA to religious freedom claims by prisoners.
- Chapter 2 adds a new vignette regarding food allergies for incarcerated persons.
- Chapter 3 adds a discussion of the application of the *Miranda* case to physical evidence in *U.S. v. Patane.*
- Chapter 4 adds new vignettes exploring inmate pen pals as well as the execution drugs used in Nevada.
- Chapter 5 is reorganized and includes three new cases, *Carpenter v. U.S.*, concerning privacy protections for cell phone location data maintained by wireless providers, *Arizona v. Gant*, limiting searches incident to arrest involving automobiles, and *Utah v. Strieff*, expanding the attenuation exception to the exclusionary rule.
- Chapter 6 adds new vignettes that discuss searches of transgendered inmates and using drones in corrections applications.
- Chapter 8 includes new vignettes about correctional officers smuggling contraband and former inmates attempting to break back into jail.
- Chapter 11 adds *State v. Houston*, with a discussion of how states are responding to the Supreme Court's juvenile sentencing jurisprudence.
- Chapter 12 adds new and timely vignettes discussing information regarding the incarceration of offenders during the COVID-19 pandemic and using the "Baby Shark" song to retaliate against inmates.

- Chapter 14 updates litigation surrounding prosecution for distributing jury nullification fliers.
- Chapter 15 includes an expanded discussion of *Buck v. Bell* as well as the formal overruling of the *Korematsu* case in *Trump v. Hawaii*.

The discussion of the cases in the following chapters are designed to help students quickly identify not just the *what* of the law, but the *why* of the law as well. Instead of lengthy excerpts, the strategy is to use everyday language so that the legal issue, court holding, and explanation of that reasoning are all readily ascertainable. The vignettes on law enforcement and corrections officials are also designed to give readily understandable examples of recent situations that reveal the ethical and moral dilemmas facing officers, administrators, and courts. The authors hope that by the end of the book students have not only been introduced to the content of the law, but also have the tools to begin to evaluate the law for themselves. We hope instructors and students alike will begin to ask questions like has the Supreme Court gone too far in the last 60 years with the Due Process Revolution through overly broad interpretations and applications of the Constitution, or not far enough to protect the rights of minorities and criminal defendants? Thus, discussion questions are provided following each case to help prompt such conversations. It is by asking such questions, and reflecting upon the legal arguments and reasoning the Court has provided, that we hope to enable students to articulate and reflect critically upon the competing values implicit in constitutional interpretation so that students will learn to value, respect, and defend these constitutional rights when in a position to do so.

Seven Deadly Sins

Chapter One

Intolerance

If she entered a church, trusting to share the Sabbath smile of the Universal Father, it was often her mishap to find herself the text of the discourse. She grew to have a dread of children; for they had imbibed from their parents a vague idea of something horrible in this dreary woman.

—Nathaniel Hawthorne, *The Scarlet Letter*

Of all the vices with which the Founders concerned themselves, perhaps none took center stage more than that of **intolerance**. Tolerance of unpopular ideas, religions, and assemblies found protection in the First Amendment to the United States Constitution. The Founders almost certainly considered freedoms of speech, religion, press, and association to be paramount among any potential declarations of basic human rights.

Today's practice among many elites, in and outside of academia, to champion concepts such as "diversity" and "inclusiveness" may seem to many observers to be nothing more than just the latest fad. But, in a way it is simply an attempt to express a very old American value.

This chapter and the next will explore ways in which the American criminal justice system honors the notion of tolerance. Constitutional law, via legal case decisions, shall be set down in this chapter. The chapter that follows shall present practical case studies that illustrate the vice of intolerance in the areas of policing and corrections. This pattern—a chapter on constitutional law followed by a chapter containing practical case studies—shall be the pattern used throughout the book.

Let us begin our examination of the constitutional taboo of intolerance by first looking at intolerance towards unpopular speech. We will then move on to other areas involving the intersection of intolerance and the criminal justice system.

Unpopular Speech

Warm and fuzzy speech needs no constitutional protection. It is unpopular speech that needs courts of law to give it safe haven, when popularly elected legislatures are too cowardly or too unreflective to do so. The First Amendment to the federal Constitution states that, "Congress [now thought to implicate state governments as well] shall make no law … abridging the freedom of speech." This would of course include "hate speech." Some countries have chosen to criminalize certain types of hateful speech. In Sweden, for example, you can be arrested for speaking out against homosexuals. In Germany, you can be arrested for publicly expressing anti-Jewish sentiments. But, in the United States, we have the First Amendment to worry about. Hence, there can be no crime in the United States for **hate speech** (merely expressing hatred for people on account of their race, religion, gender, sexual orientation, or any other attribute). However, this area can at times get a little tricky. As the case that follows illustrates, a finding of hate can be a factor in sentencing someone whose actions go beyond the mere peaceful presentation of an unpopular idea.

People v. Rokicki
718 N.E.2d 333 (Ill. App. Ct. 1999)

Ronald Rokicki entered a Pizza Hut restaurant in Illinois to order a pizza. While there he became very angry at a certain employee, culminating in his making a horrific "scene." He was subsequently convicted of disorderly conduct and sentenced.

What had made Rokicki so upset at the restaurant was his belief that the employee taking his order and handling his food was gay. Rokicki maintained that this seemingly gay employee had touched his food after having put his fingers in his mouth. This greatly upset Rokicki, and Rokicki insisted upon a refund. Rokicki also went on a ten-minute-long rant, pounding the counter while yelling words like "Molly Homemaker" and "faggot" while also pointing repeatedly at the employee. Needless to say, Rokicki's behavior disrupted the operations and atmosphere of the entire establishment. The employee who was the specific object of Rokicki's tirade was terrified. The manager refunded Rokicki's money, and Rokicki left.

Rokicki was later arrested (the store manager reported his license plate number to the police) and charged with disorderly conduct. But, interestingly, Rokicki was also charged under an enhanced penalty provision of Illinois law which provided for longer penalties for various offenses (including disorderly conduct) when the motive for the underlying crime was hatred due to someone's perceived religion, gender, race, or sexual orientation. Because of this enhanced penalty provision, Rokicki wound up getting two full years of probation as well as 100 hours of community service.

On appeal, Rokicki argued that he was being punished extra solely because of his opposition to same-sex relationships and for having expressed his opinions regarding the same. He maintained that his beliefs and expressions on the subject of sexual orientation are protected under the concept of freedom of speech.

So, the issue becomes whether a state can create an enhanced penalty situation for disorderly conduct (or certain other crimes) without violating the First Amendment when the motive behind the crime was hatred due to someone's perceived sexual orientation. The Illinois appellate court ruled that this enhanced penalty provision was indeed lawful and constitutional.

The court agreed with Rokicki that nobody can be punished (extra or otherwise) for having certain views or for calmly and reasonably expressing those views in public. This protection would cover situations involving the peaceful communication of hateful views about gay people. However, Rokicki was not being punished for hating gay people or for peacefully communicating his contempt of gay people. Rather, he was being punished for disrupting the operations of the restaurant, something he clearly had no right to do. Once having been proven guilty of disorderly conduct, the question then becomes what factors can properly be considered in ascertaining an appropriate sentence. May courts (or a legislature) consider the motive for a crime in deciding punishment? Of course they may; they have routinely done so for centuries. A thief stealing out of hunger is often properly punished less severely than one who steals out of plain greed. Motive has always mattered to judges when it comes to crafting proper sentences and legislatures (through enhanced penalty statutes) may consider motive in deciding proper sentencing legislation.

> ## Discussion Questions
>
> 1. In certain countries in Europe, merely expressing hateful ideas can be crimes in and of themselves. For example, saying bad things about Jews in Germany or gays in Sweden can get you arrested. Would you favor such laws in the United States?
>
> 2. Do you agree with the notion of "enhanced penalty statutes" for crimes which are motivated by certain types of hate?

Rokicki may have lost his battle in avoiding the **enhanced penalty statue** (allowing for an extra penalty at sentencing due to the **motive** or inspiration for the crime), but the next case shows that defendants being punished for hateful ideas are often victorious, despite their offensive expressions.

Texas v. Johnson
491 U.S. 397 (1989)

Johnson and his friends did not like Republicans, or corporate America, or Ronald Regan. So, at the 1984 Republican National Convention in Dallas he and his associates organized an outdoor protest. The group engaged in various antics finally culminating in Johnson's lighting an American flag on fire while he and the others chanted, "America the red, white, and blue, we spit on you." Nobody or no property was harmed by the burning (other than the flag itself which belonged to the group). However, many onlookers were deeply offended, and one of them even collected the remnants of the flag and buried them. Johnson was arrested by the local police on the scene and charged with "desecration of a venerated object" (basically, flag burning) in violation of Texas law. Johnson was convicted and sentenced to one year in prison and a $2,000 fine.

The issue on appeal became whether flag burning done for political protest purposes was a protected form of free speech. The state argued that many people hold the flag so sacred that Johnson's actions were tantamount to **fighting words** (abusive epithets or personalized insults which are likely to elicit an immediate breach of peace or retaliatory violence from the person to which such utterances were addressed). Some background on the fighting words exception is appropriate here. In *Chaplinsky v. New Hampshire*, 315 U.S. 568 (1942), the defendant Walter Chaplinsky, a religious protester, called the town marshal "a damned fascist," resulting in his arrest under a state ordinance prohibiting offensive or derisive speech. The Supreme Court upheld Chaplinsky's conviction, holding that his First Amendment rights to freedom of speech had not been violated, since his insults constituted fighting words. This type of speech is not protected under the First Amendment.

Later, the Supreme Court clarified that the fighting words exception applied only to personally abusive epithets as opposed to broad, offensive statements. These epithets must be so personally offensive that they would inherently provoke a violent reaction. However, to constitute fighting words the nature of the target and their threshold for such utterances must be considered. In *Lewis v. City of New Orleans*, 415 U.S. 130 (1974), Justice Powell wrote a concurring opinion noting that a police officer subject to harmful insults may be expected, by the very nature of their occupation, to have a higher threshold of restraint. Officers are less likely than the layperson to respond to such epithets with violence, and as such, minor insults directed toward police should not be considered fighting words (even if they might be for an ordinary citizen).

The Supreme Court did not buy the state's argument that flag burning should fall within the fighting words exception. It said that no reasonable observer would have interpreted Johnson's actions as a personal insult or as a challenge to exchange blows. Of course, it could be argued that the flag is something which should be protected from desecration even if the peace is not being directly threatened by its burning. The Court, however, considered the flag burning to be not only a form of speech but a form of political speech at that. Of all the types of speech that are protected, **political speech** is the most protected of all since it is being made against the very government that has the means and cover to most effectively oppress the speech-maker. The Court said that the government and society must allow the free expression of ideas that they find repugnant, even when the expression takes the form of burning the flag. "If there is any fixed star in our constitutional constellation, it is that no official, high or petty, can prescribe what shall be orthodox in politics, nationalism, religion, or other matters of opinion or force citizens to confess by word or act their faith therein." Ultimately, the Court reasoned that, "We do not consecrate the flag by punishing its desecration, for in doing so we dilute the freedom that this cherished emblem represents."

Chief Justice Rehnquist, writing for the three dissenters, had failed to convince the majority of the Court when he wrote that, "The flag is not simply another 'idea' or 'point of view' competing for recognition in the marketplace of ideas. Millions and millions of Americans regard it with an almost mystical reverence regardless of what sort of social, political, or philosophical beliefs they may have." Rehnquist believed that burning a flag was regarded by many, especially military veterans, as "evil" and that legislatures should be free to prohibit evil conduct "whether it be murder, embezzlement, pollution, or flag burning."

So we see that unlike Rokicki, who had been punished not for his speech *per se* but rather for disrupting the ambience of a private restaurant, Johnson could not be punished for the sole act of self-expression, no matter how reprehensible the content of his "speech" was. In the view of the majority of the Supreme Court, Johnson simply could not be punished for merely peacefully (albeit dramatically) expressing his views.

Discussion Questions

1. What types of speech, other than political speech, should courts be especially protective of?

2. Could a state, despite the *Johnson* case, make it a crime for someone to wash his/her car with an American flag because no rag was handy?

3. Do you know anybody who regards the flag with "almost mystical reverence," like the dissenters wrote? Who?

The next case arguably takes hate speech to a new level. Here, the protestors sink to a new low. The Supreme Court considers how far we have to go to tolerate those who are incredibly intolerant. Though it is not a criminal case, it does have clear implications for those who might like to criminalize "hate speech" here in the United States, as has been done in many other areas of the world.

Snyder v. Phelps
562 U.S. 443 (2011)

Frank Phelps was the pastor of Westboro Church in Topeka, Kansas. The church taught that God hates homosexuality and was angry with America in general and with the U.S. military in particular for being too tolerant of gays. The church also disliked the Roman Catholic Church for various reasons.

Marine Lance Corporal Matthew Snyder, a Roman Catholic, died while serving his country in Iraq. His funeral took place at his family's Roman Catholic church located in Maryland.

The Westboro Church decided to stage a protest in connection with Matthew Snyder's funeral. Members of the Westboro Church gathered on public land more than 1,000 feet from the church. They held up signs that said such things as, "Thank You God for dead soldiers," "Pope in Hell," and "God hates fags." They also sang hymns and recited Bible verses during their 30-minute presentation. Nobody in the church could hear the protestors, and the funeral was not disrupted in any way. Nevertheless, the dead soldier's father became very distraught upon watching a video of the demonstration on television news (initially resulting in his vomiting followed later by clinical depression). He sued the Westboro Church for "intentional infliction of emotional distress," a civil wrong under Maryland law. A jury awarded him $2.9 million dollars in compensatory damages plus an additional $8 million dollars in punitive damages (**punitive damages** are awarded in civil cases when the civil wrong is akin to a criminal act — the purpose of the award is to punish the "criminal-like" defendant rather than just make the victim whole).

So the issue on appeal became whether or not the protestors, who stayed on public land and out of hearing of the funeral participants, can be held liable for engaging in such arguably outrageous and hateful speech. In helping it decide this question, the Supreme Court focused on whether the speech was purely a private attack aimed to inflict pain solely on the family or whether it was more in the nature of commentary regarding broad issues of public concern. Because it found it to be the latter, it held that it was a constitutionally protected form of free speech.

"While these messages may fall short of refined social or political commentary, the issues they highlight — the political and moral conduct of the United States and its citizens, the fate of our Nation, homosexuality in the military, and scandals involving the Catholic clergy — are matters of public import." The Court went on to say that "the point of all speech protection ... is to shield just those choices of content that in someone's eyes are misguided, or even hurtful." Speech made on public land, in a peaceful manner, involving large issues of public concern, cannot be stifled in any way, even if it causes private or public pain. "We cannot react to that pain by punishing the speaker."

In his dissent, Justice Alito argued that the dead soldier's father was not a public figure. The church chose to specifically target the son, Matthew Snyder, because he was Catholic and because he was in the military. This was in effect very personal. Any public commentary was of "such slight social value" that it was dwarfed by the harm intentionally perpetrated on the family. Alito concluded that, "In order to have a society in which public issues can be openly and vigorously debated, it is not necessary to allow the brutalization of innocent victims like petitioner. I therefore respectfully dissent."

Alito of course lost this debate. Hate speech, even outrageous hate speech done in very poor taste, is still speech and is therefore protected, at least when it is "peaceful" and addresses issues of public concern.

Discussion Questions

1. Why must speech be tolerated even when it causes some people a lot of pain?

2. If the father of the dead Marine punched Pastor Phelps out for what he did, would you as a juror member be tempted to acquit the father at his assault trial?

Up to this point, we have not yet discussed "obscene speech." Should it, like hate speech, be protected? Some say, "Yes." The Supreme Court has always said, "No." But, what is the definitional line between merely naughty speech and speech that is obscene? Is all pornography obscene? What about classical paintings of nudes? What about child pornography? The next case provides us with a three-prong test to help us figure out what it means for speech to be "obscene."

Miller v. California
413 U.S. 15 (1973)

Marvin Miller was a peddler of pornography. He got in trouble when he started aggressively sending promotional pamphlets via mass mailings to people who had expressed no interest in receiving such promotions. He did this in an attempt to drum up business. His pamphlets included graphic pictures of sex between men and women which he had pulled from the books and the film he was offering for sale. One person who received such a mailing got upset and complained to the police. Miller was arrested and convicted of violating the state's obscenity laws, which banned the dissemination of obscene materials.

The first issue the Court had to decide was whether the First Amendment offered any protection to obscene speech. Like all Supreme Courts before it, the Court ruled that obscene speech was simply not protected by the Constitution. Realizing that some might see the Court's lack of interest in preventing states from cracking down on obscenity as itself a type of "repression," the Court maintained that "To equate the free and robust exchange of ideas and political debate with commercial exploitation of obscene material demeans the grand conception of the First Amendment and its high purposes in the historic struggle for freedom." It said that enlisting the First Amendment in the defense of material of no redeeming value whatsoever would be "a misuse of the great guarantees of free speech and free press."

But what exactly is "obscene speech"? This was the next and harder issue for the Court. The Court admitted that it lacked an ability to define "obscenity" with "ultimate, god-like precision." Yet, it felt a duty to address what has historically been "the intractable obscenity problem" and said that "no amount of fatigue" should tempt it to avoid its duty.

After rejecting some earlier, less than satisfactory definitions, the Court ultimately came down with a **three-prong test for obscene speech** that juries henceforth must use in deciding whether allegedly vulgar speech was indeed genuinely obscene. "The basic guidelines for the trier of fact must be: (a) whether the average person, applying contemporary community [by that the court meant local] standards would find that the work, taken as a whole, appeals to the prurient [lust-craving] interest; (b) whether the work depicts or describes, in a patently offensive way, sexual conduct ... ; and (c) whether the work, taken as a whole, lacks serious literary, artistic, political, or scientific value."

For example, the Court said that obviously offensive depictions of "ultimate sexual acts" would probably qualify under its definition. So, too would "patently offensive representation or descriptions of masturbation, excretory functions, and lewd exhibitions of the genitals." Of course, it would be up to a local jury using contemporary and local standards to decide.

So, under the Supreme Court's vision, what very well might be obscene in Jackson, Mississippi, might not be obscene in San Francisco, California. "People in different States vary in their tastes and attitudes, and this diversity is not to be strangled by the absolutism of imposed [national] uniformity." To attempt such uniformity would, in the Court's opinion, "be an exercise in futility."

Having articulated its three-prong test, the Supreme Court vacated the jury verdict so that the California courts could judge Miller's case using the newly fashioned criteria. The case was remanded to the California Superior Court for further review and assessment.

Justice Douglas in his dissent wrote that he could find nothing in the First Amendment that treats "obscene" books, pictures, etc. any differently than any other types of publications. In his view, freedom of the press covers all such publications equally. He argued that "What shocks me may be sustenance for my neighbor.... To many the Song of Solomon [in the Bible] is obscene." Justice Douglas' solution was for the people to define obscenity via a constitutional amendment, if it is even to be defined. He did not feel that judges are up to the job, nor did he believe they have the constitutional authority to do so.

Discussion Questions

1. Why should the definition of what is obscene take into account local community standards? Do you agree that it should?

2. Do you agree with the dissenter who thinks even obscene speech should be protected by the First Amendment?

3. Can you think of an example of material that flunks the first two prongs of the obscenity test (making it thus-far obscene) but which might be saved by the third prong because it has literary, artistic, political, or scientific value?

What about using the "F-word" in public? Should that word be considered obscene enough to cause its very utterance to automatically become a criminal act? In *Cohen v. State*, 403 U.S. 15 (1971), Paul Cohen was convicted in Los Angeles for disturbing the peace when he was spotted in the corridor of a county courthouse wearing a jacket bearing the words, "Fuck the Draft." Cohen claimed he wore these words to express his strong opposition to the Vietnam War. (He did not wear the jacket when he was inside an actual courtroom.) In reversing his conviction, the Supreme Court said such words could not be considered obscene (thus disturbing of the peace) since there was nothing sexual about them. "Whatever else may be necessary to give rise to the States' broader power to prohibit obscene expression, such expression must be, in some significant way, erotic. It cannot plausibly be maintained that this vulgar allusion to the Selective Service System would conjure up such psychic stimulation in anyone likely to be confronted with Cohen's crudely defaced jacket."

Even though speech is rarely found to be obscene, it sometimes is and can be prohibited. Another type of speech that can be prohibited is speech that is so inflammatory that it can cause a violent uproar. Over the years, the courts have struggled with the proper way to characterize such prohibited speech. Formulations such as "fighting words," words likely to "incite a riot," words that present a "clear and present danger," and (most recently) words likely to "incite immediate lawless action" have all been used by various courts. Whatever the exact phrase used, the principle remains: one's right to express oneself in public can be denied if it will likely provoke people to engage in serious physical violence. On the other hand, when no such immediate violence is likely, the speech — even if it is passionate and hysterical — must be tolerated. The next case demonstrates this principle quite well.

Brandenburg v. Ohio
395 U.S. 444 (1969)

Defendant Brandenburg was an Ohio leader of the Ku Klux Klan. He and fellow Klansmen held a series of rallies in which they (in full view of the press filming them) did such things as dress in full Klan regalia, burn crosses, and vocally promote racist and anti-government sentiments. At one such rally, Brandenburg stated that, "Personally I believe the nigger should be returned to Africa, the Jew returned to Israel." Brandenburg also remarked that, "We're not a revengent [sic] organization, but if our President, our Congress, our Supreme Court, continues to suppress the white, Caucasian race, it's possible that there might have to be some revengeance [sic] taken."

After reviewing these activities on film, local authorities arrested Brandenburg and charged him with violating a decades-old law from 1919 that prohibited "advocating the duty, necessity, or propriety of crime, sabotage, violence, or unlawful methods of terrorism as a means of accomplishing industrial or political reform" (the so-called "Ohio Criminal Syndicalism law"). Similar laws had been adopted by 20 other states.

The state argued that such a law made sense because a state should not have to wait until the wolf is at the gate before it can intercede to stop acts of terror. The defendant argued that his right to freely express his contempt for non-whites and for the government was being illegally suppressed.

In ruling for the defendant, the Supreme Court (reiterating language it had used in past cases) said that "the mere abstract teaching ... of the moral propriety or even moral necessity for a resort to force and violence, is not the same as preparing a group for violent action and steeling it to such action." Any law that fails to distinguish between mere abstract teachings and speech that is "likely to incite or produce imminent lawless action" is constitutionally flawed. Here, there was no reason to believe that rally attendees were being incited to immediately rise up and attack governmental institutions or the general public. Given this, their speech is protected under the First Amendment.

The Court likened this speech to that of American Communists who urge revolutionary class struggle. Such agitators are considered despicable by the vast majority of Americans, and the likelihood that they will convince any significant number of people to join them in an attempt to overthrow the government is remote at best. The KKK can rant and rave all they want. But, as long as their dark rituals do not actually **incite imminent lawless action** (the current legal test for illegal, mayhem-inducing speech), they must be tolerated.

Discussion Questions

1. Do you prefer the old test of "clear and present danger" to the new test of "inciting imminent lawless action"?

2. Can you provide an example of speech that could be a crime because it is actually inciting imminent lawless action?

3. What would be an example of a KKK leader going too far with his speech such that it is no longer merely "theoretical" in nature?

Unpopular Religion

The case discussed earlier involving the Westboro Church's protest at a Marine's funeral was primarily a free speech case. But, it had some freedom of religion undertones as well. No doubt members of that church felt a lack of tolerance for their unpopular religious expressions. Of course, most people would probably not be fans of the Westboro Baptist Church, including (and most especially) other Baptists. Yet, the First Amendment commands great tolerance for the sincere religious beliefs and practices of others. The First Amendment begins by stating that, "Congress shall make no law respecting an establishment of religion, or prohibiting the free exercise thereof."

Interestingly, a close reading of the First Amendment shows us that freedom of religion has two distinct components to it. There is a "no establishment" principle and a "free exercise" principle.

The "**Establishment Clause**" of the First Amendment means that there will be no official, government-preferred religion in any of our states. In England, for example, the Church of England is the official state-sponsored religion, with the monarch at its head. Other countries might recognize the Lutheran Church or the Roman Catholic Church or the Orthodox Church or Islam as the official religion, and payment of clergy salaries and upkeep of buildings of the favored faith can often find support by way of tax dollars. But in the United States no such official churches are to be designated by Congress or by any of the fifty state legislatures.

The "**Free Exercise Clause**" of the First Amendment means that members of religious communities must be allowed to practice their religions without any unwarranted interferences. For example, a law that forbids Muslim girls from wearing head scarves to public schools might be achievable in France, but would be unthinkable in the United States.

Most Americans have no desire to oppress religious minorities simply for the fun of it. But, where questions of tolerance really get difficult is when a religious practice comes into conflict with some meritorious societal goal, like health or safety. A literal reading of the First Amendment suggests that "free exercise" trumps everything, and that the government can never interfere with any religious practices whatsoever, no matter how harmful or outlandish. But, the Supreme Court has never read the First Amendment that literally. The language of the First Amendment may sound absolutist but its interpretation has never been found to be so. Courts have always felt compelled to use common sense. Beginning with the very old case below, courts have always differentiated between religious *beliefs* (which can never be prohibited) and religious *practices* (which sometimes can be prohibited). The case that follows involves the practice of polygamy. It has never been overturned and after a century and a half is still good law. But, given the rapidly changing sexual mores in America, and various redefinitions of marriage and family taking place, ask yourself while reading it whether or not you think it will still be good law decades from now.

Reynolds v. United States
98 U.S. 145 (1879)

George Reynolds was a Latter-day Saint who served as the personal secretary to Mormon Church president Brigham Young in Utah during the second half of the 1800s. Reynolds (who had volunteered for his church to serve as a "test case") was convicted of having more than one wife (polygamy) in violation of federal law. The federal statute in question prohibited men from "sexually cohabitating" with more than one woman at a time (the statute was worded this way in order to prevent evasion by those who underwent a religious ceremony but who made no claim of being legally married). Reynolds believed that the federal statute disallowing his polygamous lifestyle violated his First Amendment right to freely exercise the religion of his choice. Consequently, he appealed his conviction (eventually) to the United States Supreme Court.

Reynolds advanced the argument that polygamy was a sincerely held tenet of the Mormon religion and that it was unconstitutional for Congress to punish a person for practicing a principle central to one's faith. Unfortunately for Reynolds and for others like him, the Supreme Court did not agree.

The Supreme Court noted that nobody could be constitutionally punished for merely holding a religious belief of any kind. However, the First Amendment did not require the government to allow every possible religious action that one might wish to undertake. Some actions are so harmful to society that the need to outlaw them trumps the right of someone to freely exercise a religious principle (for example, nobody would expect the Supreme Court to allow refusal to pay taxes or human sacrifice in the name of religion).

The Supreme Court ultimately based its decision most squarely on the original intent of those who drafted the First Amendment in the first place. It pointed out that "polygamy has always been odious among the northern and western nations of Europe, and until the establishment of [this early form of the Mormon Church], was almost exclusively a feature of life of Asiatic and of African people." The Court went on to note that no colony or state (before or after the passage of the First Amendment) had ever recognized the right of someone to have more than one spouse. Consequently, those who drafted the free exercise guarantee of the First Amendment must have never meant for it to cover religious activities such as polygamy.

Discussion Questions

1. Do you agree that it was probably never the intent of the Framers to guarantee a right to practice polygamy when they wrote the Constitution? What about gay marriage?

2. Is there a difference between a man claiming two wives and a man living alone but sleeping around with two steady girlfriends? Which man, if either, is less moral in your view?

Though the *Reynolds* decision is helpful in reminding us that there is still a difference between **religious beliefs** (mere opinions that must always be tolerated) and **religious practices** (activities that are not always tolerated), it did not give much specific guidance as to how future courts should actually balance the right of religious minorities to practice their faith against the rights of the rest of society alleging harm by the minority religion's actions. It seemed to rely heavily on the original intent of the First Amendment's drafters. But original intent is not a favored approach in modern times (think abortion rights, gay rights, prisoners' rights, etc.).

In fact, feeling free to jettison old allegiances to "original intent," U.S. District Court Judge Clark Waddoups ruled in December 2013 that Utah's current ban on polygamy violated religious and privacy rights found within the U.S. Constitution. Though not ruling that Utah must give actual legal recognition to plural marriages, Waddoups did rule that Utah's current law making a potential criminal out of any person who "purports to marry another person or cohabits with another person" was unconstitutional. Hence, Kody Brown, of the television series *Sister Wives*, could not be prosecuted (something he feared might happen eventually) for being legally married to one woman while holding himself out in public to be "spiritually married" to three others. Weighing heavily in Judge Waddoups's decision was the fact that Utah's hostility towards cohabitation seemed targeted almost exclusively against those motivated by religion. By the assistant state attorney general's own admission, Utah probably had no interest in ever prosecuting people for "sleeping around" or for cohabitating with several mere lovers.

It is important to note that Judge Waddoups's decision was only that of a federal district court. His decision to strike down Utah's anti-polygamy legislation was appealed by the state of Utah and brought before the U.S. Court of Appeals for the Tenth Circuit. The Tenth Circuit dismissed the *Brown* case for **mootness** (the issues central to a case have been resolved or lessened in importance since the case's original filing to the extent courts should not render an opinion on the dispute). In rendering the *Brown* case moot, the Tenth Circuit reasoned that after the Browns' lawsuit was filed the county attorney's office of Utah County—the county in which Brown resided—had adopted a publicly stated policy pledging that prosecution of instances of alleged polygamy would be limited. Only cases involving alleged polygamous marriages that were the result of misrepresentation, fraud, abuse, violence, or child bigamy would be prosecuted. Also, Brown and his family had relocated to Nevada, outside the jurisdiction of any Utah anti-polygamy laws. In short, since the time of its original filing in 2011, any credible likelihood of conviction which may have been present at the time the Browns filed their lawsuit had dissolved as the case developed (*Brown v. Buhman*, 822 F.3d 1151, 1179 [10th Cir. 2016]).

Interestingly, in the Tenth Circuit's decision, no consideration was made as to the constitutionality of Utah's anti-polygamy laws, or the merits of the claims made by Brown that his First and Fourteenth Amendment rights were compromised by the criminal prohibition against cohabitating with his spiritual wives. In short, the Tenth Circuit skirted the issue of constitutionality of anti-polygamy statutes. Additionally, it should be noted that all judicial scrutiny of polygamy has been undertaken at the level of federal district and circuit courts, or in state courts, and the issue has not yet returned to the Supreme Court. As such, the original *Reynolds* decision has yet to be overturned.

While *Reynolds* remains good law, if only for reasons of mootness and pledges not to prosecute, for some decades now appellate courts have routinely balanced the religious rights of individuals against the interests of society without resorting merely to "original intent." Specifically, courts developed the idea of requiring Congress (or a state) to prove a **compelling interest** before it could interfere with a religiously motivated practice. By "compelling interest," the courts meant much more than a legitimate interest or even a substantial interest. The key word is "compelling." For example, blocking parents from preventing (on religious grounds) a life-saving blood transfusion for their minor child would probably constitute a compelling governmental interest. What about a state's interest in seeing its young citizens receive a uniform education? Does this constitute a compelling interest? The next case addresses that issue.

Wisconsin v. Yoder
406 U.S. 205 (1972)

An Amish man named Jonas Yoder refused to send his fifteen-year-old child to public school. The state of Wisconsin had made it a criminal offense for parents to refuse to send their children to school (i.e., compulsory attendance) until the age of sixteen. As a matter of religious principle, Yoder believed that children should only attend school until thirteen years of age. The Amish believed thirteen was old enough for children to learn the basics of reading, writing, and arithmetic, while education beyond that point only served to instill negative, worldly values such as pride, competition, nationalism, and excessive individualism.

At about age thirteen, Amish children were expected to leave school and start working with their hands in occupations such as farming. Amish people believed that "excessive levels of education" only tended to lure their children away from the faith and towards the values of mainstream ("English") society.

Yoder made the above arguments in the appeal of his conviction. The state countered that it had some very good reasons to require all Wisconsin children to attend school until the age of sixteen. For example, society benefits greatly when its citizenry is highly educated. Also, school attendance shields young children from being exploited by the world of work, including employment in some potentially dangerous occupations.

The U.S. Supreme Court eventually found in favor of Yoder and his fellow Amish. It said that both Yoder and the state of Wisconsin had advanced some quite good reasons for their positions. However, when dealing with a fundamental right such as the free exercise of religion, the Court refused to make use of a simple, ordinary balancing test to decide which side should win. Instead, it said that before a state could interfere with a fundamental right (like religion, speech, press, etc.), it needed not just a good reason but a "compelling state interest" before any scale could possibly tip in its favor. Only a compelling state interest could possibly have enough weight for the state's interest to outweigh a fundamental right.

In the end, the Supreme Court did not believe that the state of Wisconsin had any interest that was compelling enough to justify interference with the Amish practice of not educating their children beyond the age of thirteen. The Amish tradition of pulling children from school at age thirteen was based on core religious beliefs that were of extreme importance to members of that religious community. Wisconsin's goals were good ones, but they were not compelling ones. The Amish practice of sending children to work on farms at age thirteen was a viable alternative to attending school and posed no particular danger to the children or to society as a whole.

Discussion Questions

1. Suppose the Amish, as a matter of religious principle, wish to opt out of the national scheme to pay Social Security taxes and to later collect Social Security payments? Using what you learned above, should their decision to opt out be necessarily allowed?

2. What do you think of the notion that the state must have a compelling reason (not just a good one) to interfere with someone's religious practice? Would you be OK with the test being just a "good reason" to interfere?

From the *Yoder* case above, we saw the "compelling interest" standard in action. This standard held sway throughout much of the twentieth century. But is the standard still viable today? To the absolute horror of many religious-rights advocates (both liberals and conservatives), courts began ruling late in the twentieth century that the "compelling interest" standard (also known as "strict scrutiny") was no longer sacrosanct in the context of free exercise cases. Following the example of the U.S. Supreme Court, courts began ruling that a law hurting minority religious practices was fine whether or not there was a compelling state interest so long as it was "facially neutral and uniformly applied" (see, e.g., *Employment Division of Oregon v. Smith*, 494 U.S. 872 [1990]).

The abandonment of the "compelling interest" standard in *Employment Division of Oregon v. Smith* and its replacement with the **facial neutrality test** outraged members of Congress. Conservative and liberal politicians, concerned with traditional values and civil liberties respectively, drafted the Religious Freedom Restoration Act (RFRA) in response. RFRA sought to resurrect by statute the "compelling interest" standard. The protections provided by RFRA applied initially to both federal and state-based restrictions on religious freedom.

Despite the political agreement which led to RFRA's enactment, the Supreme Court rejected the authority of Congress to apply RFRA to state-based regulations in *City of Boerne v. Flores*, 521 U.S. 507 (1997). RFRA was overturned as unconstitutional as it applied to state-based regulations, but continues to limit federal regulations. In short, federal regulations must pass the compelling interest test imposed by RFRA, whereas state regulations would be judged under the "facial neutrality" constitutional standard of *Employment Division of Oregon v. Smith*.

Still upset with the Supreme Court's Free Exercise Clause decisions permitting states to pass regulations subject only to the facial neutrality test, Congress again sought to raise by federal statute the standard of review for some state regulations. In 2000 Congress passed the Religious Land Use and Institutionalized Persons Act (RLUIPA). Congress intended for RLUIPA to restore the "compelling interest" standard previously employed in *Yoder* to institutionalized persons in the states, including state prison and local jail inmates (as well as some zoning regulations). After RLUIPA, states could not interfere with an institutionalized person's religion unless the government demonstrates that doing so is the least restrictive means of furthering a compelling government interest. In effect, the government must not only explain why it infringed on an institutionalized person's rights, but also must explain that no alternative exists which is less burdensome to an inmate's right to practice their religion.

The next case highlights RLUIPA's impact on state prison regulations. Courts must now carefully consider the state's interests served by prison regulations. Courts must also consider whether the state's regulations are the least restrictive means (i.e., are there approaches less burdensome to an inmate's religious conduct) to advance those state interests.

Holt v. Hobbs
574 U.S. 352 (2015)

Gregory Holt, a Muslim inmate, wished to grow a beard in accordance with the teachings of his religion. The Arkansas Department of Corrections, however, had a written policy which restricted any inmates from growing facial hair, except for inmates who had skin conditions which limited their ability to shave. Holt was amenable to a compromise, offering to grow a half-inch beard instead of a full beard, to accommodate the prison's interests. Holt was refused the right to do so by the prison.

Holt sued the director of the Arkansas Department of Corrections, Ray Hobbs, arguing that the growth of a beard was central to his faith, and the Arkansas prison policy inhibited his ability to practice his religion. Arkansas replied that the grooming policy was the least restrictive alternative available to maintain the compelling interest of security of the prison, for two reasons. First, it was believed that inmates may hide items such as needles, drugs, or even Subscriber Identity Module (SIM) cards in their beards, thus limiting the control administrators had over inmates in maintaining security. Second, Arkansas argued that if inmates had beards, they may then shave them off, which may function as a disguise of sorts, to conceal their identities in escape attempts. In short, Arkansas argued that a compelling interest exists to maintain a grooming policy that restricted the growth of facial hair among religious inmates.

The Supreme Court confronted the issue of whether the Arkansas policy regarding facial hair violated the rights of Holt, who sought to grow a beard for religious purposes. The Supreme Court ruled that the policy did in fact violate Holt's religious rights under RLUIPA and reversed and remanded to the lower court's decisions.

In their decision, the Supreme Court reasoned that while Arkansas did in fact have compelling security interests regarding inmate beards—namely in preventing beards from being used to smuggle contraband or to facilitate disguise—that the implementation of the policy was not the "least restrictive alternative" available to the prison to address these concerns and thus violated RLUIPA. First, the Court acknowledged the reasonable concern that inmates might smuggle contraband in their beards. However, it is less restrictive to simply have correctional officers search inmate beards periodically (i.e., run a comb through the beard) than the policy requirement to shave them off. Also the lack of a corresponding policy requiring inmates to shave their head hair undermined the argument made for restricting beard growth.

Second, concerning the compelling state interest in preventing inmate escape and disguise through beards, the Supreme Court noted that a widely employed practice by other correctional facilities was the photographing of inmates both with and without their beards, a less restrictive alternative to strict grooming standards. Finally, the Arkansas Department of Corrections failed to articulate how its policy served a compelling interest when it simultaneously allowed inmates with dermatological conditions to avoid facial hair policies.

The next case deals with the alleged clash of gay rights, freedom of religion, and freedom of speech in the refusal of a vendor to provide certain commercial services to a same-sex couple. In reading the case, ask yourself which party you would side with in deciding the conflict.

Elane Photography v. Willock
296 P.3d 491 (N.M. 2012)

Elane Photography, a commercial photography business, was held in violation of the "New Mexico Human Rights Act" and subsequently fined about $7,000. Elaine Huguenin, who along with her husband owned the studio, had refused to photograph a gay wedding as requested by the same-sex couple. In defense of refusing to take them on as clients, she cited deeply held "Christian" religious beliefs against gay marriage. She claimed that forcing her to celebrate and affirm the marriage by photographing it would have violated her rights to free exercise of religion.

She also argued that photographing the events amounted to a type of "compelled speech," which also violated her First Amendment rights. She maintained that unlike providing ordinary goods and services that involve no elements of speech, forcing someone to engage in art against her will would violate one's freedom of expression.

Lawyers for the gay couple countered that the New Mexico Human Rights Act, which forbade the denial of goods, services, or accommodations on the basis of race, sexual orientation, etc., extended to more than just enterprises like hotels, restaurants, or public carriers. It would include basically any commercial enterprise that solicits customers or clients in the public marketplace. Their position was that by voluntarily choosing to engage in business, one cannot then pick and choose which reasonable regulations one will abide by and which regulations one will ignore. Anti-discrimination laws are designed to protect people from just that: discrimination. Attorneys for the studio disagreed, arguing that "Americans in the marketplace should not be subjected to legal attacks for simply abiding by their beliefs."

The New Mexico Supreme Court ultimately (and unanimously) ruled in favor of the gay couple and against the studio. It held that "a commercial photography business that offers its services to the public, thereby increasing its visibility to potential clients" must abide by the provision of anti-discrimination laws. It said that such a business "must serve same-sex couples on the same basis that it serves opposite sex couples." The studio's discriminating against same-sex couples would violate the Human Rights Act "in the same way as if it had refused to photograph a wedding between people of different races."

In a concurring opinion, Justice Bosson noted that owners of businesses "have to channel their conduct, not their beliefs, so as to leave space for other Americans who believe something different." He went on to write that "That sense of respect we owe others, whether or not we believe as they do, illuminates this country, setting it apart from the discord that afflicts much of the rest of the world. In short, I would say to the Huguenins, with the utmost respect: it is the price of citizenship."

Discussion Questions

1. Do you agree with the unanimous decision of the New Mexico Supreme Court? Or do you agree with a Rasmussen Survey taken around the time of this decision that found that 85 percent of lay people believed that a photographer should be allowed to refuse to photograph a same-sex wedding?

2. Suppose that a town had thirty qualified photographers and only one of them objected to photographing a gay wedding on religious grounds. Would that make any difference in your analysis as to whether or not the one photographer should be permitted to refuse to photograph the wedding?

3. Despite the ruling in the case above, could a photographer legally refuse to photograph a wedding because in his artistic view the couple is too ugly? Fat? Low class? Short? Is there a difference between these prejudices and those based on race, religion, or sexual preference?

Unpopular Assemblies

In addition to forbidding intolerance against unpopular speech and religion, the First Amendment also mandates tolerance for **unpopular assemblies** (groupings of disliked people who protest or otherwise socialize together). There is something about a group of protestors that always seems to get somebody upset just by its mere existence. People have the right to assemble and protest (subject to reasonable regulations).

Sometimes people get annoyed when others gather for purposes other than to engage in protest. For example, some readers may recall episodes in their youth when older people did not like it when they and their teenage friends would "hang out" in the neighborhood just to socialize. This next case deals with this type of youthful assembly. Or is there more to it than that?

People ex rel. Gallo v. Acuna et al.
929 P.2d 596 (Cal. 1997)

The City of San Jose, California, responded to a big gang problem by asking the California Superior Court to enter an injunction forbidding known gang members from engaging in certain activities in the city. The Rocksprings section of San Jose had become a "war zone." Gang members liked to "hang out" at all hours of the day and night on sidewalks, people's lawns, parking lots, and driveways, in carports, and in front of apartment complexes. They would openly drink, sniff, and snort various intoxicating substances. They were loud and boisterous, often engaging in fist fights and worse. Residents had to constantly put up with their loud music, vulgar speech, and echoes of gunfire. They had turned the neighborhood into a giant drive-up drug market. Such crimes as assault, murder, vandalism, theft, and arson happened all the time. Residents were prisoners in their own homes. They were threatened with physical harm if they ever dared complain. They would not allow their children to play outside. Acquaintances refused to visit them. Gang members would urinate all over the place and would use residents' houses and automobiles as "canvas" for their graffiti. Of course, whenever the police would drive by the gangsters would refrain from criminal actions until the coast was clear.

The city council asked the court to pass an injunction forbidding gang members from occupying, congregating, or otherwise loitering in their neighborhood. The court issued the injunction, and gang members appealed.

One of the many issues in this complex case involved the "right to assemble" as guaranteed by the First and Fourteenth Amendments. Does a court order that forbids street gangs from milling about violate the gang members' rights to freely assemble? The position of the gangs was that it was one thing to charge someone with a specific crime if the evidence was such to establish probable cause, but to forbid someone from merely associating with friends was unconstitutional. The California Court of Appeals agreed with the gang members and overturned the injunction. It held that injunctions could be issued forbidding activities that were independently illegal (i.e., crimes), but an injunction like the one the city was granted went too far when it included "non-criminal" conduct like mere assembly. It reasoned that you cannot equate legal acts like "hanging out" with independent crimes such as being a "public nuisance."

The California Supreme Court reversed the Court of Appeals and reinstated the injunction. It explained that the right to assemble is meant to protect groups whose assembly has either "intrinsic value" (such as cohabitating with one's relatives — such assemblies are characterized by "relative smallness ... and a high degree of selectivity" in who gets to be in the group) or "instrumental value" (such as larger groups of people who get together to pursue "a wide variety of political, social, economic, educational, religious, and cultural ends"). The California Supreme Court said that these gangs had neither intrinsic nor instrumental value. These gang members are not interested in engaging in educational, political or bona-fide cultural activities. "Freedom of Association ... does not extend to joining with others for the purpose of depriving third parties of their lawful rights. We do not, in short, believe that the activities of the gang and its members in Rocksprings at issue here ... command protection under the First Amendment."

Justice Mosk, in an angry dissent, said that "no doubt Montesquieu, Locke and Madison will turn over in their graves" when they realize they have been cited by the majority (which they indeed had been) to justify the denial of "simple rights to a group of Latino youths who have not been convicted of a crime." Justice Mosk further opined that Benjamin Franklin's famous insight applies here: "They that can give up essential liberty to obtain a little temporary safety deserve neither liberty nor safety." Mosk went on to say that this decision would allow a city to "close off entire neighborhoods to Latino youths who have done nothing more than dress in blue or black clothing." It will now be a crime to do nothing more than "ordinary, non-disruptive acts of walking or driving through a residential neighborhood with a relative or a friend." This he thought was a "blunderbuss approach" that employed "the techniques of tyranny."

> **Discussion Questions**
> 1. When you were younger did you ever "hang out" with friends in a neighborhood without engaging in "educational, political, or bona fide cultural activities"? Was your behavior, unlike that of the gang, a "bona fide cultural activity"?
>
> 2. What do you suppose made the dissent so angry in this case? Does this wealthy justice live in the real world or were his points valid?

Unpopular Media

Tolerance of unpopular media is the last topic to cover in this chapter. The drafters of the First Amendment no doubt knew that tyrannical governments have an especially strong hatred for newspapers and other media that do not support their agendas. Private citizens also can be intolerant of media outlets they dislike and may put pressure on governmental representatives to punish them for their reporting.

Some scholars consider the press to be an "**unofficial fourth branch of government**," in that it acts as a check on abuse by holding the other three, official branches accountable. Of course, sometimes the media itself can become a source of abuse and impropriety. But, thanks to the First Amendment, it is given extraordinary leeway, even when it arguably acts badly.

Freedom of the press is so strong that the government will not censor it in advance (no "**prior restraints**"). If the press is going to publish something untrue and harmful, the government will not attempt to forbid it from doing so. Instead, a victim must wait and sue the newspaper, television reporter, etc. for libel or slander after the fact. Even then, honest, good-faith mistakes will be forgiven by the courts. To win a defamation suit (lawsuit alleging character assassination) against the press, a victim would have to prove more than just harm done out of negligence: it would have to be proven that the press knowingly or recklessly disregarded the truth. One acts negligently when one does not know of a substantial risk of falsehood but reasonably should have known (this is not enough to successfully go after the press). One acts recklessly when one is indeed aware of a substantial risk of falsehood but still takes that risk anyway (that is the **press defamation standard**).

An old but good case shows the reasoning behind the rule against "no prior restraints." There are exceptions to the rule against no prior restraints (as the case below suggests) but such exceptions, in practice, are virtually unheard of in this country.

Near v. Minnesota
283 U.S. 697 (1931)

During the Great Depression, a Minnesota newspaper called *The Saturday Press* was giving local politicians fits. It had already published a series of articles in which it meant to expose corrupt and/or grossly incompetent governmental officials who were not doing anything to prevent local gangsters from profiting from illegal gambling and bootlegging enterprises. The articles claimed that the government officials were either in league with the gangsters or else outrageously derelict in their duties.

The government officials went to court and asked the court to order the journalists to cease printing any more such articles. They cited a statute allowing "abatement as a public nuisance" of any newspaper that planned to print material of a "malicious, scandalous or defamatory" nature. The trial court agreed with the governmental officials and commanded the newspaper to cease writing any more such articles.

The case eventually worked its way up to the United States Supreme Court. The Supreme Court did not like what the Minnesota court had done. In its view, the issue was not whether the government officials could sue for defamation of their character. Even if they were in fact defamed by the newspaper, the Supreme Court thought that an injunction preventing in advance the printing of a story — even a false and defamatory story — was a violation of freedom of the press. It feared that the use of prior restraints on the press by the government threatened the "very nature of a free state." In other words, the whole notion of prior restraints on the press struck the Supreme Court as really scary. There might be a rare exception in which the Court would allow a prior restraint on the press. For example, in time of war it might see the need for the government to stop a news outlet from publishing troop locations or naval ship departure dates. Some things, like publishing critical state secrets, can be enjoined in advance. But the stakes here did not involve matters of wartime national security. False allegations of malfeasance in office are alleged harms done to Minnesota officials that can be addressed after the fact through a libel suit against the newspaper. That, not dangerous governmental censorship, is the proper course of action here.

In his dissent, Justice Butler wrote that because the governmental officials were going to the court first before trying to restrain publication of the articles, it was not the kind of direct prior restraint that posed a huge danger. This was not a situation where the government officials would intervene directly as self-appointed censors engaging in editorial control. They were going through the neutral courts to get permission first. Allowing the newspapers to print false and malicious materials cannot be rectified by allowing a lawsuit after the fact. The damage has already been done.

Discussion Questions

1. What would be an example of damage that could not be corrected later via a lawsuit for money?

2. Why would the use of prior restraints on the press be a very dangerous practice that would threaten "the very nature of a free state"?

3. Other than examples given in the case, what would be an example of a critical state secret nowadays that probably could be censored in advance?

One emerging area of concern is the decline of traditional print media and the rise of vast armies of amateur "journalists" on the internet. What now constitutes the "press"? Is a journalist anyone who claims to be such? Suppose that an unpaid blogger or YouTube activist is constantly defaming and bullying someone with horrible lies. Should this amateur be protected by the rule against prior restraints just like a paid journalist would be who worked for NBC News or the *New York Times*? How would you define a member of the press in this day and age? Should we limit protections of the press to professionals who get paid for what they do? Paid journalists are often schooled in journalistic ethics and therefore know how to self-police. This is seldom the case with bloggers. Plus, unlike professional news organizations, many amateur journalists are effectively "**sue proof**" since they have no money or assets to worry about losing pursuant to an "after the fact" defamation lawsuit. Should we start requiring journalists to get licensed, the way we require doctors, lawyers, teachers, home builders, and even cosmetologists to get trained and licensed, before the "journalist" can claim "no prior restraints"? What do you think?

Chapter Key Terms

Intolerance
Hate speech
Enhanced penalty statute
Motive
Fighting words
Political speech
Punitive damages
Three-prong test for obscene
    speech
Incite imminent lawless action
Establishment Clause

Free Exercise Clause
Religious beliefs
Religious practices
Compelling interest
Facial neutrality test
Unpopular assemblies
Unofficial fourth branch of
    government
Prior restraints
Press defamation standard
Sue proof

Chapter Two

Intolerance in Law Enforcement and Corrections

Using military-grade pepper spray and police violence against non-violent student protesters violates the Constitution, and it's just wrong. When the cost of speech is a shot of blinding, burning pepper spray in the face, speech is not free.

— Michael Risher, attorney at the ACLU of
Northern California

As was mentioned in the previous chapter, this and other accompanying chapters will discuss practical case studies that are illustrative of the ethical implications regarding "the seven deadly constitutional sins." While the examples presented will often lean more heavily toward the negative (in that they will frequently demonstrate cases where something went awry) it is by no means our intention to imply that those who work in law enforcement or corrections are incompetent, biased, or unethical. Rather, we want you to think about the potential ethical dilemmas that can arise when these individuals are confronted with the responsibility of interpreting and acting upon both the law and the spirit of the United States Constitution. Moving forward, we will first discuss examples from law enforcement followed by examples from corrections that demonstrate the previous chapter's deadly sin. We will conclude the examples with discussion questions. These will allow you to further enmesh yourself in the material and think through what actions you would have taken if you were in the law enforcement or correction practitioner's shoes. With that said, lets start with the first vice of intolerance.

Law Enforcement

Warm Sands Sex Sting

The Warm Sands neighborhood is a small community in Palm Springs, California, that has been described as pro-LGBTQ+ due in large part to the nearly 30–40% gay population that resides there. However, in June of 2009, the Palm Springs Police Department executed a sex sting that many criticized as being discriminatory in nature. Through the use of undercover decoys, Palm Springs PD arrested 24 men and requested that they be charged with a misdemeanor indecent exposure charge. Palm Springs PD worked out an arrangement with the district attorney prior to the sting to have any and all arrestees charged with indecent exposure as opposed to the more lenient charge of lewd conduct (Sloss, 2011, para. 5). In a deposition, Palm Springs Police Sergeant Bryan Anderson stated that they worked this arrangement out with the DA before conducting the sting due to their displeasure with previous cases being handled too leniently. Because this is an offense often associated with flashers, the men would be required (under Penal Code Section 314) to register as sex offenders for the rest of their lives (Walsh, 2010, para. 2–3).

Advocates and lawyers for the men took issue with two things related to the sting: (1) they felt as though law enforcement used entrapment due to the use of decoys, and (2) they felt as though law enforcement was unfairly targeting gays since it is well known that there is public sex between heterosexual couples that goes unpunished (Wilson, 2011, para. 4). In total, 14 men were charged with indecent exposure. Their lawyers filed motions to have their charges dismissed due to entrapment on the part of officers; however, these motions were unsuccessful. A majority of the men were offered plea deals to plead guilty to a lesser charge of disturbing the peace or lewd conduct. A majority of them (all but one) accepted the plea deal and were imposed a $500 fine and/or sentenced to probation (Wagner, 2011, para. 9–16).

Many claimed that the Palm Springs PD acted discriminatorily. Lawyers stood firm to arguments that "if the suspects had been straight, but done the same thing, they would have never been arrested in the first place" (Kelman, 2017, para. 20). The criticisms launched at Palm Springs PD didn't stop with the men's legal counsel. After the sting hit the media, more news boiled to the surface that one of the officers conducting the sting was caught uttering anti-gay slurs on tape. Police Chief David Dominguez reprimanded the officer, and all employees of Palm Springs PD were required to take a mandatory sensitivity training (Wilson, 2011, para. 6). It appeared that things had started to settle down a bit until a second tape was discovered, this time catching the police chief making clearly derogatory and homophobic remarks. Shortly after the news of the tape broke, Police Chief David Dominguez retired and called a press conference to formally apologize. He said, "An inappropriate comment made by me did not display the utmost professional conduct expected from the chief of police and I sincerely apologize to the community at large" (Valley News, 2010, para. 2).

This example calls into question not only the potential for there being a few bad apples among a police force, but perhaps the idea that an entire department could be intolerant and homophobic. While it is likely not the case that the department openly condoned discriminatory views, one could argue that due to the selectivity of the sting, the more severe punishment worked out with the DA prior to the sting, and comments made by officers during the sting that the Palm Springs PD didn't go out of its way to minimize homophobic viewpoints. In this particular case, the saying, "Actions speak louder than words" may be fairly applicable.

Discussion Questions

1. Given what you know from the case above, do you think that the Palm Springs Police Department is intolerant of gays?

2. What would you have done if you were an officer and heard your supervisor (i.e., the police chief in this instance) making homophobic remarks?

Be Wary of Christians and Fundamentalists

On April 1, 2013, Undersheriff Ron Trowbridge attended a training session hosted by the Colorado State Patrol that was focusing on two groups, sovereign citizens and outlaw motorcycle gangs. After the training concluded he sent a letter to Red Statements (a now-defunct Christian website) alleging that he had sat through training that he felt had been discriminatory against Christians (Ahle, 2013, para. 1). He was praised by Red Statements and Christian organizations alike for blowing the whistle on structural biases that can exist in law enforcement. However, as we'll see near the conclusion of this example, those who organized the training session insisted that there was no malicious intent behind the training and rather that Trowbridge had misinterpreted the messages being conveyed by the presenter.

The section of the training that was troublesome to Trowbridge focused on sovereign citizens. The **sovereign citizens movement** consists of people who believe that they are or should be free from laws and often reject government and the notion of taxation. Although there is no clearly delineated demographic, extremely devout (i.e., radical) Christians are allegedly those who comprise the sovereign citizens movement (Seidl, 2012, para. 2 & 14). For nearly two hours, Trowbridge listened to Trooper Joe Klucznski tell those in the audience to be wary of Christians who take the Bible too literally and also fundamentalists in general because these are two large groups that tend to be part of the sovereign citizens movement. Klucznski is an analyst for the Colorado Information Analysis Center, which is funded by Homeland Security. He said during the training that he was getting his information from the Department of Homeland Security (Ahle, 2013, para. 5). Klucznski told those in the audience to "be careful of these people" and be prepared to confiscate "illegal" weapons if necessary (Hallowell, 2013, para. 11). Trowbridge noted in his letter that Klucznski told the group that the sovereign citizens had a right to their beliefs, but should be watched closely due to the potential for retaliation against those in law enforcement.

Trowbridge mentions that he felt compelled to write this letter due to his Christian beliefs because he was surprised that nobody else in the audience seemed to bat an eye. Unfortunately, after news of the letter went public Trowbridge was left high and dry by his employer. According to the Colorado State Patrol, after talking to other officers in attendance, it was learned that "None of them interpreted the instructor's comments in the manner described by the undersheriff" and that they "regret that he misrepresented the training material in a way that clearly is not the position of the Colorado State Patrol" (Hallowell, 2013, para. 24). Similarly, the Department of Homeland Security wrote a letter alluding to the session not being conducted in conjunction with DHS standards, and that the **ideologies** expressed by Klucznski did not align with those of the Department of Homeland Security. Perhaps it was just one big misunderstanding.

Discussion Questions

1. Would you have blown the whistle and told authority figures about the discriminatory messages being conveyed through your training?

2. Given the limited information that you have on this case, do you personally think it was all just a misunderstanding, or was there a hidden agenda being conveyed through the training session that day?

Perhaps one of the lesser known clauses of the First Amendment is freedom to assemble. In the case studies that follow, we will explore the boundaries of this right and debate when law enforcement should and should not be allowed to interfere with our desire to assemble. Of particular interest will be the intentions of those who assemble. Should law enforcement be allowed to dismantle peaceful demonstrations? What about violent ones? Further, should law enforcement be allowed to use tactics that prevent certain groups from assembling in the first place? These and other questions will be explored through the two case studies below.

UC Davis Pepper Spray Incident

On November 18, 2011, students of the University of California at Davis assembled in the school's quad to express their dissatisfaction with budget cuts and increases to their tuition (Kingkade, 2012b, para. 1). Nobody foresaw the turn of events that happened next. What started as a peaceful demonstration on this fall day ended up in injuries, smeared reputations, and fierce litigation. Spectators caught the entire event on their cameras, and the incident quickly gained national attention (NBC News, 2013, para. 4). Still shot images and videos on the internet show a group of students (approximately 20) peacefully sitting in a line with their arms crossed. Clad in their riot gear, UC Davis police surround them and can be heard requesting that the group disperse (ACLU, 2012, para. 10). When the students refused, Lieutenant John Pike is seen "casually dousing demonstrators in the face with a can of pepper spray as they sat on the ground" (NBC News, 2013, para. 2). Nine students were taken to the hospital and later released while 10 people were arrested (CBS News, 2011, para. 14). This caused a major uproar, and many alleged that campus police used **excessive force** (i.e., the force used exceeded the minimum amount that was necessary to resolve the dispute and protect the officers or others from harm). We will return to the event and the ethical questions that arise from it, but first, let's explore what happened in the wake of the UC Davis pepper spray incident.

The videos quickly went viral, and within days, UC Davis Chancellor Linda Katehi had people breathing down her neck. Alumni, students, and faculty demanded answers and called for something to be done. In an effort to diffuse the situation, the police chief and two officers were placed on administrative leave until further investigations could be carried out (CBS News, 2011, para. 9). It was determined that no criminal charges would be filed against the officers; however, that doesn't mean that the campus police and members of the university were free from public scrutiny.

As was mentioned above, many questioned whether or not excessive force was used. Proponents note that the demonstrators, while admittedly noncompliant, were not violent or combative toward law enforcement. As such, perhaps an alternate method aside from pepper spray could have been used. Along these same lines, people challenge how officers used the pepper spray. It was a more concentrated form that should be shot into crowds six feet or further away; however, in this case, it was administered at close range (Reynoso Task Force, 2012, p. 25). It is argued that exposure to those chemicals can result in serious medical conditions: one student at the event said that after they were all sprayed they were "coughing up blood [and] vomiting" (CBS News, 2011, para. 9). Those who were less critical of the use of pepper spray note that the campus police could have used more physically aggressive tactics to subdue the crowd. These arguments were heard the loudest among the law enforcement community. Further, those who disagree with the excessive force claim emphasize that campus police reacted the way that they did to prevent what recently happened at UC Berkeley from happening on their campus. The week prior, UC Berkeley students assembled to demonstrate their displeasure with tuition hikes. Similar to what happened at UC Davis, campus police in riot gear came in to break up the protestors; however, this event resulted in violent altercations between campus police and students, and many were hit with batons and bean bag guns (Huffington Post, 2011, para. 4). Given the social climate of recent protests, proponents of pepper spray being used note that it likely prevented a similar incident from happening at UC Davis.

In response to continued criticism and pressure to take action, UC Davis created the "Pepper Spray Incident" task force to investigate the questions (among others) posed above. The task force consisted of key stakeholders within the university such as those in upper administration, faculty, students, and alumni. The result of this task force was a 190-page document that "found that University officials and UC Davis police used poor judgment and excessive force in the confrontation" (NBC News, 2013, para. 4). Shortly after this document was published, UC Davis Police Chief Annette Spicuzza retired (Huffington Post, 2012, para. 2).

The task force and resignation of Spicuzza appeared to be just the tip of the iceberg. While all of these internal and external investigations were happening, there was a lawsuit filed against the University of California, Davis. The American Civil Liberties Union of Northern California filed a lawsuit on behalf of 21 students and alumni alleging that "police violated state and federal constitutional protections, including the First Amendment to the U.S. Constitution, when they arrested and used excessive force against these non-violent demonstrators" (ACLU, 2012, para. 1). Further, lawyers claimed that many of the plaintiffs suffered short-term physical ailments and long-term psychological ones due to their exposure to the pepper spray and the aggressive tactics used by the campus police. UC Davis settled the lawsuit for $1 million dollars, which equated to approximately $30,000 dollars to each of the 21 students and alumni who were part of the suit (Kingkade, 2012b, para. 1). There were additional stipulations aside from the money that the university had to pay out. Additionally, the chancellor had to write formal apologies to all 21 plaintiffs, students whose grades suffered in the aftermath of the event had to receive academic assistance and get their academic records adjusted, and the university had to work out a policy with the ACLU that addresses the proper procedures to follow should future peaceful demonstrations need to be broken up again (ACLU, 2012, para. 6).

Perhaps after this lengthy discussion you may be wondering, who is Lieutenant John Pike (the casual pepper spray douser) and what happened to him in the aftermath of the event? Lieutenant John Pike is a retired U.S. Marine sergeant who had a stellar career since joining the UC Davis campus police in 2001. He was honored twice for his police work when he went above and beyond the call of duty to diffuse what could have been potentially violent altercations (CBS News, 2011, para. 1–2). Given his stellar career up to this point, many questioned whether the finger should be pointed at Pike or at his supervisors. The results of the task force point to a breakdown in the entire chain of command, but additional blame is pointed at Pike, stating that his "use of force in pepper spraying seated protesters was objectively unreasonable" (Reynoso Task Force, 2012, p. 24).

Immediately following the event, Pike was put on administrative leave, and shortly thereafter, he resigned from UC Davis campus police. In June 2013, Pike filed for workers' compensation from the university because he claimed that he suffered anxiety and depression in the wake of the event. He claimed that after the videos went viral, he received death threats and approximately 17,000 emails, 10,000 text messages, and hundreds of letters (NBC News, 2013, para. 11). He won the suit and received $38,059 from the university in workers' compensation (on top of his paid leave, an estimated $110,000). Some sources point out the irony in this settlement since he received more in workers' compensation than the students and alumni did who were pepper sprayed on that November day (Peralta, 2013, para. 1 & 7).

Discussion Questions

1. Do you feel as though the UC Davis Police used excessive force?

2. Do you think that law enforcement should be allowed to dismantle non-violent protests?

3. What would you have done if you were an officer and witnessed Lieutenant Pike dousing demonstrators at close range with pepper spray?

Ogden Gang Injunction

Law enforcement and community members in the city of Ogden, Utah (a city of about 80,000 people located in Weber County) were fed up with known gang activity happening on their streets so they decided to do something about it. The specific gang that was being targeted in this case is referred to as "The Ogden Trece." Trece (also known as the Centro City Locos) is said to be one of the city's largest and longest running gangs, involved in activities ranging from graffiti to murder (Fields, 2013, para. 6–7). In an effort to curtail criminal activity, Weber County prosecutors requested an **injunction** (a court order that restrains an individual or group from carrying out certain acts) that would, among other things, control where and with whom Trece gang members could associate. In August of 2012, Second District Court Judge Ernie Jones "declared the 485-member Ogden Trece a public nuisance" and approved the Ogden Gang Injunction (Yi, 2010, para. 2). While in effect (it was later overturned), this injunction essentially prevented individuals who were allegedly part of the Ogden Trece gang from assembling. As we'll see from the discussion below, this calls into question one's First Amendment rights.

The primary goal of the Ogden Gang Injunction was to restrict gang members from hanging out together. In order to have a manageable area to patrol, officials determined that the "Safety Zone" (25 square miles) was an area that members could not associate in "regardless of whether they are in the process of committing a crime" (Reavy, 2012, para. 3). Additional stipulations were that gang members could not carry any weapons and there was a strictly enforced 11:00 pm curfew (Cutler, 2013, para. 4). The only exception to the curfew was when members were traveling to and from work or were taking part in non-gang related activities such as school events or religious services (Fields, 2013, para. 14).

Weber County attorneys said that this is something that they did not embark upon lightly and that they researched extensively prior to requesting the injunction. They saw that similar injunctions were effective in California and Texas and felt that "it will be a benefit to law-abiding citizens of this community" (Yi, 2012, para. 16). Early analyses showed that the injunction was working, and it was lauded as helping to reduce crime. According to authorities, the average number of graffiti cases dropped from 16 to 4 per month (Fields, 2013, para. 16) and they could show a 75% drop of caseloads across different crime areas (Nelson, 2013, para. 8).

Short-term data showed that the Ogden Gang Injunction was a success; however, it wasn't hailed by all community members in Ogden. Opponents challenged the injunction because they felt as though there is no definitive way to determine one's actual or alleged gang membership status. Further, they argued that the injunction would prohibit people from associating with friends and even family members if they were suspected to be part of the Trece gang. This latter point tended to be an issue for many individuals. As one man who was arrested for violating the injunction put it, "I couldn't be caught out in public with my own brother" (Nelson, 2013, para. 3).

Another party that was opposed to the injunction was the American Civil Liberties Union of Utah (ACLU Utah, 2013). After the ruling by the Second District Court to authorize the injunction, lawyers for the gang members felt confident that they would be granted an appeal to reevaluate the Second District Court's decision. "We hope that the appellate court understands the Constitution. The Trece gang argues the injunction violates their First Amendment right to free association" (Reavy, 2012, para. 6–7). This case was heard by the Utah Supreme Court, and the decision was handed down to vacate the Ogden Gang Injunction. No more than two and a half years after the injunction started it came to a screeching halt (Cutler, 2013, para. 1). Interestingly enough, this ruling was reached not due to there being a clear violation of the gang's First Amendment rights, but rather due to a technicality. According to Utah Supreme Court, the district court never had jurisdiction to authorize the injunction in the first place due to their trying to wrongfully treat the gang as an "unincorporated association" (which would wrongfully allow officials to require all alleged gang members to follow the specifications of the injunction without having to formally name individual members) (ACLU Utah, 2013, para. 1). According to lawyers for the gang members, though they viewed the decision as a huge victory, they recognized that it is most likely just the beginning of the battle. They foresaw the City of Ogden attempting to push the agenda again down the road, but countered, "You can be certain that if Weber County tries again to push for this kind of injunction, we will be on the other side pushing back" (ACLU Utah, 2013, para. 3).

Discussion Questions

1. In your opinion does the Ogden Gang Injunction violate the First Amendment?

2. Should criminals have a different set of constitutional rights than law-abiding citizens?

3. Do you agree with the Utah Supreme Court's ruling?

Corrections

Bradley or Chelsea

On August 21, 2013, Pfc. Bradley Manning was sentenced to 35 years in military prison for multiple violations of the **Espionage Act** (the U.S. federal law addressing interference with military functions, including recruitment, as well as insubordination within the military and the prevention of wartime support to the enemies of the U.S.) that included copying and then disseminating hundreds of thousands of classified military and U.S. State Department documents to the open access website Wikileaks (Tate, 2013). Upon his conviction, Manning was remanded to Fort Leavenworth, Kansas, the only facility in the military prison system designed to house those sentenced to 10 or more years. While many thought the controversies surrounding Bradley Manning would slowly fade away, a new, and for some more interesting issue, was about to surface.

In an open letter, dated the same day as his conviction, Manning declared "As I transition into this next phase of my life, I want everyone to know the real me. I am Chelsea Manning. I am a female. Given the way that I feel, and have felt since childhood, I want to begin hormone therapy as soon as possible. I hope that you will support me in this transition. I also request that, starting today, you refer to me by my new name and use the feminine pronoun (except in official mail to the confinement facility)" (Huetteman, 2013, para. 3). Lt. Col. Stephen Platt, a U.S. Army spokesman responding to Manning's declaration, stated that "Inmates at the United States Disciplinary Barracks and Joint Regional Correctional Facility are treated equally regardless of race, rank, ethnicity or sexual orientation" (Stump, 2013, para. 10). Lt. Col. Platt went on to say "The Army does not provide hormone therapy or sex-reassignment surgery for gender identity disorder. The USDB has implemented risk assessment protocols and safety procedures to address high risk factors identified with the Prison Rape Elimination Act" (Stump, 2013, para. 11).

Response to the Army's refusal to provide hormone treatment for Manning was swift and to the point as his attorney, David E. Combs, declared that if the military would not provide the treatment voluntarily, "then I'm going to do everything in my power to make sure they are forced to do so" (Huetteman, 2013, para. 7). For Mr. Combs, the need for hormone therapy extended beyond a precursor to gender re-assignment surgery because at that time, his client had not expressed a desire to pursue that option. Instead, the need for treatment centered on a psychological necessity and as such, was relevant to Manning's right to adequate medical care while confined.

The need to continue Manning's treatment for what is now known as **gender dysphoria** (an emotional and psychological discomfort with one's biological sex), was supported by two psychiatrists. According to Neal Minahan, an attorney familiar with lesbian, gay, bisexual, and transgendered (LGBT) inmates, this type of treatment is also consistent with the therapies given to other prison inmates (Huetteman, 2013). The difference, however, is that Manning is currently under military jurisdiction and subject to the Uniform Code of Military Justice (UCMJ), not the civilian criminal justice system where the inmates currently receiving hormone treatments are housed. The underlying question, therefore, is whether or not the military correctional system is being intolerant of Manning's gender dysphoria by denying his request for such treatment. According to Lt. Col. Platt, the answer is no. Inmate Manning is still a soldier and as such, eligible for psychiatric care and treatment (Stump, 2013). His attorney, however, disagrees, believing that hormone therapy is a valid and acceptable method of helping those with Manning's condition and that denying such treatment is unacceptable.

Discussion Questions

1. Do you believe employees at the Fort Leavenworth correctional facility should be required to call Bradley Manning by his preferred name—Chelsea?

2. Is hormone therapy an elective treatment or a treatment necessary for an inmate's physiological and or psychological well-being?

3. Should the government be required to pay for an inmate's hormone therapy?

Satanism behind Bars

In 1992, Robert James Howard was serving ten years for kidnapping and auto theft when he sued the Federal Correctional Institute at Englewood. In his complaint, Mr. Howard asked for a black robe, candles, candleholders, incense, a chalice, a short wooden staff, and a gong or bell. Howard's claim was that as a self-professed **Satanist** (one who worships Satan), he needed these items in order to freely practice the satanic rituals that were central to his religious beliefs and that a failure to approve his request violated his First Amendment right of religious freedom (*The New York Times*, 1994).

When Howard made his original appeal to prison officials, he was denied on the grounds that possession of such items constituted safety and security risks for the facility. The warden felt candles could be used to start fires and the robe could lead to inmate identification problems. According to Howard, however, these items were essential to perform three primary rituals that were a part of his satanic faith: (1) a compassionate ritual, (2) a personal ritual, and (3) a destruction ritual. He went on to say that at no time during these rites would he engage in such behaviors such as bloodletting or other potentially violent acts. Also, in an attempt to alleviate concerns over the destruction ritual, Howard explained that the rite was necessary to help him address any anger issues he might have towards individuals who he believed had wronged him. In the ritual, Howard stated that he visualizes killing the offending person so he is able to mentally process the desire and in doing so, eliminate any need to actually carry out those feelings in real life. Dr. Carl Raschke of the University of Denver and author on such topics as Satanism and the occult disagreed and warned "rituals of destruction are intended to kill people" (Brennan, 1994, para. 13). In fact, two of *The Eleven Satanic Rules of the Earth* are very specific on this issue and state, "4. If a guest in your lair annoys you, treat him cruelly and without mercy" and "11. When walking in open territory, bother no one. If someone bothers you, ask him to stop. If he does not stop, destroy him" (LaVey, 1967, para. 1).

Regardless of the safety concerns and intent of the rituals involved, Howard's lawyer, Darold Killmer, argued that it was his client's First Amendment right to practice Satanism while incarcerated and any failure by the system to allow him access to his rites would only highlight the intolerance of the federal correctional facility towards religious beliefs the administration deemed unacceptable. **U.S. District Court** (district courts are the general trial courts of the federal court system) Judge Edward Nottingham agreed, and for the first time a federal inmate's right to practice Satanism was upheld. In his 23-page ruling, Judge Nottingham noted that the prison's position "appears to have been based on the content of plaintiff's beliefs — an unacceptable criteria according to the Supreme Court" and that the judge would "refuse to gloss over the serious First Amendment concerns that this raises" (*The Christian Century*, 1994, para. 2). In addition, the court believed that while the prison raised some legitimate safety and security issues, "The problem is that many of the other religious groups regularly use these very same — allegedly very dangerous — implements" (para. 4). He added that while the court's decision "does not require **prison** officials to accommodate every form of Satanism, nor does it necessarily require them to allow each inmate to become a religion unto himself" (para. 4), in the end, Judge Nottingham felt that "We ought to give the devil his due" (Brennan, 1994, para. 2).

While the court had rendered its decision on Howard's request to practice satanic rituals while incarcerated, an interesting twist to this story is the position of the Church of Satan. According to Peter Gilmore, High Priest of the Church of Satan, "We do not allow Active Membership to convicted felons, particularly if the crime shows a violation of Satanic principles for social behavior. If a Church of Satan member is convicted of a felony it should be understood that membership is automatically terminated, more so if the crime is one that breaks basic tenets of Satanism" (Church of Satan, 2013, para. 2). In fact, Gilmore goes on to say that while such items as a gong and incense are used in some rituals, they, like the black robe, are not required. Ultimately, because of Howard's criminal background and his misrepresentation of satanic doctrine, the Church of Satan would have most likely denied that Howard was Satanist in the true sense of the word and therefore his self-proclamation as such would have been suspect.

Discussion Questions

1. Do you believe Satanists should be allowed to perform religious rituals in prison?

2. Does restricting the types of elements a Satanist is allowed to use in rituals constitute a violation of their First Amendment rights?

3. Should violent acts against other inmates that are clearly part of a religious doctrine be protected under the First Amendment?

Infant Inmates

Jacqueline McDougail is a young, single mother raising her son Max without any help from family or friends. She gets up every day, feeds Max, plays with him, and tries to be the best mother possible. On the surface, Jacqueline's story sounds like countless other young women across America struggling with the challenges of motherhood. The difference, however, is that Max was born and is being raised in prison while Jacqueline serves her time as an inmate at the Bedford Hills Correctional Facility for Women in Bedford Hills, New York.

While this might seem like an isolated incident, babies being born in prison and then raised by their biological mothers as they serve out their sentences are a growing trend in corrections worldwide. Historically, women who came to prison pregnant or become pregnant while **incarcerated** (which is the process or state of being confined in a lockdown correctional institution) had to either give the child up for adoption at birth or transfer custody of the child to a family member living outside of the facility (Raising a child, 2014). Pediatricians, however, like Dr. Janet Stockhelm, felt this type of response was archaic and detrimental to the psychological well-being of the mother and the proper development of the child. In fact, Dr. Stockhelm argues that "The babies aren't aware. They get excellent care" (Brown & Valiente, 2014, para. 13). She goes on to say "They are very well bonded to the mothers.... Bonding gives a baby trust in the world that they will be taken care of. The babies do better here than they would on the outside with some of these mothers" (para. 13). Most of those in favor of these arrangements, however, also agree that not everyone would qualify to raise her child in prison, and those facilities that do allow mothers to care for their newborns should only do so until the child reaches a certain age (this age and other qualifying characteristics vary from facility to facility worldwide).

The Daphne III Project (a European criminal justice organization focused on fundamental rights and justice) agrees with the concept of maternal settings in prisons and believes that Children of Incarcerated Parents (CHIP) who are not raised by their imprisoned mother (IM) are at greater risk for social isolation, devastating developmental and psychological effects, homelessness, and future incarceration (Raising a child, 2014). The group argues that creating a nurturing environment for both incarcerated mothers and their children not only promotes the overall health and safety of both mother and child, but also is more cost effective in the long run. Liz Hamilton, the nursery program director at Bedford, supports this argument and says that at her facility, the yearly cost for each child under her care is around $24,000, while the yearly housing expenses of the mother are approximately $30,000. Ms. Hamilton believes that if the mother "stays out of jail for five years, think of [those] savings" (Brown & Valiente, 2014, para. 18). She adds, "It's keeping that child from the foster care system. That's another expensive program" (para. 19).

Not everyone, however, supports the concept of mothers raising their children behind bars. James Dwyer, a law professor at the William and Mary Law School, feels that separating an incarcerated mother from her infant a birth is not an act of intolerance by the system because the child has not been charged or convicted of a crime. As such, these arrangements violate the infant's Fourteenth Amendment right to due process (Santiago, 2013). Additionally, there are already laws in place that specifically prohibit minors from being incarcerated with adults (in most cases, they must be separated by sight and sound—meaning the minors cannot see or hear the adult inmates and vice versa). Lastly, Professor Dwyer points out that to date, there have been no long-term studies addressing the effects of such arrangements on the children born and raised in prison. He questions whether the correctional system is placing the needs of the mother over the needs of the child.

In the end, this is one controversial issue for corrections that will not be going away anytime soon. According to Rebecca Baird-Remba of the Business Insider (2013), "For incarcerated mothers around the world, the best they can hope for are nursery programs, which let children live with their mothers while they're young. Beyond that they are limited to occasional visits" (para. 2). She adds that, "There are few provisions for mothers in prison in the U.S., where more than 120,000 imprisoned women have children under 18, according to a 2010 Pew Research report. Only nine states in the U.S. have prison nurseries" (para. 3). If these arrangements continue to gain support, however, one must wonder if we have opened Pandora's Box to a new type of correctional intolerance—denying the rights of incarcerated fathers to also raise their children.

Discussion Questions

1. Do you believe mothers should be allowed to raise infant children in prison?

2. In your opinion, is it cheaper for the government to provide nurseries and daycares for incarcerated mothers and their infants than to have the children cared for outside of the correctional facility?

3. Should fathers also be allowed to raise their infant child in prison if they so choose?

"Illegal" Corrections Officers

Detective Carmen Figueroa of the Arizona Department of Public Safety was a respected officer who was well liked within the agency. She began her 10-year career as a highway patrol officer and was eventually promoted to criminal investigator in 2010. By all indications, Detective Figueroa was on the fast track to a fulfilling and promising career. Things began to change, however, when her brother, an airman in the United States Air Force, applied for a passport. It was then the U.S. State Department discovered an unsettling truth—both Detective Figueroa and her brother were in the United States illegally. As a result of these revelations, Detective Figueroa resigned from the department in December 2012.

For her part, Ms. Figueroa had always believed she was a legal U.S. citizen. According to Bart Graves of the Arizona Department of Public Safety, "When she was informed by the State Department that she and her brother were not U.S. citizens, that was the first she'd heard of it" (Hassan & Castillo, 2013, para. 10). He added, "Her mother had told her she was born in this country" (para. 10). State Department records, however, told another story and showed Ms. Figueroa was in fact born in Sinaloa, Mexico, and later brought into the United States illegally as a young child. Under Arizona law, all peace officers must be U.S. citizens.

In reaction to the Figueroa incident, Arizona Representative Darin Mitchell drafted House Bill 2133 that would require all **corrections officers** (safety officers working for a local, state, federal, military, or private department of corrections) in the state to be United States citizens. The bill also stipulates that all peace officers in the state would be required to provide proof of citizenship. For Representative Mitchell, the intent of the bill is not to discriminate against non-U.S. citizens, but instead, protect the right to work of those who are. He believes that "When I represent a district that has 34 percent unemployment rate, we ought to make a really strong effort to reach out to them" (Galvan, 2014, para. 4). Mitchell goes on to say "It's about certain citizenship advantages that you have. You were a citizen, you were born there, shouldn't you at least have a first dib at that job? That's all we're saying" (Martin, 2014, para. 2).

Opponents of the bill, such as Representative Ruben Gallego, charge that such actions are discriminatory against permanent legal residents who are not U.S. citizens. He believes "We're a better country than trying to pit one class of people against another, and legal permanent residents are a type of people" (Galvan, 2014, para. 5). Representative Gallego went on to say, "I'm going to fight this all the way to the end because it's really disgusting that veterans of the Iraq and Afghanistan war that still can't become citizens because there's time requirements are going to be precluded from a good, decent paying job, especially at a time when the Department of Corrections are saying they are short of people who are qualified to take this job" (Martin, 2014, para. 10).

Officials from the Arizona Department of Corrections also disagree with the implementation of these types of intolerant policies. With 450 positions currently vacant and another 400 officers who are considered permanent legal residents currently working in the state, requiring all correctional officers in Arizona to be U.S. citizens would place an undue burden on the state in general and the department in particular. Will Barrow, a legislative liaison for the department, explains, "One of the things we know is that if we don't have officers to fill positions, we have to do other things like mandate overtime, leave positions vacant, which obviously creates a public safety risk and reduces morale among the officers" (Martin, 2014, para. 6). Legislators countered this argument by saying the bill would not be retroactive and those correctional officers who currently have permanent legal status would not be affected.

As the battle over whether or not corrections officers in the state of Arizona should be required to hold U.S. citizenship intensifies, a parallel dilemma is starting to emerge. If the employment bar is lowered and non-U.S. citizens are allowed to work as officers within the Arizona Department of Corrections, will this new dynamic hurt the professional status of corrections officers within the state? Currently, all Arizona law enforcement officers are legally required to be U.S. citizens. If corrections officers are not held to the same hiring standard, will they be viewed as less than equal members of the peace officer community?

Discussion Questions

1. Do you believe the proposed Arizona bill requiring corrections officers within the state to be U.S. citizens is a form of cultural intolerance?

2. Should permanent residents who are not U.S. citizens, but who served in the U.S. military, be employable as peace officers in the United States?

3. Should U.S. citizens be given priority status over non-U.S. citizens who are legal residents when applying for government positions, such as state corrections officers?

Sex Offender Registries

On November 22, 2003, Dru Sjodin was in a Grand Forks, North Dakota, mall parking lot talking with her boyfriend on her cell phone when a man appeared with a knife. Approximately five months later, Ms. Sjodin's body was found, dumped in a ravine after she had been repeatedly beaten, raped, and strangled over almost a three-hour period. Her attacker, Alfonso Rodriguez Jr., was convicted of the brutal **assault** (a physical attack on an individual) and sentenced to death. At the time of Ms. Sjodin's murder, Rodriguez, a Level 3 (highest risk) state of Minnesota registered sex offender, had been out of prison for approximately six months after serving 23 years for rape and attempted kidnapping (Lee, 2013).

In response to the horrific events surrounding the Dru Sjodin murder and the fact that her assailant was a registered sex offender at the time of the offenses, the Adam Walsh Child Protection and Safety Act, signed into law on July 27, 2006, by President George W. Bush, included a section that changed the name of the National Sex Offender Public Registry (NSOPR) to the Dru Sjodin National Sex Offender Public Website (NSOPW). The intent of the website is to provide information to the public on the location and personal characteristics of criminals who are required to register as sex offenders.

Since their inception in 1994 with the passage of the Jacob Wetterling Crimes Against Children and Sexually Violent Offender Registration Act, sex offender registries have come under attack as intolerant forms of overly punitive retribution whose sole purpose is to humiliate offenders who have legally satisfied the requirements of their convictions (Moraff, 2013). Organizations, such as the **American Civil Liberties Union** (ACLU) (a non-profit legal organization), also believe that publicly available sex offender registries are intolerant of sexual offenders because they interfere with effective treatment, rehabilitation, and reintegration of convicted offenders. In fact, Deborah Jacobs, director of the ACLU of New Jersey, argues that many elements of sex offender registration, such as the banishment zones that require offenders to live a certain distance from identified areas like schools, parks, and daycare centers, actually decrease public safety. Ms. Jacobs states "People who transition from prison into society face countless challenges, and most have very limited resources, financial or otherwise. People who want to lead law-abiding lives after serving a prison sentence need to establish stability in their homes, jobs and families. Those are difficult things to achieve, but add to this the consequences of Megan's Law and limits to where offenders can live, and few have hope of succeeding. Indeed, the fear of the stigma of Megan's Law can force offenders underground, out of the watchful eye of police and parole officers" (Jacobs, 2014, para. 5).

Those in favor of the sex offender registries, however, point to the fact that, in 2013, there were approximately 750,000 registered sex offenders in the United States and with dwindling correctional budgets, it would be nearly impossible to keep track of each person (Moraff, 2013). As such, it's important to keep everyone, including the general public, informed and aware. By requiring offenders to register, many believe that law enforcement and corrections officials can legally keep track of not only where they live, but also how successful they are in safely reintegrating back into society. Registration may also provide a deterrent effect because, as Seattle University law professor David Boemer points out, "They know who I am and where I am" (Farley, 2010, para. 36). Perhaps the most telling outcome, however, was shared by Kevin Hall, a deputy prosecutor of Kipsap County, who says, "I've had attorneys tell me, 'My guy will do twice the amount of time in custody — as long as they don't have to register.' That tells me that there is some value to it" (Farley, 2010, para. 31).

For the families affected by such tragedies as the Dru Sjodin case, requiring sex offenders to register will never bring back their loved ones. Society must, however, continue to grapple with the question of whether or not sex offender registries are prudent, proactive measures designed to protect society as a whole or restrictive and excessive punishments that fail to treat, rehabilitate, and reintegrate offenders back into society in a pro-social way. As Prosecutor Russ Hauge of Kipsap County, Washington, states when discussing the likelihood of a registered sex offender committing another horrific offense — "It doesn't happen very often, but when it does, it's a tragedy" (Farley, 2010, para. 21).

Discussion Questions

1. Do you believe sex offender registries are designed to be punitive or reintegrative?

2. Are sex offender registries a form of double jeopardy?

3. Is it unreasonable that sex offenders, like felons, give up certain personal freedoms and liberties upon conviction that extend beyond incarceration?

Incarcerating the Mentally Ill

Armando Cruz was a 28-year-old inmate serving time in the Psychiatric Services Unit of California State Prison, Sacramento, for the attempted murder of a police officer. Cruz, who had a long history of mental illness, both inside the California correctional system and out, was usually on some form of psychotropic drug and had tried to kill himself a number of times. On September 20, 2011, he succeeded. Correctional officers, in the course of conducting their rounds, found Cruz hanging in his cell along with a note that read simply "RE-MEMBER ME" (Rodriguez, 2013, para. 2).

As correctional facilities across the United States are forced to deal with an ever-growing inmate population that suffers from a variety of mental illnesses, the story of Armando Cruz is unfortunately not unique. In 2011 alone, 33 inmates in the California correctional system, including Cruz, committed suicide while incarcerated (Rodriguez, 2013). University of Maryland law professor Amanda Pustilnik believes "Today, our largest mental hospitals are our jails. The jail at New York's Rikers' Island functions as the nation's largest psychiatric facility. Los Angeles' jails — not its hospitals — are California's largest providers of mental health care. State prisons alone spend nearly $5 billion annually to incarcerate mentally ill inmates who are not violent" (Frances, 2013, para. 4).

Despite the growing problem, Dr. Linda Teplin of Northwestern University feels the news isn't all bad. She believes "Jails have been very good nationwide now about recognizing the need to screen for severe mental disorders when people come in, and also to provide treatment for people who are in their facility" (NPR, 2013, para. 32). The challenges for correctional facilities that are strained to meet the daily needs of the communities they serve are not only the diagnoses of mental illness among arrestees and training of correctional staff on how best to deal with them, but economic as well. Valerie Sylvester, director of medical services for the Corrections Center of Northeast Ohio, reported that in 2009 "25 percent of [the correction center's] inmates were on psychotropic medications; the cost of the drugs accounted for half of the medical budget" (Torrey et al., 2010, p. 6).

The question for many though isn't how well the jails and prisons are doing at caring for the mentally ill and at what cost, but should those suffering from a mental illness be confined to a jail or prison in the first place. Have jails and prisons become a modern-day dumping ground of all sorts for individuals with a mental illness? Unfortunately, often there is nowhere else to place them for treatment. M. J. Stephey of *Time* (2007) found that "Fifty years ago, the U.S. had nearly 600,000 state hospital beds for people suffering from mental illness. Today, because of federal and state funding cuts, that number has dwindled to 40,000. When the government began closing state-run hospitals in the 1980s, people suffering from mental illness had nowhere to go. Without proper **treatment** [care given to someone for a condition or behavior] and care, many ended up in the last place anyone wants to be" (para. 4). According to the Treatment Advocacy Center and the National Sheriff's Association, "Deinstitutionalization, the emptying of state mental hospitals, has been one of the most well-meaning but poorly planned social changes ever carried out in the United States. It was a product of the overcrowding and deterioration of hospitals; new medications that significantly improved the symptoms of about half of patients; and a failure to understand that many of the sickest patients were not able to make informed decisions about their own need for medication" (Torrey, et al., 2010, p. 2).

As a society, have we given up on the mentally ill, or do we now simply prefer the "out of sight, out of mind" mentality that seems to have become prevalent since deinstitutionalization began in the 1950s? There are always plenty of places to point fingers, but ultimately it appears the system prefers to blame corrections. Are they truly intolerant of the mentally ill or overwhelmed with the seemingly endless array of human conditions the profession is expected to correct when offenders walk through their doors? There is no easy answer, but for the Cruz family, something must be done and done quickly so another inmate isn't found hanging in his or her cell with a note that says "REMEMBER ME."

Discussion Questions

1. Are we asking too much of modern-day corrections with respect to the care and treatment of those with mental illnesses?

2. Should corrections be responsible for the care and treatment of non-violent mentally ill offenders?

3. Who do you feel should be ultimately responsible for addressing the mental health issues of those who commit crimes in the United States?

Food Allergies

Carlo Vartinelli is a man of questionable character. Serving a life sentence for first-degree criminal sexual conduct, Vartinelli, an inmate in the Michigan state prison system, claimed that the state's food service contractor, **Aramark Correctional Services** (an American food service provider commonly known as Aramark), repeatedly and intentionally served him peanut butter and fish. While on the surface these actions may not appear to be acts of intolerance, according to Vartinelli (and his most recent 2018 lawsuit against the prison's food service contractor), the company directly violated his rights to receive meals that would not incite his **food allergies** (an abnormal reaction to food that triggers the body's immune system).

According to the Federal Bureau of Prisons (2017), the term food allergies does not have a basic, universally accepted definition. For the sake of uniformity among its facilities, however, the agency uses the National Institute of Health's (NIH) classification that says a food allergy is "an adverse immune response that occurs reproducibly on exposure to a given food and is distinct from other adverse responses to food, such as food intolerance, pharmacologic reactions, and toxin-mediated reactions" (p. 1). The NIH also makes clear that food allergies differ from food intolerance, such as the inability to digest the sugar lactose.

Spanning a two-year period, from 2014 to 2015, Vartinelli's lawsuit contended that he was routinely served meals that contained either fish, peanut butter, or by-products containing fish or peanut butter (*Carlo Vartinelli v. Aramark Correctional Services*, 2019). In the legal complaint, Vartinelli's lawyer stated that exposure to those foods required multiple medical interventions and on two of those occasions, his client was forced to seek additional treatment at the local hospital. In addition, ingesting those substances has also caused permanent damage to his client's health, including chest pains, trouble breathing, and heart and nerve problems. According to Carlo, he repeatedly protested to prison officials and food service employees who, in return, acknowledged his need for nutritional accommodations and promised to do better.

In response to Vartinelli's complaints, prison officials enacted a series of modifications to help reduce/eliminate his exposure to foods that might cause him physical harm. Some of those adjustments included having him fed in his cell, the presence of **EpiPens** (epinephrine injection devices used to treat allergic reactions) during meals, and repeated reminders to the food staff and servers that Carlo was allergic to peanut butter and fish. Vartinelli's lawyer, however, argued that those adjustments were not enough, and that prison staff and Aramark Correctional Services employees showed deliberate indifference to his client's needs and the potentially lethal consequence those indifferences might cause.

On March 28, 2019, U.S. District Judge Paul Borman dismissed Vartinelli's lawsuit against Aramark Correctional Services. In his 37-page ruling, Judge Borman acknowledged the existence of Carlo's food allergies and the potential negative effects ingesting peanut butter or fish could have on his health. However, the court could not find any evidence that either Aramark Correctional Services or the Michigan prison system had intentionally given the offender any allergenic foods. In his ruling, Judge Borman stated:

> Although it is no doubt frightening for the plaintiff to have experienced these allergic reactions in a correctional environment, in the end plaintiff's complaint simply fails to adequately allege the personal involvement or the subjective awareness of any of the individual ... defendants (Bloom, 2019, para. 5).

Discussion Questions

1. What do you feel constitutes "deliberate indifference" in the care and feeding of inmates?

2. How far should correctional facilities have to go to accommodate an inmate's nutritional needs?

3. Should an inmate be held partially responsible for the costs required to accommodate special nutritional needs?

Chapter Key Terms

Sovereign citizens movement
Ideology
Excessive force
Injunction
Espionage Act
Gender dysphoria
Satanist
U.S. District Court
Incarcerated
The Daphne III Project

Corrections officers
Assault
American Civil Liberties
Union
Treatment
Aramark Correctional Serv-
ices
Food allergies
EpiPens

References

American Civil Liberties Union (ACLU). (2012, September 26). UC Davis students reach $1 million settlement with university over pepper-spraying incident. https://www.aclu.org/free-speech/uc-davis-students-reach-1-million-settlement-university-over-pepper-spraying-incident.

ACLU Utah. (2013, October 18). ACLU of Utah hails Utah Supreme Court's decision vacating Ogden's "Gang Injunction," vows to challenge further attempts to curtail rights. https://www.aclu.org/keep-america-safe-and-free/aclu-utah-hails-utah-supreme-courts-decision-vacating-ogdens-gang.

Ahle, S. (2013). Colorado State Police and Homeland Security target Christians. Red Statements. Deactivated link (retrieved 2013). http://redstatements.co/colorado-state-police-and-homeland-security-target-christians/.

Baird-Remba, R. (2013, June 2). What it's like raising kids from prison. Business Insider Australia. http://www.businessinsider.com.au/moms-in-prison-around-the-world-photos-2013-5#a-prison-in-lima-peru-opened-a-new-nursery-this-month-to-offer-better-care-for-the-40-children-there-who-are-allowed-to-stay-with-their-imprisoned-mothers-until-they-turn-3-1.

Bloom, D. (2019, March 29). Judge dismisses suit by prisoner repeatedly served peanut butter and fish despite allergies. SnackSafely.com. https://snacksafely.com/2019/03/judge-dismisses-suit-by-prisoner-repeatedly-served-peanut-butter-and-fish-despite-allergies/.

Brennan, C. (1994, October 13). Federal judge rule inmate can perform satanic rites. Deseret News. http://www.deseretnews.com.

Brown, E., & Valiente, A. (2014, February 7). Babies born, raised behind bars may keep mothers from returning to prison. ABC News. http://www.abcnews.go.com/US/babies-born-raised-bars-mothers-returning-prison/story?

id=22413184#:~:text=Babies%20Born%2C%20Raised%20Behind%20Bars%20May%20Keep%20Mothers%20From%20Returning%20to%20Prison,-By%20ELY%20BROWN&text=Jacqueline%20McDougall%20raised%20her%20son,future%20was%20on%20the%20line.

Carlo Vartinelli v. Aramark Correctional Servs., No. 19-1428 (6th Cir. 2019).

CBS News. (2011). UC Davis pepper spray cop once lauded. http://www.cbsnews.com/news/uc-davis-pepper-spray-cop-once-lauded/.

Church of Satan. (2013) F.A.Q. Prisoner issues. http://www.churchofsatan.com/faq-prisoner-issues.php.

Cutler, A. (2013, October 18). Utah Supreme Court throws out anti-gang injunction. Fox 13 News Salt Lake City. http://fox13now.com/2013/10/18/utah-supreme-court-throws-out-anti-gang-restraining-orders-in-ogden/.

Dru Sjodin National Sex Offender Public Website (NSOPW). (2014). U.S. Department of Justice, Office of Sex Offender Sentencing, Monitoring, Apprehending, Registering, and Tracking. http://www.nsopw.gov.

Farley, J. (2010). Should all convicted sex offenders be required to register? *Kitsap Sun.* http://archive.kitsapsun.com/news/local/should-all-convicted-sex-offenders-be-required-to-register-ep-419096868-357401281.html/.

Federal Bureau of Prisons. (2017, November). Management of Food Allergies. Clinical Guidance. https://www.bop.gov/resources/pdfs/food_allergy_guidance_201711.pdf.

Fields, L. (2013). Controversial gang injunction overturned by Utah Supreme Court. ABC News. http://abcnews.go.com/US/controversial-gang-injunction-overturned-utah-supreme-court/story?id=20624285.

Frances, A. J. (2013, March 10). Prison or treatment for the mentally ill? *Psychology Today.* http://psychologytoday.com/us/blog/saving-normal/201303/prison-or-treatment-the-mentally-ill.

Galvan, A. (2014, February 12). Bill requires citizenship for corrections officers. *The Washington Times.* http://www.washingtontimes.com.

Hallowell, B. (2013, April 9). Colo. Sheriff alleges shock training to TheBlaze: DHS-bound official warned against 'Christians who take the Bible literally.' The Blaze. http://www.theblaze.com/stories/2013/04/09/colo-sheriff-describes-shock-training-to-theblaze-dhs-bound-official-warned-against-christians-who-take-the-bible-literally/.

Hassan, C., & Castillo, M. (2013, December 12). Detective resigns after citizenship status revealed. CNN. https://www.cnn.com/2013/12/12/us/arizona-police-undocumented-detective/index.html.

Huetteman, E. (2013, August 22). 'I am a female,' Manning announces, asking Army for hormone therapy. *The New York Times.* http://www.nytimes.com/2013/08/23/us/bradley-manning-says-he-is-female.html.

Huffington Post. (2012). Annett Spicuzza, UC Davis Police Chief, resigned after pepper spray incident. Deactivated link (retrieved 2015). http://www. huffingtonpost.com/2012/04/18/annette-spicuzza-uc-davis_n_1436075. html.

Jacobs, D. (2014). Why sex offender laws do more harm than good. American Civil Liberties Union of New Jersey. http://www.aclu-nj.org/theissues/ criminaljustice/whysexoffenderlawsdomoreha.

Kelman, B. (2017, November). After Warm Sands gay sex sting case, judge accused of homophobic comment in secret recording. *Desert Sun.* https:// www.desertsun.com/story/news/crime_courts/2017/11/01/after-warm -sands-gay-sex-sting-case-judge-accused-homophobic-comment-secret -recording/801395001/.

Kingkade, T. (2012a, February 22). UC Davis students file lawsuit against school over pepper spraying of protesters. Huffington Post. https://www. huffpost.com/entry/uc-davis-students-file-lawsuit_n_1294411.

Kingkade, T. (2012b, September 26). UC Davis pepper spraying victims to receive nearly $1 million settlement. Huffington Post. http://www.huffingtonpost. com/2012/09/26/uc-davis-pepper-spraying-settlement_n_1916803.html.

LaVey, A. S. (1967). The eleven satanic rules of the earth. http://www.churchof satan.com.

Lee, S. J. (2013, November 13). Rodriguez was sane when he killed Dru Sjodin, experts say. Twin Cities Pioneer Press. https://www.twincities.com/2013/ 11/12/rodriguez-was-sane-when-he-killed-dru-sjodin-experts-say/.

Martin, J. (2014, February 12). Bill would require U.S. citizenship for state prison guards. KTAR News. https://ktar.com/story/82688/bill-would -require-us-citizenship-for-state-prison-guards/.

Moraff, C. (2013, May 31). Sex offender registries: Good idea gone bad? *Philadelphia.* https://www.phillymag.com/news/2013/05/31/sex-offender -registries-good-idea-bad/.

NBC News. (2013). University of California cop who pepper-sprayed student protesters awarded $38,000. NBC News. http://www.nbcnews.com/news/us- news/university-california-cop-who-pepper-sprayed-student-protesters -awarded-38-v21105239.

National Public Radio (NPR). (2013, September 15). What is the role of jails in treating the mentally ill? All Things Considered. http://www.npr.org/2013/ 09/15/222822452/what-is-the-role-of-jails-in-treating-the-mentally-ill.

Nelson, P. (2013, October 18). Injunction against 'Ogden Trece' gang over turned by court. KSL Broadcasting. http://www.ksl.com/?sid=27299251.

Peralta, E. (2013). UC Davis' 'pepper spray cop' wins $38K in workers' comp. NPR. http://www.npr.org/blogs/thetwo-way/2013/10/23/240343882/uc-davis-pepper-spray-cop-wins-38k-in-workers-comp.

Raising a child through prison bars. (2014). The DAPHNE III Project. http://www.mothers-in-prison.eu.

Reavy, P. (2012, August 12). Ogden gang injunction made permanent; appeal expected. *Deseret News*. http://www.deseretnews.com/article/865560947/Ogden-gang-injunction-made-permanent-appeal-expected.html?pg=all.

Reynoso Task Force Report: UC Davis November 18, 2011 "pepper spray incident" task force report. (2012). https://demonstrationreviews.ucdavis.edu/local_resources/pdf_documents/reynoso-report.pdf.

Rodriguez, S. (2013, January 17). Suicide in solitary: The life and death of Armando Cruz (Part I). Solitary Watch. http://www.solitarywatch.com/2013/01/17/suicide-in-solitary-the-life-and-death-of-armando-cruz-part-1/.

Santiago, K. M. (2013, June 3). Babies behind bars: Motherly love or abuse? HLN. Deactivated link (retrieved 2015). http://hlntv.com.

Schwartz, C. (2011, November 10). Occupy U.C. Berkeley protesters face violent confrontation with campus police (video). Huffington Post. http://www.huffingtonpost.com/2011/11/10/occupy-uc-berkeley-police_n_1086195.html.

Seidl, J. (2012, February 7). FBI increasing its monitoring of 'Sovereign Citizens'—but why? The Blaze. https://www.theblaze.com/news/2012/02/07/fbi-increasing-its-monitoring-of-sovereign-citizens-but-why.

Sloss, J. (2011). Court motion claims sex stings unfairly target gays. http://www.kesq.com/Court-Motion-Claims-Sex-Stings-Unfairly-Target-Gays/499986.

Stephey, M. J. (2007, August 8). De-criminalizing mental illness. *Time*. http://www.content.time.com/health/article/0,8599,1651002,00.html.

Stump, S. (2013, August 22). Bradley Manning: I want to live as a woman. *Today News*. http://www.today.com/news/bradley-manning-i-want-live-woman-6C10974915.

Tate, J. (2013, August 21). Judge sentences Bradley Manning to 35 years. *The Washington Post*. http://www.washingtonpost.com.

The Christian Century. (1994, November 16). Prison ordered to allow satanic rituals. *111*(33), 1072.

The New York Times. (1994, October 18). Court ruling allows satanism in prisons. http://www.nytimes.com/1994/10/18/us/court-ruling-allows-satanism-in-prisons.html.

Torrey, E. F., Kennard, A. D., Eslinger, D., Lamb, R., & Pavle, J. (2010, May). More mentally ill persons are in jails and prisons than hospitals: A survey of the states. The Treatment Advocacy Center. http://www.treatment advocacycenter.org/storage/documents/final_jails_v_hospitals_study.pdf.

Valley News. (2010). Palm Springs police chief apologizes for insensitive remarks during sex sting. Deactivated link (retrieved 2015). http://www.my valleynews.com/story/53424/.

Wagner, G. (2011, March). Most Defendants in Palm Springs Sex Sting Expected to Accept Plea Deals. https://www.nbclosangeles.com/news/local/most-defendants-in-palm-springs-sex-sting-expected-to-accept-plea-deals/1918599/.

Walsh, E. (2010). Firestorm erupts over Palm Springs sex sting. https://www.ebar.com/news///240767.

Wilson, P. (2011). Palm Springs police chief resigns over gay sex sting. http://articles.latimes.com/2011/jan/11/local/la-me-palm-springs-20110111.

Yi, S. (2010, September 28). Ogden enforcing ban on street gang. KSL.com. http://www.ksl.com/?sid=12610904&fm=related_story&s_cid=article-related-2.

Chapter Three

Subterfuge

The Florida Klan has a better plan than lynching to be rid of those they label communistic: it is mysterious disappearance with no traces left. Frank Norman was an organizer of the United Citrus Workers' Union and a thorn in the side of the dominant whites. One of his aims was that blacks and whites should stick together.... Frank Norman did not return. Nor has his body been discovered. It may have been buried in an unknown grave, or burned in a mysterious fire that occurred a few days later. It may have been weighted and sunk in one of the many lakes in the vicinity, or dropped into one of the flooded phosphate pits close by.

—Frank Shay, *Judge Lynch*, pp. 243, 244–45 (1938)

People who wish to act badly prefer darkness to light. As the expression goes, sunlight is a powerful disinfectant. A large body of constitutional legal cases concerns itself with the necessity for criminal justice actors to act transparently. Stained glass may be beautiful in cathedrals, but society is much better off when our police stations, courthouses and prisons have windows that are clear.

This chapter (and the next) deals with the constitutional taboo of subterfuge. **Subterfuge** encompasses such concepts as concealment, deception, evasion, and non-accountability. Our country is one that is unalterably opposed to such historical pathologies as the secret police, the Star Chamber, or the gulag. To prevent such ills, a body of constitutional law has developed in this nation which guards against officials acting stealthily.

Many of the cases in this chapter will concern themselves with issues of subterfuge in the context of our courts. However, we shall begin by dealing with the need for straightforwardness in the conduct of our police and for accountability in what is taking place behind the imposing walls of our penal institutions.

Subterfuge and the Police

Police carry handcuffs, batons, stun guns, and pistols. They must be held to high levels of accountability. The cases in this section are attempts by the courts to "check" the police so that they continue to walk the path of constitutionally acceptable behavior.

Miranda v. Arizona is quite possibly the most famous Supreme Court case world-wide. Thanks to the American entertainment industry, nearly everyone on the planet with access to television or a movie theater knows the warnings American police normally have to give those they arrest and interrogate. But why must officers give these warnings? What happens if they do not? And must officers give warnings regarding other constitutional rights? These and other questions are addressed in our next three cases.

Miranda v. Arizona
384 U.S. 436 (1966)

One of the most famous cases that attempts to get police to stop engaging in "off the grid" dirty antics is *Miranda v. Arizona*. Miranda was an accused rapist who, after being arrested, was questioned extensively by the police. During the two hours of questioning, he wound up eventually confessing to the rape. He did not allege that the police used any torture to extract this confession. However, what upset Miranda was that the police never bothered to inform him that he had a constitutional right to refuse to answer their questions or to have a lawyer present if he chose to continue.

So, the issue on appeal was whether the police should be required to inform suspects of their right to avoid self-incrimination before any **custodial questioning** (interrogation of someone who is not free to leave) occurs. The police took the position that such a requirement was ludicrous. After all, they are not defense attorneys. Their job is to fight crime, not to teach people about their rights. Advising suspects of their Fifth Amendment right to avoid self-incrimination might only help the guilty to evade successful prosecution. Why would the police want to do that? The police did not deny that such a Fifth Amendment constitutional right existed. They just did not think it was their responsibility to highlight the right to a criminal suspect.

The Supreme Court disagreed. It ruled that henceforth, police must advise anyone subject to questioning while in custody of certain "procedural safeguards" that they possess which will help them to secure their right to not self-incriminate. The *Miranda* **rights** or warnings which police must give include the right to remain silent, that anything said can be used negatively in court, and the right to have an attorney present before voluntarily choosing to answer questions (including a free lawyer if one is too poor to afford one). If the police fail to advise someone in custody of these rights prior to the interrogation, then any incriminating statements that are given will be kept from the jury at trial (**suppressed**).

What the Court was really worried about was the police taking advantage of the inherently "coercive" and "police dominated" atmosphere produced by a custodial interrogation to cheat people out of their right to not have to self-incriminate. It felt that requiring police to advise someone of her rights would greatly help dispel some of this coercion and help balance the scales. This is so for two reasons. First, people are not legally trained and do not necessarily know their constitutional rights. Second, just hearing the police recite these rights will help people feel better and less intimidated. The suspect will not only know his or her rights, but will know that the police know these rights and apparently are willing to honor them.

It should be noted that the police cannot try to dodge this "procedural safeguard" by trying to talk someone out of a decision to remain silent or have a lawyer present once it is chosen. That sort of underhandedness will not be tolerated. Once a suspect invokes the right to remain silent, the interrogation must end. Once a suspect asks to have a lawyer present, the interrogation must end until a lawyer is present (this is known in police jargon as the suspect's having "**lawyered up**").

Discussion Questions

1. Do you agree that custodial questioning is so inherently high-pressured that *Miranda* rights are necessary to help dissipate the pressure? What is it about this situation that is so high-pressured?

2. What do you make of the fact that none of the other Western democracies always require their police to advise people in custody of their

> right to remain silent or to have a lawyer present? Are these countries
> all dropping the ball?

The *Miranda* decision is remarkable because police can no longer use subterfuge as easily as had been the case in the past to get people to self-incriminate. It is our first case in which the Supreme Court seems to want to use its influence to guard against forms of police subterfuge. Although a very famous case, *Miranda* has proven controversial in application. The justices have disagreed mightily about exactly when evidence should be suppressed if its requirements are not followed. Now, let us examine a case that illustrates this type of situation and reveals just how divided the justices are about how *Miranda* should be applied.

United States v. Patane

542 U.S. 630 (2004)

In June 2001, officers were called to investigate a reported violation of a restraining order prohibiting Samuel Francis Patane from contacting his ex-girlfriend. Simultaneously a county probation officer reported that Patane, a convicted felon, was in illegal possession of a firearm (specifically a Glock pistol). After questioning Patane at his residence, officers arrested Patane for violation of the restraining order. Patane interrupted the officers giving him the *Miranda* warnings, stating that he knew his rights.

Following the interruption, the questioning continued. The respondent was initially reluctant to respond to questions about the firearm, stating "I am not sure I should tell you anything about the Glock because I don't want you to take it away from me." Officers persisted with their questioning, and Patane told them where it was and gave them permission to retrieve it. The Glock pistol was found and seized.

A grand jury indicted the respondent for possession of a firearm by a convicted felon. The district court granted Patane's motion to suppress the Glock pistol, and the Tenth Circuit Court of Appeals affirmed the suppression. The Tenth Circuit reasoned the firearm was inadmissible under the **fruit of the poisonous tree doctrine** (evidence discovered because of an unconstitutional action). Patane gave his unwarned statement (i.e., a statement given without full *Miranda* warnings) about the Glock pistol, which led to the discovery and seizure of the Glock pistol itself. This presented the Supreme Court with the question of whether the fruit of the poisonous tree doctrine, developed in the Fourth Amendment context, applies in the context of statements given voluntarily, but without the recitation of full *Miranda* warnings. Was the physical evidence (the Glock pistol) admissible or subject to the exclusionary rule?

Before proceeding it is important to make clear that Patane's *statements* about the Glock pistol to officers were clearly inadmissible at trial. He made unwarned statements during custodial interrogation—his interruption of the warnings was irrelevant regarding the admissibility of the statements. The Supreme Court wants a clear bright line rule for officers (and also for lower courts, in order to avoid lengthy evidentiary hearings on motions to suppress). The Court provides clarity for offers—either complete, full *Miranda* warnings or lose any statements from custodial interrogations. The precise question confronted by the Supreme Court here was whether this reasoning extended to the physical evidence derived from these unwarned statements.

The Supreme Court reversed the judgment of the lower courts and ruled the Glock pistol was admissible. The plurality opinion (written by Justice Thomas and joined by then Chief Justice Rehnquist and Justice Scalia) reasoned there was no breach in Patane's constitutional rights. The physical fruit of a voluntarily statement (albeit unwarned) does not need to be suppressed. Rather the Self-Incrimination Clause of the Fifth Amendment applies only to statements. The physical evidence was non-testimonial, and therefore does not need to be suppressed. The plurality even goes so far as to suggest *Miranda* warnings are effectively optional: "[P]olice do not violate a suspect's constitutional rights (or the *Miranda* rule) by negligent or even deliberate failures to provide the suspect with the full panoply of warnings prescribed by *Miranda*. Potential violations occur, if at all, only upon the admission of unwarned statements into evidence at trial." Thus, if officers anticipate finding physical evidence, such as drugs, as the result of interrogation, officers could choose not to Mirandize such defendants. Only statements are covered by the *Miranda* exclusionary rule. If this distinction between statements and physical evidence seems odd, it might be useful to remember the purpose for *Miranda* warnings—to help mitigate the psychological coercion of officer interrogations. Statements can be psychologically coerced, leading to false confessions and thus wrongful convictions. Physical evidence, however, is inherently reliable as it is not subject to psychological pressures.

Justice Kennedy and Justice O'Connor delivered a concurring opinion distancing themselves from some of the reasoning in the plurality decision. They did not want to encourage officers to view *Miranda* warnings as discretionary depending upon the type of evidence they might anticipate discovering. However, they agreed that Patane's Glock pistol was admissible since its admission "does not run the risk of admitting into trial an accused's coerced incriminating statements against himself." Rather, exclusion would ignore "the important probative value of reliable physical evidence." Thus, they also refused to extend the fruit of a poisonous tree doctrine to *Miranda* violations, at least for physical evidence. They were not concerned with the admissibility of physical evidence, but were looking ahead to other categories of "fruit of the poisonous tree" evidence, such as statements from other witnesses discovered as the result of a defendant's unwarned statements.

Four justices dissented. They would have extended the exclusionary rule for *Miranda* violations to fruit of the poisonous tree, including physical evidence derived from unwarned statements. They wanted to maintain the incentive for officers to consistently give *Miranda* warnings during custodial interrogations. "There is no way to read this case except as an unjustifiable invitation to law enforcement officers to flout *Miranda* when there may be physical evidence to be gained." Unless officers are incentivized to give the prescribed warnings meant to counter the coercive atmosphere of custodial interrogations, lower courts will have to again engage in the previous [pre-*Miranda*] time-consuming and difficult inquiries of assessing the voluntariness of statements (that Patane's statements were obviously voluntary does not address the difficulty of making this determination in other instances). Officer incentives to provide *Miranda* warnings "can only atrophy if we ... recognize an evidentiary benefit when an unwarned statement leads investigators to tangible evidence."

Discussion Questions

1. Do you think the justices in the majority took too literal of an interpretation here regarding *Miranda* protections?

2. Do you anticipate ways that law enforcement could use the outcome of this case to impact when and how they deliver *Miranda* warnings to criminal suspects?

The Supreme Court in *Miranda* used warnings reminding suspects of their Fifth Amendment rights ("right to remain silent") to help guard against psychological coercion leading to wrongful confessions. But is there a general obligation for officers to remind people of their constitutional rights contained in other amendments before seeking cooperation in investigating a crime?

Now, let us turn to a case which considers whether officers must warn regarding other constitutional rights.

Schneckloth v. Bustamonte
412 U.S. 218 (1973)

During a routine night patrol, Sunnyvale police officers observed a car with one headlight out and with a burned-out license plate light. The police pulled the car over (legally) to investigate. Once stopped, six men were observed in the vehicle, including Bustamonte, who was sitting on the front seat near the driver. The driver was unable to produce a driver's license when asked. One of the officers asked the driver if he could search the car. The driver said, "Sure, go ahead." The officer had no probable cause to believe that contraband or criminal evidence would be found in the car; hence consent of the driver would be needed in order for the search to be legal. During the search, the police found three stolen checks under the rear seat. Bustamonte was eventually implicated in the crime and at his trial asked that the three stolen checks be suppressed as the fruits of an illegal search. His motion was denied, the checks were admitted into evidence, and Bustamonte was convicted of possessing the stolen checks.

On appeal, Bustamonte argued that the trial judge erred in not suppressing evidence of the checks. Bustamonte said that the driver's consent was the product of police coercion and therefore not truly voluntary. This was so, according to Bustamonte, because the driver had never been told that he had the right to refuse his consent. Consent, to be truly valid, must be informed consent. In other words, Bustamonte argued that a type of "*Miranda* warning" should have been given to the driver so that he could refuse consent and also told that his refusal would not be used against him in any way (including resulting in his arrest or in the refusal being used to develop probable cause for a search). Without the requirement for such a warning, Bustamante argued, the right to refuse would be relegated to the "special province of the sophisticated, the knowledgeable, and the privileged."

Like in *Miranda v. Arizona*, the police countered that it was not their job to explain to people their rights. Advising suspects of their right to refuse consent would only encourage them to invoke it. This would prevent the police from doing potentially fruitful searches when full-blown probable cause was lacking and even though they had a bona fide hunch that something was amiss.

This time (unlike in the *Miranda* decision) the Supreme Court sided with the police. It would not require police to demonstrate that a suspect knew of his or her right to refuse consent before the consent could be deemed to be valid. True, consent must be voluntary for a **consent search** to be legitimate. But knowledge of the right to refuse consent is not necessarily required for voluntariness to be established. Ignorance of one's right can be one factor in deciding voluntariness, but it is just one factor in a host of factors. The courts should look to a "**totality of the circumstances**" (the overall, big picture) in ruling on voluntariness.

The Court went on to say that certain rights must be explained to someone for the right to really exist. But a situation involving the consent search of a car is a "far cry" from rules requiring trial judges to inform defendants of rights during court proceedings, or even the rule established in *Miranda* of requiring police to advise a custodial suspect of the Fifth Amendment right against self-incrimination. *Miranda* warnings (since they occur after someone is taken into custody) address an inherently police-dominated coercive atmosphere. The Court said the Fifth Amendment right against self-incrimination, and the Sixth Amendment right to a fair trial, are categorically different and in greater need of scrupulous attention than the Fourth Amendment right against unreasonable searches. To require police to advise people of their right to refuse a request for their consent to search would simply prove too burdensome and too "impractical" in the day-to-day routine of police work.

Justice Marshall, in his dissent, expressed his view that "when the Court speaks of practicality, what it really is talking of is the continued ability of the police to capitalize on the ignorance of citizens so as to accomplish by subterfuge what they could not achieve by relying only on the knowing relinquishment of constitutional rights."

Justice Marshall's fear regarding the potential for police "subterfuge" may have carried the day in the *Miranda* decision, but failed to persuade the majority of the Court in the present case. Even so, given the *Miranda* decision and the fact that the busy Supreme Court agreed to even hear Bustamante's appeal proves that wariness of the potential for police subterfuge remains a feature of the Court.

Discussion Questions

1. Do you agree with the Court that a police officer pulling you over and asking to search your car is a significantly less pressure-filled situation than a custodial interrogation? Can people be expected to think straight in either situation?

2. Would your friends and family members know that they have the right to refuse a police request to search their car during a traffic stop, with no negative consequences?

3. Why do you suppose people with something to hide so often give consent for police to search their cars?

One essential concern of the Drafters of our Constitution was that police not be permitted to go overboard in their zeal to find contraband or criminal evidence. Consequently, the Fourth Amendment requires, among other protections, that the police "particularly describe" the place they want to search when seeking a search warrant. It would simply not do for the police to say they would like to search an entire city block or the east side of town. Normally, what a reviewing magistrate would like in most situations is an exact address or something akin to that. If police were allowed to search huge areas for contraband or evidence, they could easily evade the spirit of the Fourth Amendment's prohibition against unreasonable searches. Conducting large-scale and unreasonable searches is precisely what agents of King George, looking for smuggled goods that were never taxed, liked to do in colonial America and was one of the major causes of the Revolution. This "**particularity requirement**" is the subject of the next case. Though the Court ultimately sides with the police, this is a situation in which the exception clearly proves the rule: subterfuge will not be tolerated.

Maryland v. Garrison
480 U.S. 79 (1987)

Baltimore police officers wished to search the apartment of a man named McWebb who occupied the third floor of the apartment house located at 2036 Park Avenue. The police wanted to search his apartment because of their belief that marijuana and drug paraphernalia would be found there. The problem was that the police honestly, but erroneously, believed that McWebb occupied the entire third floor, when in fact the third floor included two apartments: one occupied by McWebb and the other by Garrison. So, in their application for a search warrant they described the place to be searched as the entire third floor of 2036 Park Avenue. It was not until their search of the wrong apartment (the one occupied by Garrison) was underway, and after they had discovered illegal drugs in the wrong apartment, that the police discovered their error and realized that the third floor was composed of two separate apartments. Nevertheless, having found the illegal drugs, they arrested Garrison for possessing them.

Garrison was convicted of the crime and appealed. He argued that the police failed to correctly describe the place to be searched and that consequently evidence of the illegal drugs should be suppressed. So, the issue here is whether a mistake by the police in describing the place to be searched negates the validity of the search warrant.

The Supreme Court ruled that the police had done nothing sinister and that the search was lawful. It said that it "recognized the need to allow some latitude for honest mistakes that are made by officers in the dangerous and difficult process of ... executing search warrants." The key is whether the "over breadth" in the description of the place was "objectively understandable and reasonable." Here, it was clearly understandable and reasonable. At the time officers made an application for a warrant they believed, based on the facts known to them, that the entire third floor belonged to McWebb. They reasonably thought that there was no subdivision of the floor into two separate apartments until after they had discovered the neighbor Garrison's illegal drugs. Of course, if the mistake had been realized before the drugs were seen, the police would have had the duty to immediately discontinue their search. In sum, the officers' conduct was not an attempt to evade the particularity requirement through subterfuge but a good faith and reasonable mistake that need not be punished by excluding the evidence.

Discussion Questions

1. Would you consider laziness and carelessness on the part of a police officer in particularly describing the place to be searched as a mistake that is reasonable and understandable?

2. Can you think of another scenario (other than the one in the case above) in which police might understandably mess up in particularly describing a place to be searched?

Another opportunity unscrupulous police have to evade the Constitution is to misrepresent themselves while trying to justify their actions retroactively in court. Fear of this type of subterfuge has prompted our courts to invent the "articulable facts" doctrine. This doctrine, which also applies to the Fourth Amendment, is illustrated in the case that follows.

United States v. Pavelski

789 F.2d 485 (7th Cir. 1986)

Rick Pavelski and three other men were spotted by a Portland, Oregon, officer while on routine motorized patrol. The four were driving in a car with out-of-state plates and avoided eye contact with the officer (Deputy Fitz). Not liking the lack of eye contact, Deputy Fitz began to follow the car while trying to find a reason to legitimately pull it over. Before he found such a reason, the car pulled into a parking lot and came to a stop.

At this point, Deputy Fitz still had no reason to believe that the men had violated any laws. But, in fact, they had previously robbed two banks in Wisconsin and were driving around the country spending their $80,000 in loot.

Approaching the car in the parking lot, Deputy Fitz asked the men what they were doing. They said they had become lost while looking for a female acquaintance's house. Though Deputy Fitz still had no evidence of any crime, he testified later in court that he had a "gut feeling that things were real wrong." Because of this gut feeling, Deputy Fitz (now joined by other officers) wound up searching the car. During this search, the police found various guns, police scanners, stocking caps with eye holes punched in them, pillowcases, rubber gloves, and other suspicious items. At this point, Fitz arrested the men for possessing illegal weapons. Portland police eventually identified them as the suspects wanted in connection with the two Wisconsin bank robberies. They were extradited to Wisconsin and eventually convicted of robbing the two banks.

On appeal of the convictions, Pavelski argued that the guns and all of the other incriminating items that Deputy Fisk found in the car should have been suppressed during the trials as fruits of an illegal stop. Pavelski argued that when the various police cars had boxed his car in the parking lot, he no longer felt free to leave and this therefore constituted an investigatory stop, a type of Fourth Amendment "seizure." Though investigatory stops do not require probable cause like a full-blown arrest, they still legally require "reasonable suspicion" to be valid under the Fourth Amendment.

The federal court that heard the appeal agreed that Pavelski had been "stopped" and hence seized, and that such a seizure would indeed require reasonable suspicion on the part of the police. When testifying about the basis for his reasonable suspicion in the trial-level court, the federal appellate court noted that Deputy Fisk could not point to any specific bases for his suspicion that these men had engaged in illegal activity. All he had was the before-mentioned "gut feeling"—essentially his instinct as an officer. The issue was whether a "gut feeling" could be enough to ever constitute "reasonable suspicion" as the basis for a legitimate investigatory stop.

The appellate court ruled that investigatory stops always require "reasonable, articulate suspicion of criminal activity." This **articulable facts doctrine** means that an officer in court (e.g., during a suppression hearing) must be able to point to specific, objective facts that had earlier formed the basis of his suspicion. A "gut feeling" or a "hunch" simply does not satisfy this requirement. Since Officer Fitz failed to articulate specific, objective facts to back up his claims that suspicious activity was afoot, the investigatory stop—the seizure—was unreasonable and any fruits of it (like items found during the search of the car) had to be suppressed. "Inarticulate hunches and un-particularized suspicion may not form the basis for an investigatory stop."

So, we see from the decision above that reviewing courts are unwilling to simply take an officer's word for it that reasonable suspicion existed. This would invite every officer to simply say that he had a "hunch," and any officer could evade the Fourth Amendment with impunity.

Luckily for Deputy Fitz, the appellate court went on to "save" the robbery convictions by further ruling that other independently and legally obtained evidence against Pavelski was so overwhelming that any error resulting from the trial court's failure to suppress the evidence in the car was simply "harmless error." It was "harmless" because Pavelski would have been certainly convicted anyway, without a doubt.

This harmless error finding, though curiously convenient, does not take away from the fact that at least the "articulable facts" doctrine was itself confirmed by this decision as being a needed one in the battle against police attempts to evade the requirements of the Fourth Amendment. Let us hope that the "harmless error" finding of the appellate court was not itself a subterfuge to achieve some form of "rough justice."

Discussion Questions

1. Would it be acceptable in your view for a police officer with a mere hunch to follow a motorist closely for an extended period of time until the motorist did something wrong to "justify" an actual stop? Or would this "harassment" constitute a type of seizure in your view?

2. Have you or anyone you know been pulled over by the police for apparently nothing more than a police officer's hunch?

Despite the above "anti-subterfuge" cases, some level of police trickery apparently is still permitted in our constitutional system. The case that follows demonstrates this fact, though a strong and stinging dissent accompanies the case. In reading the summary of the majority and the dissenting opinions below, consider which side you take on this particular use of subterfuge.

Miller v. Fenton
796 F.2d 598 (3d Cir. 1986)

Miller was the prime suspect in the murder of Mrs. Margolin. After his arrest, Miller was taken to the police station, where Detective Boyce questioned him for about an hour. The detective's goal was to obtain a confession to the crime, thus making a conviction nearly certain. During this hour-long interrogation, performed after the defendant had signed away his *Miranda* rights, Miller confessed to the killing. No threats or physical force were used during the questioning. However, the detective did engage in various acts of deceit and trickery to illicit the incriminating response.

For example, Detective Boyce repeatedly pretended to be very sympathetic to Miller. He spoke to him in a kind and friendly manner. Sometimes, his feigned kindness seemed to extend to extraordinary levels. For example, Boyce told Miller such things as, "This hurts me more than it hurts you because I love people.... I'm on your side, Frank.... I'm your brother, you and I are brothers, Frank, [and] I want to help my brother."

In addition, Boyce lied to Miller by telling him that the victim was still alive. Later he told Miller that the victim had just died in order to achieve an emotional reaction. Boyce also told Miller several times that Miller was merely an ill individual who should not be punished. Miller was told that confessing would help him to purge his conscience and that he would then feel much better. When Miller finally confessed to the murder 53 minutes into the interrogation, he subsequently collapsed in a state of emotional shock.

After his conviction of murder, Miller appealed to the federal court of appeals claiming that he was tricked into confessing to the murder and that use of trickery caused his confession to have been given involuntarily. It therefore should never have been used against him at trial.

The issue for the court was whether Miller's confession was indeed voluntary. The court held that Miller was correct in that only voluntarily given confessions are admissible, but could voluntariness survive trickery? The court ruled that it could.

In deciding whether or not a confession was voluntarily given, the **"rule regarding tricked confessions"** holds that a court will look to the "totality of the circumstances" in determining the propriety of the tactics used to obtain a confession. Trickery used during interrogation is part of this, but standing alone trickery does not automatically constitute a constitutional violation. The question in the court's mind was whether the detective's "statements were so manipulative and coercive that they deprived Miller of his ability to make an unconstrained autonomous decision to confess."

Turning its attention to that question, the court ruled that Miller did indeed voluntarily confess. Miller was able to make a rational choice. He was a "mature adult, thirty-two years of age." Additionally, he had earlier served a jail sentence, no doubt making him knowledgeable of what happens to people when they confess to crimes. Also, the detective's "good guy" demeanor during questioning was merely an "approach recognized as a permissible interrogation tactic."

Lies also do not necessarily cause a confession to become involuntary. It depends on the type of lie and whether or not the lie was such to overcome a suspect's will. The detective's lies about the victim still being alive, or then later claiming the victim had just recently died did not seem to destroy Miller's free will. Indeed, Miller remained rather impassive upon being told these false details.

The court had its biggest problem with the detective having told Miller that he was sick and therefore not responsible for what he had done. Such a statement could be inferred to constitute a promise on the detective's part to not seek to have the case prosecuted criminally. However, a much more likely interpretation by the defendant would have been that though the detective as an individual was personally sympathetic to the defendant, the state's attitude might still ultimately be quite different. Hence, it was unlikely that the confession was motivated by a mistaken belief on the part of Miller that the state would simply let the murder charges drop.

In light of the totality of the circumstances, including Miller's continued guarded and suspicious demeanor throughout the interrogation, the court ultimately concluded that Miller had made an unforced decision to relieve his inner tensions rather than to have succumbed to manipulation amounting to a coerced and involuntary confession.

Judge Gibbons, in his dissent, took strong exception to the decision of the majority above. The dissent agreed with the majority that the test should be whether, "in the totality of the circumstances [Miller's] will was overborne." However, it disagreed with the majority's conclusion that Miller's confession was voluntary.

First, the sympathy extended to Miller by the detective's tone and friendly manner was not done out of any desire to help Miller to relieve his inner tensions. Rather, they were all directed at the single purpose of making Miller admit his guilt. "The repeated assurances, the friendly, understanding manner, and the soft tone…. Every word, every nuance of expression, every change in tone of voice was calculated toward one end, and one end only—obtaining an admission of guilt."

Second, lying to the defendant that the victim had survived, followed by the lie that she had just recently died, was a tactic meant to evoke an emotional response on the part of the defendant. The confession itself is evidence of Miller's will having been overcome, the exact goal of the detective.

Finally, repeatedly telling Miller that he was sick and that "you are not responsible, you are not responsible, Frank," constituted an implied promise of leniency. Confessions obtained through false promises of leniency are totally out of bounds.

So, we see from the above that the dissent argued that Miller's Fifth Amendment right to remain silent was violated. The majority however thought that the questioning simply amounted to clever, albeit perhaps sketchy, police work. Which side do you agree with?

Discussion Questions

1. Is trickery in the pursuit of obtaining a "bad guy's" confession a virtue or a vice?

2. Do you admire the detective's tactics in the case above or do you think less of him ethically because of them?

3. What are some common tactics you are aware of that police commonly use to "trick" people into confessing to crimes?

Subterfuge in Corrections

There was a time, not too long ago, that courts trusted wardens to do the right thing regarding prison inmates. This **"hands off doctrine"** lasted until about the 1960s. Prior to that courts often used language describing inmates as being "civilly dead" or even "slaves of the state," to justify washing their hands of abuses taking place behind closed prison doors. After all, nowhere in the Bill of Rights is there any mention of inmates having constitutional protections. Of course, all along prisoners had the right to file a petition for a writ of habeas corpus (thanks to Article I, Section 9 of the Constitution). But these petitions were only available to challenge illegal confinement itself (e.g., an innocent person was being imprisoned) and not the conditions of the confinement, no matter how horrendous these conditions might be.

Nowadays, courts have come to realize that the Constitution does not stop at the prison door. Prisoners, even those who belong there, still have some human rights left and these rights must be protected by courts of law. Prisoner access to courts is a crucial first step in ensuring that rights are being protected. The old days of "hands off" simply allowed too much opportunity for prison officials to subvert the Constitution.

Access to courts was an issue first raised in habeas corpus matters where prison officials interfered with petitions being delivered to the courts. For example, in the case of *Ex Parte Hull*, 313 U.S. 546 (1941), Michigan prison officials had developed a rule that only "properly drawn" petitions for a writ of habeas corpus would be sent to a court. A prison review committee would pre-screen petitions drafted by inmates, and if the petition was deemed to be improperly written, it would be returned to the inmate. Hull's petition had been returned to him, but he managed later to sneak it out to the court by getting it to his father. The issue in *Hull* became whether or not inmates had the right to submit petitions free of interference from prison officials. The U.S. Supreme Court ruled that prison staff had no right to intercept a petition for a writ of habeas corpus meant for delivery to the courts. Article I, Section 9 of the U.S. Constitution guarantees the right to file a petition for a writ of habeas corpus, and by definition only a person in custody would want to file such an instrument. The purpose behind the right of habeas corpus would be defeated if prison officials could decide which petitions are worthy of being forwarded on to the courts.

The case that follows shows further refinement in the notion that prisoners should have access to the courts to address perceived wrongs. By 1969, when this case was decided, the right to sue for relief has come to be understood to include unjust conditions of confinement and not just the legality of being confined at all.

Johnson v. Avery
393 U.S. 483 (1969)

A Tennessee prison had a regulation that provided that, "No inmate will advise, assist, or otherwise contract to aid another, whether with or without fee, to prepare Writs or other legal matters." Johnson, an inmate, sued, and the case wound its way up to the U.S. Supreme Court. The issue was whether or not such a regulation was constitutional.

The prison claimed that it had legitimate reasons for such a rule. It wanted to preserve prison discipline and also prevent the practice of law without a license. Johnson on the other hand argued that so-called "jailhouse lawyers" should be tolerated in order to give unsophisticated inmates a fair shot at justice.

So, is such a prison regulation constitutional? The Court ruled that it was not. It said that many inmates needed help for the right of access to the courts to have real meaning. Many inmates are low functioning, and many are even illiterate.

Specifically, the Court held that unless a state provides some alternative means for ignorant or illiterate inmates to get help drafting their petitions, **jailhouse lawyers** (self-taught inmates helping other inmates with legal matters) must be permitted. Inmates must have access to the courts in order for their rights to be protected. We cannot rely on prison officials to always self-police. Access to the courts means meaningful access.

Prisons can still have rules prohibiting inmates from charging money for their services. They can also have reasonable regulations regarding the time and place where help can be obtained. If states really want to do so, they can ban inmates from giving legal help to each other as long as they are willing to provide other means of assistance. For example, states could provide public defenders to assist inmates. They could even just provide senior law students. But banning jail house lawyers without providing any other means of assistance would prevent the ability of courts to review allegedly improper confinement or conditions of confinement.

Discussion Questions

1. Would you need the help of a "jailhouse lawyer" with legal matters if you were an inmate? Or are you smart enough to do it yourself?

2. If you faced long years in prison would you consider developing enough knowledge to become a "jailhouse lawyer"?

In addition to trying to shut down inmate access to courts, another way prisons might attempt to silence inmate complaints is by disallowing non-legal related mail. Or a prison might allow mail but attempt to heavily censor what can be said in a letter to the outside. The next case addresses this concern.

Procunier v. Martinez
416 U.S. 396 (1974)

Prison officials in California developed rules that were meant to prevent inmates from exaggerating the bad conditions of their confinement or unduly complaining about their treatment. Specifically, inmates were forbidden to send any letters "expressing inflammatory, political, racial, religious or other views or beliefs." Additionally, inmates could not send or receive letters that were "lewd, obscene, or defamatory; contain foreign matter, or are otherwise inappropriate." Do you see any problems with words such as "political," "defamatory," and "or otherwise inappropriate"? Apparently the Supreme Court did.

In writing its opinion, the Court began by referring to the old "hands off doctrine." It made it clear that this doctrine was now officially dead. "When a prison regulation or practice offends a fundamental constitutional guarantee, federal courts will discharge their duty to protect constitutional rights."

It then went on to address the main issue: To what degree can prisons censor mail? The Supreme Court felt it needed to address this issue because states had widely varied standards. Some simply were invoking "hands off" when it came to prison rules regarding mail (letting wardens do whatever they pleased) while others went so far as employing an incredibly high "clear and present danger" test (the standard being used to protect the free speech rights of civilians).

The Court decided to come up with a standard between the extremes. It held that restrictions on mail were acceptable if they were "in furtherance of legitimate governmental objectives and go no further than is necessary to achieve those objectives." **Legitimate penological objectives** could include such things as maintaining security, maintaining order, and effectuating rehabilitation. Of course, even if one of these goals is being sought, the regulation on mail could go no further than is necessary to achieve the stated goal.

Applying this test to the Tennessee mail-censorship rules, the Court ruled that Tennessee was violating the First Amendment right of free speech. The Tennessee rules limiting the sending and receiving of mail were too broad and too vague. They could easily be used to shut down unwanted criticism of what was taking place inside the prison.

The Court went on to say that one lower court had it right by requiring that an inmate be notified if a letter is rejected and that the inmate then be given the right to protest and to a review by a different official in the prison. Prison staff can of course read all incoming and outgoing mail since that is a legitimate security need. But prison staff cannot simply censor criticism of the institution by using vague and overly broad language like the Tennessee officials tried to do here.

> ## Discussion Questions
>
> 1. What would happen if prisons were allowed to censor all outgoing mail and other communications to the outside world to whatever degree they thought was proper?
>
> 2. What is an example of a clearly inappropriate, non-vague communication to the outside world that a prison should be allowed to censor and stop?

Hands off doctrines, interfering with inmate access to courts, and unjustified restrictions on inmate mail can all facilitate subterfuge within a prison context. But so can internally punishing inmates in serious ways for alleged prison rule violations. The next case addresses the need for inmates undergoing serious internal punishment for alleged rule-breaking to be given some sort of fair procedures first. One's liberty can be further reduced even while incarcerated, and officials could get away with punishing inmates they simply don't like if no due process is provided.

Wolff v. McDonnell

418 U.S. 539 (1974)

Nebraska prison inmate McDonnell was accused by prison officials of engaging in serious misconduct. His punishment included the loss of his accumulated "good time" credits.

"**Good time**" in prisons is an inmate incentive program for good behavior. Depending on the state, inmates typically receive a certain number of days off their sentence for each month they serve without receiving any disciplinary write-ups. This "good time" accumulates and can add up to quite a few months off one's sentence if one is generally a "good" inmate.

McDonnell sued, claiming that he was being denied his right to due process as guaranteed by the Fourteenth Amendment. He argued that Nebraska officials could not just take away his "liberty" without due process of law. He further argued that loss of good time amounted to not merely a loss of liberty, but a serious loss of liberty.

So, the first issue on appeal became whether "liberty" and "due process" as guaranteed by the Fourteenth Amendment cover inmates being disciplined internally by a prison. The U.S. Supreme Court ruled that it does. Even inmates cannot be deprived further of liberty without due process of law. The Court said, "A prisoner is not wholly stripped of constitutional protections. There is no iron curtain between the Constitution and the prisons of this country."

Is there a "liberty interest" implicated in the taking of good time? There indeed is a liberty right attached to good time according to the Supreme Court. It is true that the Constitution itself does not give a right to so-called "good time." However, the Constitution is not the sole source of **liberty interests**. States can voluntarily (through statutes and otherwise) create liberty interests on their own. Since the state of Nebraska chose to create a right to good time, this liberty interest could only be taken away pursuant to some sort of due process.

Once the existence of a liberty interest was established, the next issue becomes, exactly what process is due? The taking of small liberties would only require a minimum amount of due process. Big losses of liberty would require a lot of due process. Which is the taking of good time? The Court ruled that since the loss of good time involved a big liberty loss, a lot of process was due.

Specifically, the Court ruled that before a prison could take away good time (or any other "big" loss of liberty), it first had to provide all of the following: (1) 24-hour notice prior to a disciplinary hearing including a written summary of the evidence against the inmate; (2) a right of the inmate to call witnesses on his behalf; (3) a right to have a fellow inmate help him present his case if he needs it; and (4) impartial staff to serve as the decision maker (not the offended guards).

In addition to listing what due process is required before taking away an inmate's good time, the Court also noted what is not required in the way of due process (even for "big" losses of liberty): (1) no right to an appeal; and (2) no right to cross-examine witnesses (confrontation can lead to special hazards in a prison context).

So, we see that prison staff cannot just "ruin an inmate's life" (what is left of it) without providing some due process first. We learned that loss of good time constitutes a "big liberty loss" and therefore requires "big due process." What other internal prison punishments would you consider to be big enough liberty deprivations to require all of the due process rights listed in the above opinion? (If you are stumped, see the discussion questions below for some possibilities to consider.)

Discussion Questions

1. Should long stays in solitary confinement count as a "big loss," triggering the full list of due process rights mentioned in the case above?

2. Should loss of visitation privileges, in your opinion, count as a "big loss"?

3. Should loss of television, in your opinion, count as a "big loss"?

Subterfuge and the Courts

It is not just the police and correctional officials who might attempt to act with secrecy, evasion, or stealth. Courthouse actors (e.g., judges, prosecutors, defense attorneys) also face temptations to accomplish their goals without the burdens of transparency or accountability.

One of the most basic constitutional safeguards that exists to prevent courthouse subterfuge is the requirement regarding **public trials**. The Sixth Amendment states that "in all criminal prosecutions, the accused shall enjoy the right to a ... public trial." This right reflects the nearly instinctual Anglo-American distrust of secret trials and accompanying governmental persecution of citizens it happens to dislike.

Sometimes, however, a legitimate need may exist to "clear the courtroom" during trials when, for example, witnesses face intimidation from onlookers in the audience. This next case teaches us when courtroom security can be found to trump the requirement for open trials.

People v. Kin Kan
574 N.E.2d 1042 (N.Y. 1991)

Kin Kan, an American resident of Chinese origin, stood trial with her co-defendant, Harry Ip, in a New York state trial court on the charges of selling two pounds of heroin to undercover police officers in a Manhattan apartment. Prior to the trial, the judge had ordered that the courtroom would have to be cleared of all spectators during the upcoming trial. This closure would affect all potential spectators, including members of Kan's family. The judge entered this pre-trial ruling at the request of the prosecution who had convinced the judge of the necessity of this action during a pre-trial hearing on its motion for closure.

During that pre-trial hearing, the trial judge had been told that a confidential informant feared retaliation by Kan's "people" (though he did not express any fear of her actual family). This informant also said that he was involved in other ongoing informant activity and that he feared retaliation from gang members connected with that other activity should he show his face in public.

Over Kan's objections, the trial took place in a virtually empty courtroom, and both Kan and Ip were found guilty of the felonious sale of drugs. Pursuant to his conviction, Ip filed a habeas corpus petition in federal court and was awarded a new trial on the grounds that his trial with Kan had not been a public one. Kan then appealed separately to the state appellate court and the state court ruled that since Ip was awarded a new trial in federal court, Kan must get one as well since "the constitutionality of the closure was no longer open to determination by state courts." The People appealed this decision regarding Kan to New York's highest court (which in New York happens to be called the New York Court of Appeals instead of the New York Supreme Court).

The New York Court of Appeals affirmed the decision of its lower state court granting Kan a new trial. It said this case pits Kan's desire for a public trial against the state's desire to protect a key cooperating witness. It ruled that the state had failed to prove its case that the dramatic step of closing the courtroom to all spectators, including even Kan's family members, was proper.

The Court agreed that though the Sixth Amendment right to a public trial is "fundamental" it is "not absolute." Closure is a possibility in some rare cases. But it is an "exceptional authority that must be sparingly exercised only when necessitated by unusual circumstances." It also noted that "the balance of interests must be struck with special care."

The Court said that the United States Supreme Court had actually developed a **four-prong courtroom closure test**: (1) an overriding need to protect against harm; (2) the closure must be "no broader than necessary;" (3) "reasonable alternatives" must be considered; and (4) justifications for the closure must be stated on the record.

The New York Court of Appeals concluded that all four of the above prongs failed to be met. There was no evidence that Kan's family members wanted to do any harm to the witness. The closure seemed too broad, and the trial judge never specifically explained why members of Kan's family had to be excluded. The identity of the confidential informant was already known to Kan and to her family anyway, so what would be the point? And, the judge never seemed to explore any alternative possibilities, such as clearing everyone except the defendant's family members.

On the other side, Kan really needed her family present because she could not speak English and had difficulty understanding the proceedings and testimony. Though interpreters were used in court, they apparently did not sufficiently help Kan to understand what was taking place.

Because the trial court failed to satisfy any of the four prongs (let alone all of them) Kan had to be given a new trial. She had a constitutional right to not only a trial, but a public one. This right was not provided.

Discussion Questions

1. Can you think of a situation in which a trial closed to the public indeed would be justified out of legitimate necessity?

2. Have you ever gone to a courthouse just to watch a trial you had no personal stake in?

3. Why do you suppose most jury trials are done in nearly empty "echo-chambers" even though they are nearly all open to the public?

Requiring courts to hold their trials open to the public is one thing, but some court-related work by its very nature must be done in private. For example, prosecutors generally do not have totally "open file" policies with regards to cases they are working on and strategizing over. Even so, should we require prosecutors to turn over pro-defense evidence that they happen to discover to a defendant that they still believe to be guilty? After all, defense lawyers do not have to enlighten prosecutors about incriminating evidence they come across in their investigations that clearly helps prove their client's guilt. Defense lawyers who divulge such materials would be seen as failing their clients as a lawyer. So, should the same rule hold true with prosecutors? Or is prosecutorial subterfuge worse than defense attorney subterfuge when it comes to evidence in the lawyer's possession? The case that follows addresses this issue.

Kyles v. Whitley
514 U.S. 419 (1995)

An older woman was shot to death while putting groceries in her car in the parking lot of a supermarket. Her murderer then took her car keys and drove off in the vehicle. For quite some time the case remained unsolved. However, eventually, a man named "Beanie" came forward and told the police that Kyles had committed the crime. The police searched Kyles's apartment and found the gun used to kill the victim plus various items belonging to her. Based on this evidence found in Kyles's apartment, plus testimony from three of six eye-witnesses to the crime identifying Kyles as the assailant, Kyles was convicted of the murder.

At first blush, this might seem like a pretty open and shut case against Kyles. But, prior to the trial the prosecutor had learned some things that could have quite possibly helped the defendant beat the murder conviction. For example, the eyewitnesses had initially given various differing descriptions of the murderer. This was never highlighted by the defense attorney during the trial because the prosecutor had never told him about these conflicting descriptions. Additionally, Beanie had visited Kyles's apartment before it was searched and could have planted the incriminating gun and other evidence. This was not implausible because Beanie was a suspect in multiple other robberies at the time. Again, the defense attorney was never told about this pre-search visit by Beanie even though the prosecutor knew about it. This information could have greatly bolstered the defendant's defense at trial that he was being framed by Beanie.

Kyles was ultimately found guilty of murder and sentenced to death. Eventually, he became aware of the evidence helpful to his case in the prosecutor's file and sought a new trial claiming he had been denied due process of law.

The Supreme Court reversed Kyles's conviction and Kyles was awarded a new trial. In so holding, the Court reaffirmed earlier cases in which it ruled that prosecutors have a legal duty to disclose so-called "exculpatory evidence" to the defense, whether or not the defense even asks for it (in Kyles's case, the defense actually did ask for any exculpatory evidence but was turned down). The Supreme Court reminded us that information is considered to constitute **exculpatory evidence** "if there is a reasonable probability that, had the evidence been disclosed to the defense, the result of the proceeding would have been different." It goes on to clarify that the word "probable" does not have its usual mathematical definition of more likely than not. Rather, "reasonable probability of a different result is accordingly shown when the Government's evidentiary suppression undermines confidence in the outcome of the trial."

The Court went on to stress that analyzing evidence in the prosecutor's possession for exculpatory value should not be done using an item-by-item approach but rather should be done with the evidence being considered "collectively." Of course, this means that prosecutors still have to be trusted to exercise proper discretion. "The prosecution, which alone can know what is undisclosed, must be assigned the consequent responsibility to gauge the likely net effect of all such evidence and make disclosure when the point of reasonable probability is reached." The Court cautioned prosecutors that they have the solemn responsibility to not allow the "adversary system of prosecution ... to descend to a gladiatorial level unmitigated by any prosecutorial obligation for the sake of truth." The Court pointed out that prosecutors who are unsure whether or not evidence is exculpatory should not take the chance of keeping it to themselves.

Given these standards the Court found quite a bit of exculpatory evidence in Kyles's murder case that should have been turned over to the defense prior to trial. The informant Beanie's "visit" to Kyles's apartment prior to the police search, the differing descriptions of the murderer initially given by eyewitnesses, and the fact that Beanie was a suspect in several robberies all could have easily bolstered Kyles's defense that he had been "set up" by Beanie and was not the murderer. It was clear to the Supreme Court that this undisclosed evidence, taken as a whole, undermined confidence in the verdict.

Discussion Questions

1. What are some other examples of exculpatory evidence that you can think of in a criminal case investigation that should always be disclosed to the defense?

2. Is it possible for a prosecutor to have exculpatory evidence yet still believe a defendant is guilty and should go to trial?

3. How is it fair that a prosecutor must divulge exculpatory evidence of which his side alone has knowledge to the defense attorney but the defense attorney does not have to divulge incriminating evidence of which her side alone has knowledge to the prosecutor?

As we have learned, prosecutorial subterfuge can take place by failing to disclose evidence favorable to the accused. An even more blatant form of subterfuge occurs when prosecutors fail to correct material false impressions given the jury by prosecution witnesses during trial. The case that follows illustrates that situation.

Miller v. Pate
386 U.S. 1 (1967)

An eight-year-old little girl was sexually assaulted and murdered. Lloyd Miller, Jr. was charged with the crimes. The case against Miller was purely circumstantial—there were no eyewitnesses to the events. There was, however, one piece of powerfully emotional physical evidence admitted at trial: a pair of red-stained shorts found about a mile from the crime scene.

The prosecutor's theory was that these shorts must have belonged to Miller. During Miller's trial, the prosecution put a chemist on the stand who testified that the red stains on the shorts were blood, the blood was human blood, and the blood was "Type A," the same blood type of the murdered little girl. The defendant's blood type was "O," not "A."

Other prosecution witnesses referred to the "blood-stained shorts" repeatedly during Miller's trial. Also, the prosecutor "made the most" of the blood-stained shorts during his closing arguments to the jury and emphasized how the shorts were stained with the blood of the dead little girl.

Ultimately, the jury convicted Miller, and he was sentenced to death. He remained on death row for many years awaiting execution. Eventually, his attorneys filed a writ of habeas corpus claiming that his confinement violated the U.S. Constitution. Apparently, Miller's trial attorney had filed a motion to be able to inspect the red-stained shorts prior to trial years before. This motion was resisted by the prosecution at the time and the trial judge ultimately refused to grant the defense attorney's request.

During the habeas proceeding years later in federal court, the state was ordered by the federal judge to produce the shorts and to allow defense experts to analyze them. A chemical microanalyst (an expert specializing in identification and quantitative analysis of very small amounts of chemical substances) working for the defense analyzed the red stains and determined that they were red paint, not blood. It was further established that the prosecutor knew of this at the time of trial (he had confided in various police officers at the time).

The federal district court overturned Miller's convictions for rape and murder and ordered that either the charges be dropped or that he be given a prompt new trial. The state appealed this decision to the U.S. Court of Appeals, which reinstated Miller's convictions. The appellate court thought that there was enough clean evidence for the decision to stand despite the perjured testimony that had been admitted. The case then found itself before the U.S. Supreme Court.

The U.S. Supreme Court reversed the decision of the Court of Appeals and ratified the district court's decision to overturn the conviction. It said that "more than 30 years ago this Court held that the Fourteenth Amendment [referring to due process] cannot tolerate a state criminal conviction obtained by the knowing use of false evidence." The Court gave no further explanation for its decision other than to say, "[t]here has been no deviation from that established principle. There can be no retreat from that principle here."

The shortness of the Court's rationale for its decision is itself quite something. One grasps that this case was a "no brainer" for the high court. The Court's message to the national criminal justice community apparently is that such subterfuge on the part of prosecutors can have no place in our system of justice. There was no entertaining the idea of "harmless error" here on the part of this Court.

The above case illustrates two acts of malfeasance on the part of the prosecutor: his own lying to the jury during closing argument and his earlier failure to correct **material false impressions** (significant, misleading statements) made by state witnesses on the stand. Both acts not only constitute grounds for reversal of the verdict but grounds for disciplinary action against the prosecutor as well.

Discussion Questions

1. Why do you suppose the Court was completely unwilling to "budge" on this one even though there may have been plenty of "clean" evidence to support the conviction anyway?

2. If you were a prosecutor, do you think you could ever be tempted to fail to correct a material false impression coming from one of your own witnesses?

Another type of devious constitutional evasion which must be guarded against can occur in the courtroom even before the actual trial begins. This type of subterfuge has to do with concealing one's racist agenda for stacking juries by hiding behind protections traditionally afforded lawyers during the pre-trial, jury selection process.

In order to ensure that both sides get an unbiased jury, lawyers are allowed to have a hand in selecting who will and who will not serve in a particular case. During a process known as **voir dire**, attorneys for both sides are permitted to ask questions of potential jurors assembled in the courtroom prior to the trial for the purpose of exposing potential biases. After this questioning is over, lawyers can ask the judge watching the proceedings to remove anyone whose answers showed obvious bias (so called "challenges for cause" which are un-limited in number). The lawyers are also given a certain number of so-called "peremptory challenges" which they can use to eliminate potential jurors whose answers, mannerisms, or tone merely worries them. The lawyers do not have to justify these **peremptory challenges**. Therefore, traditionally, prosecutors could strike a potential juror just based on their intuition or hunch that the person might be biased without having to provide the judge with any specific, articulable reasons for getting rid of the prospective juror. Again, these unex-plained strikes are very limited in number and are allowed in order to help en-sure the seating of an unbiased jury.

What if a prosecutor wishes to use the lack of accountability of peremptory challenges not to get rid of a juror merely suspected of being biased, but rather to simply get rid of all potential jurors of the same race? Should that misuse of peremptory challenges be tolerated? Peremptory challenges, if not checked in some way by the judge, could enable prosecutors to evade the diligent and long-term efforts we as a society have made to ensure racial equality and fairness in our court systems. The case that follows addresses these concerns.

Batson v. Kentucky
476 U.S. 79 (1986)

James Batson was a black person charged with burglary. During jury selection, four African Americans sat in the courtroom as potential jurors for the upcoming trial. As part of the jury selection process, the prosecutor wound up using his peremptory challenges to strike all four black prospective jurors from the venire. This resulted in an all-white jury for Batson's trial.

Batson's lawyer objected to the use of peremptory challenges in this manner, claiming that his client was denied both equal protection and a jury composed of a fair cross-section of his peers. The trial court and ultimately the Kentucky Supreme Court rejected Batson's concerns, saying that the "sanctity of peremptory challenges" required them to do so. Historically peremptory challenges have never had to be explained or justified in any way by the attorney exercising them.

The U.S. Supreme Court agreed to hear this case, which puts the practical utility of peremptory challenges up against the desire to avoid race-based jury selection. The issue, as the Court itself put it, was simply this: "May prosecutors use their peremptory challenges to eliminate prospective jurors of a specific racial group?"

The Court held that such use of peremptory challenges could not be tolerated. It noted the nation's long march towards eliminating all-white juries, which once had been standard in many parts of the country. Hence previous decisions struck down various state practices that limited jury service to whites only. The Court expressed confidence that no state had such an official policy anymore. However, if prosecutors were allowed to use the secretive nature of peremptory challenges to stack juries with members of the same race, then the Court's efforts to afford minorities the right to serve on juries (and the right of minority defendants to have them serve) could easily be thwarted.

The Court concluded that the Equal Protection Clause must be interpreted to mean that there are "some limits on the state's exercise of peremptory challenges." It is simply "impermissible for a prosecutor to deny to blacks the same right and opportunity to participate in the administration of justice enjoyed by the white population."

How can a trial judge enforce such a ruling without abolishing peremptory challenges entirely? The Supreme Court said that trial judges should look for "patterns" of strikes that suggest that racial exclusion is going on. One pattern could be the use of racial strikes repeatedly by a member of the same office (or by the entire office of prosecutors) in case after case over time. However, a pattern can be established in just one particular case as well. For example, if a prosecutor uses several peremptory challenges to strike minority prospective jurors (especially if there are not many minorities present to begin with), then a "prima facie case" of racial discrimination has been established. The judge should then call the prosecutor to side bar and demand that he or she give "neutral," non race-based explanations for the strikes. If the prosecutor cannot give specific, credible justifications for striking the jurors, then the judge should intervene and disallow the prosecutor's efforts.

The Supreme Court said it trusted the ability of trial judges to clamp down on purposeful discrimination in the jury selection process. In requiring this of judges, the Supreme Court believed that the "mandate of equal protection" and the "ends of justice" would be better served. It said that "public respect for our criminal justice system and the rule of law will be strengthened."

Two justices dissented. In writing for both, Justice Rehnquist said that he saw nothing sinister in using race as a basis to get rid of a prospective juror. To him, it just was common sense. As he put it, "The use of group affiliations, such as age, race, or occupation as a proxy for potential juror partiality ... has long been accepted as a legitimate basis for the State's exercise of peremptory challenges." He went on to say that "I do not believe there is anything in the Equal Protection Clause, or any other constitutional provision, that justifies such a departure" from prior thinking.

In a concurring opinion, Justice Marshall would have gone much further than the majority opinion. He argued that the majority's decision would not end the racial discrimination that peremptory challenges inject into the jury-selection process, but rather "[t]hat goal can only be accomplished by eliminating peremptory challenges entirely." He worried about the ease of generating pre-textual reasons for strikes that could not be effectively challenged, as well as "conscious or unconscious racism" which might lead a prosecutor to conclude a prospective minority juror is "sullen" or "distant," a characterization that would not come to mind if a white juror had acted similarly.

A subsequent U.S. Supreme Court case expanded the above ruling to include defense attorneys as well as prosecutors. Defense attorneys also were notorious for using peremptory challenges to strike jurors of a particular race. Now, they too must explain themselves at side-bar should racial patterns in their strikes emerge. Later, this doctrine was expanded even further to forbid gender-based use of peremptory challenges by either the prosecution or the defense.

Discussion Questions

1. Some legal scholars suggest that all peremptory challenges be abolished in our system. If a lawyer can convince a judge that a prospective juror's answer shows actual bias then they can exercise the so-called "challenge for cause," but peremptory challenges based merely on intuition or gut feelings should be eliminated. What do you think?

2. Race and gender aside, what types or categories of people might prompt you to use a peremptory challenge if you were a prosecutor?

Chapter Key Terms

Subterfuge

Custodial questioning

Miranda rights

Suppressed

Lawyered up

Fruit of the poisonous tree doctrine

Consent search

Totality of the circumstances

Particularity requirement

Articulable facts doctrine

Rule regarding tricked confessions

Hands off doctrine

Jail house lawyers

Legitimate penological objectives

Good time

Liberty interests

Public trials

Four-prong courtroom closure test

Exculpatory evidence

Material false impressions

Voir dire

Peremptory challenges

Chapter Four

Subterfuge in Law Enforcement and Corrections

It happened because a clique within that anti-gang unit went beyond its "gunslinger" mentality and gangster tactics to become gangsters themselves. It happened because fear of CRASH rogues and the code of silence licensed officers who were aware of CRASH brutality to look the other way.

> — *Rampart Reconsidered: The Search for*
> *Real Reform Seven Years Later*

What we found is that the problem of police corruption extends far beyond the corrupt cop. It is a multi-faceted problem that has flourished in parts of our City [New York] not only because of opportunity and greed, but because of a police culture that exalts loyalty over integrity; because of the silence of honest officers who fear the consequences of "ratting" on another cop no matter how grave the crime; because of willfully blind supervisors who fear the consequences of a corruption scandal more than corruption itself.

> — "Commission to Investigate Allegations of
> Police Corruption and the Anti-Corruption
> Procedures of the Police Department"

Law Enforcement

L.A.P.D. CRASH

An unfortunate side effect of our consumer driven society is that often times the only "newsworthy" stories are those that depict law enforcement officers as villains. This is even more prevalent when there are issues of corruption, deception, or various abuses of power by law enforcement. In the following discussion, we will examine the events that transpired among an elite task force of the Los Angeles Police Department (LAPD) known as the CRASH unit. In the wake of the Rodney King incident and the OJ Simpson trial, CRASH left its citizens feeling further dejected and questioning the ability of the LAPD to effectively and ethically combat crime (The Rampart CRASH Unit, 1999, para. 1–3).

Rampart is a densely populated area (33,790 people per 7.9 square miles) on the west side of downtown Los Angeles that experienced a significant increase in violent street gang activity in the mid-1980s. In an effort to address this trend, the LAPD created the gang unit called CRASH (Community Resources Against Street Hoodlums). "The primary mission of the CRASH unit is to gather intelligence on the criminal street gangs ... and to monitor their activities" (*Frontline*: CRASH Culture, n.d.a, para. 4). Initial data showed that this unit was successful in reducing crime: "gang-related crimes in [the] Rampart Area fell from 1,171 in 1992 to 464 for 1999, a reduction that exceeded the city-wide decline of violent crime over the same period" (*Report of the Rampart*, 2000, p. 1).

Although the CRASH unit appeared to be effectively addressing gang violence within the Rampart area, it eventually came to light that some of their officers did so through unethical police tactics. Officers of the CRASH unit were accused of things like drug dealing, intimidating witnesses, planting evidence, framing suspects, robbery, perjury, and false imprisonment (Knowland & Nebbia, 2000, para. 1). Furthermore, this problem was not an isolated issue inherent to a few "bad seeds" within the department. It appeared to be systemic and deeply rooted in the practices of those involved with the CRASH unit. For example, investigations conducted in the aftermath of the scandal showed that those involved operated like a subcultural gang themselves, both through their criminal actions and their customs. Allegedly, they would give out plaques with shell casings on them designating when a fatal shooting had occurred and they had tattoos and patches on leather jackets with images of things like a skull and aces and eights on them (which stood for the dead man's hand of "Wild Bill" Hickock) (*Frontline*: CRASH Culture, n.d.a, para. 32).

In the following sections, we will discuss a timeline of the CRASH scandal followed by an overview of post-scandal reports. These investigations not only aired the dirty laundry that had been occurring among the CRASH unit for years, but also demonstrated that an unspoken **"code of silence"** had permeated throughout the ranks of the LAPD. Additionally, it was alleged that those in positions of authority turned a blind eye to the corruption and never intervened when they should have. Ultimately, these reports called for (and resulted in) more internal and external oversight to ensure that corruption like this never happened again.

Perhaps the most notorious name associated with the Rampart CRASH scandal is that of Officer Rafael Perez. Perez blew the whistle and exposed a lot of the corruption occurring within the LAPD CRASH unit; however, his motivations came from a place of self-preservation rather than valor. Officer Perez was on the CRASH unit, and along with his colleagues, engaged in less than ethically sound practices. He was charged with possession of cocaine with the intent to sell (he stole six pounds from the property locker), grand theft, and forgery. In exchange for leniency with his sentence (five years and immunity from further misconduct charges), Officer Perez provided the prosecution with nearly 4,000 pages of sworn testimony implicating approximately 70 other officers of misconduct (*Frontline*: Rampart Scandal Timeline, n.d.b, para. 11–13).

Unfortunately, there had been a string of prior incidents within the CRASH unit that led the administration to question Perez's activities. The first prominent case involved the shooting of one off-duty LAPD CRASH officer by another off-duty LAPD officer. Officer Frank Lyga shot and killed Officer Kevin Gaines, who was alleged to have pointed his gun at Lyga after having a road rage moment. Lyga told authorities that he was acting in self-defense and was exonerated of all charges. The investigation turned up troubling information about Officer Gaines: he had allegedly been involved in previous road rage incidents where he pulled his gun out on drivers and that he was said to be working as an off-duty security guard for a well-known rapper (something which was discouraged among the LAPD CRASH unit) (*Frontline*: Rampart Scandal Timeline, n.d.a, para. 1–2). A second issue involving a CRASH officer dealt with bank robbery. Officer David Mack was allegedly the mastermind behind a robbery where he conspired with his girlfriend (the bank manager) to have extra cash on hand when the incident occurred. He was sentenced to a little over 14 years in federal prison. In yet another incident, Officer Brian Hewitt brought a suspected gang member to the station for questioning and beat him to the point where he was vomiting blood and needed medical attention.

One of the more well-known heinous incidents of corruption involved Perez and his partner Nino Durden attempting to murder an innocent gang member named Javier Ovando. Perez and Durden accused Ovando of pulling a weapon on them while they were trying to apprehend him. The officers then allegedly shot Ovando in self-defense and along with the 23-year sentence that he received for assaulting two officers, Ovando wound up paralyzed from the waist down. Follow-up investigations revealed that Ovando never assaulted either officer and that a weapon was planted near him after he was shot to make it appear as if the shooting was a legitimate case of self-defense. Due to the previously established plea deal, Officer Perez was not charged with this crime. Officer Durden on the other hand was, and like Perez, worked out a plea deal and was sentenced to 5 years in federal prison. Given that Ovando did nothing wrong, his sentence was overturned, and he was released from prison after serving two and a half years (*Frontline*: Rampart Scandal Timeline, n.d.b, para. 14). He was awarded $15 million in damages (the largest individual police misconduct settlement for the LAPD to date), and it is estimated that by the time all the civil cases come to a close, the city of Los Angeles will have paid out nearly $125 million dollars in damages (*Rampart Reconsidered: Executive Summary*, n.d.b, p. 11).

Once those in administration caught wind of the various incidents discussed above, they formed a board of inquiry to investigate the scandal. This board consisted of command staff members that were part of the LAPD. Their report pointed fingers at the management structure that oversaw the CRASH unit. Even after this report was produced there were concerns about the LAPD's ability to be truly reflective about their behaviors. As such, the Rampart Independent Review Panel was created in 2000 and consisted of a broader spectrum of community members such as those in law enforcement, education, and business. Similar to the board of inquiry report, this report emphasized ineffective administration:

> Supervisors effectively deferred to CRASH to monitor itself. This lack of control over Rampart CRASH sent a clear message to its officers that they were a police force unto themselves, governed only by their own rules, and free to take the law into their own hands if that would further the mission of CRASH. At Rampart, the failure to impose adequate supervision and controls over CRASH officers resulted in a heighted sense of insularity which reinforced and perpetuated an "us versus them" mentality among Rampart CRASH officers. (*Report of the Rampart Independent Review Panel*, 2000, p. 8)

Additionally, this report called for external supervision of the LAPD, arguing that through their actions they had proven their inability to self-police and monitor misconduct. In 2000, the Department of Justice threatened the city and LAPD with a lawsuit alleging that they not only engaged in, but also actively practiced civil rights violations through the behaviors of those involved with the CRASH unit. In order to avoid litigation, the city agreed to a **consent decree** (a settlement where neither party admits fault or guilt, yet both parties agree to specific terms of said agreement) where a federal court (U.S. District Court for the Central District of California) would assume jurisdiction over the LAPD and ensure that they were properly addressing the glaring misconduct that was occurring within the CRASH unit (*Rampart Reconsidered*, n.d.a, p. 6 & 47). Follow-up investigations highlight that a lot of positive steps have been taken to address police misconduct; however, it will most likely still be quite some time before the public fully trusts the LAPD.

Discussion Questions

1. Do you feel as though the plea deal that Perez was given was fair?

2. What additional steps do you think administrators could take to prevent misconduct from happening in their departments?

3. Do the ends justify the means? In other words, are you willing to overlook these officers' transgressions since their actions lead to a noticeable reduction in crime?

Serpico

Officer Frank Serpico is perhaps one of the best well-known **whistleblowers** to date who risked life and limb to expose the corruption that was an epidemic in the NYPD of his time (the 1960s and 1970s). Serpico became an officer for the NYPD in 1959, and he worked his way up from patrol to the plainclothes unit (Marcou, 2014, para. 2–3). Similar to undercover officers today, this unit dressed in disguise and worked undetected within the community to apprehend criminal suspects. It wasn't long after Serpico was assigned to the plainclothes unit that he learned about "pads" or payoffs that officers received in exchange for turning a blind eye to criminal activity (Messing, 2012, para. 18). These "pads" would go to individual officers but also be pooled among the unit and divvied up between officers later. As such, this corruption was on a grand scale and either directly or indirectly impacted nearly every officer who was part of the plainclothes unit.

Serpico was unwilling to be a part of "pad" and tried on numerous occasions to tell those in authority about the corruption that he was witnessing. Unfortunately, Serpico was repeatedly told to stay quiet. It would come out later that those in positions of authority not only knew about but also partook in the corruption that he was describing. For example, when Serpico confronted a supervisor to disclose the things he witnessed, he was told that "he risked being found floating dead in the East River if he persisted" (Messing, 2012, para. 21). This was one of many interactions that Serpico had with those in positions of authority. Realizing that the corruption infiltrated all the way up the ranks, Serpico teamed up with fellow Officer Durk and in 1970 they reached out to *The New York Times* with their news of corruption (Wilde, 2013, para. 14).

It didn't take long after the story aired for the city and NYPD to take notice. Within months, Mayor John V. Lindsay appointed Whitman Knapp to lead an investigation into the corruption. This spawned the Knapp Commission, which was charged with documenting the extent of corruption occurring within the NYPD. The outcome of that commission (mainly supported through the testimony of Serpico) determined that the corruption was "an extensive, Department-wide phenomenon, indulged in to some degree by a sizable majority of those on the force and protected by a code of silence on the part of those who remained honest" (Ortega, 2011, para. 3). As such, those few honest officers like Serpico either chose to not speak up or they were threatened into silence.

After Serpico broke the "blue wall of silence" his remaining 12 months on the force ended up being a living hell. He was often verbally assaulted by other officers, being called things like a "rat" and "snitch," and he received many life-threatening letters and calls at both work and home. Serpico's career with the NYPD came to a screeching halt when he was shot point-blank in the face by a suspect during a drug raid. Miraculously, he survived the shooting, but Serpico is permanently deaf in one ear and has a bullet lodged in his brain. Although there was never any proof of this, it was believed that Serpico was set up by fellow officers and that the shooting was a hit (Wilde, 2013, para. 6). Serpico (and others) felt this to be the case because his fellow partners did nothing to back him up, and rather than call an ambulance they took him to the hospital in the back of their patrol car (Dvorak, 2010, para. 40). Actions taken in the aftermath of Serpico's shooting also verified that it could have been a hit for hire, or that at a bare minimum, a majority of his fellow officers wished him dead. He received condolence cards while recovering at the hospital that read things like, "Die you scumbag" and "With sincere sympathy … that you didn't get your brains blown out, you rat bastard." Also, as news spread throughout the precinct of Serpico's shooting, anonymous notes starting showing up on chalkboards asking for funds to hire a lawyer to defend the "guy who shot Serpico" and to get the person who shot him lessons "to teach him to shoot better" (Wilde, 2013, para. 13–15). There were investigations into the shooting of Serpico, and there was never enough evidence to conclusively say whether anyone affiliated with the NYPD was involved. To this day, Serpico lives a solitary life and only comes out of hiding to make brief appearances about public reform relating to **police corruption**.

Discussion Questions

1. Do you think you would have blown the whistle if you were in Serpico's position?

2. What sanctions do you think are appropriate for officers engaged in corruption?

3. Do you think that the issues facing the NYPD during the 1970s are isolated or is police corruption more common than we would like to assume?

Abner Louima

On August 9, 1997, Abner Louima was out with friends at Club Rendezvous which was a Brooklyn dance club where the Haitian immigrant community liked to hang out. After the club let out, a scuffle ensued between two women in the parking lot. Supposedly, Louima was trying to help break these two women up, and it was at this stage that law enforcement was called to the scene. During the course of trying to regain order, an officer named Justin Volpe was allegedly sucker punched by someone in the crowd. Officer Volpe identified Louima as one of the men who had punched him, and he was "arrested on charges of assault, resisting arrest, disorderly conduct and obstruction of justice" (Hinojosa, 1997, para. 11). These charges were later dropped when they determined there was no evidence substantiating these claims and also given the turn of events that transpired in the aftermath of Louima's arrest.

It was from this point on that Louima's night took a turn for the worse. While taking Louima into custody, law enforcement allegedly yelled racial slurs at Louima and beat him in the patrol car before going to the 70th Precinct. Once at the precinct the beating continued and got more violent as time went along. The abuse reached a climax when Officer Volpe drug Louima into a bathroom, sodomized him with a broomstick handle, and then shoved the bloodied broomstick in his face while taunting him (Chan, 2007, para. 3). After Volpe was done sexually assaulting Louima, he allegedly "paraded through the stationhouse with the stick in his hand, and bragged how he had 'broken a man down'" (Vann, 2000, para. 8). As a result, Louima suffered a raptured bladder and colon and had to spend two months in the hospital recovering.

While the abuse itself is horrifying, perhaps more alarming is that nobody in the precinct intervened. At one point in time, there were supposedly four different officers involved with beating Louima at the dance club and then an additional two joining in at the precinct. This doesn't include the number of other officers who would have seen Volpe with the broomstick after the fact. A scary reality is that the "code of silence" surrounding this incident would have likely remained unbroken had it not been for a nurse treating Louima reaching out to his family, the media, and the Internal Affairs Bureau of the NYPD (Chandler, 2012, para. 5).

There was a significant amount of public outcry for the abuse that Louima suffered at the hands of the NYPD. He went on the air and recounted the event while in the hospital, and it was hard to find anyone willing to side with the officers in this instance. In fact, then Mayor Rudolph Giuliani (who had a track record of siding with law enforcement up to this point) was quoted as saying, "These allegations are shocking. The alleged conduct involved is reprehensible done by anyone at any time. Allegedly done by police officers, it's even more reprehensible" (Hinojosa, 1997, para. 15). It wasn't long after the news broke that the officers were being formally investigated and criminal charges were being brought against them.

The courts focused their efforts on four officers in total, and Volpe in particular, given his role of being the primary aggressor in this case. Volpe was charged with aggravated sexual abuse and first degree assault and received a sentence of 30 years in prison without the possibility for parole. The charges and subsequent trial of Volpe were rather straightforward, and there was little doubt about his **culpability** (guilt or wrongdoing). However, it was less clear how the courts should prosecute a second officer who was said to be Volpe's accomplice. It was alleged that Officer Charles Schwartz assisted Volpe by holding Louima down during the assault. These facts were less cut and dried than the allegations against Volpe, and Schwartz went through four rounds of trials in an attempt to clear his name. He claimed that he was wrongfully accused and mistaken for another officer because he was working at his desk during the assault. After five years of litigation, Schwartz took a plea to a five-year sentence for perjury in exchange for all the other charges being dismissed (Chan, 2007, para. 3). Schwartz was released from prison after four years and allowed to serve out the last year of his sentence in a halfway house (Marzulli,

2007, para. 1). Two additional officers (Thomas Weise and Thomas Bruder) received five years in prison for charges of conspiracy to obstruct a federal investigation (Vann, 2000, para. 2).

The events that transpired in the precinct bathroom that evening altered Louima's life in more ways than he would have ever imagined. Whether intentional or not, he became a poster child for **police brutality** and the spokesman for overcoming police corruption. Amazingly, he said that he forgave the officers for what they did and said that "Maybe God figured I was the one to make it public. God wanted me to suffer; he had a plan for me" (Chan, 2007, para. 10). Louima filed a suit against the city and won an $8.7 million settlement, the largest brutality settlement in the city's history.

Discussion Questions

1. Do you agree with the sentences that Volpe and Schwartz received?

2. What do you feel the NYPD needed to do in order to regain the trust of its citizens?

Amadou Diallo

Amadou Diallo was a 23-year-old immigrant from Guinea who came to America to pursue a better life. He lived in the Bronx, making ends meet by street peddling items such as socks, gloves, and videos (Cooper, 1999, para. 21). Amadou lived a simple life and was saving his money to attend college and work on a computer science degree. Unfortunately, no more than two and a half years after he came to the U.S., Diallo's life was cut short at the hands of law enforcement.

On the evening of February 4, 1999, Amadou was approached by four plainclothes New York police officers who were members of the Street Crimes Unit. While this unit normally focuses "largely on taking illegal guns off the streets" their purpose for being in Diallo's neighborhood this evening was to track down information about a serial rapist (Cooper, 1999, para. 7). At 12:44 am, the four officers approached Diallo (who was in the front stoop of his apartment complex) and asked for identification. It is unclear what happened next, but the officers each fired rounds at Diallo because they said that he was not complying with their requests and was reaching for a weapon. In total, 41 shots were fired at Diallo, and 19 ended up hitting and ultimately killing him (Starr, 2014, para. 2).

The events transpired so quickly that it took a lot of post-shooting investigatory work to parcel out all of the details. It was determined that all of the officers fired at Diallo: two of them emptied their weapons (firing 16 times each) while the third fired his gun five times and the fourth did so four times. It also came to light that three of the officers had been involved in shootings before, which was strange since the majority (~90%) of officers in that department had never fired their gun in the line of duty (Cooper, 1999, para. 8–10). Some alleged that this might have demonstrated that these officers were "trigger happy," or even worse, that the Street Crimes Unit used violence as a means to get its desired results. The officers stood behind their story that their use of **deadly force** was warranted due to their fear that Diallo was reaching for a weapon. It ended up that Diallo did not have a weapon and that he was most likely reaching for his wallet (a wallet and pager were found next to his dead body).

The four officers were charged with second-degree murder. After three days of jury deliberation, they were found not guilty. The verdict rocked the greater New York area, with some praising the jury for **acquitting** the four officers while others were critical of the decision. For example, one officer's lawyer was quoted as saying "Police officers have to be able to do their jobs. When the evidence supports them, a jury will support them" (Fritsch, 2000, para. 20). However, others, such as former Mayor David N. Dinkins, disagreed. He was quoted as saying, "This will send the wrong message to those members of the Street Crime Unit who walk around saying, 'We own the night'" (Fritsch, 2000, para. 12).

In the aftermath of the trial, nearly 300 people congregated near the stoop where Diallo was shot to show their discontent with the outcome of the trial. Leading the pack was Reverend Al Sharpton, who said that he would be pushing for the U.S. Justice Department to bring federal civil rights charges against the four officers and the city of New York (because the four officers were white and Diallo was black). Federal charges were never filed because the U.S. Justice Department found the accusations to be unwarranted. Although the officers were not deemed criminally liable for the death of Diallo, his family filed a civil suit against the city alleging that "racial profiling by the Police Department was the cause of their son's death" (Feuer, 2004, para. 4). Those in administrative positions staunchly defended the actions of the officers and "neither the city nor the Police Department admitted any wrongdoing in the case" (Feuer, 2004, para. 6). While the NYPD was unwilling to admit any fault, the city eventually settled with the family for $3 million dollars, and shortly thereafter, the Street Crimes Unit was dismantled.

Although this case may seem less egregious than those discussed above, it calls into question nonetheless whether these officers abused their power and/or worked in a department that endorsed secrecy. Does the fact that three of these four officers were among the few to have fired their weapon in the line of duty before suggest that they were probably "trigger-happy" cops who should have had more administrative oversight? Additionally, did anyone in a position of authority question the motivation behind the shooting and challenge the officers' accusation that they believed Diallo had a weapon? Furthermore, why is so little known (still to this day) about the interactions that occurred that evening between Mr. Diallo and the four officers? And lastly, does the department's unwillingness to admit any fault demonstrate that they truly supported their officers' decisions, or that they were willing to cover their officers' backs (and theirs) at any cost?

Discussion Questions

1. How do you think you would have voted if you were a jury member in the trial of the four officers?

2. Given what happened to Diallo, and what is so often happening around the country today, do you feel as though we should reexamine the policies and procedures behind the use of deadly force by law enforcement?

The cases above demonstrate issues of police corruption that occurred on a grand scale as well as two isolated incidents of police misconduct and potential secrecy among the NYPD. One can assume given the national attention that CRASH garnered and the repeated media exposure that the NYPD received in the 1970s and then again in the mid-1990s that law enforcement agencies have curtailed police misconduct. Unfortunately, it appears as though the NYPD was not yet out of the spotlight and that the mid-1990s would usher in an entirely different set of police corruption/misconduct issues.

Mollen Commission

It was assumed that the corruption of the 1970s identified in the Knapp commission was in the NYPD's past. Unfortunately though, a new and more heinous type of corruption was ushered in around the early portion of the 1990s among New York's law enforcement. Similar in scope to what occurred on the opposite coast with the CRASH scandal, officers from the NYPD started receiving accusations of selling drugs and beating up suspects (*Shielded from Justice*, 1998, para. 3). There was little delay between these accusations and action, and in July of 1992, then Mayor David N. Dinkins called for a commission (headed by Milton Mollen) to investigate the allegations (Raab, 1993, para. 7).

The outcome of the report was damning in that, contrary to popular belief, the corruption did not occur exclusively at the hands of a few "rogue cops." Rather, officers from the 30th, 9th, 46th, 75th, and 73rd Precincts were swept up in these allegations (*Shielded from Justice*, 1998, para. 3). While it's hard to determine the extent of corruption (due to the "blue wall of silence"), the Mollen Commission found that some precincts had more problem officers than others (e.g., the 30th Precinct alone had 14 officers arrested on various charges) (Mollen Commission, 1994, p. 11). Also, similar to the issues that the NYPD faced 20 years prior, the Mollen Commission noted that those in positions of authority, while not actively engaging in the corruption themselves, should be held accountable because they knew about and did nothing to stop it.

According to Michael Armstrong, chief counsel for the Knapp Commission, the crimes committed by those being accused here differ in scope from the corruption of the 1970s:

> The Crooks, however, that you have uncovered, the criminals seem to be a different breed of criminals [than twenty-years ago] … the guys you're digging up, these guys are walking around with lead-lined gloves and riding shotgun for organized crime people. Instead of taking money to look the other way while someone else commits a street crime, they're out there competing with the criminals to commit street crime themselves, and it seems to me that is a very big difference (Mollen Commission, 1994, p. 10).

As such, rather than being complacent, these officers were accused of actively engaging in criminal behavior.

The commission found officers guilty of not only lower-level corruption schemes like **planting evidence** and stealing money, but large-scale crimes like actively committing robbery and burglary alongside convicted criminals. Perhaps the most habitual offender among the officers was Michael Dowd. Prior to being arrested on charges of drug dealing, officer Dowd had 16 complaints filed against him alleging that he was robbing drug dealers and then selling their cocaine (Treaster, 1994, para. 1). The Mollen Commission turned up additional dirt on various officers, who did things like stealing (drugs, guns, and money), "tuning" people up (beating them for information), bribing, planting evidence, and committing perjury (Mollen Commission, 1994, p. 2).

As was the case with the Rampart Independent Review Panel and the Knapp Commission, the Mollen Commission called for both internal and external oversight to address corruption occurring within these problem precincts. Among other things, the commission suggested that departments should improve screening and recruitment efforts, strengthen first-line supervision (those who should be detecting and punishing corruption), and put in place disincentives for corruption (Mollen Commission, 1994, p. 7). These efforts focus on internal detection and catching the problem early. Additionally, the commission called for external oversight to ensure that these policies were being implemented and to help ensure that they become a lasting staple among the NYPD.

Discussion Questions

1. What do you feel that police departments can do to help prevent corruption and misconduct before it happens?

2. Do you feel as though corruption and misconduct is something that only happens in larger departments like the NYPD and LAPD?

Corrections

Joyce Mitchell and the New York Prison Break

On September 26, 2015, Joyce Mitchell, a civilian worker for the New York State prison system, was sentenced to a range of no less than 28 months and no more than 7 years for supplying inmates David Sweat and Richard Matt with tools that helped them break out of the Clinton Correctional Facility. Throughout the approximately three-week manhunt that eventually led to Mitchell's arrest, Matt's death, and Sweat's capture, Mitchell changed her story numerous times as to what happened and her level of involvement. As CBS News stated in July of 2015, Joyce Mitchell's confession was one of sex and subterfuge (CBS News, 2015).

David Sweat began his criminal career early in life. From computer theft, **involuntary confinement** (holding a person against his or her will), and felony attempted burglary, Sweat spent most of his life in and out of courtrooms and confinement. In July of 2002, however, his criminal activities "graduated" to murder. On that day, at approximately 3:45 am, Sweat, with his accomplice Jeffrey A. Nabinger Jr., fired two bullets into the head of Broome County Sheriff's Deputy Kevin J. Tarsia, killing him at the scene (Dooling, 2015). It was for this crime that Sweat would eventually end up at the Clinton Correctional Facility and make his way into the **tailor shop** (a place in prison where clothing is made) of Joyce Mitchell.

Like Sweat, Richard Matt began his criminal career at an early age. Adopted by foster parents, Matt had a history of crimes ranging from weapons charges to harassment to felony assault. The events, however, that would eventually lead him to the Clinton prison began in North Tonawanda, New York. Matt had heard that his former boss, William Rickerson, had a large sum of money hidden somewhere. So, he and his accomplice, Lee Bates, kidnapped Rickerson and repeatedly beat him in the trunk of Bates' car in an effort to get him to tell them where the money was (DuVall, 2015). Eventually, Matt became frustrated and broke Rickerson's neck, killing him. After the murder, Matt dismembered the corpse and threw the body parts into the Niagara River.

Unfortunately, Matt's murder spree was just beginning. After the Rickerson killing, he crossed over into Mexico. There, he met a man in a bar and killed him over some money (Shepherd, 2015). Once again Matt fled, but was eventually caught by Mexican police and spent nine years in prison before being transferred back to the U.S. for the Rickerson murder.

With all three members of the notorious escape eventually arriving at the Clinton Correctional Facility, Mitchell's involvement with convicted murders Sweat and Matt began in the prison's tailor shop. Working as a supervisor for the prison, Mitchell supposedly became involved first with Sweat and then later with Matt during the course of their almost daily interactions. While she denied any type of relationship with Sweat, former inmate Erik Jensen said that Mitchell and Sweat were much more than friends and their relationship was the standing joke among prisoners working in Tailor Shop 3, a location where inmates made items such as pants, jackets, and other clothing. By Jensen's account, Mitchell and Sweat had sex in the 8 by 15 foot shop stockroom at least 100 times during his stay at Clinton (Schram & Golding, 2015).

While prison officials suspected a relationship between Mitchell and Sweat had developed, they were unable to prove it and, as a result, transferred him out of the unit. With Sweat out of the picture, Matt began to groom his own connection with the supervisor. According to Mitchell, "Inmate Matt and I got along well. We talked every day, and he treated me with respect and was nice to me. He made me feel special" (LoTemplio, 2015, para. 4 & 5). Slowly, however, Matt "began with seemingly innocent requests for help, but soon escalated into sexual contact, she said, including sending him nude photos to give to the other inmate,

David Sweat" (Lantz et al., 2015, para. 4). Ultimately, in discussions with investigators, Mitchell said her relationship with Matt became so close she eventually "admitted to smuggling hacksaw blades by hiding them in frozen hamburger meat and having the meat delivered to Matt" (CNN Wire, 2015, para. 25).

Eventually, Sweat and Matt were assigned to adjacent cells and their plan to escape began to take shape. After a month spent cutting through his cell wall at night, Sweat said "He would wait each night until after the 11:30 head count to crawl through the hole, shimmy down a series of pipes going down several stories and begin roaming the tunnels. He would return to his cell each morning before the 5:30 a.m. count, camouflage his portal to the maze below and start his daily routine" (Rashbaum, 2015, para. 12). Finally, on June 6, 2015, Sweat and Matt crawled out of their cells, down a 24-inch steam pipe, and through a manhole just outside of the Clinton facility. Mitchell had planned to meet them at the manhole, where the three of them would then drive away and start a new life together. The tailor shop supervisor, however, got cold feet and never picked the two convicts up.

Finally, after almost three weeks on the run, the escapees, who were likened to the main character in the popular movie **Shawshank Redemption**, had their luck run out. (In the prison movie starring Morgan Freeman and Tim Robbins, a man was wrongly convicted of murder and eventually escaped prison.) On June 26, Matt was the first to be sighted and after raising his shotgun towards one of the officers, was killed by a federal agent assisting in the search (Rashbaum & Mueller, 2015). Sweat was found two days later near the Canadian border and, after being shot twice, was taken into custody.

In the end, Joyce Mitchell's tale of sex and subterfuge ended almost like a Hollywood movie. Mitchell was caught and convicted of assisting in the inmates' escape; Matt was killed in a confrontation with law enforcement; and Sweat is now housed in a maximum-security facility.

Discussion Questions

1. Do you feel Joyce Mitchell should have to pay the costs associated with the three-week manhunt to find Sweat and Matt?

2. While Mitchell was a main contributor to the inmates' escape, where else did the correctional system fail during the course of events?

3. Should female civilian employees be allowed to work with male inmates?

The Washington Redskins Ticket Sting

One of the classic acts of subterfuge in corrections occurred when a variety of Washington, D.C., law enforcement and probation agencies, along with the **U.S. Marshals Service** (the law enforcement branch of the federal court system), conducted the Washington Redskins ticket sting in December of 1985. Working from an interagency database, the Marshals Service FIST (Fugitive Investigative Strike Team) sent out letters to the last known addresses of approximately 3,000 wanted offenders who had over 5,000 outstanding warrants, including charges of murder, rape, robbery, and assault (U.S. Marshals Service, 2014). The letters informed the lucky "winners" that they have won two free tickets to the upcoming game between the Washington Redskins and the Cincinnati Bengals. To make the offer even more enticing, those who showed up would also be entered into a drawing for Redskins season tickets and the possibility of winning the grand prize of an all-expenses-paid trip to Super Bowl XX (United Press International, 1985).

On the morning of December 15 at around 9:00 am, approximately 100 offenders arrived at the Washington, D.C., convention center to participate in the **Flagship International Sports Television** (FIST — the Marshals' name for the fictitious sports company running the "giveaway" — the same acronym of the Marshals fugitive apprehension unit) event. As the invitees wandered in, they were greeted by agents and officers disguised as masters of ceremony, waiters, and bus boys. One officer was even outfitted as a giant chicken with red boots and a concealed gun under his wing. The attendees were dressed in everything from business suits to official Redskins shirts, jackets, and hats. All were excited about their good fortune and some even began singing the Redskins fight song. After waiting as long as they felt comfortable, officers secured the area and began the "event." The offenders were excited, expecting to receive a free brunch, tickets, and rides to and from the game. Instead of a fun afternoon watching football, however, the attendees were greeted by 166 officers from Eastern New York, Maryland, Northern Virginia, the District of Columbia, and the Marshals Service (U.S. Marshals Service, 2014). After the initial shock of what was really happening began to wear off, reality for the offenders set in.

As the arrestees were being processed, many started to protest. According to the United Press International (1985), one individual was heard saying, "They said we were going to a football game — that's false advertising" (para. 7). Another handcuffed prisoner was heard muttering, "This ain't fair, this just ain't fair" (Associated Press, 1985, para 6). Hebert M. Rutherford III of the U.S. Marshals Service, however, didn't seem to be too upset over the comments. In his opinion, "It was party time and they fell for it, hook, line, and sinker" (Associated Press, 1985, para. 5). While some complained that the Washington Redskins Ticket Sting was a legal, but unethical operation, the feeling of the officers that day focused on the fact that it's always better and safer for everyone concerned if these types of offenders are arrested away from their homes or when they don't expect it. In the end, this type of subterfuge accomplished both.

Discussion Questions

1. Do you feel the Washington Redskins ticket sting was unethical?

2. What restrictions, if any, should be placed upon correctional officers when tricking offenders who have absconded from correctional supervision, such as probation or parole?

3. Was the Washington Redskins ticket sting a form of entrapment?

Uncovering Jail Corruption

The Los Angeles County Sheriff's Department was the focus of an FBI undercover sting operation designed to investigate accusations of prisoner abuse occurring within the Los Angeles County Men's Central Jail. Beginning with an anonymous tip from a facility inmate, the FBI began working with the informant in an effort to uncover allegations of officer **misconduct** (behavior that is deemed socially unacceptable or improper) and abuse. Initially, communication between the agency and the inmate occurred through the jail's in-house phone system, but fearing deputies might be listening in on their conversations, a plan was devised to smuggle a cell phone into the inmate's unit (Faturechi, 2011a). During one of the interviews, the inmate, later identified as Anthony Brown, told agents that he knew of a deputy in the jail who, for the right price, would smuggle contraband into the facility for offenders. Contact was made with the officer, Gilbert Michel, who covertly delivered a cell phone to inmate Brown for $1,500.00 (Faturechi, 2011b). At the time he brought the device into the facility, Michel did not know the offender was working with the **FBI** (Federal Bureau of Investigation — the main investigative branch of the U.S. Department of Justice). Officer Michel later resigned from the L.A. Sheriff's Department and was charged with one count of bribery of a public official. He accepted a plea deal and served six months in prison in exchange for his continued involvement in subsequent investigations of misconduct by his previous employer (Ex-LA County, 2016, para. 1–4).

While the FBI was pleased with their initial efforts, Los Angeles County Sheriff Lee Baca believed the Bureau not only crossed the line with their covert actions, but also may have in fact broken the law by willfully enticing and encouraging the introduction of contraband into his facility. Sheriff Baca explained that deputies found the cellphone on Brown during a routine pat down and before he was able to use the devise to record any alleged abuse by officers. The sheriff also detailed how after an initial interview with the inmate, sheriff's deputies suspected he was working with the FBI (Kim, 2014a). Of particular concern for Sheriff Baca, however, was the FBI's apparent lack of knowledge and expertise regarding not only his jail and jail procedures, but the inmate they had selected as their informant. The FBI agent handling inmate Brown on behalf of the Bureau, Agent Leah Marx, had only been with the FBI for a little over a year and deputies claimed that she was very aware that Brown "had been convicted of 15 felonies and sentenced to more than 400 years" (Kim, 2014b). Laura Eimiller, a spokeswoman for the FBI, countered the concerns of Sheriff Baca by saying "With regard to the investigation, FBI agents at all times were acting within the course and scope of their duties and were in compliance with FBI policy and practices" (Faturechi, 2011b, para. 13).

Unfortunately, the battle between the FBI and the Los Angeles Sheriff's Department was not over. After the sheriff's department discovered Brown was an FBI informant, the bureau alleges the department made a concerted effort to conceal and hide Brown from its agents (Kim, 2014b). Seven Los Angeles County sheriff's deputies, including two lieutenants and two sergeants, were charged with obstruction of justice and conspiracy for supposedly changing Brown's name on the inmate rosters to various aliases and continually relocating him within the facility in an attempt to keep him away from his FBI handlers. Sheriff's deputies admit they did change Brown's name and moved him within the facility at various times, but that they did so at the request of the FBI (Stampler, 2013). The sheriff's deputies claimed that the actions were the result of a phone call from Steve Martinez, the acting chief of the FBI's Los Angeles field office at the time, to Sheriff Baca, requesting that Brown be placed into protective custody for his own safety. Fearing for the inmate's safety, and as requested by the FBI, the deputies contended that their actions were in accordance with department policy and that both the FBI and Los Angeles County sheriff command officers were aware of their actions.

Discussion Questions

1. Do you believe the FBI violated the law by willfully smuggling a cell-phone into the Los Angeles County Jail?

2. Should the FBI or other federal agencies be allowed to circumvent the Los Angeles County Sheriff's Department policies and procedures in order to conduct a civil rights violation investigation?

3. What criteria do you believe an agency should use when conducting covert investigations in a lockdown facility using inmates as informants?

Illegal Relationships

In one of the more notorious acts of subterfuge by officers with inmates, four female corrections officers from the Baltimore City Detention Center carried on long-term sexual relationships with Tavon White, the incarcerated leader of the city's **Black Guerrilla Family** (BGF) (a prison and street gang) gang. Even more shocking, however, than the sexual relationships between the four officers and White was that all four females allegedly became pregnant by the inmate, with a second suspected of having two children by the convicted felon (Fuchs, 2013). All of the babies were conceived while White was incarcerated at the Baltimore facility.

The uncovering of the secret affairs began in 2009 as part of a federal investigation into the BGF's activities at the Baltimore City facility (Marimow & Wagner, 2013). What began as an effort to assess how and to what extent the BGF was continuing its criminal activities within the walls of the detention center, later turned into a full-blown investigation that focused on the corruption and crime committed by the officers themselves. White, sentenced in 2009 for attempted murder, instructed incarcerated members of the BGF to seek out vulnerable female officers with "low self-esteem, insecurities, and certain physical attributes" (Fuchs, 2013, para. 10). He found them in the form of Jennifer Owens, Katera Stevenson, Chania Brooks, and Tiffany Linder, the four officers who were impregnated by White. Owens and Stevenson even went as far as having the name "Tavon" tattooed on their bodies.

On the surface, the sexual activity between White and the four female corrections officers might seem like an isolated incident. Unfortunately, according to a United States Department of Justice report released just after the indictments of the four officers, the Baltimore City Detention Center had one of the highest rates of officer/inmate sexual contact in the nation (Duncan, 2013). Duncan went on to say that second only to Indiana's Marion County Jail Intake Facility, almost 7% of the inmates at the Baltimore City Detention Center claimed to have had sexual relations with an officer or staff member. The Indiana facility had almost 8% of the inmate population making the same claim. The national average, according to Allen Beck, one of the primary authors of the **Department of Justice** (a primary investigative and enforcement branch of federal law enforcement) study, is just under 2% (Duncan, 2013).

Unfortunately for the Baltimore facility, sex between inmates and female officers was not the only problem. In addition to the sexual favors provided by Owens, Stevenson, Brooks, and Linder, they and nine other female corrections officers at the detention center were also engaged in smuggling cell phones, money, drugs, and other types of contraband into the facility so White and the BGF could sell the items to the other inmates (Ritchie, 2013). For the most part, the officers were able to get the contraband into the facility by concealing the items in their hair, underwear, and shoes (Marimow & Wagner, 2013). According to White's indictment, he bragged in a telephone conversation that "This is my jail. You understand that? I'm dead serious.... I make every final call in this jail ... and nothing go past me. Any of my brothers that deal with anybody, it's gonna come to me. Before (somebody) stab somebody, they gotta run it through me" (Mungin, 2013, para. 10). White even claimed that he was making over $16,000 a month selling the smuggled contraband to other inmates (Marimow & Wagner, 2013).

In the end, 44 people were charged with crimes (correctional officers and detainees at the facility) and 35 of those individuals plead guilty (including White). Four defendants opted to go to trial and three of those were acquitted while one died prior to the conclusion of their trial (Shaffer, 2016, para. 18–21). The then Governor Larry Hogan decided to permanently close the facility in 2015 claiming that the facility was a long-standing "black eye" for the state (Fenton and Broadwater, 2015, para. 1).

Discussion Questions

1. Legally, the inmates who had sexual relationships with the officers are considered victims. Do you agree?

2. Where do you think the primary failure of the system occurred in the Tavon White case?

3. Many argue that because of the sexual tensions between male inmates and female officers (and vice versa), only officers of the same sex should oversee inmates. Do you agree?

Strip Searches

Strip searches (the removal of a person's clothing in an attempt to locate concealed items) within correctional facilities are a common occurrence in today's jails and prisons. In most cases, the officers involved conduct themselves in a professional and respectful manner. There have been, however, accusations that strip searches in some facilities have taken on a more prurient purpose.

One such case involved two female inmates at the St. Clair County Jail in Illinois. During 2012, Leticia Jackson and Teresa Hale, both convicted of driving under the influence, were serving weekend sentences in the facility. The two offenders alleged that during strip searches in the jail, they were repeatedly humiliated and abused by two of the officers involved, including acts of sexual misconduct (Kelley, 2014b). Jackson and Hill also stated that the same two officers would strip them on a regular basis during their shifts. A third inmate, Sandra Russell, claimed that she was not only strip-searched multiple times by the facility officers, but that her strip searches were conducted in front of other inmates in an attempt to humiliate her. On one day, Russell alleged that officers strip-searched her on three separate occasions.

St. Clair County Sheriff Rick Watson, however, did not agree with the accusations, stating that his officers never humiliated inmates during any strip search and all searches were performed with dignity and in a professional manner. As defined by the United States Court of Appeal, a strip search constitutes "an inspection of a naked individual without any scrutiny of the subject's body cavities" (Ryan, 2013, para. 3). According to Sheriff Watson, "We're doing everything according to state standards and doing it with respect. Of course we don't like doing it anymore than they do. We do it for the safety of jail staff and inmates. We don't want somebody sneaking a shank in here and see an inmate stabbed or killed. We don't want staff getting killed" (Kelley, 2014a, para. 4). Kelley went on to say that Jail Superintendent Phillip McLaurin believed that "Normally those searches come around based on the fact that an inmate threatened suicide or other inmates identified the individual as having contraband in their possession. Nobody enjoys being strip-searched. No matter whether it is with one person or 10 people, you feel uncomfortable" (para. 10).

Unfortunately for St. Clair County, 29 additional inmates have filed a joint federal lawsuit also claiming abuses from illegal strip searches. At the heart of the complaint is the contention that inmates disagreed with the department's use of group strip searches where inmates were lined up and stripped searched at the same time. Inmates also alleged that officers would conduct **cavity searches** (a visual or invasive inspection of a person's body cavity designed to find contraband) of suspected inmates in front of the entire group during these group strip searches (Bell, 2013). The complainants claimed they had repeatedly tried to use the detention facility's grievance process to express their displeasure with the process, but their concerns about the humiliation and abuse went unanswered. As a result, they felt they no other alternative than to file a $10 million lawsuit in federal court seeking compensatory and punitive damages. Not long after the inmates had filed their suit, a federal judge in a different group strip search case ruled that group strip searchers were not unconstitutional as long as they weren't done to humiliate or embarrass the inmates involved (Kelley, 2014a). In his ruling, Judge J. Phil Gilbert said of the defendant whose case was denied "He does not describe any harassing, or demeaning comments or behavior on the part of the prison staff, nor does it appear that the search was performed with the intent to degrade him, or that is was unnecessary in light of legitimate security concerns" (Bell, 2013, para. 12). According to Sheriff Watson, as was evident in the case above, at no time were strip searches in his jail ever used to humiliate or embarrass inmates.

Discussion Questions

1. Do you agree with the judge that it's all right to strip search inmates in groups as long as there is no intent to humiliate or degrade the individuals involved?

2. Should officers be allowed to strip search inmates of the opposite sex in certain circumstances, such as when there are immediate security concerns?

3. What challenges to transgendered inmates are present when discussing the policies and procedures of strip searches?

Inmate Pen Pals

As part of the rehabilitative process, many inmates attempt to find **pen pals** (individuals who correspond with each other via mail or electronic means) with which to correspond while they're incarcerated. To facilitate these inter- actions, there are a number of inmate pen pal websites, such as Women Behind Bars, Jail Babes, and PrisonPenPals, where inmates can post their pictures, bios, and contact information in the hope that an interested person on the out- side will make contact and start writing. These long-distance relationships often allow inmates the opportunity to develop personal contacts outside of the prison environment and practice their pro-social behavioral skills. Unfor- tunately, what those on the outside see isn't always what they get.

Take, for example, Aaron Douglas, a maximum-security inmate. According to Douglas' online biography, he enjoys "listening to music, working out and playing cards, Considering I'm locked in my cell 22 hours a day I also watch a lot of T.V. as well." He also says, "This is my first time doing anything like this, so bare [sic] with me. I've been incarcerated since 2014 and I'm looking for someone that I can start a new friendship with because sitting in here gets to be pretty lonely. I would love to be able to talk to someone about how their day went and hear about what's going on in the outside world. Maybe I can bring some happiness into your life and vice versa" (Henderson, 2019). What Douglas fails to mention is that he was convicted of a cold-blooded **murder** (the illegal killing of one human being by another) and accused of another.

And then there are inmates like Matt Johnston who "loves to play and watch hockey, he's loyal and he's looking for a special girl with whom to share his love and strength" and Nathan Zuccherato who is "looking for female friends to write and get to know. He likes the Blue Jays, and he likes to read and work out." Even Tyler Sturrup "enjoys camping, hiking, swimming and dogs. He also hopes to own his own business someday." They don't sound too bad, right? What Johnston fails to mention, however, is that he murdered six individuals in the infamous Surrey Six slaughter, while Zuccherato, a gang assassin, was guilty of multiple murders during his reign of terror in the 2000s. Sturrup also left out the small detail that he is a **neo-Nazi** (an individual associated with an organization similar to the German Nazi Party) killer serving a life sentence. Needless to say, some pen pals are quite surprised to find out the sweet "in- nocent" person behind bars who is so willing to share their life and dreams with them may also have a very dark and sometimes violent past.

Victims and victim's rights groups are also outraged at the ability of offenders, some of whom have been convicted of very serious offences, to have access to Internet and social media outlets that allow them to have contact with the outside world. Roberta Roper is one such example. Her daughter, Stephanie Roper, was the victim of a horrific murder in an abandoned farmhouse in 1982. Ms. Roper's killer, Jerry Lee Beatty, is now one of the thousands of inmates seeking a pen pal with which to develop a relationship. According to Beatty, "I really am asking for a second chance—my family has either died or left me after 25 years of imprisonment. I need finances for attorneys, art supplies, and some everyday essentials." Roberta, however, finds the whole situation offensive. For her and her family, "It compounds everything (victims) have to endure" (Sylvain, 2012).

Discussion Questions

1. In your opinion, should inmates be allowed to have pen pals while incarcerated?

2. Do you agree with Roberta Roper that allowing inmates pen pals victimizes their victim's families all over again?

3. Should inmates be required to fully disclose their criminal history when setting up their profiles on online pen pal sites?

Nevada's Execution Drugs

Use of the death penalty as a final sanction against horrific crimes is one of those moral dilemmas that will be continually debated. Even more problematic, in some cases, is the manner in which the execution is administered. Within the United States, the primary methods of ending an offender's life are hanging, electrocution, the gas chamber, firing squad, and lethal injection (with lethal injection being the primary method used in every state that actively enforces the death penalty) (Death Penalty Information Center, 2020).

As the debate over whether or not the death penalty should be allowed continues, some drug companies are making it clear they do not want their **pharmaceuticals** (a compound or compounds used for medical purposes) used to end the life of a convicted inmate. One such company is Alvogen, an American-based corporation with global clients. Alvogen sued the state of Nevada for what it claims was the illegal acquisition of its drug midazolam, a substance used in the execution of Nevada death row prisoner Scott Dozier

(Gonzalez, 2018). Nevada, however, contested the accusation, saying the drug was not illegally obtained, and its use was consistent with accepted medical practice.

Dozier, convicted of multiple murders, was also an apparent drug dealer and user. His first victim, Jansen Green, was Dozier's roommate in 2001. When Green threatened to expose Dozier's **methamphetamine** (a highly addictive stimulant that affects the central nervous system) business, he was shot in the back of the head with a .22-caliber rifle (Erickson, 2018). After Green's execution, Dozier broke both of his legs so he could stuff Green's body into a black toolbox and buried him in a shallow grave out in the Nevada desert.

Dozier's second victim, Jeremiah Miller, was also killed in a drug-related incident. Miller wanted to make methamphetamine and approached Dozier for assistance. Miller had borrowed $12,000 to buy the necessary ingredients, but instead, like Green, was executed, mutilated, and stuffed into a large suitcase. The suitcase containing Miller's body was later found in a dumpster by a local maintenance man. For this crime, Dozier received the death penalty.

After his conviction and subsequent death sentence in 2007, Dozier told the court in 2016 to expedite his execution. In his opinion, "Life in prison isn't a life and if people say they're going to kill me, get to it" (Stanley-Becker, 2019, para. 3). As the prison prepared for Dozier's death, they intended to try a never-before-used drug cocktail of midazolam (a sedative), fentanyl (a pain-killer) and cisatracurium (a muscle-paralyzing agent). The pharmaceutical company Alovogen, upon hearing of Nevada's plan to use its drug midazolam in the execution, filed a legal complaint arguing the state had obtained its drug "by **subterfuge** [deceit used to achieve a goal] with the undisclosed and improper intent to use it for the upcoming execution" (Stanley-Becker, 2019, para. 13). As a result of this lawsuit, Dozier's original execution date of October 16, 2017, was postponed. After a second hearing in August 2017, a new execution date was set for November 13, 2017. Alovogen once again appealed the use of its drug and was joined in the suit by Sandoz, a Swiss-based pharmaceutical company that also didn't want any of its drugs used in U.S. executions.

Ultimately, as lawsuits and legal battles over his fate continued, Dozier grew tired of the delays and life inside of a Nevada prison. Prison officials had noticed his changing demeanor and had him placed on suicide watch. As his mental state continued to decline, Dozier finally committed suicide in his cell on January 5, 2019.

Discussion Questions

1. Should pharmaceutical companies have to state what their drugs can and cannot be used for?

2. Was Nevada's failure to disclose its intended use of midazolam an act of subterfuge?

3. In your opinion, is it possible to have a humane execution?

Chapter Key Terms

"Code of silence"
Consent decree
Whistleblower
Police corruption
Culpability
Police brutality
Deadly force
Acquittal
Planting evidence
Involuntary confinement
Tailor shop
Shawshank Redemption
U.S. Marshals Service
Flagship International
    Sports Television

Misconduct
FBI
Black Guerrilla Family
Department of Justice
Strip searches
Cavity searches
Pen pals
Murder
Neo-Nazi
Pharmaceuticals
Methamphetamine
Subterfuge

References

Associated Press. (1985). Redskins ticket sting nets 101 fugitives. Associated Press. www.apnewsarchive.com.

BBC. (2014, March). Australia: Drone used to carry drugs near prison. www.bbc.com.

Bell, K. (2013, December). Inmates at St Clair County jail file federal lawsuit over strip searches. *St. Louis Post-Dispatch*. www.stltoday.com.

Blue Ribbon Rampart Review Panel. (n.d.a). *Rampart reconsidered: The search for real reform seven years later*. http://www.lapdonline.org/assets/pdf/Rampart%20Reconsidered-Full%20Report.pdf.

Blue Ribbon Rampart Review Panel. (n.d.b). *Rampart reconsidered: The search for real reform seven years later. Executive summary.* http://www.lapd online.org/assets/pdf/rampart_reconsidered_executive_summary.pdf.

Burks, B. (2014, January). 4 arrested outside of central MS correctional facility. WLOX13. www.wlox.com.

Carrera, J. B. (2014, May). Woman accused of trying to smuggle "Ice" into DOC for jailed boyfriend, inside her baby's diapers. Guam News. http://www.pacificnewscenter.com.

CBS News. (2015, July). Joyce Mitchell's confession: A tale of sex, subterfuge. CBS News. www.cbsnews.com.

Chan, S. (2007). The Abner Louima case, 10 years later. *The New York Times.* http://cityroom.blogs.nytimes.com/2007/08/09/the-abner-louima-case -10-years-later/?_php=true&_type=blogs&_php=true&_type=blogs&_php=true&_type=blogs&_r=2&.

Chandler, D. L. (2012). Abner Louima was savagely beaten by NYPD 15 years ago today. NewsOne. http://newsone.com/2029939/abner-louima-case/.

CNN Wire. (2015, July). NY prisoner David Sweat claims he and partner escaped twice, split apart over alcohol, bickering. KTLA5. www.ktla.com.

C1 Staff. (2014, March). Inmate smuggles drugs into jail with artificial leg. CorrectionsOne.com. http://www.correctionsone.com.

C1 Staff. (2014, May). Woman caught smuggling meth in baby diapers. CorrectionsOne.com. http://www.correctionsone.com/.

Cooper, M. (1999). Officers in Bronx fire 41 shots, and an unarmed man is killed. *The New York Times.* http://www.nytimes.com/1999/02/05/ny region/officers-in-bronx-fire-41-shots-and-an-unarmed-man-is-killed. html.

Death Penalty Information Center. (2020). Methods of execution. https://deathpenaltyinfo.org/executions/methods-of-execution#:~:text=The%20 primary%20means%20of%20execution,firing%20squad%2C%20and%20 lethal%20injection.&text=The%20predominance%20of%20lethal%20injec tion,the%20Court%20regarding%20older%20methods.

Dooling, N. (2015, June). David Sweat's brutal path to prison. www.press connects.com.

Duncan, I. (2013, May). Baltimore has high rate of staff-inmate sex. *The Baltimore Sun.* www.baltimoresun.com.

DuVall, E. (2015, June). Richard Matt's troubles began early in life. *Democrat & Chronicle.* www.democratandchronicle.com.

Dvorak, K. (2010). Frank Serpico of NYPD fame carries the torch for lamp lighters. https://thekdreport.me/2010/01/24/frank-serpico-of-nypd-fame -carries-the-torch-for-lamplighters/.

Erickson, B. (2018, July 20). Nevada death row inmate committed 2 drug-related killings. *Las Vegas Review-Journal*. https://www.reviewjournal.com/crime/homicides/nevada-death-row-inmate-committed-2-drug-related-killings/.

Ex-LA County sheriff's deputy sentenced for accepting bribe. (2016, June). https://abc7.com/los-angeles-county-sheriffs-department-gilbert-michel-lee-baca-leroy/1384174/.

Faturechi, R. (2011a, September). FBI paid deputy to smuggle cellphone in jail sting. *Los Angeles Times*. www.articles.latimes.com.

Faturechi, R. (2011b, September). L.A. County Sheriff Lee Baca gives details of FBI sting. *Los Angeles Times*. www.articles.latimes.com.

Fenton, J. & Broadwater, L. (2015). Gov. Hogan announces 'immediate' closure of Baltimore Jail. *The Baltimore Sun*. https://www.baltimoresun.com/maryland/baltimore-city/bs-md-hogan-city-jail-20150730-story.html.

Feuer, A. (2004). $3 Million deal in police killing of Diallo in '99. *The New York Times*. http://www.nytimes.com/2004/01/07/nyregion/3-million-deal-in-police-killing-of-diallo-in-99.html.

Fritsch, J. (2000). The Diallo verdict: The overview; 4 officers in Diallo shooting are acquitted of all charges. *The New York Times*. http://www.nytimes.com/2000/02/26/nyregion/diallo-\verdict-overview-4-officers-diallo-shooting-are-acquitted-all-charges.html.

Frontline: CRASH Culture. (n.d.a). PBS. http://www.pbs.org/wgbh/pages/frontline/shows/lapd/scandal/crashculture.html.

Frontline: Rampart Scandal Timeline. (n.d.b) PBS. http://www.pbs.org/wgbh/pages/frontline/shows/lapd/scandal/cron.html.

Fuchs, E. (2013). This man allegedly impregnated four of his guards while running a criminal empire from prison. *National Post*. www.news.nationalpost.com.

Gander, K. (2014, April). Teenager Dallas Archer tried to smuggle gun into prison inside her body. *The Independent*. http://www.independent.co.uk.

Gatti, W. (2009, December). Pigeons used to smuggle drugs. The Pigeon Insider. http://www.pigeonracingpigeon.com.

Gerber, C. (2014, May). Kokomo woman accused of hiding gun in bra while visiting Miami Correctional. *Kokomo Tribune*. http://www.kokomotribune.com.

Gonzalez, R. (2018, July 11). Why Nevada's execution drug cocktail is so controversial. Wired.com. https://www.wired.com/story/the-untested-drugs-at-the-heart-of-nevadas-execution-controversy/.

Henderson, P. (2019, December 18). Chilliwack murderer among inmates looking for pen pals online. The Abbotsford News. https://www.abbynews.

com/news/chilliwack-murderer-among-inmates-looking-for-pen-pals
-online/.

Hinojosa, M. (1997). NYC officer arrested in alleged sexual attack on suspect. CNN. http://www.cnn.com/US/9708/14/police.torture/.

Jauregul, A. (2014, April). Teen arrested with loaded gun in vagina: Cops. The Huffington Post. http://www.huffingtonpost.com.

Kelley, D. (2014a, January). 'Humiliating': Female inmates at St Clair County Jail plan to sue over strip searches. *Belleville News-Democrat*. www.bnd. com.

Kelley, D. (2014b, March). Lawsuit: Ex-inmates allege illegal strip searches at St. Clair County Jail. *Belleville News-Democrat*. www.bnd.com.

Kim, V. (2014a, May). Federal trial begins for deputy accused in L.A. County jail abuse case. *Los Angeles Times*. www.latimes.com.

Kim, V. (2014b, May). In jails trial, FBI agent explains smuggling cellphone to informant. *Los Angeles Times*. www.latimes.com.

Knowland, D., & Gerardo, N. (2000). The Los Angeles police scandal and its social roots. World Socialist Web Site. https://www.wsws.org/en/articles/ 2000/03/lapd-m13.html.

Lantz, D., Katershy, A., & Margolin, J. (2015, July). Inside Joyce Mitchell's relationships with escaped prisoners and fantasy of a new life. ABC News. www.abcnews.go.com.

LoTemplio, J. (2015, July). Mitchell's statements to police reveal relationship with Matt, Sweat. *Niagara Gazettte*.www.niagara-gazette.com.

Marcou, D. (2014). Police history: Frank Serpico and the preservation of honor. Police1. http://www.policeone.com/patrol-issues/articles/6729848-Police -History-Frank-Serpico-and-the-preservation-of-honor/.

Marimow, A. E., & Wagner, J. (2013, April). 13 corrections officers indicted in Md., accused of aiding gang's drug scheme. *The Washington Post*. www. washingtonpost.com.

Marzulli, J. (2007). Loima liar set free. *New York Daily News*. http://www.ny dailynews.com/news/crime/louima-liar-set-free-article-1.232918.

Messing, P. (2012). New York's foulest. *New York Post*. http://nypost.com/ 2012/08/05/new-yorks-foulest/.

Miller, D. (2013, November). Mini-chopper drops tobacco into state prison yard. WALB News. www.walb.com.

Mollen Commission. (1994). *Commission to Investigate Allegations of Police Corruption and the Anti-Corruption Procedures of the Police Department Commission Report*. Police Assessment Resource Center. Deactivated link (retrieved 2015). http://www.parc.info/client_files/Special%20Reports/4% 20-%20Mollen%20Commission%20-%20NYPD.pdf.

Montaldo, C. (2011, December). Top ten list of dumb criminals in 2011. About. com Crime. http://crime.about.com.

Mungin, L. (2013, November). Jail officers accused of accepting bribes, teaming with gang to bring in drugs. CNN Justice. www.cnn.com.

Ortega, T. (2011). What Frank Serpico started: The Knapp Commission Report. *The Village Voice*. http://blogs.villagevoice.com/runninscared/2011/04/what_frank_serp.php.

Raab, S. (1993). New York's police allowed corruption, Mollen Panel says. *The New York Times*. http://www.nytimes.com/1993/12/29/nyregion/new-york-s-police-allow-corruption-mollen-panel-says.html.

Schaffer, C. (2016). Former Baltimore corrections officer pens book on prison sex scandal. *WMAR Baltimore*. https://www.wmar2news.com/news/region/baltimore-city/former-baltimore-corrections-officer-pens-bookon-prison-sex-scandal.

The Rampart CRASH Unit: Blood on the hands of the LAPD. (1999, October 3). *Revolutionary Worker* #1024. http://www.revcom.us/a/v21/1020-029/1024/lapd.htm.

Rashbaum, W. K. (2015, July 20). New York prisoner's keys to escape: Lapsed rules, tools and luck. *The New York Times*. https://www.nytimes.com/2015/07/21/nyregion/in-new-york-prison-escape-patience-timing-and-luck-for-david-sweat.html?searchResultPosition=48.

Rashbaum, W. K., & Mueller, B. (2015, June 26). Richard Matt, escaped prisoner in New York manhunt, is fatally shot. *The New York Times*. www.nytimes.com.

Report of the Rampart Independent Review Panel: A report to the Los Angeles Board of Police Commissioners concerning the operations, policies, and procedures of the Los Angeles Police Department in the wake of the Rampart scandal. Executive summary. (2000). http://www.clearinghouse.net/chDocs/public/PN-CA-0002-0008.pdf.

Ritchie, R. (2013, April). Jailhouse soap opera: 13 female guards indicted for smuggling drugs & phones; 4 impregnated by same inmate. CBS Baltimore. www.baltimore.cbslocal.com.

Ryan, J. (2013). Strip search and substitute/subterfuge. Legal and Liability Risk Management Institute. www.llrmi.com.

Salina Staff. (2014, March). Artificial leg used to smuggle drugs into jail. *Salina Post*. http://salinapost.com.

Schram, J., & Golding, B. (2015, June). Shaw-skank had closet sex with killer at least 100 times: Ex-inmate. *New York Post*.www.nypost.com.

Shepherd, K. (2015, June). Who are Richard Matt and David Sweat? N.Y. prison escapees have violent history. *Los Angeles Times*. www.latimes.com.

Shielded from justice: Police brutality and accountability in the United States. (1998, June). Human Rights Watch. http://www.hrw.org/legacy/reports/reports98/police/uspo100.htm.

Stampler, L. (2013, December). FBI sting exposes Los Angeles jail corruption; 18 sheriff's deputies arrested. *Time.* www.nation.time.com.

Stanley-Becker, I. (2019, January 7). "Life in prison isn't a life": A Nevada inmate whose execution was delayed is found dead in an apparent suicide. *The Washington Post.* https://www.washingtonpost.com/nation/2019/01/07/life-prison-isnt-life-nevada-inmate-whose-execution-was-delayed-is-found-dead-apparent-suicide/.

Starr, A. (2014). How the legacy of Amadou Diallo lives on in New York's immigrant community. The World. http://www.pri.org/stories/2014-02-05/how-legacy-amadou-diallo-lives-new-yorks-immigrant-community.

Sylvain, A. (2012, March 12). Victims blast inmate pen-pal sites. *USA Today.* https://www.corrections1.com/communications/articles/victims-blast-inmate-pen-pal-sites-px3DHhOZqTBYee7w/.

The Telegraph. (2009, March 30). Pigeons fly mobile phones to Brazilian prisoners. https://www.telegraph.co.uk/news/newstopics/howaboutthat/5079580/Pigeons-fly-mobile-phones-to-Brazilian-prisoners.html.

Treaster, J. B. (1994, July 7). Corruption in uniform: The *Dowd* case; Officer flaunted corruption and his superiors ignored it. *The New York Times.* http://www.nytimes.com/1994/07/07/nyregion/corruption-uniform-dowd-case-officer-flaunted-corruption-his-superiors-ignored.html.

United Press International. (1985, December). Police net 100 fugitives with football ticket ruse. *Chicago Tribune.* www.articles.chicagotribune.com.

U.S. Marshals Service. (2014). History-Fugitive Investigative Strike Teams (FIST). U.S. Marshals Service. www.usmarshals.gov.

Vann, B. (2000). The Abner Louima case: Three New York cops guilty in cover-up of torture. World Socialist Web Site. https://www.wsws.org/en/articles/2000/03/loui-m09.html.

Wilde, J. (2013). Frank Serpico: The true story of the corruption busting cop. http://caught.net/FrankSerpico.pdf.

Chapter Five

Intrusiveness

The telescreen received and transmitted simultaneously. Any sound that Winston made, above the level of a low whisper, would be picked up by it; moreover, so long as he remained within the field of vision which the metal plaque commanded, he could be seen as well as heard. There was of course no way of knowing whether you were being watched at any given moment. How often, or on what system, the Thought Police plugged in on any individual wire was guess-work. It was even conceivable that they watched everybody all the time. But at any rate they could plug in your wire whenever they wanted to. You had to live — did live, from habit that became instinct — in the assumption that every sound you made was overheard, and, except in darkness, every movement scrutinized.

— George Orwell, *Nineteen Eighty-Four* (1949)

The year 1984 may have come and gone, but George Orwell's concerns about the dangers of governmental intrusiveness still resonate loudly. The kind of technological snooping that formerly had been thought to be entertaining science fiction has now become stark reality. One can only imagine the technological wizardry possessed by such agencies as the American National Security Agency and various other public and private entities worldwide.

Americans have never liked snoops. In fact, a major cause of the American Revolution was anger over warrantless searches being conducted by British agents hired to enforce the hated stamp tax laws.

This chapter will cover the constitutional vice of "**intrusiveness**" (violations of our privacy or autonomy). To illustrate this ethical concern, we will examine some interesting cases involving such things as unreasonable searches, unreasonable seizures, and the so-called (and highly controversial) "general right to privacy."

What Is a Search?

Few Americans know it, but the American Revolutionary War was, to a large degree, an anti-tax revolt. Colonists hated paying British taxes, especially in light of the fact that they were not represented in Parliament (hence the famous war cry of "no taxation without representation"). The **stamp tax** was particularly considered heinous. Agents of the British king routinely searched warehouses, stores, and even homes looking for goods lacking the proper stamps that showed that the tax on the goods had been paid. These agents were armed with nothing more than mere "**writs of assistance**" (watered-down versions of search warrants that lasted for the life of the monarch, and which did not require the agent seeking one to first describe where exactly he wanted to search, what exactly he expected to find, or even why he believed he would indeed find anything).

It is no wonder that upon winning their war for independence the Framers insisted upon language creating a right to be free from such invasions of their privacy. Hence, the **Fourth Amendment** declares that:

> The right of the people to be secure in their persons, houses, papers and effects against unreasonable searches and seizures shall not be violated, and no warrants shall issue but upon probable cause, supported by oath or affirmation and particularly describing the place to be searched and the persons or things to be seized.

What the Framers really were concerned about was governmental intrusiveness. Respecting privacy is an ethical value that helped start a war. The case that follows explores the ramifications of this concept of privacy.

Katz v. United States
389 U.S. 347 (1967)

Katz was suspected by the FBI of using the telephone lines to conduct illegal gambling operations, a federal offense. To gather evidence against Katz, agents attached an electronic listening device to the outside of a telephone booth used by Katz to make phone calls. The booth was made of glass and had a door that could close. The FBI listened in on a phone call made by Katz and later used a recording of this incriminating call against Katz at trial.

On appeal to the U.S. Supreme Court, Katz argued that the spying done by the FBI on his phone calls resulted in an illegal search (given that no search warrant was first obtained), and that all such evidence should have been suppressed at trial pursuant to the so-called exclusionary rule. The government, on the other hand, countered that no search had been performed for two reasons: the booth was never physically penetrated, and it was made of glass, thus enabling anyone to look inside at will. Since no search took place, no search warrant was required for the governmental eavesdropping.

The Court took this opportunity to pin down a clear definition for a "search" (invoking Fourth Amendment protections). It ruled that a **search occurs** whenever the government violates a "**reasonable expectation of privacy**." Using this standard it then went on to rule that Katz's reasonable expectation of privacy had indeed been violated, and since no search warrant was obtained, the recordings of the incriminating phone calls must be suppressed.

Regarding the lack of physical penetration of the phone booth, which the government thought proved that no search took place, the Court responded, "The Fourth Amendment protects 'people' and not simply 'areas.'" As to the government's argument that booths made out of glass afford no privacy expectation, the Court reasoned that what Katz sought to avoid by entering the booth was "not the intruding eye—it was the penetrating ear." The bottom line was that the government's use of an electronic listening device to listen in on a private telephone conversation violated an objectively reasonable expectation of privacy held by Katz.

One of the interesting lessons that could be learned from the *Katz* decision is that even though the Framers could never have envisioned all of the coming advancements in surveillance technologies, the Court is fully capable of protecting the timeless and enduring core value that the Framers clearly understood and sought to protect: freedom from governmental intrusiveness. Snooping is snooping regardless of what era one happens to live in or what sophisticated equipment one happens to employ.

Discussion Questions

1. What are some of the new technologies that scarily expand modern governments' abilities to violate their citizens' "reasonable expectations

of privacy"? Do you think that countries without the Fourth Amendment in play are in grave danger of their future governments invading peoples' privacy?

2. If we have nothing to hide, why should we care about protecting our privacy?

3. Does the Fourth Amendment protect us from private businesses using technology to invade our privacy and learn all about us? If not, where might this one day lead?

California v. Greenwood
486 U.S. 35 (1988)

Police officers in Laguna Beach, California, received information that Greenwood might be dealing drugs. So, on trash pick-up day, they went to Greenwood's street and spoke to the trash collector working the area. Like everyone else, Greenwood had left his trash at the curb for pick up that day. The police asked the trash collector to segregate Greenwood's trash that was about to be collected from that of his neighbors and to then proceed to the end of the block where the police could examine it. The trash collector complied with the officers' requests. Sure enough, the police found evidence in Greenwood's trash, establishing that Greenwood had indeed been trafficking in illegal drugs. Greenwood was tried and convicted of this crime.

Greenwood argued on appeal to the Supreme Court that the police violated a reasonable expectation of privacy when they looked through his trash. Hence, this inspection constituted a search and, as such, would have required a search warrant based on probable cause, which was never obtained. According to Greenwood, the illegally obtained evidence should have been suppressed, and his conviction should be overturned.

So, does a person have a reasonable expectation of privacy in trash left at the curb for pick-up? The Supreme Court did not think so. It said that the standard is not whether Greenwood subjectively felt violated but rather what society would find objectionably reasonable in terms of a privacy expectation. It said that "plastic garbage bags left on or at the side of a public street are readily accessible to animals, children, scavengers, snoops, and other members of the public." Since anyone can lawfully go through someone's abandoned trash, so too can the police without a warrant. No constitutionally protected "search" had occurred.

The majority's reasoning did not sit well with two dissenters (Justices Brennan and Marshall). They wrote, "The mere *possibility* that unwelcome meddlers *might* open and rummage through the containers does not negate the expectation of privacy" [italics in original]. They went on to suggest that "Most of us … would be incensed to discover a meddler — whether a neighbor, a reporter, or a detective — scrutinizing our sealed trash containers to discover some detail of our personal lives." They pointed out that, "A single bag of trash testifies eloquently to the eating, reading, and recreational habits of the person who produced it…. [It] can relate intimate details about sexual practices, health and personal hygiene…. [It] can divulge the target's financial and professional status, political affiliations and inclinations, private thoughts, personal relationships, and romantic interests." In short, trash contains a lot of highly personal traces of one's private life, and nobody reasonably expects anyone to inspect their garbage on pick-up day.

Which side of this case do you come down on: that of the majority or that of the dissent? It is interesting to note that despite the belief of the dissenters that a mere possibility of snooping should not negate a reasonable expectation of privacy, courts have consistently held that police can eavesdrop on conversations conducted out in public since nobody can reasonably expect privacy absent the taking of any precautions. Additionally, police can use devices easily obtained by members of the public to observe people (e.g., watching people through their uncovered windows while using binoculars in a building across the street — since anyone can easily obtain binoculars). No reasonable expectation of privacy has been violated. Of course, using exotic equipment (electronic listening devices, thermal imaging equipment pointed at peoples' homes, etc.) would be another matter.

Discussion Questions

1. How would you feel if you caught a neighbor going through your curbside trash can late at night in order to learn more about you? Would you feel violated or just shrug it off?

2. If an employee of yours went through your trash at work just out of curiosity about you, would you fire that employee? Why or why not?

As mentioned earlier, police use of exotic equipment not available to the general public to spy on people usually violates a reasonable expectation of privacy. But how might a court feel about the use of specially trained drug-sniffing dogs? Everyone knows someone who owns a dog, but who do you know that owns a professionally trained sniffer dog? The next case analyzes this twist.

Florida v. Jardines
569 U.S. 1 (2013)

A detective with the Miami-Dade Police Department received a tip that Jardines was growing marijuana in his house. The detective watched the house for some time and then, with the help of a fellow officer trained to use a drug-sniffing dog, approached Jardines' front porch and allowed the dog to do its job. After sniffing around the porch, the dog sniffed the base of the closed front door and promptly sat down. The dog's sitting down was the signal to the police of where the dog thought the smell was the strongest. Based on the dog's response, the officers obtained a search warrant to search the interior of the house. Pursuant to the search of the premises, various marijuana plants were located.

Jardines was charged with trafficking in marijuana. Prior to trial, Jardines filed a motion to have the evidence regarding the marijuana plants suppressed. This motion to suppress was granted by the trial court. The state appealed this pre-trial ruling, and the decision to suppress the evidence was overturned by the Florida Court of Appeals. The defense then appealed to the Florida Supreme Court, and it reinstated the original order of the trial court suppressing the evidence.

The U.S. Supreme Court ultimately agreed to hear the matter, evidently considering it to be one of national importance. The issue simply was whether the use of a specially trained drug dog to sniff around someone's front porch constitutes a "search" within the meaning of the Fourth Amendment. In a five-to-four decision, the Supreme Court ruled that a search had indeed taken place on that porch.

True, the Court had ruled in a previous decision that a drug dog's sniffing around the exterior of a car (and a consequential detection of drugs) did not violate a reasonable expectation of privacy as long as the stop was legal and the sniffing was brief. It is also true that the Court had previously held that the use of a trained dog to sniff luggage at an airport (thus alerting airport security to the presence of contraband) did not constitute a search. How then was the encounter on Jardines' front porch a search?

The Court's majority reasoned, "the area immediately surrounding and associated with the home is part of the home itself for Fourth Amendment purposes." The legal concept here is that of "curtilage." **Curtilage** is that area outside the home that is so intimately connected to family life and activities that it can fairly be considered part of the home. A front porch is an obvious, classic example of curtilage. Because the drug dog sniffed upon the curtilage it violated the defendant's property interests. The area surrounding the home is not the exterior of an automobile or a piece of airport luggage, rather, it is an area owned by the suspect and considered part of the home. Nobody anticipates drug dogs wandering on to their property (and effectively into their home) as an ordinary and expected occurrence. The officer did not even have implied permission to enter the property with a drug-sniffing dog. The officer's search warrant was only obtained after the home (the curtilage) had already been searched.

In a concurring opinion, Justice Kagan argued the issue was not so much trespass upon the curtilage, but whether a reasonable expectation of privacy had been violated. Writing separately but in support of the majority's decision, she reasoned that a drug dog, like thermal imaging equipment, is something that the general public would not possess. Since drug dogs are exotic, their use by someone would violate an expectation of privacy.

Justices Alito, Roberts, Kennedy, and Breyer all dissented. They argued the officers did have implied permission to enter the curtilage to approach the front door and knock or ring the doorbell, just as a Girl Scout selling cookies might do. Bringing the drug dog along did not change the situation. Furthermore, they argued that no reasonable expectation of privacy had been violated on the porch. They reasoned, "A reasonable person understands that odors emanating from a house may be detected from locations that are open to the public, and a reasonable person will not count on the strength of those odors remaining within the range that, while detectable by a dog, cannot be smelled by a human."

Discussion Questions

1. Would you feel personally violated if you looked out the window of your house and saw the police using a sniffer dog to sniff around your front porch?

2. Besides a porch, can you think of any other outside area of a house that might constitute "curtilage"? What about a carport? Flower beds between the edge of the lawn and the house? A tool shed next to the driveway?

The police violating the privacy of our front porches may be bad enough, but what about tracking us using our beloved mobile phones and smartphones? Before you answer "of course," what if police only use the information we voluntarily provide to our cell phone companies continuously throughout the day by way of normal daily usage? That is the issue in the next case.

Carpenter v. United States

585 U.S. ___, 138 S. Ct. 2206 (2018)

The police arrested four men in connection with a series of armed robberies. One of the men confessed to the crimes and gave the FBI his cell phone number and the phone numbers of fifteen other accomplices, including Timothy Carpenter. Prosecutors applied for court orders under the Stored Communications Act for records "relevant and material to an ongoing criminal investigation" to obtain **cell-site location information** (CSLI) for the phone used by Carpenter. Whenever a smartphone is on, regardless of whether the owner is using it, it taps into the wireless network several times per minute and transmits data that wireless carriers collect and store for their own business purposes. CSLI may be used by law enforcement to ascertain whether a cell phone was on at a certain time within the general area of the cell tower pinged (within several hundred city blocks of a crime scene). Using in part the CSLI derived from Carpenter's phone, prosecutors charged him with six counts of robbery and related firearms charges. FBI agent Christopher Hess testified at Carpenter's trial, offering expert testimony about CSLI and showing maps placing Carpenter near four of the charged robberies. Carpenter was convicted on all but one of the firearm charges and was sentenced to more than 100 years in prison.

Prior to trial Carpenter had moved to suppress the CSLI on Fourth Amendment grounds. Carpenter argued law enforcement needed a full warrant based on probable cause in advance of obtaining CSLI, instead of the lower relevance standard (which is lower even than the reasonable suspicion standard) authorized by Congress in the Stored Communications Act. The district court denied Carpenter's motion to suppress, and the Sixth Circuit affirmed his conviction, reasoning that Carpenter lacked a reasonable expectation of privacy in the CSLI since he had shared that information with his wireless carrier. Carpenter asked the Supreme Court to rule that a subpoena of CSLI is a search within the meaning of the Fourth Amendment necessitating a full search warrant based on probable cause.

The Supreme Court held in a 5–4 decision that the government generally needs a warrant to access privately held CSLI. The Supreme Court reaffirmed that the Fourth Amendment protects not only property, but also reasonable expectations of privacy. The Supreme Court ruled that when the government obtains CSLI (even though CSLI is not as precise as GPS tracking) this intrudes upon reasonable expectations of privacy. Expectations of privacy in the digital age do not fit neatly into existing precedents. The Court refused to extend application of the **third-party doctrine** (information disclosed to a third-party is generally no longer clothed with a reasonable expectation of privacy). The Court had previously relied upon the third-party doctrine to permit government agents to obtain data, such as credit card transactions, bank records, and telephone numbers dialed, without a warrant. However, the Court reasoned that tracking a person's movements and location through long-term monitoring of private cell tower records is far more intrusive than what previous precedents authorized. Additionally, the third-party doctrine generally applies to voluntary exposure, and while a user might be abstractly aware that their cell phone provider keeps logs, location tracking happens without any affirmative act on the user's part.

The dissenters argued that cellphone records are no different from any other business records that the government has the lawful right to obtain with legal process, such as a subpoena, but without probable cause and a warrant. Typically, the government is entitled, as part of a criminal investigation, to subpoena information from third parties. In fact, Congress had specifically addressed this issue by legislation and established a system by which judges had to sign off on the government obtaining such data, although Congress chose a lower standard of suspicion than probable cause. They also emphasized that Carpenter's property was not searched, as the cellphone location data did not belong to Carpenter, but rather the cell phone company.

Justice Thomas went further, arguing that the fundamental problem with the Court's majority opinion is its use of the reasonable expectation of privacy test. The test was articulated in *Katz v. United States* and, according to Justice Thomas, has no basis in the text or history of the Fourth Amendment. Its use invites courts to make judgements about policy, not law. Justice Gorsuch also laments the Court's departure from the original understanding of the Fourth Amendment in adopting the reasonable expectation of privacy test. Gorsuch suggested the Court consider returning to a Fourth Amendment jurisprudence more tied to property interests than one connected to the more nebulous and unpredictable reasonable expectation of privacy test.

As noted by the dissenters, application of this case (and more broadly issues of data privacy and the reasonable expectation of privacy test) promises to be an ongoing area of litigation. Recent developments have only amplified the dissenters' point, because in 2020 Justice Ginsburg lost her long battle with cancer. Her death, and the subsequent nomination and confirmation of Justice Barrett in the waning months of the Trump administration, promise to bring changes in many areas of constitutional law. Five-to-four decisions, such as this one where Justice Ginsburg was one of the five justices in the majority, are ripe for reconsideration.

Discussion Questions

1. What are your reactions to this case? Do you think Carpenter had a reasonable expectation of privacy given the information that law enforcement was collecting?

2. Where do you think the line in the sand should be drawn? What data that we transmit should be publicly accessible versus protected by the Fourth Amendment?

3. Do you think the majority was right in this case to protect Carpenter given that law enforcement was in essence tracking his movements?

Searches without a Warrant

Smartphones and the huge volumes of personal information often stored within them present a whole new potential area of worry for privacy rights advocates. Yet the next case is not just another cell phone case; it asks whether the traditional rules permitting officers to search through your purse, backpack, and wallet for personal information without a warrant when you are arrested apply to the even more information-packed smartphone in your pocket. The case that follows may very well become a "landmark" case in this critical area.

Riley v. California
573 U.S. 373 (2014)

This case actually involves two similar cases, consolidated into one case for Supreme Court review. The first case, *Riley v. California*, involved a man named Riley who had been stopped for driving with expired tags. Riley was arrested and his car impounded. During the arrest, the police found a cell phone in Riley's pants pocket. The contents of this phone were examined by the arresting officer and by a detective supposedly as part of the "**search incident to a lawful arrest**" (one of the recognized exceptions to the search warrant requirement). Based on contents viewed within the phone, Riley was later successfully convicted of a gang-related shooting that occurred several weeks before the traffic stop and arrest.

The companion case of *U.S. v. Wuhrie* also involved the search of a mobile phone. Wuhrie was arrested after the police watched him apparently selling crack cocaine. They seized his smartphone and accessed its contents, again using the justification of a warrantless search incident to a lawful arrest. During the examination of the smartphone's contents, the officers were able to discover the location where the defendant was secretly living. The police then obtained a search warrant for this residence and discovered drugs, weapons, and cash. Wuhrie's subsequent conviction resulted in a sentence of imprisonment of over twenty years.

The issue in both of these cases was the same: Does the search of the contents of a mobile phone (a "flip phone" in the case of Riley and a "smartphone" in the case of Wuhrie) violate the Fourth Amendment, despite the long-recognized exception that searches incident to lawful arrests do not ordinarily require search warrants?

Searches normally do indeed require search warrants. However, over the years the Supreme Court has carved out various exceptions to this **general search warrant requirement**. These exceptions are based on practicality and reasonableness. The **search warrant requirement exceptions** include such things as consent searches, seizure of evidence in plain view, searches of automobiles (probable cause still needed but no search warrant), exigent (urgent) circumstances, frisk of suspect's outer clothes for weapons inside, and thorough searches incident to lawful arrests. In the case of the latter, courts allow warrantless searches of the persons of arrestees in order to find weapons that could be used to harm officers or to effectuate an escape, and also to prevent the destruction of evidence. These compelling goals outweigh any right to privacy and thus the warrantless search is deemed to be reasonable.

However, in reviewing the searches of Riley's phone and Wuhrie's phone, the U.S. Supreme Court now took the opportunity to hold that searches incident to arrest will *not* be deemed to cover the internal data of mobile phones. Unlike most physical things found on a person, modern cell phones have extraordinary privacy implications. Chief Justice Roberts, who wrote the opinion in this 9–0 decision, emphasized that "Modern cell phones are not just another technological convenience" but rather "they hold for many Americans the privacies of life." He noted that "allowing a search of that phone without a warrant allows police to search more information than most people keep in their houses." Since the privacy concerns are so huge, police must get a warrant before making the search. Otherwise, the Fourth Amendment is offended.

True, cell phones could theoretically be used as a weapon. For this reason, police officers may inspect the phone for such things as hidden razor blades within its case. But "digital information stored on a cell phone cannot itself be used as a weapon to harm an arresting officer or to effectuate the arrestee's escape.... Data on the phone can endanger no one."

Also true is that data on a cell phone that is not immediately seized could potentially be wiped clean by the arrestee while being transported to jail or even wiped clean by others remotely. But this is not so likely as to overpower the huge privacy concerns. In any event, officers can often retrieve such wiped data after the fact.

So, the bottom line here, according to Chief Justice Roberts, is that officers who wish to examine data stored within our cell phones, including private data that "can date back for years," need to "get a warrant."

Discussion Questions

1. Should there be any exceptions to the rule established in the above case? If so, what would be an example of such an exception?

2. What are some of the "privacies of life" that are housed in your own mobile phone?

The next case will dive into the restrictions and parameters of searches conducted without a warrant. What happens when a police officer is justified in arresting the driver of a car—are they able to search the vehicle as well? This also is an opportunity to explore the differences between a probable cause search of a vehicle and a search of a vehicle incident to arrest.

Arizona v. Gant
556 U.S. 332 (2009)

Officers visited a residence prompted by an anonymous tip of possible drug activity. Gant opened the door, told officers he expected the owner to return later, and officers left. Officers then conducted a background check and discovered Gant had an outstanding warrant for driving with a suspended license. Officers went back to arrest Gant, but Gant was not there when officers arrived. While officers were investigating others, Gant came back. Officers saw Gant drive into the driveway and arrested him. After he was apprehended they searched Gant's car incident to his arrest and found a bag of cocaine and a gun.

Gant moved to suppress the cocaine and gun found in his car, claiming it was an unconstitutional search. As noted in the previous *Riley* case, searches incident to arrest without a search warrant have been long recognized by the Court, along with a group of other search warrant exceptions. Under the automobile exception, which the state argued for prior to Gant's trial, if officers would have had probable cause to search Gant's vehicle for contraband, they could have searched the entire car, bumper to bumper, inside and out (e.g., under the hood, in the trunk and inside the gas cap, within the vent covers and seat cushions). However, under the narrower search incident to arrest exception, usually the area to be searched is the area within the person's immediate control — typically the area into which a person could reach or lunge at the time of arrest. For a vehicle this is usually the area of the passenger compartment. In Gant's situation, this included the inside of the jacket pocket lying on the backseat where the cocaine was found.

For Gant, the issue was the timing of the search, since at the time officers searched Gant's car, Gant had already been secured in the back of an officer's squad car. The State argued the search of Gant's car was warranted and justified due to the arrest warrant, noting that for safety reasons, a search incident to arrest is still justified after the suspect has been apprehended. Also searches incident to arrest are justified in order to preserve evidence. The trial court rejected admission under the vehicle exception to the warrant requirement and ruled officers lacked probable cause for such a search, but admitted the evidence as a permissible search incident to arrest. The Arizona Supreme Court reversed and ruled the evidence should have been suppressed, but were divided over the meaning of prior Supreme Court precedent.

The Supreme Court, in a 5–4 decision, suppressed the evidence found in Gant's car after Gant had been apprehended, handcuffed, and removed from the immediate scene to a secure location, therefore posing no imminent threat. Also, since Gant was arrested on the basis of a pre-existing warrant for driving on a suspended license there was no possibility of destruction of evidence related to that crime. The Court rejected the broad reading of prior precedent and clarified that searches of a vehicle, incident to a recent occupant's arrest, is generally only constitutional when the arrestee is still within reaching distance of the passenger compartment at the time of search.

The Court did recognize one caveat concerning the preservation of evidence. They concluded that "circumstances unique to the vehicle context justify a search incident to a lawful arrest when it is reasonable to believe evidence relevant to the crime of arrest might be found in the vehicle." In previous cases, the Court had upheld searches incident to arrest following drug arrests. In such situations, where evidence pertaining to the crime of arrest might be found, then strict requirements of timing would be relaxed (the search incident to arrest could occur after the suspect was securely confined). That caveat, however, did not assist the state regarding the search of Gant's car.

The four dissenting justices noted that it is much safer for an officer to conduct a search once a suspect has been securely detained. The new rule creates a "perverse incentive for an arresting officer to prolong the period during which the arrestee is kept in an area where he could pose a danger to the officer." This 5–4 decision is yet another that might be subject to reconsideration in light of recent changes to the makeup of the Court.

Discussion Questions

1. How should the courts balance officer safety against individual rights to privacy?

2. Do you agree with the majority vote on this case? In your opinion, should the evidence have been suppressed?

Improper Seizures of the Person

As we have seen, searches are one way that agents of the government can be intrusive. Seizures of people are yet another way. The Fourth Amendment concerns itself with both searches and seizures. Whereas searches directly implicate violations of our privacy, seizures of our persons (e.g., traffic pull-overs, other investigatory stops, and full-blown arrests) implicate perhaps a different aspect of intrusiveness: violations of our autonomy and liberty of movement — perhaps the most basic affront of all to our desire to be left alone.

There are two basic types of **seizures of persons**: stops and arrests. Police may stop a person (e.g., a motorist or a pedestrian) for investigative purposes as long as the officer has "reasonable suspicion." Police may arrest a person (take a person into custody) as long as the officer has "probable cause" (a much higher standard). Sometimes it is difficult to draw a line between a mere "stop" and a full-blown "arrest." This can be as much art as it is science. The courts will look at two things in determining whether a seizure was a stop or an arrest. These **two "stop v. arrest" criteria** are: (1) the duration of the encounter, and (2) the level of intrusiveness that has occurred. The case that follows illustrates these concepts.

Dunway v. New York
442 U.S. 200 (1979)

The police suspected that a man named Dunway was involved in an attempted robbery and homicide. They lacked probable cause to arrest him. But they did suspect him. The police found Dunway at a neighbor's home and "picked him up" for questioning. After transporting him to the police station, police read Dunway his *Miranda* rights and started their interrogation. Dunway eventually made incriminating statements and was ultimately convicted of the crimes.

On eventual appeal to the U.S. Supreme Court, Dunway sought to have his convictions overturned on the grounds that police had arrested him without probable cause and that anything he might have admitted thereafter (despite *Miranda* warnings having been given) would be fruit of this unlawful detention and, therefore, should have been suppressed. The state countered that they had not arrested the defendant but rather only took him in for questioning. The state bolsters its argument by noting that the defendant had been told that he was not under arrest when he was taken to the police car and that he had consented to their request to be taken in for questioning. The police also noted that they had relied on a state statute that permitted police to "detain an individual upon reasonable suspicion for questioning for a reasonable and brief period of time."

The issue before the Supreme Court was whether the transportation and questioning of the defendant constituted an **arrest** (a significant interference with physical liberty requiring probable cause, which was lacking) or merely an **investigative stop** (a less intrusive interference with movement requiring only reasonable suspicion, which was present). The Supreme Court ruled that it was a full-blown arrest. Since it was an arrest lacking in probable cause, the defendant's incriminating statements should have been suppressed, and his convictions must be overturned.

The Court noted that the encounter was not brief. Additionally, the defendant was not questioned where he was found but rather transported elsewhere. Though he supposedly had "consented" to go with the police, he was never subsequently told that he was "free to go" at any time. In fact, if he had tried to leave the police station before they were through with him he would have been restrained.

The Court said that "an intrusion of this magnitude" constitutes an arrest despite what the police or even a state statute deems to call it. The fact that the defendant had never been "booked" was of no consequence. In effect, he had clearly been arrested.

In a concurring opinion, Justice Brennan noted that "the treatment of the petitioner, whether or not it is technically characterized as an arrest, must be supported by probable cause." He explained that "detention for custodial interrogation — regardless of its label — intrudes so severely on interests protected by the Fourth Amendment as necessarily to trigger the traditional safeguards against illegal arrest."

In his dissenting opinion, Justice Rehnquist (joined by one other justice), argued that no arrest had taken place. "After learning that the person who answered the door was petitioner, the officer asked him if he would accompany him to police headquarters for questioning, and petitioner responded that he would." Since Dunway had consented to go with the officers, he was not under arrest.

Discussion Questions

1. Have you (or someone you know) ever been "merely" transported by the police against your will (e.g., out of a neighborhood, shopping plaza, etc.) without ever being subsequently booked? If so, did the police have probable cause for this "arrest"?

2. Suppose the police stop someone (based on reasonable suspicion) but never transport them anywhere? At what point would stopping someone and holding that person there turn into an arrest in your view?

Sometimes, laypeople (or even police officers) have a hard time understanding what "**probable cause**" means. It has been described as facts which would lead a reasonably prudent person to believe contraband, fruits of a crime, or evidence will be found in a particular place or to draw a conclusion that a suspect has committed a crime.

A definition for "**reasonable suspicion**" is even harder. What is clear is that it is something less than probable cause, but still something "reasonably" more than a zero percent chance. What is crystal clear is that a mere hunch or "gut feeling" is not enough to establish "reasonable suspicion." Being stopped may not be as intrusive as being arrested, but it is still intrusive. The case that follows illustrates these principles.

Delaware v. Prouse
440 U.S. 648 (1979)

On a night in November, a New Castle County police officer on patrol was looking for something to productively occupy his time. So, he pulled over a man named Prouse just to check him out. As the officer later explained, "I saw the car in the area and wasn't answering any complaints, so I decided to pull them off." Prouse, the driver of the car, had not been violating any traffic laws nor acting in any suspicious manner. After having pulled Prouse over, the officer noticed some marijuana "in plain view" on the floor of the vehicle. Prouse was subsequently arrested for possessing marijuana, a controlled substance.

Prior to the start of any trial, Prouse asked the local court to order that the evidence of the marijuana be suppressed on the grounds that the stop had been illegal since it was not based on any reasonable suspicion. The court agreed with the defendant and granted his request. The state then appealed this pretrial ruling and the matter eventually landed in the U.S. Supreme Court.

The U.S. Supreme Court ruled that the local judge acted correctly in suppressing the marijuana evidence. It confirmed the understanding that a police officer may only stop a person for investigative purposes if the officer has "reasonable suspicion" to believe that a law had been broken by that person. In order to convince a reviewing court that the officer indeed had reasonable suspicion, the officer would have to put forth "**specific and articulable facts**" in court. In other words, he would have to be able to convey clear, sound, and credible reasons justifying his suspicions. Intuition, hunches, or mere feelings are not good enough.

The state's attempt to characterize the marijuana as having been "in plain view" on the automobile floor also will not stand. The contraband would not have been "in plain view" if the officer had not illegally pulled Prouse over in the first place. Hence, the evidence constituted "fruit" of the illegal stop and is subject to the exclusionary rule.

The state also had attempted to argue that randomly "checking out" motorists was no more intrusive than what the police routinely and legally did in stopping motorists at drunk driving checkpoints. Checkpoints do not require "reasonable suspicion," and yet the courts tolerate them. The Supreme Court, however, said that checkpoints were perceived by citizens as being much less intrusive than the stopping of just one solitary motorist. "At traffic checkpoints the motorist can see other vehicles being stopped ... and he is much less likely to be frightened or annoyed by the intrusion."

Discussion Questions

1. Why was the marijuana not in plain view when the cop could plainly see it just sitting right there on the floor of the car?

2. What would be some different examples of "reasonable suspicion" to justify pulling a car over?

3. How easy would it be for a dishonest officer to come up with reasonable suspicion between the illegal stop and the suppression hearing in court? Would the rule requiring "specific and articulable facts" slow a dishonest cop down much in court? An honest cop?

So far in this chapter we have considered what constitutes a search, as well as examined some types of improper seizures. Next, we will examine what happens after an illegal seizure and explore one of the exceptions to the exclusionary rule.

Utah v. Strieff
579 U.S. ___, 136 S. Ct. 2056 (2016)

Utah detective Douglas Fackrell received an anonymous tip about the possibility of drugs being sold out of a South Salt Lake residence. Officer Fackrell began intermittent surveillance of the residence, and over the course of a week observed visitors who left a few minutes after arriving, leading Fackrell to speculate the tip had been accurate. Fackrell saw Edward Joseph Strieff Jr. leaving the residence and stopped him for questioning. However, Fackrell did not know when Strieff had arrived nor how long he had stayed at the residence before leaving. This was not a consensual encounter, but rather an investigatory stop. After asking for identification and checking to see if he had a previous criminal record, Fackrell discovered Strieff had an outstanding warrant for a traffic violation and arrested him. During the search incident to his arrest, Fackrell found methamphetamine and drug paraphernalia on Strieff.

The prosecutor conceded at the suppression hearing that Fackrell did not have enough evidence to conduct an involuntary seizure of the defendant. Even though the prosecutor conceded the stop was unconstitutional, the state trial court refused to order the suppression of the evidence as a remedy for the illegal stop. Instead, the trial court ruled the **attenuation exception** (attenuation is time or other factor that helps dissipate the taint of the illegal stop upon the legitimacy of evidence subsequently found) to the exclusionary rule applied, reasoning the existence of a valid arrest warrant attenuated the connection between the unlawful stop and discovery of the drugs and paraphernalia obtained during the search incident to arrest. The Utah Supreme Court disagreed—it reversed the trial court and determined that the evidence should have been suppressed because the warrant that was the basis for the arrest was only discovered during an unlawful investigatory stop. According to the Utah Supreme Court, attenuation had traditionally required a significant passage of time between an illegal stop and the subsequent discovery of evidence. Also, attenuation had traditionally required a voluntary act by the defendant to return and speak with officers.

In a 5–3 vote (there was no ninth vote since Justice Scalia had unexpectedly died four months before), the Supreme Court overturned the Utah Supreme Court decision. The Supreme Court ruled that evidence obtained in violation of the Fourth Amendment's protections should nevertheless be admitted into evidence when application of the three-part attenuation test suggests the costs to society of its exclusion outweighs the benefits of its deterrent effect to change officer behavior. In the absence of police misconduct, the discovery of a valid, pre-existing arrest warrant attenuates or weakens the connection between the unconstitutional investigatory stop and the evidence seized incident to the lawful arrest. To apply the attenuation exception courts must examine the (1) temporal proximity of the discovery of the evidence to the unconstitutional conduct (i.e., the time elapsed), (2) intervening circumstances, and (3) level of police misconduct. Applying these factors, the Court acknowledged that the temporal proximity factor weighed in favor of the defendant and exclusion of the evidence as almost no time had lapsed between the illegal stop and the search.

The Court went on, however, to conclude that the other two factors weighed in favor of the state's position. When a pre-existing valid warrant is discovered after an unconstitutional investigatory stop, this intervening circumstance "strongly favors" admission of the evidence. "In this case, the warrant was valid, it predated Officer Fackrell's investigation, and it was entirely unconnected with the stop. And once Officer Fackrell discovered the warrant, he had an obligation to arrest Strieff." The conduct of Officer Fackrell also weighed in favor of the admission of the evidence since the Court found he was at most negligent in not doing more to confirm the defendant was a short-term visitor at the suspected residence. The Court noted that the trial court had "stressed the absence of flagrant misconduct by Officer Fackrell, who was conducting a legitimate investigation of a suspected drug house." According to the majority, there was no indication the unlawful stop was part of any systemic or recurrent police conduct, rather all the evidence suggested the stop was merely "an isolated instance of negligence."

The dissenters objected, arguing that the Fourth Amendment's exclusionary rule was intended to prevent police officers from taking advantage of their own unconstitutional conduct. Since the officer lacked adequate reasonable suspicion to stop the suspect, as conceded by the prosecution, exclusion of evidence works as a remedy to ensure officers are scrupulous in their adherence to constitutional rules. "When courts admit only lawfully obtained evidence, they encourage those who formulate law enforcement policies, and the officers who implement them, to incorporate Fourth Amendment ideals into their value system." Failure to do this instead rewards manifest neglect, if not an open defiance, of constitutional protections.

According to the dissenters, the effect of this ruling is to lower even further the protections and standard for investigatory stops if officers are willing to gamble the suspect has an outstanding warrant, which might be a good bet in certain areas. Allowing evidence to be admitted under these circumstances essentially creates a group of second-class citizens in areas of high outstanding warrants (warrants issued for failure to appear on traffic offenses, or failure to pay fines, especially in areas of low socio-economic status or where law enforcement is aggressive in raising revenue for city operations through traffic fines). The dissenters rejected the idea that this was an isolated incident, stressing the "astounding numbers of warrants" which can be used to justify searches after stops without cause. The dissenters pointed out that in a single year in New Orleans "officers made nearly 60,000 arrests, of which 20,000 were of people with outstanding traffic or misdemeanor warrants from neighboring parishes for such infractions as unpaid tickets." After the Ferguson incident, investigators found that in the St. Louis metropolitan area "officers routinely stop people — on the street, at bus stops, or even in court — for no reason other than an officer's desire to check whether the subject had a municipal arrest warrant pending." The Utah Supreme Court had also described as "routine procedure" the decision of Salt Lake City officers to run warrant checks on pedestrians detained without reasonable suspicion.

The dissenters emphasized that the Fourth Amendment does not tolerate illegal searches and seizures just because an officer did not know any better. Rather, even officers prone to negligence may learn from the exclusion of illegally obtained evidence. Indeed, it is negligent officers "most in need of the education, whether by the judge's opinion, the prosecutor's future guidance, or an updated manual on criminal procedure." If officers are in doubt what the Constitution requires, exclusion gives officers an incentive to err on the side of constitutional behavior.

Discussion Questions

1. Do you feel as though having an outstanding warrant should make a suspect subject to a search incident to arrest? Does this unnecessarily expand the boundaries of when and where subjects can be searched?

2. Do you personally align more so with the majority or minority vote in this case?

So far in this chapter we have examined "intrusiveness" in the context of the Fourth Amendment (searches and seizures). We shall now consider "intrusiveness" in a totally different way: alleged governmental violations of the so-called "general right to privacy." Unlike searches, seizures, and self-incrimination rights—which involve black letter concepts—the general right to privacy can only be discovered by using what some might label "a more creative approach" to constitutional interpretation (hence its ongoing controversy).

The General Right to Privacy

What do the First Amendment right to worship, the Third Amendment right to be free from soldiers lounging about in your house, the Fourth Amendment right against unreasonable searches and seizures, and the Fifth Amendment privilege against self-incrimination all have in common? Many would argue just one word: privacy! As we shall see in the case below, there are many individual privacy rights found in the Bill of Rights. Can it, therefore, fairly be said that a larger, more comprehensive, "general" right to privacy must somehow exist as well? If so, what might this general right cover in addition to the specific privacy elements unquestionably found in the Bill of Rights?

The general right to privacy, now most famously associated with the abortion rights case of *Roe v. Wade*, 410 U.S. 113 (1973), was actually first "discovered" eight years prior in a case that very few laypeople have ever heard of: *Griswold v. Connecticut*, 381 U.S. 479 (1965). We shall first look at *Griswold*, then *Roe,* then the twenty-first century case of *Lawrence v. Texas*, 539 U.S. 558 (2003). Through all of your readings, ask yourself whether you agree with the legal analysis or believe it to be a matter of constitutional jurisprudence getting a bit too creative.

Griswold v. Connecticut
381 U.S. 479 (1965)

In the early 1960s, Estelle Griswold was the executive director of the Planned Parenthood League of the state of Connecticut. She also served as acting director of one of Planned Parenthood's local state centers. At this center, Griswold and a physician named Buxton (her co-defendant) provided clients with various instructions on how to prevent pregnancies and also with certain birth control devices. This violated state law, which at the time forbade anyone from using "any drug, medicinal article or instrument for the purpose of preventing conception" and also made a criminal of anyone who "assists, abets, counsels, causes, hires or commands" another to violate this prohibition. Both Director Griswold and Dr. Buxton were convicted of assisting three women in violating this anti-birth control statute, and each was fined $100.

The defendants appealed, arguing that women have a constitutional right to engage in birth control and that Planned Parenthood has the right to assist them. This right was argued to fall under a constitutional "right to privacy."

Ultimately, the U.S. Supreme Court had to decide whether or not a general right to privacy indeed exists in the Constitution. This is not a simple question because no such general right to privacy had ever been discovered to exist up to this point in our history. So, is there a general right to privacy? The Supreme Court found that there was such a right.

It reasoned that the Bill of Rights clearly enumerated several specific rights that could be considered rights to privacy. For example, the First Amendment guarantees of free speech and religion clearly contain elements of privacy. The Third Amendment prohibition against the quartering of soldiers "in any house" in peacetime without the permission of the owner obviously is meant to protect one's privacy. The Fourth Amendment protections from unreasonable searches and seizures and the Fifth Amendment privilege against self-incrimination also speak to "privacy." One could even perhaps read "privacy" into the Ninth Amendment's provision that, "The enumeration in the Constitution, of certain rights, shall not be construed to deny or disparage others retained by the people." The Court decided that these individual, mini-privacy rights combine to create a larger, more **general right to privacy** that must be the ultimate source of all of the explicit, individual rights. It spoke of a "zone of privacy created by several fundamental constitutional guarantees." It said that all of these individual, smaller rights of privacy collectively cast off enough light to reveal the larger, more general right to privacy that had been lurking all along within the penumbra (*Latin* for "almost a shadow") of the Bill of Rights. This "**penumbral right**" of privacy is "older than the Bill of Rights — older than our political parties, older than our school system."

Having found this formerly shadow-obscured, general right to privacy, the only remaining question was whether birth control constituted one of its elements. The Court thought that it most certainly did. It asked, "Would we allow the police to search the sacred precincts of marital bedrooms for telltale signs of the use of contraceptives? The very idea is repulsive to the notions of privacy surrounding the marriage relationship." The majority concluded by stating that, "Marriage ... is an association that promotes a way of life, not causes; a harmony of living, not political faiths; a bilateral loyalty, not commercial or social projects. Yet it is an association for as noble a purpose as any involved in our prior decisions." In the poetic language one can clearly sense the Court's heartfelt belief that marriage and its associated practices are not any of the government's business.

In his dissent, Justice Stewart (joined by Justice Black) agreed with the majority that Connecticut's anti-contraception law was "uncommonly silly." Stewart wrote "As a philosophical matter, I believe the use of contraceptives in the relationship of marriage should be left to a personal and private choice." Yet the Court's job was not to decide whether the law was "unwise or even asinine," but whether or not it violated the Constitution somehow:

> What provision of the Constitution makes this law invalid? The Court says it is the right of privacy "created by several fundamental constitutional guarantees." With all deference, I can find no such general right of privacy in the Bill of Rights ... or in any case ever before decided by this Court.

Stewart concluded by saying that if the people of Connecticut believe this law no longer reflects modern standards, they should ask their legislators to repeal it. This would be the "constitutional way to take this law off the books."

Discussion Questions

1. How can a justice both think a law is stupid and "even asinine" yet not be willing to strike it down as unconstitutional? Are asinine laws that interfere with people's lives necessarily unconstitutional?

2. If someone were to ask you to point out where in the Constitution the general right to privacy can be found, what would you now tell that person?

3. Why did the court use the word "penumbral" to describe a right such as the right to privacy? Besides privacy, could there be other "penumbral rights" in the Constitution yet to be discovered? Like what?

As we have just seen, the *Griswold* case led to the discovery of the general right to privacy. Having discovered the right to privacy, the Court then considered what it might encompass. It found that birth control within a marriage relationship fell within its reach. What other behaviors or actions might also fall within this newly discovered right to privacy?

Few people today would think that government should interfere with a married couple's choice to use birth control pills or other forms of contraception. Perhaps that is why almost nobody has ever heard of the *Griswold* decision, as ground-breaking as it was. But, what if a woman wanted to terminate an unwanted pregnancy that posed no health threat to her? Would the right to privacy cover that as well? If it did cover it, would the "right to life" nevertheless trump this "right to privacy"? Unlike the case of birth control, the determination that there is a constitutional right to an elective abortion continues to be a source of seemingly unending, heated debate within American society. Almost nobody has heard of *Griswold*, but almost everyone has heard of *Roe*. For many, *Roe v. Wade* represents the healthy and virtuous evolution of legal doctrine first articulated in the *Griswold* case. For many others, *Roe* is evidence of a Pandora's Box opened by a deceptively harmless *Griswold* decision.

Roe v. Wade
410 U.S. 113 (1973)

"Jane Roe" (an alias used to protect the woman's identity) became pregnant. Thinking that it would help qualify her for a legal abortion in Texas, Roe first claimed that she had been raped. However, this rape story ultimately did not hold up. In any event, Roe still wanted a legal abortion but could not have one due to a Texas law criminalizing elective abortions when the pregnancy was not the result of rape or incest. Roe filed suit against Henry Wade, the Dallas district attorney, seeking a judgment declaring the anti-abortion statute to be unconstitutional.

On eventual appeal to the U.S. Supreme Court, the big issue became whether or not the "right to privacy," first articulated in *Griswold v. Connecticut* eight years earlier, covered not only laws criminalizing birth control (the *Griswold* finding) but also laws criminalizing elective abortions. The Supreme Court ruled that elective abortions (at least up to a point in the pregnancy) were indeed protected by the general constitutional right of privacy.

The Court reasoned that two competing interests were at stake: the right of a woman to control her choice whether or not to proceed with a pregnancy (her privacy right) versus a state's arguably legitimate wish to protect the life of the potential, developing human life. The bottom line was that the Court ruled that prior to the end of the **2nd trimester** (roughly the sixth-month mark or the point of "**viability**" — the point at which the developing fetus has a chance to survive outside the womb), states could not outlaw abortions. Prior to "viability," the woman's right to privacy outweighs the state's interest in protecting the potential human life. However, once viability is reached, states are free to criminalize elective abortions if they so desire (so long as states always grant an exception if the mother's health is in danger).

Two justices strongly dissented from the decision of the majority to strike down pre-viability abortion statutes. Justice White wrote that he could "find nothing in the language or history of the Constitution to support the Court's judgment.... The upshot is that the people and the legislatures of the 50 states are constitutionally disentitled to weigh the relative importance of the continued existence and development of the fetus, on the one hand, against a spectrum of possible impacts on the woman on the other." Justice White concluded that the majority's opinion was an "exercise of raw judicial power."

Justice Rehnquist wrote that the Court had just found "a right that was apparently completely unknown to the drafters" of the Constitution and its various amendments. Up until this point in time, there apparently "was no question concerning the validity of this provision or of any other state statutes" of similar nature.

Discussion Questions

1. Why do you suppose the majority settled on "viability" as the point in the pregnancy where a state can start criminalizing elective abortions? What other point in the pregnancy might it have considered in lieu of that?

2. Some people still do not believe in the idea of a general right to privacy in the Constitution that covers elective abortions or anything else. Others believe there is a general right to privacy in the Constitution, but it should not cover elective abortions. Others believe it should include elective abortions but not quite so late as six months into a pregnancy like *Roe* decided. Still, others like the holding of *Roe* and agree that elective abortions should be protected up until viability. Others think that *Roe* does not go far enough and believe that elective abortions should be allowed through the entire nine months of the pregnancy. Where exactly do you stand?

3. Would it surprise you that although many countries allow elective abortions, almost no other country in the world allows elective abortions as late as the *Roe* decision does? What, if anything, do you make of that?

So, we see in *Roe* the expansion of the right to privacy from its original domain involving the protection of birth control devices and medicines to a broader reach now covering elective abortions as well (at least up to the point of "viability"). In the case that follows, the Supreme Court will be asked to expand the reach of the right to privacy yet further. It will involve the matter of gay sex between consenting adults.

Lawrence v. Texas

539 U.S. 558 (2003)

Officers of the Harris County (Houston, Texas) Police Department responded to the residence of John Lawrence after having received a report of a weapons disturbance. Upon arriving, the officers legally entered the home and witnessed Lawrence engaging in a sexual act with another man. The officers arrested Lawrence and his partner and charged them both with the crime of "deviate sexual intercourse, namely anal sex, with a member of the same sex (man)." Lawrence and his friend were convicted and ultimately fined $200.

The U.S. Supreme Court ultimately agreed to hear this matter to consider whether or not Lawrence's constitutional rights had been violated due to the enforcement of this statute. Interestingly, the Supreme Court had ruled seventeen years previously that states could indeed criminalize homosexual acts between consenting adults. In this earlier case of *Bowers v. Hardwick*, 478 U.S. 186 (1986), the Court had said that "proscriptions against this conduct have ancient roots," and that given the history and traditions of our country, "no fundamental right" to gay sex existed, whether it be housed under the right to privacy or otherwise. It further opined that upholding morality was clearly a legitimate function of government (otherwise there would be many criminal laws that would have to be invalidated).

In reconsidering the matter, the Court decided that it had erred in deciding the *Bowers* case the way it had. It noted that the majority in *Bowers* were wrong when they thought that the heart of the issue involved nothing more than the right of an individual to engage in a particular type of sex. Rather, the Court realized that the issue really involved the right of someone to engage in a "personal relationship" that it now ruled was clearly private and part of the "fundamental liberty" guaranteed by the Due Process Clause of the Fourteenth Amendment.

It went on to say that "at the heart of liberty is the right to define one's own concept of existence, of meaning, of the universe." *Bowers* was, therefore, "not correct when it was decided, and is not correct today."

Focusing on privacy concerns, the Court noted that the government must respect the "private lives" of citizens, that the State cannot "control their destiny by making their private sexual conduct a crime," and that "there is a realm of personal liberty which the government may not enter." Finally, the Court made clear that no legitimate state interest can justify governmental "intrusion into the personal and private life of the individual."

In essence, the Court confirmed that the Fourteenth Amendment's Due Process Clause protects two types of liberties: non-fundamental liberties (which can be taken away if fair process is first given) and **fundamental liberties** (basic human rights that no amount of court process could ever take away). Privacy (including gay sex) falls under the domain of fundamental liberty.

Justice Scalia (joined by two others) dissented. Outraged, Scalia accused the majority of taking sides in the culture wars and of allying itself with the liberal agenda of the academic legal community. He said that it was true that "social perceptions of sexual and other morality change over time" but that it was up to democratically elected legislatures to update laws if needed and not the role of a "governing cast that knows best." Scalia said the *Bowers* decision thirteen years earlier was correct when it said that the government had a legitimate interest in upholding "majoritarian sexual morality" through criminal laws. To hold otherwise would be to invalidate the basis for criminalizing such practices as "fornication, bigamy, adultery, adult incest, bestiality and obscenity." Scalia feared that the Court now "effectively decrees the end of all morals legislation."

Discussion Questions

1. Why do you suppose that dissenter Scalia got so outraged at this decision? In your view, was his outrage justified or an over-reaction?

2. In your view, is all sex between consenting adults constitutionally protected (no exceptions)?

3. What did the Court mean when it said that "at the heart of liberty is the right to define one's own concept of existence, of meaning, of the universe"? In what way does consensual sex figure into this?

So, now that you have read the privacy trilogy of *Griswold*, *Roe*, and *Lawrence*, where do you stand on the notion that there exists within the Constitution a (fairly recently) discovered and still evolving general right to privacy that so far covers birth control, elective abortion, and gay sex? Are you comfortable with this line of cases or do you worry about what specific privacy protections might come next?

One area that "might come next" has to do with polygamous style relationships. As mentioned in an earlier chapter, U.S. District Court Judge Clark Waddoups ruled in December 2013 that a Utah law banning certain polygamy-style relationships was an unconstitutional invasion of privacy (and an affront to the free exercise of religion). Kody Brown (the star of a reality television series on polygamy known as *Sister Wives*) sued Utah for putting him in continued fear of prosecution for living with several women at the same time. Utah had not only made it a crime to fraudulently portray oneself as being legally married to more than one person at the same time (e.g., without the other "spouse" being aware of another "marriage"), but also made it a crime if one merely "purports to marry another person or cohabits with another person." Brown held himself out to be legally married to just one woman but did purport to be "spiritually married" to three additional women (all with one another's knowledge and consent).

Judge Waddoups ruled that Utah (which apparently would have no trouble tolerating a man "sleeping around" or even living with several "non-wives" at the same time) "can't dictate [the Browns'] living arrangements." Waddoups opined that "encouraging adulterous cohabitation over religious cohabitation that resembles marriage in all but State recognition seems counterproductive to the goal of strengthening or protecting the institution of marriage." Government just cannot create a situation in which "it's the expression of the fact that a person is a wife that makes it illegal." The bottom line is that the government has no right to tell people how to run their private sex lives or what private, non-legally binding terms they wish to employ in describing their status towards one another.

Chapter Key Terms

Intrusiveness
Stamp tax
Writs of Assistance
Fourth Amendment
Search occurs
Reasonable expectation of
   privacy
Curtilage
Cell-site location informa-
   tion
Third-party doctrine
Search incident to a lawful
   arrest
General search warrant re-
   quirement

Search warrant requirement
   exceptions
Seizure of persons
Two "stop v. arrest" criteria
Arrest
Investigative Stop
Probable Cause
Reasonable Suspicion
Specific and articulable facts
Attenuation exception
General right to privacy
Penumbral right
2nd trimester
Viability
Fundamental liberties

Chapter Six

Intrusiveness in Law Enforcement and Corrections

We can't keep bending the Fourth Amendment to the resources of law enforcement … particularly when this stop is not incidental to the purpose of the stop. It's purely to help police get more criminals, yes. But then the Fourth Amendment becomes a useless piece of paper.
— Justice Sotomayor, Transcript of Oral Argument,
Rodriguez v. U.S. (2014)

Law Enforcement

Sandusky Traffic Stop

Law enforcement has a responsibility to ensure that individual rights are upheld while executing searches and seizures as well as questioning alleged suspects. These are rights which are clearly spelled out for us in the Fourth and Fifth Amendments; however, many cases call into question whether or not agents of the criminal justice system are doing so within the bounds of our rights or in an intrusive manner. We will explore some of these cases below starting with perhaps one of the more trivial and routine practices that law enforcement engages in on a daily basis: traffic stops.

On October 1, 2014, Officer Christopher Denny pulled Andre Stockett (passenger) and Kathryn Denslow (driver) over, alleging that Denslow's headlights were not on and suspecting that her Ohio driver's license was suspended (Sandusky officer placed on leave, 2014, para. 2). Stockett was starting to get irritated with how long it took officer Denny to check the status of Denslow's Michigan license, so he decided to start recording their conversation once Officer Denny returned to their car. What followed was a 7-minute-long video that documented the interactions between Officer Denny, Stockett, and Denslow. After Officer Denny returned, he confirmed that Denslow's Michigan license was in fact valid, but he claimed that Stockett looked very similar to Jeremy Newell, a wanted felon who had warrants out for his arrest. Stockett asserted that he was not Newell, so Officer Denny requested that Stockett provide identification in order to prove that he was in fact not Newell. Stockett refused to provide his identification because he claimed that he had done nothing wrong and that he was sick of being harassed by the cops (Astolfi, 2014, para. 1–9).

The dialogue between Stockett and Officer Denny slowly escalates and you can see on the video that Officer Denny is annoyed at Stockett's unwillingness to provide ID and get out of the car as requested. Stockett claims that if the original reason that they were pulled over had been resolved, then Officer Denny has no probable cause (language which he uses in the video) to continue questioning them. Officer Denny threatens to arrest Stockett on obstruction of justice charges and reminds him that it was a "lawful stop" (Astolfi, 2014, para. 12). Officer Denny then proceeds to bring in a K9 drug sniffing dog, alleging that Denslow (female driver) seemed suspicious and nervous. The dog sniffed the perimeter of the car, and Officer Denny tells Stockett that the dog alerted to there being drugs in the car. After requesting that Stockett step out of the car one last time, Denny tells him that he better cooperate so that his child (a 2-week-old baby strapped in a car seat in the back) won't be taken by protective services. It is at this point in time that Officer Denny calls for backup from two other officers.

Stockett and Denslow eventually step out of the car and are both arrested on **obstruction of justice** charges (behavior of a person of interest that interferes with law enforcement duties). Officer Denny and his backup proceed to search the car for drugs, but none are found. Stockett claims that he will (and eventually does) file a complaint with the Sandusky Police Department claiming that he was racially profiled and that Officer Denny had no probable cause to confine and continue questioning the couple (Ouriel, 2014, para. 9–13). Due to the amount of national attention that the video received as well as the nature of Stockett's allegations, the Sandusky Police Department requested that an external review be conducted by the Lucas County Sheriff's Office. Two weeks later, the report came out and noted "several inconsistencies or omissions from Officer Denny's report" (Inconsistencies found in Sandusky officers, 2014, para. 3).

One area in which there were discrepancies between the video and Denny's report was Denny's assertion that he had pulled the couple over for driving without their headlights when it was dusk. The video however indicates that when the couple was initially pulled over, it was still light outside and that they therefore legally would not need to have their headlights on. Regardless of this fact, reports indicate that the couple was in fact driving with their headlights on anyway so this point proved to be moot. Another issue involving inconsistencies was with Officer Denny's claim that Stockett looked a lot like Newell, a wanted felon in the area. Records indicate that four minutes before the stop occurred, Officer Denny called into dispatch and requested that they run Stockett's name through the database to see if he had any outstanding warrants (Wright & Gallek, 2014, para. 2). And perhaps one of the most damning pieces of evidence against Officer Denny's motivation for pulling them over is that Stockett himself claims that Denny knew who he was before pulling them over. He told one newspaper source that "He Knew who I was. He talked to me moments before my girlfriend came to pick me up. I had my 2-week-old son in the back of the vehicle. I was doing nothing wrong" (Wright & Gallek, 2014, para. 6).

Once all of this information came to light, the charges against the couple were quickly dropped, and Officer Denny was placed on a month-long unpaid suspension. He was allowed to return to work as long as he signed an agreement stating that if he had any complaints filed against him through November 2016 that he would be immediately terminated. Additionally, this document stipulated (among other things) that he would (1) undergo additional training about how to properly write reports as well as conduct legitimate searches and seizures, (2) not apply for internal promotions for at least two years, and (3) volunteer 208 hours to help build a stronger relationship between the department and the community (Ouriel, 2014, para. 30–34).

Discussion Questions

1. Given the information that you know about this case, does it seem as though Officer Denny had any probable cause to pull over Stockett and Denslow?

2. If you were Officer Denny, would you have arrested the couple on obstruction of justice charges?

Drug-Sniffing Dogs

As the case above demonstrates, there is often a lot of gray when interpreting the *unreasonable* clause of the Fourth Amendment's protection against searches and seizures. The previous chapter discussed the legality of using drug-sniffing dogs on a person's property; however, this case calls into question the use of said dogs to sniff a car pulled over for a routine traffic stop. Within the past decade, courts have weighed in on many issues involving drug-sniffing dogs used on motor vehicles on the side of the road. However, in the 2005 case of *Illinois v. Caballes*, the Supreme Court drew a line in the sand and determined that the police do not need a warrant to use a drug-sniffing dog during a lawful routine traffic stop. The Court established that when a dog alerts to "the location of a substance that no individual has any right to possess [this] does not violate the Fourth Amendment, so long as the traffic stop is not unnecessarily prolonged" (Root, 2015, para. 1).

In the wake of this decision, many lower courts are left to grapple with the boundaries of defining "unnecessarily prolonged" searches. This issue came to the forefront of attention after a man was pulled over for driving haphazardly outside of Valley, Nebraska. Dennis Rodriguez was pulled over just after midnight in 2012 for swerving onto the shoulder lane. He claimed that he did so to avoid a pothole. About 21 minutes after the traffic stop started, Rodriguez was issued a written warning and asked to step out of the vehicle so that a K-9 dog could sniff the perimeter of his car. Rodriguez indicated his lack of consent but still stepped out of the car. He waited with Officer Struble by the patrol car for backup to arrive. Shortly after backup arrived, the dog searched the perimeter of the car and alerted to something being in the trunk. A search of the trunk revealed a large bag of methamphetamine. Rodriguez was arrested shortly thereafter (Skelton, 2014, para. 4–7).

Rodriguez appealed his conviction claiming that he had been subjected to an unreasonable search and seizure. The Eighth Circuit Court of Appeals determined that the length of delay that Rodriguez was subject to before the dog actually executed its search was not unreasonably prolonged. The court argued that his "detention without reasonable suspicion was only a minor violation of Rodriguez's personal liberty, and therefore, the evidence could be used" in court (Skelton, 2014, para. 11). Unsatisfied with this ruling, Rodriguez's team of lawyers appealed the decision all the way to the United States Supreme Court. The Court granted certiorari and heard the case of *Rodriguez v. United States* in October of 2014.

Illinois v. Caballes had already set precedent when it came to the use of drug-sniffing dogs during lawful traffic stops; however, the Court stated that the parties would be arguing a different question in this case:

> This Court has held that, during an otherwise lawful traffic stop, asking a driver to exit a vehicle, conducting a drug sniff with a trained canine, or asking a few off-topic questions are "de minimis" intrusions on personal liberty that do not require reasonable suspicion of criminal activity in order to comport with the Fourth Amendment. This case poses the question of whether the same rule applies after the conclusion of the traffic stop, so that an officer may extend the already-completed stop for a canine sniff without reasonable suspicion or other lawful justification (*Rodriguez v. United States*, No. 13-9972 [2014]).

As is evident from the passage above, the question now becomes whether a K-9 search can happen after the ticket has been issued and the traffic stop is viewed as complete. In attempting to quantify how much longer Rodriguez was actually held, the Eighth Circuit Court of Appeals viewed the additional seven- to eight-minute detention as **de minimis** (inconsequential, insignificant, or minor) (*United States v. Rodriguez*, 2014). However, the Supreme Court of Nevada ruled in a similar case that nine minutes are too long (Kerr, 2014, para. 7). The Supreme Court of the United States now had the task of deciding how long is too long and at what point in time a search has become "unnecessarily prolonged."

In oral arguments, attorneys for Rodriguez claimed that once a stop is finished, the individual in question should be allowed to go free. Justices Alito and Bader Ginsburg opposed this viewpoint, claiming that any competent officer will delay handing over the ticket until the drug-sniffing dog search has been executed. Additionally, Justice Bader Ginsburg is quoted as saying, "It just seems to me that you're not going to accomplish any protection for individuals if that's your position" (Transcript of oral argument, *Rodriguez v. U.S.* [2014]). According to Orin Kerr from the George Washington University Law School, the real question in this matter would likely revolve around "whether there should be a 'de minimus' rule at all, not how long it should extend" (Kerr, 2014, para. 12). In April of 2015, the Court reached a decision and sided with Rodriguez. The justices decided that bringing in the K9 unit after the completion of a lawful traffic stop violates the Fourth Amendment protections against unreasonable searches and seizures. Additionally, the seizure "becomes unlawful if it is prolonged beyond the time reasonably required to complete the mission" (*Rodriguez v. United States*, 2015).

Discussion Questions

1. What is your opinion about using drug-sniffing dogs during a lawful routine traffic stop? The Court has ruled that if it is promptly done it does not violate our rights. But what do you think?

2. If you were a judge and had to weigh in on this, how would you define an "unreasonably prolonged" traffic stop?

North Dakota Cattle Dispute

As technology advances, law enforcement is finding that they can use new and cutting-edge forms of technology to help aid their investigations. As the previous chapter illustrates, the use of electronic surveillance by law enforcement through mechanisms such as wire-tapping has been used and debated among the courts for decades. However, newer technological advancements are starting to come out that make police observation not simply audio or text based (as is the case with wire or electronic data tapping), but also visual and dimensional. For example, law enforcement is now starting to use drones for aerial surveillance as well as infrared or Range-R imaging to sense heat and/or movement through walls. As these technological advancements are being used more and more frequently, it begs the question of whether or not these practices infringe on our protections against unreasonable searches and seizures or if their use is justified. We will explore this and other questions below as we discuss two cases where law enforcement used these newer forms of technology to help solidify their investigation and press charges against the suspects in question.

The first case in question used a drone to help settle a cattle dispute. However, before we get into the particulars of the case, let's further discuss this new technology as well as some of the debate revolving around its use. Drones essentially look like mini-helicopters and allow law enforcement to get a visual look at items or spaces, usually from the top down. The Grand Forks County Sheriff's Department in North Dakota was one of the first agencies to adopt the use of drones, and in 2015 it was estimated that there were only about a dozen departments across the country that were using them. It is speculated that the use of drones by law enforcement across the U.S. will continue to grow as departments are beginning to recognize the potential cost savings that they can gain from using drones rather than helicopter surveillance (thousands as opposed to millions of dollars).

As more agencies are turning to the use of drones, there seems to be an increasing uneasiness among American citizens. Namely, some question "whether drones are a powerful way to improve public safety or a threat to individual privacy" (Pilkington, 2014, para. 4). Proponents of their use cite the cost-saving benefit, not to mention officer safety, in that they can collect **criminal intelligence** from afar. Opponents, on the other hand, argue that drones are too intrusive and provide law enforcement access to see things they wouldn't otherwise be able to see. For example, Birrell summarizes the opposition side nicely when she states, "with the aid of new technologies, privacy protection has been eroded in favor of law enforcement" (Birrell, n.d., p. 1). Perhaps in an effort to make both sides happy, many states have enacted or are considering legislation that regulates their use (Galizio, 2014, para. 2). Additionally, and as has always been the case, any agency (be it local, state, or federal) must get Federal Aviation Administration approval prior to using a drone (Koebler, 2013, para. 7).

Now let's turn our attention to the case at hand, where a drone was used to help settle a dispute over wandering cows. In 2011, Rodney Brossart was arrested when he refused to send six cows that had walked onto his land back to his neighbor's property until his neighbor paid him for the feed the cows had consumed (Gallagher, 2012, para. 3). It is unclear from reports whether or not the cattle had truly wandered from the neighbor's land or if they had been stolen, but when officers showed up with a search warrant, Brossart and his family put up a fight. The family engaged in an armed standoff with law enforcement officers that lasted for nearly 16 hours. Due to concern for their safety, a local sheriff requested the services of the U.S. Border Patrol to bring in a drone to conduct surveillance of the farm (Fox News, 2014, para. 3). Once they gathered enough information to know the whereabouts of people within the house, law enforcement moved in and arrested the family members.

On January 14, 2012, a jury found Brossart not guilty of theft and criminal mischief (the charges related to the cow dispute) but guilty of terrorizing the police. Initially, they charged his three sons with terrorizing the police as well, but they wound up pleading to the lesser charge of menacing law enforcement officers, resulting in a sentence of one year of probation (Peck, 2014, para. 4). Rodney (the father) was sentenced to three years for his role in the armed police standoff with all but six months of that sentence being **suspended** (served via probation and with the charges often dismissed after an offender fulfills the conditions of their probation). Rodney Brossart's attorney appealed the conviction based on "the warrantless use of an unmanned surveillance aircraft," which he argued violated Rodney's Fourth Amendment rights (Gallagher, 2012, para. 6). However, a federal judge upheld the use of the drone, saying that "there was no improper use of an unmanned aerial vehicle" in this case (Koebler, 2013, para. 5).

While the absurdity of the dispute and the twists and turns that followed make it a memorable case, many argue that the more significant point to take away is that this is the first case in which a domestic drone was used against an American to help execute an arrest. There have been previous cases in which drones have been used by law enforcement to help collect evidence against criminal suspects, but never before have the courts upheld their use in aiding an arrest. Many argue that this case may drastically alter the way that courts view the use of drones and how their use impacts our Fourth Amendment right to be protected from unreasonable searches and seizures (Minkoff, 2014, para. 1–3).

Discussion Questions

1. Do you feel that the use of drones by law enforcement infringes on our right to privacy?

2. If you had been the federal judge when this case came before you, how do you think you would have ruled on the use of the drone to collect information about the whereabouts of the Brossart family?

Using Technology to "See" through Walls

Thus far, we have explored intrusiveness in the context of searches and seizures during the course of law enforcement procedures that are seemingly mundane (e.g., routine traffic stops) as well as more unique in scope (e.g., using a drone to help discern a suspect's whereabouts). The drone case illustrated how technology is increasingly calling into question the boundaries between individual rights and public safety. However, one could argue that the next two cases that will be discussed pushed the boundaries of law enforcement powers even further when the technology being used allows officers to "see" inside a suspect's home without having to actually step foot inside the premises. The first case will explore the use of infrared (or thermal) imaging, which is used to help law enforcement see the location of heat imbalances within a residence (namely, heat associated with the growing of marijuana plants). The second case will explore the use of Range-R technology, which is used to sense where a suspect is physically located within a dwelling. What will be interesting to note is the different outcomes for the defendants in question when courts ruled on their privacy concerns.

Danny Kyllo was suspected of growing marijuana plants in his home. Law enforcement used a thermal imaging device to scan his triplex to see if they could detect if/where he might be growing the plants. Infrared (or thermal) imaging picks up on the amount of heat being put off by an object and displays different colors based on variations in heat (Ruppe, n.d., para. 4). This technology allows the user to scan through walls for heat distributions to see, for example, the outline of a body, or in this case, a concentration of heat that may be indicative of heat lamps.

In Kyllo's case, law enforcement used the scans to discover that the roof over his garage and the interior wall of his house were hotter than the rest of his house as well as adjacent neighboring homes (*Kyllo v. Unites States*, 2001, para. 8). Using this information as a basis for probable cause, law enforcement then requested and was granted a search warrant. Upon executing the search, law enforcement found that Kyllo was growing approximately 100 marijuana plants in his garage. He was arrested and charged with one count of manufacturing marijuana.

Shortly after his conviction Kyllo's attorney's appealed, claiming that his Fourth Amendment rights had been violated. The intermediate court of appeals (Ninth Circuit) saw no problem with how law enforcement used the technology to aid their investigation, reasoning that the imager did not expose any intimate details of his life. The case eventually made its way to the U.S. Supreme Court, and drawing upon the *Katz* decision (discussed in the previous chapter), it overruled the lower court's decision and ruled in favor of Kyllo by a vote of 5 to 4 (*Kyllo v. United States*, 2000, para. 3). The Court ruled that "authorities scanning a home with an infrared camera without a warrant constituted an unreasonable search barred by the Fourth Amendment" (Ruppe, n.d., para. 5). In other words, you cannot get a search warrant to physically enter a home based on an earlier search using infrared technology that itself was not authorized by a search warrant.

In a similar yet newer case, law enforcement used Range-R technology to help them apprehend a fugitive who had violated his parole. The Range-R instrument is described as looking like a stud finder and is used to detect movement that is within 50 feet on the other side of a wall. It is said to be a powerful tool (i.e., it can detect movement as subtle as breathing as well as motion), but not nearly as advanced as other devices that can show 3-D displays of where people are located on the other side of a wall (Heath, 2015, para. 9–10). The case in question revolves around the arrest and subsequent confiscation of firearms illegally owned by a parolee.

Steven Denson was not abiding by the stipulations of his parole because he left town and his parole officer was unable to contact him. Armed with an arrest warrant, authorities tracked him to an address located in Wichita, Kansas. They used the Range-R technology to let them know if and where Denson was located inside the house. During the subsequent course of arresting him, the police found that he was in possession of two illegal firearms (Rivero, 2015, para. 8–10).

Denson plead guilty to charges of illegally possessing firearms but later tried to appeal both his arrest and the subsequent search that ensued. The Tenth Circuit Court of Appeals sided with the government, noting the legality of both the arrest warrant and the search that resulted in the apprehension of the firearms. In parceling out the two arguments, they reasoned that the arrest was executed via a legitimate search warrant. Further, the justices argued that law enforcement could have used other tactics (such as high-electricity output, suspect being unemployed, and the early time of day) to assume the suspect's presence as probable cause for requesting the search warrant. Regarding the search that followed, the justices argued that law enforcement is entitled to a "**protective sweep**" to ensure that nobody else is present in the house and that this was especially warranted given that Denson's roommate had an outstanding warrant (Louwagie, 2014, para. 4–8).

What is interesting about this case is that though the appellate court in the *Kyllo* case discussed earlier ruled in favor of Kyllo when it came to the use of infrared, the appellate court ruled against Denson when it came to the use of Range-R. One could speculate a variety of reasons as to why this is the case. It could be that in the first case, law enforcement did not have a search warrant to use the infrared technology whereas they did have an arrest warrant to use the Range-R technology in the second case. A second potential explanation is the time-lag between these two cases and the amount of government intrusiveness cases that have been debated among the courts between 2001–2014 (for example, relating to thermal imaging, drug-sniffing dogs, various forms of radar devices, etc.) (Richardson, 2015, para. 9–12). And a third potential explanation among many may be due to the differing opinions that justices at all levels of the appeal process have regarding cases where police powers are juxtaposed against individual rights.

Discussion Questions

1. Do you find the use of thermal and/or Range-R imaging too intrusive?

2. Do you feel as though there should be a line drawn in the sand regarding intrusive technologies (i.e., only used when there is probable cause, only used when proper search/arrest warrant is present, etc.)?

Third-Party Doctrine

In the wake of the terrorist attacks on 9/11, the government has increasingly expanded the scope of electronic information that can be searched in the name of public safety. As an example, the National Security Agency and the hotly debated USA PATRIOT Act expanded the scope of what electronic information can be searched and monitored under the guise of public safety. Proponents of increasing the powers that we provide the government and law enforcement officers to monitor our electronic activities argue that it does not unnecessarily infringe upon our privacy rights and that it has led to an increase in information that has been collected related to terrorist activities. Opponents, on the other hand, feel as though it gives the government and law enforcement excessive power and unduly infringes upon our rights to privacy. While this last example (discussed below) is not a direct reflection of electronic surveillance collected to combat terrorism, it does call in to question the debate about privacy related to electronic surveillance. In this case, we will explore when and if individuals have a right to privacy if the information has been shared with another party.

In 1976, a woman reported that she had been robbed, and she provided law enforcement with a description of both the robber as well as the vehicle that he was driving. Days later, she started receiving threatening phone calls from a man who said he was the robber, and she also saw the same vehicle driving in front of her home. Law enforcement monitored her neighborhood and when they saw a vehicle matching the one described by the victim, they traced the license plate number to "Michael Lee Smith." The police then asked the phone company to install a "pen register" on Smith's telephone that would create a record of all the telephone numbers that he was dialing. This confirmed that Smith was in fact calling the victim, and he was arrested shortly thereafter (Villasenor, 2013, para. 1–4).

Smith tried to challenge his conviction on the grounds of his Fourth Amendment protection against unreasonable searches being violated; however, in *Smith v. Maryland* (1979), the Court ruled that there had been no such violation. In fact, the Court established that installing the pen register did not constitute a search under the Fourth Amendment. Further, the justices argued that a Fourth Amendment search "only occurs when a citizen has a reasonable expectation of privacy" and that people do not have an expectation of privacy in the numbers that they dial (Friedersdorf, 2013, para. 4). What came out of this ruling has often been referred to as the **third-party doctrine**. According to this doctrine, information that is shared with a third party (usually for business purposes) such as credit card information, telephone records, etc., "doesn't carry with it a reasonable expectation of privacy under the Fourth Amendment" and that one has assumed a risk in disclosing this information to a third party (Salam, 2013, para. 1). Essentially what this means is that any information that we disclose to a third party, regardless of how sensitive in nature that information may be, can be monitored or seized by law enforcement and/or the government.

In the wake of *Smith*, those most familiar with the doctrine feared that it would cause a ripple effect and allow law enforcement more access to data that previously required a search warrant to access. Additionally, opponents feared that the courts would not be adequately prepared to apply the *Smith* ruling to technological advances that would likely present themselves in the future. Justice Sotomayor captured this sentiment well in a 2010 case where she stated that *Smith* "is ill suited to the digital age, in which people reveal a great deal of information about themselves to third parties in the course of carrying out mundane tasks" (Watzel, 2014, para. 5). A variety of cases are now challenging varying forms of technology and our expectations to privacy (i.e., e-mail interactions, cell phone data, third-party data, etc.), so it will be interesting to see where the Court stands on these issues of personal rights and public safety in the coming years.

Discussion Questions

1. What is your opinion about law enforcement and governmental powers having access to our electronic data? Do you feel as though public safety trumps our individual rights to privacy?

2. What is your reaction to the third-party doctrine? Is this too intrusive or do you see legitimacy to the argument that a reasonable expectation of privacy is "lacking" in those types of communications?

Corrections

Strip Searches of Inmates

As mentioned in a previous chapter, strip searches can sometimes be viewed as prurient activities designed to circumvent departmental policies and procedures. As such, inmates might be strip searched for the officer's erotic pleasure or as a way to justify humiliating the offender in front of other inmates. Strip searches, however, can also be viewed as intrusions on an inmate's privacy and self-esteem. The difference would center on the intent of the officer's actions.

In May 2013, Dana Holmes of Coal City, Illinois, was driving home when she was pulled over by a LaSalle County deputy for suspicion of drunk driving (Caufield, 2013). While at the county jail, Holmes claimed she was unnecessarily strip searched by four deputies (three men and one woman). During the event, Holmes believed her civil rights were violated and that the deputies caused her undue emotional harm by performing the search without any legal justification. Video of the search showed Ms. Holmes being carried into a cell by the four officers, placed on the floor, her clothes removed, and then housed alone in the cell with only a blanket to cover herself. The arrestee claimed that she was forcibly dropped to the ground and was left for a period of time without clothing or a means of covering herself from view.

LaSalle County Sheriff's Department, however, had a different view of the events as they unfolded on the day of Ms. Holmes' arrest. Upon arrival at the jail, deputies claim that Ms. Holmes became combative during a routine **pat-down search** (a cursory search of an individual's outer clothing for contraband and weapons) and because of her perceived over-reaction to standard safety protocol, had reasonable suspicion to believe that Ms. Holmes was hiding contraband on her person. Due to her demeanor, corrections deputies performed a strip search of Ms. Holmes. Under Illinois law, officers are allowed to strip search inmates or arrestees if they have "reasonable belief" that the individual is in possession of a weapon or controlled substance (Perez, 2013). In addition, state law requires the search to be performed by an officer of the same sex and that the search cannot be viewed by those not conducting the search.

The deputies believed they were following department policy for a combative female believed to be in possession of a weapon or illegal substance (Coffey, 2014). Prior to the placement, Ms. Holmes had kicked the female officer twice. As a result of her violent and aggressive actions, the arrestee was placed in a padded cell, a location different than a traditional cell and designed for the occupant's safety, and had her clothes removed to reduce the possibility of the individual hurting herself. At no time was Ms. Holmes strip searched again by any of the officers. Sheriff officials also stated that within a few minutes of the officers leaving the cell, the female officer provided Ms. Holmes a tear-proof or "suicide" blanket.

A lawsuit, filed by Ms. Holmes and four other arrestees, claiming civil rights violations, resulted in the county settling with the plaintiffs for $355,000. While admitting no wrongdoing, the county sheriff remarked in response to questions regarding the officers' actions that "It isn't written. It's a procedure as opposed to a policy" (Meincke, 2014, para. 5).

Discussion Questions

1. Should officers have the right to remove the clothing of violent inmates or arrestees for the offender's own safety?

2. In your mind, does the simple act of removing an inmate's or arrestee's clothing constitute a strip search?

3. Is there ever a time when a member of the opposite sex should be allowed to be present during a strip search?

Cell Searches

In April 2015, Jamell Cureton, a reputed gang leader being charged with plotting the killings of Debbie and Doug London, claimed his cell had been search illegally by the Federal Bureau of Investigations (FBI) and because of this, all materials acquired in the search must be excluded from his trial (WBTV Web Staff, 2015). According to court records, federal agents searched Cureton's cell in April of 2015 and took with them a number of documents and writings Cureton claimed were **legal correspondence** (legal communication between a defendant and their legal representative) and therefore excluded from seizure during a cell search. Chiege Okwara, attorney for the defendant, believed the actions by federal officials violated the attorney-client right to privacy rules.

The right for correctional officials to search an inmate's cell was established in the case of *Hudson v. Palmer* (1984). In the Court's opinion, written by Chief Justice Burger, the Court held "A prisoner has no reasonable expectation of privacy in his prison cell entitling him to the protection of the Fourth Amendment against unreasonable searches" (p. 1). The Court went on to say, "The unpredictability that attends random searches of cells renders such searches perhaps the most effective weapon of the prison administrator in the fight against the proliferation of weapons, drugs, and other contraband" (p. 1).

According to correctional officials, however, the documents seized by the FBI represented a clear threat to those inside the facility, as well as evidence of ongoing criminal activity by Cureton and other incarcerated gang members (Gordon, 2015b). Documents detailing interactions between Cureton, a member of the United Blood Nation, and other members of the gang currently being held in other facilities were often written in cryptic code. Federal prosecutors were later able to decipher the messages that talked about the failed robbery attempt on the London's furniture store that eventually led up to their murder.

Of particular concern to federal agents was a collection of pictures, also seized in the raid, of U.S. District Judge Frank Whitney, Superior Court Judge Richard Boner, and Charlotte City Attorney Bob Hagemann, as well as documents that appeared to be a file on a local reporter covering the murder case. Officials believed the collage found in Cureton's cell may have been a "**hit list**" (a list of individuals targeted for murder) of sorts and because of this, all three officials were placed in protective custody (Gordon, 2015b). Even though Cureton was incarcerated at the time for a charge of attempted robbery, his ties to local gangs prompted the U.S. Marshalls to watch the homes of the two judges and city attorney.

Cureton and his attorney, however, refuted those allegations and argued the seizure of the materials by the FBI not only interfered with his ability to have fair legal counsel, but also prejudiced possible jurors by defaming his name (Gordon, 2015a). In addition, Cureton believed the federal government had shared his legal material with local prosecutors, potentially inhibiting his ability to have a fair trial. Okwara told reporters, "I believe that they had access to our documents that includes his questions to me as his attorney" (WBTV Web Staff, 2015, para. 17). If this were true, she contended, prosecutors were now aware of their defense strategy.

Discussion Questions

1. Given Cureton's violent criminal past, were federal agents justified in seizing the materials in his cell?

2. When should the safety of a facility and or those outside of the facility override attorney-client privilege?

3. If legal documents were shared with the prosecution, do you feel Cureton's right to a fair trial was compromised?

College Courses for Inmates

Over the years, there has been a growing debate on whether or not inmates should: (a) be allowed to take college/university courses while incarcerated and (b) if so, who should pay for them. On one hand, proponents of education behind bars believe an educated inmate will not only be more compliant and focused on proactive activities while incarcerated, but once they leave, the former convicts will be in a much better position to secure meaningful employment. Proponents also assert that denying inmates the right to this type of education is a form of extreme intrusiveness, akin to withholding reading or other materials designed to improve the offender's character and mental outlook. Those who oppose providing inmates with higher education often argue that the purpose of incarceration is punishment and rehabilitation, not the opportunity to acquire a college degree that many law-abiding citizens either don't have the time to earn or cannot afford to obtain.

Those who advocate for access to higher education while incarcerated firmly believe that doing so is a wise investment. Stephen Streurer, executive director of the **Correctional Education Association** (a professional association for educators in a criminal and juvenile justice setting) stated that, in general, had offenders not been imprisoned, they would, on average, have earned 40% more than they are currently capable of bringing home (Deruy, 2013). Skorton and Altschuler (2013) agree and argue that a system that intrudes on an offender's ability to improve him or herself is doing a disservice to not only the inmate, but to society at large. From their perspective, college-educated offenders are less likely to reoffend, saving the taxpayer upwards of 2.7 billion dollars per year. Streurer, however, admits that educating inmates is often a hard sell to the public. After all, "Who wants to send a crook to college when they're having a hard time getting their own kids through?" (Deruy, 2013, para. 5).

Not everyone, however, is sold on the value of providing a college education to those who have willfully violated the laws of society and victimized its members. First and foremost in their arguments is the issue of cost. In May 2014, New Jersey Advance Media asked its readers "Should prisoners receive a free college education behind bars?" Of the 3,356 respondents, only 418 said "Yes, taxpayers should help foot the bill" (Johnson, 2014). For Kara Henson, the issue is also a matter of equity. Henson (2009) stated, "Hardworking American citizens fight every day to be their best, striving to succeed as far as they can. Why is it fair that inmates, citizens who have committed crimes, are able to receive a college education for free?" (para. 7). Even former President Bill Clinton agreed when he signed a bill in 1994 defunding federal assistance to inmates wishing to pursue a college education behind bars. As he put the new legislation into effect, President Clinton said "People who commit crimes should be caught, convicted, and punished. This bill puts government on the side of those who abide by the law, not those who break it" (Johnson, 2014, para. 9).

Discussion Questions

1. Do you feel it's an intrusion on an inmate's right to treatment and re-habilitation if the government denies offenders access to higher education while incarcerated?

2. If inmates should be allowed to take college/university courses while incarcerated, who should pay for this education?

3. Is access to higher education while incarcerated a right or privilege?

Strip Searching Jail/Prison Visitors

As controversial as strip searching inmates and arrestees can be, an even more intrusive form of invasive practices by corrections is the strip searching of visitors to jails and prisons. The most common reason for strip searching a visitor is to control the introduction of drugs, weapons, and other forms of contraband into the facility. Many question, however, if the practice is going too far.

Take, for example, the case of a female visitor to the South Central Correctional Facility in Clifton, Tennessee. The unnamed plaintiff in a lawsuit against the Nashville-based **Corrections Corporation of American (CCA)** (a private prison corporation) claimed that as she was going through the prison's security checkpoints, one of the officers noticed a sanitary napkin in her pocket. When questioned about the item by officers, the plaintiff informed them that she was menstruating and needed the sanitary napkin for her person hygiene (Sisk, 2015). As officers continued to question her on the item, the plaintiff offered to leave the facility or leave the sanitary napkin behind during her visit.

Correctional officials, however, instructed the women to enter a nearby bathroom. Once inside, the visitor was ordered to lower her pants and allow a female officer to inspect her genitals to ensure that she was in fact menstruating (Associated Press, 2015). According to the head of security at the South Central Correctional Facility, a prison run by CCA for the Tennessee Department of Corrections, standard policy dictates the strip search of menstruating visitors. The plaintiff contended, however, that there was no reasonable justification for the search and if she would have refused to be searched, she could have been permanently banned from all future visitations. While strip searching children prior to entering a correctional facility might seem like an anomaly, these events happen more often than people realize. For example, in 2001, at least five students from a Washington, D.C., middle school were moved into a room and strip searched while on a tour of the local jail (Blum & Woodlee, 2001). As a result of these actions by correctional officials, Warden Patricia Britton and three male officers, all long-time employees of the department, were fired from their positions.

On the West Coast, the California Department of Corrections and Rehabilitation (CDCR) has a policy in place that allows the strip search of a juvenile should they test positive for contraband during a **canine search** (the search of persons and/or property by dogs trained to detect drugs and other contraband) (Enty, 2014). According to Enty, deputy director for the Center on Juvenile and Criminal Justice, "Should the search result in a positive alert (even a false positive, which research has shown comprise as many as 80 percent of all positive identifications), the visitor in question must submit to a strip-search or else forgo the visit. The regulations make no exception for children, and existing CDCR paperwork regarding unclothed searches explicitly includes accompanying minors" (para. 2).

Many, however, argue that such intrusive policies do not help keep illegal items from entering a correctional facility and, in fact, do nothing more than deny family and other visitors from spending time with those who are incarcerated (Hartman, 2015). Compounding the frustration and issues surrounding strip searches of visitors is how in many cases, staff and visitors are treated differently. In California, both scanners and canine searches are used as part of the initial screening prior to entering a state prison. Should a staff member trigger a positive alert, he or she receives a simple pat down of the outer clothing. Visitors, however, are required to submit to a strip search or forfeit their visit, even if they had traveled hundreds of miles to get there (Clayton, 2015).

Discussion Questions

1. Given the need to keep a correctional facility safe and secure, are institutional needs more important than visitors' rights?

2. Are strip searches nothing more than legalized voyeurism?

3. Should visitors under the age of 18 be subjected to the same search techniques as their adult counterparts?

Solitary Confinement

The use of **solitary confinement** (isolation from other inmates) by correctional facilities has long been questioned as an intrusive form of discipline that exceeds the standard necessary for institutional safety and security and interferes with the effective treatment and rehabilitation of incarcerated offenders. Inmates are often isolated for a number of reasons, such as the safety and security of the inmate, the safety and security of other inmates, and the segregation of severely mentally ill inmates. To compound the issues of solitary confinement, Fatos et al. (2014) found that of the 244,699 inmate files reviewed from the New York City jail system over a four-year period (2010–2013), inmates in solitary confinement (roughly 7% of the jail population) committed approximately 53% of the facility's acts of self-harm and approximately 45% potential acts of fatal self-harm.

Take the example of Joe Giarratano, an inmate at Virginia's Red Onion State Prison, serving time for the murder of his girlfriend and the rape and murder of her 15-year-old daughter. Moved around the country from one special housing unit (SHU) to another, Giarratano, in a letter to the American Civil Liberties Union (ACLU), talked about the intrusive nature of living in solitary. Speaking of his time in the Utah prison system, he said:

> The cell was a bit larger: 8' x 12'. Solid slider door with small window in it. They kept the window covered with a magnetic flap (picture a large, flexible, refrigerator magnet). The cell had a concrete form bunk with very thin mattress. Stainless steel toilet/sink combo. There was a cell window, approximately 3' x 5", which let some natural light in for a few hours in the morning/afternoon. I was allowed a small amount of legal material, and religious materials, and writing material. I was allowed 2 hours of "outside" rec and 2 10-minute showers per week. The outside rec was in a small, high-walled cube area with no roof. Maybe a little larger than a cell. Yelling to other prisoners was not permitted. If you did it you would lose your rec period and shower. Only human contact was with guards or counselor. If the counselor wanted to see you, the guard would shackle you, cuff you behind your back, place you on a short leash and sometimes put a hood over your head. You would be escorted to a room and chained to a wall where the counselor would speak. Then you would wait to be escorted back—could take a few minutes, could be 2 hours chained to the wall" (Giarratano, 2015, para. 3).

To many, the experiences of Giarratano are typical of life in solitary confinement and exhibit a direct correlation between the intrusive manner in which a SHU can affect an inmate and the outward manifestations identified in the research of Fatos et al. (2014).

To this end, there appears to be a growing social and political concern over the use of solitary confinement. The state of California recently agreed to reduce the number of inmates housed in SHUs and end the use of indefinite solitary confinement for gang leaders. For Jules Lobel, a lawyer for the **Center for Constitutional Rights** (a non-partisan, U.S. constitutional awareness organization established by the U.S. Congress), "There clearly has been a fundamental shift in our society in recognizing that solitary confinement does present serious constitutional and psychological problems" (Johnson, 2015, para. 16).

Discussion Questions

1. Do you feel the use of solitary confinement is cruel and unusual punishment?

2. If you were to place stipulations on the use of solitary confinement, what would they be and why?

3. Can a prison operate effectively, while still maintaining the safety and security of inmates, officers, and staff, without the use of solitary confinement?

Transgendered Inmates

A growing issue for many correctional facilities today is where to house their **transgendered** (a person who does not identify with their biological sex) inmates. From an institutional perspective, correctional officials must be concerned about the safety and security of such individuals and the effects and possible negative outcomes that might develop when housing those who self-identify as a gender that differs from their biological sex. From the offenders' standpoint, however, denying inmates the right to be housed based upon preferred gender and not biological sex is an intrusion into their lives that denies them the constitutional rights of life, liberty, and the pursuit of happiness.

One such high-profile case was that of Ashley Diamond of Rome, Georgia. Sentenced to 11 years for a burglary-related parole violation, Diamond claimed to have been the "victim of no less than seven brutal sexual assaults" (Stelloh, 2015, para. 16). Diagnosed with gender dysphoria prior to incarceration, Diamond was placed in a male correctional facility upon conviction. According to Diamond, however, the Georgia Department of Corrections (GDC) showed "its disregard for her gender by placing her in a male prison" (Hensley, 2015, para. 13).

While housed in various facilities across the state, Diamond claimed continued harassment by male inmates. Diamond also claimed that correctional staff made derogatory remarks, referring to Diamond as "he-she thing" and being told to "act like a man" and to "guard her booty," a remark Diamond claimed was a warning to possible sexual assaults (Kellaway, 2015a, para. 6). Fighting Diamond's efforts to be housed in a female correctional facility, a move lawyers felt was more in line with the inmate's gender preference, GDC instead moved the offender to a medium-security facility in Columbus, Georgia. The move, according to GDC, placed the inmate in an environment where correctional officials could better maintain the offender's safety and security. Diamond, however, disagrees and feels that being housed with male inmates interferes with Diamond's desire to live as a female and has filed suit against the GDC and the state of Georgia. Diamond settled that lawsuit in February 2016 after being paroled, but then she was returned to prison in October 2019 for a parole violation. Diamond alleges she was again sexually assaulted and has again filed a lawsuit against Georgia corrections officials. The U.S. Department of Justice has filed a brief in Diamond's latest case (Brumback, 2021).

A similar case in Texas has also made national headlines. Joshua Zollicoffer (also known as Passion Star), a black transgendered woman, felt that placement in a male maximum-security correctional facility showed a "**deliberate indifference**" (the conscious or reckless disregard of the consequences of one's act or omissions) to Zollicoffer's safety and as such, qualified as "cruel and unusual punishment" under the Eighth Amendment (Kellaway, 2015b, para. 4). According to Zollicoffer, "Look, I got 36 stitches and have scars on my face that prove the prisons are not safe and the current system does not work. Somebody needs to be intrusive into this state's business. Because if somebody was intruding, probably these things would not happen" (Sontag, 2015, para. 5).

The challenge for corrections, however, is where to place a transgendered inmate that meets the needs of everyone involved. Placing a biological female who identifies as a male in a male facility exposes that inmate to possible rape and abuse. Placing a biological male who identifies as a female in a female facility opens up the possibility of illegal consensual sexual activity and may intrude on the other female offenders' rights. Placing both transgendered male and female inmates in housing units inconsistent with their preferred gender may be viewed as an intrusion on their ability to live a life consistent with who they feel they truly are. In the end, correctional officials must ensure the safety and security of all inmates. The question, however, is how to do so while accommodating the needs of transgendered offenders.

Discussion Questions

1. Where do you feel transgendered inmates should be housed within a correctional facility?

2. Should the rights of a transgendered inmate override the rights or feelings of those inmates whose biological sex is consistent with the preferred gender of the transgendered offender?

3. Is placing a transgendered inmate in a housing unit consistent with their biological sex an act of "deliberate indifference" by correctional officials?

Searching Transgendered Inmates

American jails and prisons are faced with a number of challenges in today's world. Among these are the housing, care, and treatment of their transgendered populations. Agencies across the U.S. continue to struggle with the balance between individual rights and freedoms versus the population's and facility's needs for safety and security. As such, the question of searching a transgendered offender often comes into play. Should inmates in general, and transgendered inmates in particular, be searched by officers consistent with their biological and/or preferred gender identifications? More importantly, is it offensive or intrusive to have an officer who identifies as male search an offender who identifies as female or vice versa.

According to the U.S. Department of Justice, Federal Bureau of Prisons (BOP) *Transgender Offender Manual* (2017), all offenders housed in BOP facilities will be searched in a manner consistent with the offenders' institution or housing gender designation. For example, if an inmate is housed in a unit designated for male offenders, policies and procedures relevant to male inmates will be used, regardless of the inmate's biological characteristics. The same, therefore, is true of offenders housed in an institution or housing unit designated for females. During the search of all inmates, including transgendered offenders, officers will use **gender neutral pronouns** (a pronoun that does not correspond to a known gender) and names (such as the inmate's last name or "Inmate" and the last name).

Many, however, feel this type of policy does not go far enough in its effort to protect transgendered inmates and their rights and privacy while incarcerated. According to the National Center for Transgender Equality's publication

Policies to Increase Safety and Respect for Transgender Inmates: A Guide for Agencies and Advocates (2018), agencies should ask a transgender offender which gender that person feels comfortable with during a search and state the reason for such a search. The center often cites the U.S. Department of Justice standards outlined in the **Prison Rape Elimination Act** (PREA) (legislation designed to reduce or eliminate the occurrences of rape within a correctional facility), which state:

> The facility shall not search or physically examine a transgender or intersex inmate for the sole purpose of determining the inmate's genital status. If the inmate's genital status is unknown, it may be determined during conversations with the inmate, by reviewing medical records, or, if necessary, by learning that information as part of a broader medical examination conducted in private by a medical practitioner. (f) The agency shall train security staff in how to conduct cross-gender pat-down searches and searches of transgender and intersex individuals in a professional and respectful manner, and in the least intrusive manner possible, consistent with security needs.

In the end, each agency must decide on the policies and procedures that meet both the safety and security needs of the facility, as well as the privacy and confidentially expectations of the transgendered inmate. The challenge, however, comes as the number of identified genders continues to grow. With over 100 recognized genders, American jails and prisons, along with their officers and staff, may well end up spending enormous amounts of time and resources navigating the legal landmines laid out to address a very small portion of the correctional population.

Discussion Questions

1. Should inmates, in general, be allowed to dictate who is and isn't allowed to search them?

2. What should a facility do if a transgendered inmate says they don't feel comfortable allowing any officer to search them or see the offender naked?

3. How much power should an inmate have in deciding the type of care and treatment they receive while incarcerated?

Drones in Corrections

Imagine sitting in a jail or prison yard, enjoying the sun on a clear day and suddenly you hear a low hum in the background. As you sit there, the hum becomes louder and you notice your fellow inmates starting to get up, looking skyward as they do. Suddenly, a small **aerial drone** (an unmanned aircraft) appears from behind a housing unit, hovers for a few seconds over the yard, and appears to drop something onto the ground. Inmates run to the object, while officers seem confused as the drone flies away. You have just witnessed a new technological way to introduce contraband into the facility — a drone drop-off.

While this might seem like some far-fetched plot from a sci-fi movie, drones and their contraband drops have been a problem for corrections for years (Vincent, 2020). According to the Department of Justice's (DOJ) Office of the Inspector General (OIG), the Federal Bureau of Prisons (BOP) began formally tracking the use of drones against their facilities in 2018 (U.S. Department of Justice, 2020). During that year, there were 23 incident reports involving drones. In 2019, that number climbed to 57. In one such incident, BOP officers recovered a drone with a package containing 20 cell phones, 23 vials of drugs ready for injection, multiple syringes, and multiple packages of tobacco, as well as a number of other types of **contraband** (items that are illegal in a lockdown facility or in too great a quantity for a lockdown facility). The OIG and the BOP, however, felt those numbers were most likely underreported because the BOP had yet to establish formal reporting procedures for drones that intruded into facility airspace.

One such example of these intrusions is the case of Nicolo Denichilo and Adrian Gooicharran, two men from New Jersey. Beginning in July 2018, New Jersey officials say Denichilo and Gooicharran completed no less than seven contraband drops using a modified drone designed to airlift packages into the Fort Dix federal prison (Gibbon, 2020). Each drop contained items that included marijuana, steroids, syringes, and cell phones. Upon learning of the deliveries, prison officials conducted an extensive search of the facility and found over "160 cell phones, 150 **SIM cards** (an electronic identification device), 74 cell phone batteries, 35 syringes, and two saw blades, as well as marijuana and steroids" (para. 8). Denichilo and Gooicharran were both charged with "conspiring to smuggle contraband and to defraud the government and smuggling contraband into a federal prison." (Gibbon, 2020, para. 11). If convicted, each offender faces five years in prison and up to $100,000 in fines.

In another incident, authorities in Florida arrested Casandra Kerr and her daughter Cencetta Didiano outside of a Florida state prison. The mother/daughter duo wanted to cheer up a family member who was incarcerated inside of the facility, so they decided to buy a drone on eBay and pack it with tobacco and cell phones (Darrah, 2018). Unfortunately for them, alert prison officers notified the local sheriff whose deputies found Kerr and Didiano driving around the outside of the prison. Kerr, who was allegedly operating the drone, was charged with introducing contraband into a correctional facility, while her daughter was charged with aiding and abetting.

To help combat the growing problem of aerial drones being used to introduce contraband into a federal prison, the Federal Aviation Administration (FAA) enacted air space restrictions for drones. In a June 2018 press release, FAA officials stated, "This is the first time the Agency has placed specific flight restrictions for unmanned aircraft, or 'drones,' over Federal Bureau of Prisons and U.S. Coast Guard facilities. The FAA has placed similar flight restrictions over military installations that remain in place, as well as over ten Department of Interior facilities and seven Department of Energy facilities" (para. 4).

Discussion Questions

1. What do you feel would be an appropriate punishment for those who introduce contraband into a correctional facility using an aerial drone?

2. What reactive measures do you feel correctional officials should be allowed to use to deter aerial drones over facility airspace?

3. Should the use of an aerial drone be an aggravating factor when charging incarcerated offenders with receiving contraband?

Chapter Key Terms

Obstruction of justice
De minimus
Criminal intelligence
Suspended sentence
Protective sweep
Third-party doctrine
Pat-down search
Legal correspondence
"Hit list"
Correctional Education Association
Corrections Corporation of American (CCA)

Canine search
Solitary confinement
Center for Constitutional Rights
Transgendered
"Deliberate indifference"
Gender neutral pronouns
Prison Rape Elimination Act
Aerial drone
Contraband
SIM cards

References

Associated Press. (2015, January). Prison guard strip-searches visitor to prove she was menstruating: Lawsuit. HuffPost.www.huffingtonpost.com.

Astolfi, C. (2014). Sandusky cop stop causes stir. *Sandusky Register*. http://www.sanduskyregister.com/news/law-enforcement/6222396.

Birrell, E. (n.d.). Technology and the Fourth Amendment: Balancing law enforcement with individual privacy. Deactivated link (retrieved 2015). http://www.eecs.harvard.edu/cs199r/fp/Eleanor.pdf.

Blade Staff. (2014, November 10). Inconsistencies found in Sandusky officer's statements. *The Blade*. http://www.toledoblade.com/Police-Fire/2014/11/10/Inconsistencies-found-in-Sandusky-officer-s-statements.html.

Blum, J., & Woodlee, Y. (2001). Boys strip-searched on jail tour. *Los Angeles Times*. www.articles.latimes.com.

Brumback, K. (2021, April 23). DOJ weighs in on suit filed by trans woman in Georgia prison. *Raleigh News & Observer*. https://www.newsobserver.com/news/nation-world/national/article250891889.html.

Caufield, K. (2013, October). County fires back against strip search lawsuit. *NewsTribune*.www.newstrib.com.

Clayton, G. L. (2015, January). Dogs, strip searches greet prison visitors. SFGATE. www.sfgate.com.

Coffey, C. (2014). LaSalle County settles strip search lawsuits. NBC News.www.nbcchicago.com.

Darrah, N. (2018, December 19). Florida mom, daughter sent contraband to prison via drone delivery, deputies say. Fox News. https://www.foxnews.com/us/florida-mom-daughter-sent-contraband-to-prison-via-drone-delivery-deputies-say.

Deruy, E. (2013, May). What it costs when we don't educate inmates for life after prison. ABC News.www.abcnews.go.com.

Enty, D. M. (2014, December 23). When did it become legal to strip-search a child? The Imprint. https://imprintnews.org/featured/when-did-it-become-legal-to-strip-search-a-child/9004.

Fatos, K. et. al. (2014). Solitary Confinement and Risk of Self-Harm Among Jail Inmates. American Journal of Public Health, 104(3) 442–447.

Federal Aviation Administration (FAA). (2018, June 7). FAA establishes restrictions on drone operations over DOJ and USCG facilities. United States Department of Transportation. https://www.faa.gov/news/updates/?newsId=90545.

Fox News. (2014, January 28). Predator drone helps convict North Dakota farmer in first case of its kind. https://www.foxnews.com/us/predator -drone-helps-convict-north-dakota-farmer-in-first-case-of-its-kind.

Friedersdorf, C. (2013). The Supreme Court logic that could destroy privacy in America. *The Atlantic.*http://www.theatlantic.com/politics/archive/2013/ 12/the-supreme-court-logic-that-could-destroy-privacy-in-america/282697/.

Galizio, G. (2014, April 10). Will drones infringe upon your Fourth Amendment rights? DRONELIFE. http://dronelife.com/2014/04/10/will -drones-infringe-upon-your-fourth-amendment-rights/.

Gallagher, R. (2012, June 12). Did a surveillance drone help in the arrest of a North Dakota farmer? Slate. http://www.slate.com/blogs/future_tense/ 2012/06/12/rodney_brossart_north_dakota_farmer_arrested_in_case_ involving_predator_surveillance_drone_.html.

Giarratano, J. (2015). Joe Giarratano — Stories from solitary. American Civil Liberties Union. https://www.aclu.org/issues/prisoners-rights/cruel -inhuman-and-degrading-conditions/joe-giarratano-stories-solitary.

Gibbon, J. F. (2020, March 15). Two charged for making drone drug drops at New Jersey federal prison. *New York Post.* https://nypost.com/2020/03/15/ two-charged-for-making-drone-drug-drops-at-new-jersey-federal-prison/.

Gordon, M. (2015a, February). Apparent threat prompts protection of Charlotte judges, city attorney. *The Charlotte Observer.* www.charlotteobserver.com.

Gordon, M. (2015b, May). Reputed gang leader: Throw my charges out. *The Charlotte Observer.* www.charlotteobserver.com.

Hartman, K. E. (2015, April). Strip-searches will keep helpful visitors, not illegal drugs, out of prison. *Los Angeles Times.* www.latimes.com.

Heath, B. (2015). New police radars can 'see' inside homes. *USA Today.* http:// www.usatoday.com/story/news/2015/01/19/police-radar-see-through-walls/ 22007615/.

Honoloy, N. (2015, April). Justice department supports transgender inmate's lawsuit against Georgia Department of Corrections to seek hormone therapy. *New York Daily News.* www.nydailynews.com.

Henson, K. (2009, December). Prison inmates shouldn't receive free college education. The Round Table (Middleton High School, Middleton, MD). www.mhsroundtable.com.

Hudson v. Palmer, 468 U.S. 517 (1984).

Illinois v. Caballes, 543 U.S. 405 (2005).

Johnson, B. (2014, May). Poll: Should prisoners receive a free college education behind bars? NJ.com. www.nj.com.

Johnson, C. (2015, September). California prisons to limit number of inmates in solitary confinement. National Public Radio. www.npr.org.

Kellaway, M. (2015a, May). Georgia trans inmate Ashley Diamond relocated after receiving threats. The Advocate. www.advocate.com.

Kellaway, M. (2015b, March). Incarcerated Texas trans woman finally wins safer housing after repeated rapes, threats. The Advocate. www.advocate. com.

Kerr, O. (2014). Supreme Court takes case on duration of traffic stops. *The Washington Post*. http://www.washingtonpost.com/news/volokh-conspi racy/wp/2014/10/02/supreme-court-takes-case-on-duration-of-traffic -stops/.

Koebler, J. (2013, March 1). Maine state police purchase $300 'toy' drone; using it would be illegal. U.S. News & World Report. http://www.usnews.com/ news/articles/2013/03/01/maine-state-police-purchase-300-toy-drone -using-it-would-be-illegal.

Kyllo v. United States (2001). http://www.oyez.org/cases/2000-2009/2000/2000_ 99_8508/.

Kyllo v. United States, 533 U.S. 27 (2001). https://supreme.justia.com/cases/ federal/us/533/27/case.html.

Louwagie, L. (2014). Police radar carries risk of abuse, court says. Courthouse News. http://www.courthousenews.com/2014/12/31/police-radar-carries -risk-of-abuse-court-says.htm.

Meincke, P. (2014, April). LaSalle County jail strip-search lawsuit settled: LaSalle County to pay Dana Holmes $125K. ABC 7 News.www.abc7 chicago.com.

Minkoff, M. (2014). First Ever Domestic Drone Arrest Upheld in Court. https://michaelminkoff.com/first-ever-domestic-drone-arrest-upheld- court/.

National Center for Transgender Equality. (2018). Policies to increase safety and respect for transgender inmates: A guide for agencies and advocates. https://transequality.org/sites/default/files/docs/resources/PoliciestoIncrea- seSafetyandRespectforTransgenderPrisoners.pdf.

Ouriel, A. (2014). Stockett: Denny works in dysfunctional department. *Sandusky Register*. http://www.sanduskyregister.com/news/law-enforcement/6618611.

Peck, M. (2014). Predator drone sends North Dakota man to jail. Forbes. http:// www.forbes.com/sites/michaelpeck/2014/01/27/predator-drone-sends -north-dakota-man-to-jail/.

Perez Jr., J. (2013, October). Lawyer: More women claim illegal strip-searches. *Chicago Tribune*. from www.articles.chicagotribune.com.

Pilkington, E. (2014). 'We see ourselves as the vanguard': The police force using drones to fight crime. *The Guardian*. http://www.theguardian.com/world/2014/oct/01/drones-police-force-crime-uavs-north-dakota.

Richardson, L. (2015, January 20). Exposed: Police radars can 'see' inside homes—No warrant needed. Truth Uncensored. http://truthuncensored.net/exposed-police-radars-can-see-inside-homes-no-warrant-needed/.

Rivero, D. (2015). Police are using a new device that can 'see' through walls. https://splinternews.com/police-are-using-a-new-device-that-can-see-through-wall-1793844799.

Rodriguez v. United States No. 13-9972 (2014). Transcript of oral argument. http://www.oyez.org/cases/2010-2019/2014/2014_13_9972.

Rodriguez v. United States, No. 13-9972 (2014). http://www.washingtonpost.com/news/volokh-conspiracy/wp-content/uploads/sites/14/2014/10/2014_WL_3725024.pdf.

Rodriquez v. United States, No. 13-9972. 575 U.S. (Apr. 21, 2015). http://www.supremecourt.gov/opinions/14pdf/13-9972_p8k0.pdf.

Root, D. (2015, January 21). Traffic stops, drug-sniffing dogs, and unreasonable searches and seizures. *Reason*. http://reason.com/blog/2015/01/21/today-at-scotus-traffic-stops-drug-sniff.

Ruppe, D. (n.d.). Supreme Court rules on police using infrared. ABC News. http://abcnews.go.com/US/story?id=93127&page=1.

Salam, R. (2013, June 12). The third-party doctrine. *National Review*. http://www.nationalreview.com/agenda/350896/third-party-doctrine-reihan-salam.

Sandusky officer placed on leave after traffic stop. (2014). WKYC Studios https://www.usatoday.com/story/news/local/ohio/2014/10/08/sandusky-officer-on-leave/16929189/.

Sisk, C. (2015, January). Lawsuit says CCA prison guards strip-searched visitor to prove she was having period. www.nashvillepublicradio.com.

Skelton, A. (2014). Nebraska traffic-stop case headed to U.S. Supreme Court. *Omaha World-Herald*. http://www.omaha.com/news/crime/nebraska-traffic-stop-case-headed-to-u-s-supreme-court/article_ee37b94a-4e56-11e4-a08a-001a4bcf6878.html.

Skorton, D., & Altschuler, G. (2013, March). College behind bars: How educating prisoners pays off. *Forbes*. www.forbes.com.

Sontag, D. (2015, May). Push to end prison rape loses earlier momentum. *New York Times*. www.nytimes.com.

Smith v. Maryland, 442 U.S. 735 (1979).

Stelloh, T. (2015, August). Transgender inmate suing Ga. Prison system granted surprise early release. NBC News. www.nbcnews.com.

United States v. Rodriguez, 741 F.3d 905 (8th Cir. 2014).

U.S. Department of Justice. (2017). *Transgender Offender Manual*. Federal Bureau of Prisons. https://www.bop.gov/policy/progstat/5200-04-cn-1.pdf.

U.S. Department of Justice. (2020, September 15). Audit of the Department of Justice's efforts to protect Federal Bureau of Prisons facilities against threats posed by unmanned aircraft systems. Bureau of Prisons.

Villasenor, J. (2013). What you need to know about the third-party doctrine. *The Atlantic*. http://www.theatlantic.com/technology/archive/2013/12/what-you-need-to-know-about-the-third-party-doctrine/282721/.

Vincent, J. (2020, September 16). Federal prison officers are worried drones could one day be used to airlift inmates to freedom. The Verge. https://www.theverge.com/2020/9/16/21439372/drones-prisons-doj-bop-report-smuggling-contraband.

Watzel, R. (2014). *Riley's* implications for Fourth Amendment Protection in the cloud. *Yale Law Journal*. http://www.yalelawjournal.org/forum/rileys-implications-in-the-cloud.

WBTV Web Staff. (2015, July). FBI document reveals details on jail cell search, killing of Lake Wylie couple. WBTV. www.wbtv.com.

Williams, T. (2015, September). Prison officials join movement to curb solitary confinement. *The New York Times*. www.nytimes.com.

Wright, M., & Gallek, P. (2014, October 9). New details revealed on controversial traffic stop. The Blade. https://fox8.com/news/controversial-traffic-stop-tapes-reveal-officer-knew-driver/.

Chapter Seven

Craftiness

He [the prosecutor] may prosecute with earnestness and vigor — indeed he should do so. But, while he may strike hard blows, he is not at liberty to strike foul ones.
—Supreme Court Justice George Sutherland,
Berger v. United States, 295 U.S. 78, 88 (1935)

Life may not be fair, but we expect our criminal justice system and its officials to be so. Indeed, the Fourteenth Amendment to the Constitution demands that before the government takes away our life, liberty, or property, it must first give us "due process," or fundamental fairness. We expect the system to have fair rules and that officials within the system will act in accordance with them. We like the idea of having smart people among our criminal justice officials, but we do not want them to be too **crafty** (that is, too sly, clever, cunning, or deceitful in achieving their ends). We simply do not want our criminal justice officials to engage in abusive tactics in their pursuit of "justice."

Three classes of officials who can really upset us when they act craftily are police officers, prosecutors, and judges. In this chapter, we shall look at constitutional examples of cunning foul play with regards to each of these.

Police Craftiness

We expect police officers to fight crime, but to fight cleanly. One way that police officers can exercise power in an abusive manner is through entrapping people. Another way is for them to make use of sketchy statutes to pick on people they simply do not like. Yet, a third way is for them to be a bit too clever in their use of lineups. This section will look at three cases regarding the police. The first case deals with entrapment, the second with police use of so-called "vague statutes," and the third with the use of overly suggestive line-ups.

Jacobson v. United States
503 U.S. 540 (1992)

A Midwestern farmer named Keith Jacobson had a subscription to some very offensive magazines involving photographs of naked, preteen boys. These magazines were entitled "Bare Boys I" and "Bare Boys II." Amazingly, at the time of purchase and use, these magazines (and others like them) were not against the law in the jurisdiction where Jacobson lived. However, this later changed with the passage of federal legislation, which made it a crime to possess child pornography. By the time this law came into effect, there was no evidence that Jacobson any longer purchased or viewed such materials.

Enforcement of this new federal legislation (known as the "Child Protection Act") was the responsibility of agents working for the Postal Service and also for the Customs Service. These agents became aware of Jacobson's earlier (and lawful) purchases and decided to target him with special attention.

Pretending to represent civilian groups opposed to sexual censorship, the federal agents started sending Jacobson solicitations through the mail urging him to purchase child pornography. These offers included promises to use the profits from any sales in the organizations' various fights against governmental prohibition of child porn.

For example, one mailing came from a pretend organization called "HINT" (the "Heartland Institute for a New Tomorrow"), which held itself out to be an "organization founded to protect and promote sexual freedom and freedom of choice." Another mailing came from a different made-up organization called the "American Hedonist Society" which, in a letter to Jacobson, claimed that "we have the right to seek pleasure without restrictions being placed upon us by outdated puritan morality." What all the mailings sent by the federal agents to Jacobson had in common was that they offered to sell him pornographic images of underage boys and to use proceeds to combat any political opposition.

Jacobson at first ignored such offers to purchase, but after more than two years of constant bombardment he finally gave in and placed an order. He was promptly arrested and charged with violating the federal act prohibiting such a purchase.

During his trial before a jury, Jacobson presented an entrapment defense, but the jury refused to excuse his crime on that basis. He appealed, claiming that no reasonable jury could possibly have found him to be anything but entrapped.

On eventual appeal to the U.S. Supreme Court, Jacobson saw his conviction overturned. The Court agreed with Jacobson that proof of entrapment was plain and overwhelming. In finding that Jacobson had clearly been **entrapped** (lured into committing a crime), the Court made use of the same test that had been used during Jacobson's trial, the so-called "predisposition test."

Under the "**predisposition test**," a jury is supposed to determine whether or not a defendant had been "predisposed" to commit the crime in question. If the defendant was predisposed already to commit the crime, then a police "sting" involving that suspect was simply good police work. On the other hand, if a subject was not predisposed, then police solicitations amounted to tempting an innocent person into breaking the law, something that person ordinarily would probably not do but for the police enticement. So, for example, it might be legitimate for an undercover police officer dressed and acting as a prostitute to proposition "Johns" circling the red-light district repeatedly in an obvious search for paid sex. But it would probably be inappropriate for that same undercover police officer to approach a citizen minding his own business while sitting and reading on a park bench with enticing offers of cheap, paid sex. The "Johns" were predisposed; the book-reading citizen was not.

In the case of Jacobson, the Supreme Court opined that there simply was no evidence whatsoever that Jacobson was predisposed already to purchase the forbidden materials. True, Jacobson had purchased such materials years before, but such purchases had been legal then. According to the Supreme Court, "evidence of predisposition to do what once was lawful is not, by itself, sufficient to show a predisposition to do what is now illegal, for there is a common understanding that most people obey the law even when they disapprove of it." The Court went on to further say that "government agents may not originate a criminal design, implant in an innocent person's mind the disposition to commit a criminal act, and then induce commission of the crime."

Noting that Jacobson only placed an order for the materials after two and a half years of constantly being solicited by the undercover agents, the Court concluded by ruling that no reasonable jury could have concluded beyond a reasonable doubt that Jacobson was already predisposed to engage in the illegal activity. Since sufficient proof of predisposition was lacking, the jury clearly should have acquitted Jacobson under the entrapment defense he had put forth. His right to due process had been violated.

Discussion Questions

1. What would be an example of a "clean" drug sting that would constitute good under-cover police work rather than entrapment?

2. Why is entrapment wrong? What is so bad about the police testing people's integrity?

3. Do you think there is any crime that the police could lure you into committing that you are not currently predisposed to commit?

As we see from the above case, luring innocent citizens into breaking the law is one unfair way for the police to make an arrest. Another unfair way is for the police to profit from poorly worded and ill-defined statutes to target people whom they simply dislike or personally disapprove of. When legislatures drop the ball by drafting statutes that lack reasonable amounts of clarity (so-called "**vague statutes**"), they enable certain bad actors among the police to abuse their power. The case that follows illustrates this type of police foul play.

Minnesota v. Reha

474 N.W. 2d 360 (Minn. App. 1991)

The city of Minneapolis decided to make sure people performed their duty to keep a tidy house. So, it passed a law making it a crime for anyone occupying a dwelling within the city to fail to keep their home in a "clean and satisfactory condition." Members of the local health department were charged with enforcing this law. When they received a citizen complaint regarding Reha's home, they went over to her place to investigate.

What they found upon their inspection was not pretty. Interior walls contained embedded dirt, food was left lying around in various places, and a stack of boxes leaned against an inside wall. Agents also spotted clothes strewn about the interior of the residence. Some of the clothes even contained roaches and mice droppings. Outside, agents noticed five plastic garbage bags on the back porch and "severe clutter" in the yard.

Reha took exception to the health department's assessment that her house was slovenly kept. Instead, she asserted that it was merely "disorganized." Nevertheless, she was charged with failing to keep her home in the required "clean and satisfactory condition" and convicted of such pursuant to a jury trial. At sentencing, the court sentenced her to serve 35 days in jail or else pay a $700 fine.

Reha appealed her conviction to the Minnesota Court of Appeals. She argued that the Minneapolis ordinance was unconstitutionally "vague." Specifically, she maintained that it was so vague as to deny her due process of law as required by the Fourteenth Amendment.

The Minnesota Court of Appeals agreed with Reha and reversed her conviction. The Court was upset by the fact that the phrase "clean and satisfactory condition" lacked sufficient specificity for ordinary people to "understand what condition is prohibited." In other words, the verbiage failed to put people on **proper notice** of what was required of them.

The Court also was upset because the statute was so unclear that it empowered the police to engage in "**arbitrary and discriminatory enforcement**." In other words, it gave agents of the state a handy and convenient tool to persecute people they simply dislike or don't approve of. This, the Court felt, it could not tolerate.

The Court emphasized that the phrase "clean and satisfactory" is not some shorthand or "term of art" with a widely understood meaning. These words could mean very different things to different people. In fact, it had been established at trial that even members of the local Health Department charged with enforcing the law had trouble agreeing on what constituted an acceptable level of keeping a dwelling in a "clean and satisfactory condition."

Because the statute failed to put people of ordinary intelligence on notice of what was required of them and because the law empowered the police to engage in discriminatory enforcement, it violated the Due Process Clause of the Fourteenth Amendment as being fundamentally unfair. In other words, the statute was "**void for vagueness**."

Discussion Questions

1. What did the court mean when it said that "clean and satisfactory" is not some "term of art"?

2. What are the two evils associated with vague statutes?

3. How could Minneapolis fix its law by making it sufficiently clear to give adequate notice of what is expected?

4. What part of the Constitution do vague statues violate?

United States v. Wade

388 U.S. 218 (1967)

A man with a strip of tape on each side of his face entered a bank and robbed it at gunpoint. He made off with a pillowcase full of cash. Only two employees were present in the bank at the time: a cashier and the bank's vice-president. Both had witnessed the robbery.

Half a year later, FBI agents arrested Wade on suspicion of robbing that bank. He was taken to a local courthouse where a lineup had been arranged. It was hoped that the cashier and vice-president would be able to positively identify Wade as the person who had held up their bank.

Half a dozen prisoners were placed in the lineup, including Wade. Each was forced to wear strips of tape on the sides of their face and to say something along the lines of "put the money in the bag." Both the cashier and the vice-president picked Wade out as the robber of their bank. Later, at trial, they again identified Wade as the robber to the jury.

There were a couple of problems, however, with the initial lineup in the local courthouse. First, the lineup was allowed to take place without Wade's lawyer being given the opportunity to be present. Second, prior to the lineup in the courthouse, both the cashier and the bank vice-president had spotted Wade "standing in the hall" next to an FBI agent. Minutes later, they saw him again in the lineup and identified him as the one who had robbed them many months before.

Wade was convicted by the jury and appealed, claiming that he was denied a fair trial due to the tainted lineup and denied the right to counsel when his lawyer was not invited to attend the lineup. The prosecution maintained that there is no right to counsel at lineups, and any taint was cured by the two witnesses identifying Wade "independently" during the trial.

So, was Wade denied a right to a fair lineup, a right to an attorney at a lineup, and ultimately to a fair trial? The Supreme Court ruled that this was so.

Calling a post-indictment lineup a "critical stage" of the prosecution, the Court ruled that the defendant had the right to an attorney present. A post-indictment lineup, like any other "**critical stage**," is a step in the process that can determine the entire outcome of a case. Since the lineup was so critical, the defendant had a right to an attorney present to make sure that the lineup was conducted fairly. It does no good for the government to argue that the lack of an attorney at the lineup was cured by the new identification of the defendant during the trial. By then, the damage was done, and the witnesses were **tainted**.

The Court also noted that the observation by the witnesses of the defendant in the hallway in the company of an FBI escort just prior to the lineup is a good example of why an attorney is needed at lineups to make sure that every-thing is done correctly. It rejected the FBI's attempt to characterize the lineup as being a "**mere preparatory step**" like fingerprinting that required no lawyer be present. Again, it was a crucial stage of the process — a stage that could affect the entire outcome of the case.

The Court went on to give other examples of how police have been known to run unfair lineups. For example, reports have been made of the police using members of a lineup who were all familiar to the identifying witness (except for the suspect); using members of a lineup who looked "grossly dissimilar" to the suspect; having a lineup in which only the suspect wears clothing that the criminal had worn during the crime; and lineups in which the police suggest whom they think the witness should choose.

Because Wade was not given an attorney at the lineup to make sure that it was fairly done, and because the lineup, in fact, was not fairly done, Wade's con-viction was overturned. Both Wade's Sixth Amendment rights (fair trial, counsel) and Fourteenth Amendment rights (due process) had been denied him.

Discussion Questions

1. How might dishonest cops intentionally signal who they want a witness to pick during a line-up without using any words?

2. How might honest cops unconsciously signal who they think a witness should pick during a lineup?

3. How does having a defense lawyer present help prevent the dangers in the two questions above?

Prosecutorial Craftiness

Most people think that judges are the ones who wield the most power in the courthouse. But the case is often made that prosecutors wield even more day-to-day power than do the judges. When you think of it, the prosecutor decides who will get charged, what the charges will be, and usually what punishment the person will get (think of plea bargaining). And as a practical matter, these decisions are largely unreviewable by anyone outside the prosecutor's own office. No wonder then that Attorney General (later Supreme Court Justice) Robert Jackson once said that that "The prosecutor has more control over life, liberty, and reputation than any other person in America" (from "The Federal Prosecutor," an address delivered by Jackson in Washington, D.C., on April 1, 1940, at the Second Annual Conference of U.S. Attorneys).

Fortunately, most prosecutors (like most people) are ethical most of the time. But, with power comes the temptation to misbehave. The cases that follow explore situations involving crafty and abusive tactics on the part of prosecutors.

First, we shall look at the problem of "selective prosecution," and we shall consider two cases in that area. Then we shall consider the problem of "vindictive prosecution." Next, we shall look at clever efforts on the part of prosecutors to take two bites of the apple, thus demonstrating the need for prohibitions against double jeopardy. Finally, we shall consider prosecutorial attempts to gain unfair advantage by inflaming the passions of a jury during a trial.

Yick Wo v. Hopkins
118 U.S. 356 (1886)

Yick Wo, a Chinese-born resident of San Francisco in the 1880s, operated a laundry in a wooden building. In 1880, San Francisco passed an ordinance making it illegal for any person to operate a laundry in a building made of wood, supposedly to reduce the risk of fire (laundries in brick or stone buildings were legal). Under authority of this ordinance, San Francisco refused to grant Yick Wo a license that would allow him to continue his laundry operations, even though he had been engaged in that business in the same building for the past twenty years. In fact, the licensing board denied laundry licenses to all Chinese applicants even though it granted licenses to 79 of 80 non-Chinese Americans who wished to run laundries out of wooden buildings.

Yick Wo continued to run his business despite lacking a license. Consequently, he was fined ten dollars. Unable or unwilling to pay the fine, he was sentenced to jail. He appealed his conviction all the way up to the U.S. Supreme Court, claiming unfair, selective prosecution on the part of California authorities.

The U.S. Supreme Court agreed with Yick Wo that he had been unfairly selected for prosecution and reversed his conviction. The Court saw through San Francisco's pretense of being concerned about fire prevention and rather believed it was more concerned about reducing Chinese participation in the laundry business than it was about reducing the risk of fire.

The Court noted that prosecutors have broad authority to prosecute whom they like, but this power does not "leave room for the play and action of purely personal and arbitrary power." The Court opined that "whatever may have been the intent of the ordinances ... they were applied ... with a mind so unequal and oppressive as to amount to a practical denial by the State" of equal protection of the law as guaranteed by the Fourteenth Amendment. The Court concluded that "though the law itself be fair on its face and impartial in appearance, yet ... it is applied and administered by public authority with an evil eye and an unequal hand." The discrimination had no reason for its existence except "hostility to the race and nationality" to which Yick Wo belonged.

Discussion Questions

1. Other than racial minorities, what other types of minorities might unscrupulous prosecutors target for selective prosecution?

2. Do you think a new prosecutor who wants to begin prosecuting a legitimate but previously unenforced crime should be able to start doing so without the first person selected for prosecution successfully claiming "selective prosecution"?

Despite the decision in *Yick Wo*, selective prosecution wrongs are very hard in practice to establish in court. Over-extended prosecutors with limited resources are generally given the benefit of the doubt in attacking what crime they can, even if it be in piecemeal fashion. Prosecutors are given broad discretion in their judgment calls of which cases are easiest to prove, which constitute the most serious violations, etc.

In order to prevail, an alleged victim of **selective prosecution** must not only prove that a certain group of people appears to have been singled out for prosecution but that it was the prosecutor's subjective intent to discriminate against people because of their race, religion, gender, etc. In other words, the alleged victim must not only prove an apparent **discriminatory effect** but an actual **discriminatory intent**. Proving the subjective, discriminatory intentions of someone is not very easy to do.

The case that follows shows how difficult it is to convince an appellate court that "selective prosecution" has taken place. It involves a defendant who believed that people of his race were being singled out during the "war on drugs."

United States v. Armstrong
517 U.S. 456 (1996)

Armstrong was arrested for the distribution of crack cocaine after confidential informants working for the Inglewood, California, police department bought crack from him on several separate occasions. A total of 124 grams had been purchased.

After being indicted for the sale of the crack, Armstrong filed a motion for discovery and also to have the indictment quashed on the grounds that members of the black race were being targeted for prosecution in the local drug war. Specifically, Armstrong pointed out that every one of the 24 cases involving the sale of crack cocaine in his area involved African Americans. Not a single white person was arrested for selling crack cocaine, nor were whites arrested for selling drugs that white people preferred in his area (e.g., LSD) in numbers anywhere near those for arrests involving the sale of crack. Armstrong asserted that because the prosecutor was dealing in "selective prosecution" based on race, the indictment violated his rights to equal protection.

In support of his allegations, Armstrong cited the 24 cases referred to earlier, an affidavit obtained from an intake official at a local drug rehabilitation center claiming that "equal numbers" of local drug dealers were white and black, and a newspaper article reporting that people caught selling crack are punished much more severely nationally than people caught selling powder cocaine (with the insight that almost everyone who sells crack is black).

The United States Supreme Court ultimately agreed to consider Armstrong's claim of selective prosecution. It noted that in order to prove a selective prosecution claim, a defendant had to prove that the government's actions had both a "discriminatory effect" and were motivated by a "discriminatory purpose." It must be shown by "clear evidence" that "the decision whether to prosecute" was "based on an unjustifiable standard such as race, religion, or other arbitrary classification." The Court also said that there was a strong "presumption of regularity" on the part of the prosecution because the government must be given a lot of leeway and deference to get its job done with the limited resources at its disposal. Prosecutors are presumed to be competently discharging their constitutional duties, and absent a clear showing that the matter is otherwise, an accusation of selective prosecution shall not stand.

In the end, the Court ruled that Armstrong failed to prove his claim of selective prosecution. He could not prove that the government's actions had a discriminatory effect (let alone a discriminatory motivation). To prove a discriminatory effect, Armstrong would have to show that similarly situated people of other races were not being prosecuted when they were caught with crack cocaine. But people of races other than African American simply were not committing the same crime of selling or using crack cocaine in numbers like those among the black community. Statistics showed that at the time over 90% of crack cocaine users were African American. Since there was no discriminatory effect, there was no selective prosecution and hence no denial of equal protection.

Discussion Questions

1. If you were an African American on a jury in this jurisdiction, would you be tempted to nullify the law by finding black defendants not guilty even when proven to be guilty?

2. Even though local prosecutors in the case above ultimately managed to avoid a "selection prosecution" finding, why might it have been a bad idea for them to continue going after crack cocaine users so heavily after their appellate court victory?

Do you agree with the outcome of the case above? In the Bronx, during the 1990s, many African-Americans, upset over the state's policy of punishing dealers of crack cocaine much more harshly than dealers of powder cocaine, reportedly began to "nullify the law" by refusing to convict local people caught selling crack cocaine despite clear proof of guilt. It was their way of fighting back against what they perceived to be race-motivated, selective, harsher punishments. What do you think of such actions?

Prosecutors can fight unfairly not only in being selective in their prosecutions but in being vindictive in their prosecutions as well. "Selective prosecution" typically involves the targeting of a group of people based on their race, gender, religion, or some other impermissible category. "**Vindictive prosecution**," on the other hand, typically targets an individual against whom a prosecutor seeks revenge for that individual's having had the boldness to exercise some right or another. The case that follows illustrates the concept of "vindictive prosecution."

Blackledge v. Perry
417 U.S. 21 (1974)

Perry got into a fight with another inmate while both were serving time in a North Carolina prison. Initially, Perry was charged and convicted of misdemeanor assault. He was convicted pursuant to a bench trial (no jury), as was the custom in North Carolina in such matters. The judge who convicted him sentenced him to six months for the assault, to be served after he was done serving his current prison sentence.

North Carolina law allowed anyone convicted of a misdemeanor of this magnitude to appeal. The appeal would constitute a *trial de novo*, meaning the slate would be wiped clean, and a jury (not just a judge) would now be presented with the evidence from scratch. In other words, a trial by jury would constitute the "appeal" of the non-jury trial conviction.

The prosecutor assigned the case apparently was not very happy with Perry's assertion of his right to a *trial de novo* before a full-blown jury. The prosecutor dropped the misdemeanor case and rather caused Perry to be charged with felony assault with a deadly weapon in the jury-level court (replacing the old charge of misdemeanor assault). This new, more serious charge was based entirely on the same set of facts that had led to the earlier charges.

Perry pled guilty to this felony charge and was sentenced to five to seven years, to run concurrently with the prison sentence he was currently serving. Perry later changed his mind about having agreed to this "deal" and filed a writ of habeas corpus in federal court. Eventually, the U.S. Supreme Court agreed to hear this case.

Perry's arguments before the Supreme Court concerned two issues: double jeopardy and vindictive prosecution (the latter being a violation of due process). The Court found in Perry's favor on the vindictive prosecution claim and never had to address the double jeopardy argument.

In ruling that Perry had been the victim of vindictive prosecution, the Court found that the State appeared to have retaliated for Perry's assertion of his right to a new trial by bringing more serious charges against him. Retaliation for the exercise of a constitutional or statutory right is not a permissible basis for a prosecution.

The Court found a similarity to what the prosecutor had done to Perry with what a judge had done to someone in the case of *North Carolina v. Pearce*, 395 U.S. 711 (1969). In *Pearce*, a defendant had successfully appealed his conviction and sentence and was granted a new trial. Upon reconviction, the judge gave him a new sentence that was more severe than he had received the first time around. In that case, the Supreme Court had ruled that "imposition of a penalty upon the defendant for having successful pursued a statutory right of appeal or collateral remedy would be ... a violation of due process of law." The Court in that same case went on to further say that "vindictiveness against a defendant for having successfully attacked his first conviction must play no part in the sentence he receives after a new trial." The Court went on to note that a judge theoretically could increase the sentence following a successful appeal and re-conviction, but only if he or she could place a convincing, independent justi-fication for the harsher sentence on the record—e.g., important, new facts not known the first time around.

The "lesson" that the Court thought was demonstrated by the *Pearce* case was that the Due Process Clause is offended by retaliation-based increases in sentences following retrial after appeal. The question then becomes whether a prosecutor can be vindictive when a judge may not be so? The Court said that the answer must be "no." Either way, retaliation on the part of a court officer for the assertion of a right is a violation of due process. Vindictive pros-ecution simply is not constitutionally permissible.

Discussion Questions

1. What is an example of some other right that a person might assert only to have an angry prosecutor then attempt to engage in vindictive pros-ecution?

2. Should prosecutors who are found to have engaged in vindictive pros-ecution not only have the damage they caused be corrected but also be personally punished? If so, how?

The above case appears comforting, but defendants should not get too com-placent. Despite Perry's success, courts are reluctant to find vindictiveness on the part of prosecutors in the arena where it allegedly exists with the most prevalence: plea bargain negotiations. The whole idea behind plea bargaining is to persuade defendants to give up an important right, that being the right to a trial. Persuading defendants to plead guilty can involve some very tough ultimatums.

For example, in *Bordenkircher v. Hayes*, 434 U.S. 357 (1978), a prosecutor demanded that Paul Hayes, charged with passing an $88.30 bad check, either agree to do five years or else face life in prison under a three-strikes law that the prosecutor could invoke at will. Hayes balked at doing five years for such a tiny check. The prosecutor invoked the three-strike rule, and the case went to trial. Hayes lost the trial and got the life sentence the prosecutor had promised.

On appeal, Hayes' argument to the Supreme Court that he was the victim of a vindictive prosecutor who punished him too harshly for having exercised his right to a trial was rejected. The Court noted that the prosecutor simply did what the law allowed him to do, and plea bargaining must permit such rough-and-tumble practices if it is allowed to exist. As long as the prosecutor openly laid his cards on the table, all was fairly done.

Vindictive prosecution, when it occurs, is not fair. Another "dirty trick" occurs when prosecutors who have lost a case try to get a second crack at a defendant by dodging the prohibition against double jeopardy. The next case explores this type of craftiness.

Ashe v. Swenson
397 U.S. 436 (1970)

Ashe and several acquaintances allegedly burst into a room and robbed six people who were engaged in a game of poker. All of the robbers wore masks so as to obscure their identities. The robbers fled with the cash, and the police were called. Ashe was found walking down the side of a highway near the point where the alleged get-away car apparently had been abandoned.

Ashe was accused of being one of the poker game robbers and was brought to trial.

Interestingly, for whatever reason, the prosecutor chose to try Ashe for the robbery of just one of the six poker players and not the others. The evidence at trial linking Ashe to the robbery was rather weak. None of the six poker players could visually identify who had robbed them due to the masks the robbers had worn. One of the six could identify Ashe in a way, but only supposedly by recognizing his voice as that of one of the robbers. Another of the six players could identify Ashe, but only supposedly by recognizing Ashe's body shape and mannerisms as being similar to those of one of the robbers.

Because only two of the six poker players could identify Ashe at all, and then only based on fuzzy, non-visual criteria, the jury felt compelled to acquit Ashe of the robbery, feeling that there simply was too much reasonable doubt.

However, the prosecutor was not about to concede defeat. He next recharged Ashe for the robbery of one of the other poker players who was present. The prosecutor claimed that this did not constitute a violation of double jeopardy since he was alleging the robbery of someone completely different than the individual poker player designated as the victim in the first trial.

Apparently having had the chance to "get his act together," the prosecutor managed to convince the second jury that Ashe had robbed the newly designated victim in question. The trial judge subsequently sentenced Ashe to 35 years in prison!

Ashe appealed this conviction all the way to the U.S. Supreme Court. The Supreme Court ultimately sided with Ashe and reversed his conviction. The Supreme Court emphasized that the prohibition against **double jeopardy** exists so that people can be protected from having to "run the gauntlet a second time." Prosecutors are not permitted to use a first trial as a "dry run" to help them prepare for a second trial on the same set of facts. This is exactly what the prosecutor seems to have accomplished.

The Court went on to point out that the state cannot break up one criminal incident into a number of separate crimes and then increase its odds of victory by taking each piece of the incident to a separate jury. This is precisely the type of unfair process that double jeopardy was meant to prohibit.

When the first jury acquitted Ashe, it basically had reasonable doubt regarding whether or not Ashe was present during the collective robbery of the six poker players. The state, unhappy with that determination of reasonable doubt, cannot ask a second jury to reconsider the same issue all over again.

The state was allowed to name all six poker players as robbery victims, but it had to do so in a single trial against Ashe. It simply cannot prosecute someone repeatedly until it gets the result it is after. The judgment of the trial court was reversed, and Ashe ordered to be set free.

Discussion Questions

1. Is double jeopardy always bad? Would you allow someone to be tried twice if new, overwhelming evidence came to light for the first time after someone had already been acquitted?

2. Should double jeopardy prevent the retrial even of a defendant who was acquitted because the judge or jury had been bribed by that defendant? (Current law says the acquittal must stand.)

So far, we have looked at prosecutorial attempts to employ abusive tactics in terms of selective prosecution, vindictive prosecution, and serial prosecution (double jeopardy). The case that follows considers the problem of prosecutors attempting to fight dirty by **inflaming a jury** (causing passions to overwhelm reason).

People v. Shazier
151 Cal. Rptr. 3d 215 (2012)

Daniel Shazier, a person convicted years earlier of multiple sex crimes, was now alleged by the state of California to be a dangerous, "sexually violent predator" whom the government sought to have civilly committed to a mental institution. This action, made pursuant to California's "Sexually Violent Predator's Act," entitled him to a jury determination of whether or not he posed a danger to others of violent, sexual behavior, in that such a finding was tantamount to a "conviction" of sorts.

The state attempted to prove its case of sexual danger by putting on two expert medical witnesses (doctors) who both testified that in their opinions, Shazier was attracted to underage teenage boys. They also both testified that they believed he posed a "moderate to moderate-high risk" of engaging in sexually violent offenses towards such boys. Both doctors admitted that their diagnoses would not be without some controversy in the mental health field. But they believed that Shazier qualified for commitment as a potentially dangerous sexual predator.

After a lengthy trial, the jury found Shazier to be potentially dangerous to the degree that he should be committed to an indefinite period in accordance with California law. Shazier appealed this determination, arguing that during the trial the prosecutor had engaged in multiple acts of prosecutorial misconduct, including several instances in which he inappropriately inflamed the passions of the jury. Such misconduct on the part of the prosecutor was alleged to deny him a fair trial and due process of law. He asked the California Court of Appeals to reverse the judgment of the trial court.

After reviewing the evidence, the Court of Appeals agreed with Shazier and reversed the judgment of the trial court. It concluded that the prosecutor had engaged in so many instances of misconduct that the trial had become "so infected … with unfairness as to make the resulting conviction a denial of due process."

Specifically, the Court was disturbed by the following, multiple instances of apparent misconduct. First, it ruled that the prosecutor had acted unfairly when he asked the jury during closing argument what their friends and family would think of them if they let this defendant go free. This constituted "blatant misconduct" on the part of the prosecutor because juries are not to be influenced by such things as "passion," "prejudice," "public opinion," or "public feelings"; correct verdicts should be reached "regardless of the consequences."

Next, the Court was upset when the prosecutor implied that Shazier was a "prolific child molester" without any such proof being before the court. The prosecutor suggested that Shazier only escaped additional criminal convictions because he had never been caught. The Court ruled that "statements of supposed facts not in evidence ... are a highly prejudicial form of misconduct and a frequent basis for reversal."

The Court also was offended by the prosecutor's attempts to scare the jury by reminding them of the proximity of schools to the defendant's home if he were released. This was improper because juries are not supposed to consider the consequences of their verdicts. The Court ruled that "such considerations are wholly improper, and cast doubt on the jury's ability to properly consider the evidence in this case."

Next, the Court expressed concern over the prosecutor's questioning of defense experts by bringing up stories of child molestations completely unrelated to the defendant's life. For example, the prosecutor asked one defense expert (a doctor) about an unrelated case involving a child molester who molested every child in his apartment complex, including his own three-and-a-half-year-old son. Bringing up this and other completely irrelevant cases could have no purpose other than to "incite the passions and prejudice of the jury."

The prosecutor also acted unfairly in the Court's opinion when he badgered a defense expert by telling him two different times, "Mr. Ross, you don't know what you're talking about, do you?" The Court saw these as "speeches to the jury masquerading as questions." The prosecutor also impugned the character of the defense attorney when, during closing argument, he told the jury that the defense lawyer "had been deceptive during the trial" without any basis for such a remark.

The bottom line for the appellate court was that even if any one of the above examples of misconduct standing alone was not by itself enough to compel a reversal, the cumulative effect of all of them was such as to render the trial fundamentally unfair. The Court concluded that "the prosecutor engaged in a pervasive pattern of inappropriate questions, comments and argument, throughout the entire trial, each one building on the next, to such a degree as to undermine the fairness of the proceedings."

Discussion Questions

1. What sorts of things might inflame your passions such that you could not think clearly and fairly? What sorts of crimes easily push your buttons?

2. How might the omnipresence of modern recording technology create more opportunities for prosecutors nowadays to attempt to inflame the passions of juries?

3. Shouldn't prosecutors be expected to try to get juries to develop "righteous anger" when hearing about dastardly crimes? What is the difference between getting a jury passionately engaged in a trial and inflaming a jury's passions?

Interestingly, the court in the case above was not only upset with the prosecutor but with the trial judge as well. It noted that the defense attorney repeatedly had lodged objections to the bad incidents as they took place but was repeatedly overruled by the judge. Judges too can be guilty of foul play. The next section of the chapter explores this idea.

Judicial Craftiness

We might expect some police and prosecutors to engage in unfair maneuvering. But we do not expect judges to ever do so. Judges are not supposed to have personal agendas of any kind. They are expected to be completely neutral, non-combatants.

The sad reality is that judges, just like other criminal justice actors, can sometimes be darkly artful in achieving certain desired goals. The cases that follow illustrate constitutional aversion to judges acting craftily.

United States v. Booker
543 U.S. 220 (2005)

A man named Freddie Booker was found guilty by a federal jury of possessing 92 grams of cocaine. Federal courts at the time made use of mandatory sentencing guidelines. Given the amount of cocaine determined by the jury to have been in Booker's possession, the guidelines required a sentencing judge to give Booker a sentence of 22 years in prison.

However, the sentencing judge wound up sentencing Booker to 30 years (not 22) based upon facts he discovered during the sentencing hearing. The judge determined that, despite what the jury thought, Booker had really possessed 655 grams of cocaine (not merely 92). Because of this much larger amount of cocaine, the federal sentencing guidelines instructed the judge to sentence Booker to the much longer prison term.

Since the judge considered the amount of cocaine to be a "sentencing fact" rather than a "trial fact," he felt authorized to use a mere "preponderance of the evidence" standard in finding the fact. So, since the amount of cocaine was deemed a "sentencing fact" rather than a "trial fact," not only could the judge decide the fact rather than a jury, but the judge could find the fact using a standard of proof well below that of "beyond a reasonable doubt," like a jury would be required to employ.

Booker's judge was quite correct that "**sentencing facts**" do not require a jury determination and that "preponderance of the evidence" is all that is needed to establish such facts. For example, sentencing judges are supposed to consider the "whole person" in deciding an appropriate sentence. Hence, they take many facts into consideration, such as the educational level of the defendant, his employment history, family background, medical condition, addiction issues, apparent motivation for the crime, indications of remorse, etc. All of these constitute typical "sentencing facts," which do not require a jury determination and only require proof by preponderance of the evidence.

The question on appeal to the U.S. Supreme Court became whether a fact that can increase a sentence by eight years could be fairly deemed to be a mere "sentencing fact" rather than a full-blown "trial fact." Remember, the jury had thought that the state had only proven (beyond a reasonable doubt) the possession of 92 grams of cocaine (not hundreds more like the sentencing judge had determined).

Ultimately, the Supreme Court ruled that a fact so critical as to increase a sentence by eight years was properly a "**trial fact**" that should have been determined by a jury beyond a reasonable doubt. Because this critical trial fact was decided by a judge rather than a jury (and using the preponderance of evidence standard rather than proof beyond a reasonable doubt), Booker had been denied his Sixth Amendment right to trial by jury. Specifically, it held that the "Federal Constitution requires that any fact (other than a prior conviction) which is necessary to support a sentence exceeding the maximum authorized by the facts established by a plea of guilty or a jury verdict must be admitted by a defendant or proved to a jury beyond a reasonable doubt." So, for example, if the maximum penalty for generic simple assault is two years in prison, but the maximum for simple assault based on hatred of someone's race is double that, a finding of racial hatred would be a "trial fact" and not a mere "sentencing fact." This is so because it would result in a maximum penalty greater than what non-hate-based assault would have called for. In essence, simple assault and hate-based simple assault are two entirely different crimes since they have two entirely different maximum penalties.

Discussion Questions

1. What are some typical examples of mere "sentencing facts" in ordinary cases?

2. Why would it be too burdensome to expect judges to be convinced beyond a reasonable doubt when it comes to mere sentencing facts? Or should they be so convinced in your opinion?

We see in the *Booker* case that the Sixth Amendment right to a jury trial will stand in the way of judges who wish to hide behind "sentencing facts" in a sly way to find someone guilty of critical facts that might not pass muster with a jury. If Booker's eight years of extra prison time disturbed you, the case that follows might prove even more upsetting. Here, a judge seems to take advantage of a defendant's lack of comprehension in sentencing him to life in prison.

Boykin v. Alabama
395 U.S. 238 (1969)

Boykin allegedly committed a series of five armed robberies back in an era when Alabama still made use of the death penalty in punishing armed robbery. Boykin gave up his right to a jury trial on the robberies and agreed to simply plead guilty to all of them. In accepting his guilty pleas, the judge never bothered to tell Boykin of his right to a jury, his right to have the charges proven beyond a reasonable doubt, his right to an attorney to assist him with a trial, or even the potential sentences he could receive in pleading guilty. In fact, the judge did not ask Boykin any questions at all. Instead, he quickly accepted his pleas of guilty and subsequently sentenced him to death on each of the five robbery counts.

As you can imagine, Boykin was not happy with this outcome. He decided to appeal his "convictions" (guilty pleas count as convictions) and sentences all the way to the United States Supreme Court. The issue before the Court was whether a judge could accept a guilty plea made by a woefully ignorant defendant without violating that defendant's right to receive due process of law. In ruling that the judge's conduct was a constitutional violation, the Supreme Court ruled that the judge not only committed error but "plain error." It held that a judge cannot lawfully accept a plea of guilty from someone until the judge is convinced that the guilty plea is being entered "knowingly and voluntarily."

In order for a guilty plea to be a "**knowingly entered plea**," a defendant must understand the nature of the charges (in this case, the legal elements of armed robbery), the rights he is giving up by pleading guilty (e.g., the right to a jury trial, guilt beyond a reasonable doubt), and the possible range of penalties he is exposing himself to (in this case, the death penalty). In other words, his act of pleading guilty must be an informed act, one that is made with proper understanding of its consequences.

In order for a guilty plea to be a "**voluntarily entered plea**," a defendant must be deemed to be entering the plea of his own free choice and will. In other words, the court must assure itself that the defendant is not acting under any coercion or improper threats of any kind, nor due to any secret promises that are not part of the plea bargain (if there is a plea bargain).

The Court emphasized that a guilty plea is not simply some minor event. It constitutes a full-blown conviction that can result in dire consequences. A guilty plea "supplies both evidence and verdict, ending controversy."

Because this judge so cavalierly accepted Boykin's guilty pleas while promptly sentencing him to his demise, he denied Boykin his due process rights. Consequently, Boykin's sentences were vacated, and his cases remanded for new trials or for properly executed guilty pleas.

Discussion Questions

1. What is the difference between "knowingly entered" and "voluntarily entered"?

2. Don't many defendants only plead guilty because they are threatened with much longer sentences if they go to trial and lose? Are such defendants truly "voluntarily" pleading guilty in your view?

3. Is it appropriate for a judge to accept a guilty plea from an angry, emotionally upset defendant who technically says the right things when asked if he is "voluntarily" giving up his right to a jury trial?

Thanks to the *Boykin* case above, many jurisdictions now make use of what are generically known as "***Boykin* forms**." These forms are filled out by a defendant before going to court to enter a plea of guilty. The defendant is given a check-list of rights and potential consequences to initial within the form. The defense lawyer then presents the form to the judge during the guilty plea hearing. The judge then typically goes over the points orally with the defendant, making sure he or she has understood each one. Courts do not have to use such *Boykin* forms. But it is clear that they have to use some procedure to ensure that any guilty plea is both "knowingly entered" and "voluntarily entered."

It is not just adults who have to worry about judges sometimes treating them in an unfair and cunning manner. Even juveniles can face such challenges at times. The case that follows is the seminal case of a juvenile court judge treating a child with gross unfairness.

In re Gault
387 U.S. 1 (1967)

Gerald Gault, a fifteen-year-old boy, and his friend were accused by a neighbor of having made a lewd telephone call to her. Police came to the neighborhood and took Gerald to the detention home. Gerald's parents were not home at the time, and when they returned they wondered where Gerald was. After making inquiries, they learned that he had been taken away by the authorities.

The very next day, the juvenile judge held a hearing to determine Gerald's culpability and fate. The charging document filed against him by a juvenile probation officer alleged no facts, only that Gerald was "delinquent." This document, as sketchy as it was, was never even served on either Gerald or his parents.

The hearing that took place was very informal indeed. Mrs. Cook, the alleged victim of the offensive phone call, never even came to court to testify. Instead, the court relied upon hearsay summaries of what she had told the authorities. Because Mrs. Cook was not there, Gerald had no way to confront her or to cross-examine her.

In fact, no witnesses were ever sworn in, and neither was a transcript of the hearing ever made. The judge adjudicated the fifteen-year-old Gerald delinquent and placed him in the Arizona State Industrial School (a type of juvenile jail) until he was to turn twenty-one. If Gerald had been an adult, the most he could have possibly received for this offense was a mere two months in jail.

Arizona provided no appellate rights to juveniles at the time, so Gerald got his case before the appellate courts (and eventually the U.S. Supreme Court) via a writ of habeas corpus alleging that his confinement violated the U.S. Constitution. The U.S. Supreme Court considered his plight and ruled in his favor.

The Court rejected claims advanced by the State that children like Gerald Gault had no due process rights because juvenile courts only had their best interests at heart. The State tried to argue that juvenile courts merely acted as surrogate parents, never seeking retribution but only rehabilitation—what was in the "best interests" of the child. Since no punishment was ever meted out in juvenile courts, no due process rights had to be provided. In fact, it was the State's position that affording juveniles due process rights would only hinder the mission of juvenile courts to help youngsters.

The Supreme Court found all of the State's various arguments to be essentially phony. First, it held that juveniles had the right (like adults) to adequate and timely notice of the charges so that they could prepare a proper defense. The argument that notice was a bad idea because it interfered with the State's goal to keep the episode secret (thus protecting the child's privacy) was rejected and deemed to be completely unpersuasive.

Second, the Court ruled that juveniles facing a delinquency hearing had the right to an attorney to represent them. It did not like the State's argument that a juvenile probation officer could see that the juvenile's rights to the regularity of proceedings were protected. After all, the juvenile probation officer is the one who has brought the charges against the child. Thus, the officer is acting in a capacity that is very akin to that of a prosecuting attorney. An accusatorial juvenile probation officer simply cannot be trusted to assure that the juvenile's rights are protected.

Next, the Court held that juveniles like Gerald Gault have the right to confront and cross-examine their accusers in court. The stakes are just too high not to test the evidence in this proven-effective manner.

Finally, the Court ruled that juveniles, like adults, have the privilege against self-incrimination. Juvenile courts typically believed that confessions were "good for the soul" and were an indispensable first step towards rehabilitation. Consequently, juvenile judges would strongly encourage those in trouble to admit their delinquent acts to the court. In rejecting this rationale, the Supreme

Court noted first that confessions from children are notoriously unreliable. It then went on to express its view that a child who is convinced by adults to confess, only to then be severely punished, often feels bitterness at having been tricked rather than helped. This is especially true in a case like that of Gerald Gault, who was given nearly six years of confinement in a very unpleasant institution for a rather minor offense.

In sum, the Court ruled that Gerald's due process rights regarding notice, counsel, confrontation, and self-incrimination did indeed exist and were not honored. His delinquency adjudication was vacated and his placement in the industrial school rescinded.

Discussion Questions

1. If, like Gault, you were sent to reform school for six years for one obscene phone call, how rehabilitated would you be when you finally were set free?

2. Would any real parent ever send their own child to a state industrial school for six years for a lewd phone call? If not, what was this judge really trying to do to Gault?

We see in the *Gault* case just discussed that a mean-spirited judge, unbound by due process restraints, can find a way to punish a child, even outrageously so, by hiding behind the old doctrine of **parens patriae** (the state acting as an ultimate, concerned parent). Not all judges can be trusted to act as a loving parent in situations involving wayward youth. Nor can they be trusted to act as physicians of sorts, along some sort of misguided "medical model" of justice. Unlike physicians, judges can force their "medicine" on people whether they consent to it or not. And, unlike physicians, judges sometimes inflict pain for its own sake rather than as part of legitimate treatment.

This completes the chapter on "craftiness." We have seen examples of police officers employing sly tactics when they attempt to entrap people, target people using vague statutes, or take advantage of suggestive lineups. We have seen examples of prosecutors employing cunning tactics when they engage in such machinations as selective prosecution, vindictive prosecution, serial prosecution (double jeopardy), and inflaming the passions of the jury. Finally, we have seen judges abusing their power when they artfully do such things as pretend that an important trial fact is a mere sentencing fact, accept guilty pleas from defendants who do not understand what they are getting themselves into, or deny juveniles all due process rights under the pretense of acting as their concerned, surrogate parents.

Though most professionals who work in our criminal justice system play fairly and shun all schemes, we have seen that a few actors (be they police, prosecutors, or judges) do not. Fortunately, the Constitution's hostility to any "monkey business" or use of manipulative and injurious tactics is there to help keep them in check.

Chapter Key Terms

Crafty
Entrapped
Predisposition test
Vague statutes
Proper notice
Arbitrary and discriminatory enforcement
Void for vagueness
Critical stage
Tainted
Mere preparatory step
Selective prosecution

Discriminatory effect
Discriminatory intent
Vindictive prosecution
Double jeopardy
Inflaming a jury
Sentencing facts
Trial fact
Knowingly entered plea
Voluntarily entered plea
Boykin forms
Parens patriae

Chapter Eight

Craftiness in Law Enforcement and Corrections

The function of law enforcement is the prevention of crime and the apprehension of criminals ... criminal activity is such that stealth and strategy are necessary weapons in the arsenal of the police officer.
— *Sherman v. United States*, 356 U.S. 369, 372 (1958)

Law Enforcement

Operation Blue Shepherd

At times, law enforcement may need to deceive their suspect in order to fully get out of them the information that they are after. However, there is no clearly defined boundary of what is an acceptable amount of deception versus a blatant case of entrapment. The first case in question will explore this topic through a discussion of an undercover internet sting called Operation Blue Shepherd. This sting was designed to catch adults who were allegedly contacting minors online to meet up with them for sexual encounters.

If you have ever watched the television series *To Catch a Predator* (*TCAP* from here on) which aired from 2004–2007, then you will see that the following story is reminiscent of how they ran their undercover operations on this television show. *TCAP* was widely successful perhaps due to the dramatic nature of the encounters that happened between suspects and the host of the show, Chris Hansen. The producers of the *Dateline* show partnered with Perverted-

Justice (a self-proclaimed internet watchdog group) and local law enforcement officers to set up undercover stings where the adult males thought they were coming to meet the underage boy or girl whom they had been chatting with online. When they showed up, they were surprised to find an adult who quickly started grilling them on their internet conversation with the minor and asking them for an explanation. When they left the house, they were greeted by law enforcement and quickly taken into custody. Many of them would later face and be convicted on various charges related to soliciting sex from a minor (Cook, 2011, para. 1–4).

Similar to *TCAP*, Operation Blue Shepherd was an undercover sting held in Pensacola, Florida, in 2011. Operation Blue Shepherd was just one example of many stings that were being run across the state of Florida during this time-frame. The operations were coordinated under the Internet Crimes Against Children (ICAC) task forces, which brought together law enforcement entities from numerous levels as well as judges and prosecutors to combat internet sex crimes against children. The ICAC was also heavily funded, which allowed law enforcement agencies to apply for grants to help run the undercover stings (Anderson, 2013, p. 2, para. 12–13).

One man who started searching around on the "Casual Encounters" section of Craigslist encountered Amber (19 years old) who was advertising "2 sisters seeking a man to handle both [of] us." A 43-year-old Army veteran named Edwin "Trey" Gennette replied to the post, and he was told on numerous occasions that Amber was of age but her sister, Erin, was only 14 years old. While Gennette showed some reservation through his chat log, he eventually agreed to meet the sisters at their home. When he showed up, he was confronted by police officers in bulletproof vests and taken into custody. He ended up being one of 25 suspects caught in Operation Blue Shepherd during the week-long operation (Twenty-five men arrested, 2011, para. 1–2).

While the undercover stings were proven to be effective due to the sheer number of arrests that occurred, there were some who were critical of the way that the operations were run. For example, a local Florida news station investigated a number of stings overseen by ICAC and found that law enforcement targeted both adult websites (like MeetMe.com, Fling.com, and SpeedDate.com) as well as some more ambiguous ones regarding the typical age of their clients (such as Craigslist, Backpage, Facebook, and Twitter). Furthermore, they found that law enforcement would oftentimes introduce a child into the conversation later on or switch the age of the child after the suspect and child in question had established a bit of a chat history (Pransky, 2015, para. 35–39). Additionally, Florida police investigated some of the more well-known sex stings and found over 1,200 cases where innocent victims were entrapped and had their property illegally seized. Ret. Army Col. Mike Pheneger, chair of the Greater Tampa Chapter of the American Civil Liberties Union, expressed concern over the *To Catch a Predator*-style stings, stating that, "The Justice Department (should) be asked to look into this ... to find out if they are following the rules, because it would appear they are not" (Pransky, 2014 para. 3).

Others are critical of the dramatic public displays that often happen after a large number of arrests occur at one of these stings. Gennette discussed how this was the case with Operation Blue Shepherd, and that in a matter of days, his as well as the 24 other suspects' mug shots were advertised in the local newspaper. Other agencies throughout Florida have even released videos of the arrests on their YouTube pages and put the offenders' names and home addresses on their homepage (Anderson, 2013, p. 3, para. 5). These public displays of humiliation can ruin the lives of the suspect, and while there are likely more unreported cases out there, two suspects who were swept up in one of Florida's sex stings ultimately committed suicide (Lewis, 2012; Man facing child solicitation, 2013).

Gennette said that he found support through his family to prevent him from following the fate of the two men discussed above. He claimed that his life was practically destroyed in the wake of the sting because, among other things, he had to find the means to pay off his $300,000 bond and he found himself practically homeless at times. He claimed that he suffered "due to police injustice" and that he was entrapped because the undercover officer incessantly pushed a sexual agenda on him that he did not set out to engage in (Anderson, 2013, p. 2, para. 4). After having a motion to dismiss his charges denied, Gennette plead guilty to less severe charges that would keep him out of jail. Because he entered a plea of **nolo contendere** (i.e., I will not contest), he was allowed to appeal the denial of the motion to dismiss the charges. He claimed that his arrest was the product of entrapment, and the First District Court of Appeals agreed. The court reversed the denial of the motion to dismiss and **remanded** (appellate court action sending an appealed case back to the trial court for further action) the matter back to the trial court to dismiss the charges (*Gennette v. State*, 124 So. 3d 273 [Fla. Dist. Ct. App. 2013]). In the wake of his experiences, Gennette created an outreach website (called Florida Action) for both victims and family members of victims who felt, as he did, that they had been wrongfully entrapped by an internet sex sting.

Discussion Questions

1. Do you feel as though these undercover sex sting operations are an appropriate use of deception by law enforcement?

2. If you were the judge in Gennette's case, do you think you would have viewed the circumstances surrounding his arrest as entrapment?

Entrapped Autistic Teen

The following discussion is similar to the one presented above; however, in this case, law enforcement is deceiving (mostly) minors instead of adults and luring them with drugs instead of sex. In this section, we will be discussing undercover agents who went into high schools and posed as students looking to buy and sell illegal substances. For those who have either seen the 1980s television series or the newer 2012 movie titled *21 Jump Street*, this undercover tactic is going to sound familiar. But, unfortunately, it will lack the comedic elements.

Undercover drug stings have been going on all over the U.S., but California in particular has begun really cracking down on drug sales that occur throughout their high schools (some speculate due to the legalization of medicinal marijuana). For example, in 2010, 14 students were arrested in an undercover sting at Palm Desert High School. In 2011, 24 students were arrested on drug-dealing charges in Moreno Valley and Wildomar. And in 2012, 22 students were arrested in Riverside County in a multi-school sting (Miles, 2013, para. 8–10).

One of the more controversial stings was carried out in Riverside County and dealt with law enforcement targeting an autistic youth. In this sting, an undercover agent posed as a recent transfer student to Chaparral High School who goes by the name of "Daniel Briggs." He quickly meets and befriends a 17-year-old boy named Jesse Snodgrass, who is shy and also recently moved to the area to finish his senior year of high school (Rubin Erdely, 2014, para. 11). They met on Jesse Snodgrass' third day of class, and Jesse thinks that he has tackled a feat that has challenged him his entire life: making a new friend. Jesse struggled to find and keep friends throughout his youth. Due to his noticeable handicap and emotional disorders (autism, bipolar disorder, Tourette's syndrome, and a variety of anxiety disorders), he was bullied and tormented by his peers during his childhood (Winkler, 2014, para. 5). In order to protect himself, Jesse often got into physical altercations with those who bullied him. He also engaged in a variety of maladaptive coping mechanisms such as banging his head against walls, punching, and scratching himself (Rubin Erdely, 2014, para. 17). This ultimately led to Jesse having a discipline record for the various ways that he has acted out over the years.

Shortly after they met, Daniel asked Jesse if he knew where he could get some weed. In an effort to keep their friendship going, Jesse replied that he could get him some even though he had no experience with buying, selling, or smoking the drug. Daniel continued to probe Jesse over the coming weeks about needing the pot, and Jesse started receiving contact from Daniel outside of school via text messages. In follow-up reports, Jesse reports that he tried to stall and/or thwart Daniel's requests because he started to feel anxious with how persistent he was getting. Jesse estimated that he received approximately 60 text messages over the span of a couple weeks and got to the point where he felt as though Daniel was stalking him. As was typical, Jesse coped with the stress by engaging in self-harm practices (e.g., he fled to the boys' bathroom where he burned his arm with a lighter) (Rubin Erdely, 2014, para. 21). His parents conversed with the school about the incident and what his social life was like at school lately, but nobody seemed to notice the relationship that was developing between Jesse and Daniel.

Daniel continued to press Jesse to buy him some drugs and slipped Jesse a $20 bill. Jesse knew that he couldn't access his prescription medication since his parents kept it locked, and he also didn't know where to turn to buy it on the streets. He bought a half-joint from a homeless man and gave it to Daniel. He did this again one more time and then refused to provide Daniel additional drugs. Their friendship ended shortly thereafter (Miles, 2013, para. 5).

Once Deputy Daniel Zipperstein had collected enough evidence, he arrested Jesse along with 21 of his peers. While the charges for the other students varied by severity and quantity of drugs being sold, Jesse was arrested and charged with selling .6 grams of pot (Downs, 2014, para. 5). He was taken to the police station and not allowed to see his parents until his court date, which was sched uled for two days later. His parents described the look in his eyes as "haunting" and said that after his arrest, he suffered from post-traumatic stress disorder, insomnia, panic attacks, and depression. Beyond the criminal sanctions, Jesse was expelled from school. This prompted his parents to sue the Temecula Valley Unified School District (TVUSD) since they willingly participated with the undercover sting and subjected their son to the traumatic event. In a unique twist of events, TVUSD filed a **cross complaint** with the Riverside County Sheriff's Department (RCSD). They claimed that if they were found liable, then the RCSD should have to pay damages due to their "negligent, unlawful and tortious conduct … [and] unconstitutional entrapment, search, and seizure" of Jesse (Snodgrass, 2014, para. 3–4). Later a judge overturned the expulsion, and a separate judge dropped the criminal charges against Jesse (Ackerman, 2014, para. 5).

Jesse's parents reported being pleased with the final outcome; however, they are still upset with how their son was treated in the first place. They stated that it is obvious by his behavioral patterns and socialization skills that Jesse has the cognitive level of an 11-year-old and that Deputy Zipperstein should have known better than to target their son. While they are thankful that their son was able to finish out his schooling and get his degree, his parents said that he is "permanently scarred" from the event.

Numerous newspaper stories highlight these *21 Jump Street*-like undercover stings happening across the U.S. in states such as Texas, California, and Tennessee. While they appear to be used frequently, some have highlighted inherent problems with how the stings are run. Furthermore, others question whether or not they are even effective and produce desired results. For example, a 2007 Department of Justice study reported that these undercover stings can sometimes help track down low-level offenders, but they usually force those higher up in the ranks, such as suppliers, underground. Additionally, there are those who question the ethics behind the undercover operations and the emotional inequity that exists between the officers and the youths that they are trying to buy or sell from. The officers usually have five or more years on the students, and they know how to manipulate the youths. Many question whether or not this deception is worth it (Mahoney, 2013, para. 7–9). It is a tough call to make, but perhaps the better way to frame the question is to ask, "Does the end justify the means"?

Discussion Questions

1. Given the limited information that you have on this case, does it seem as though Deputy Zipperstein unconstitutionally entrapped Jesse?

2. Do you think that Jesse's limited cognitive development should make him less culpable for his actions?

Coerced Confessions

At times, law enforcement has to use deception, coercion, and other psychological strategies to aid them in apprehending and convicting criminal suspects. While the courts have weighed in on numerous issues regarding these tactics and criminal procedures, there is unfortunately no gold standard that can be applied across the board. However, many claim that the courts often support law enforcement using these strategies. According to Shealy, "the Supreme Court has routinely and consistently upheld the use of deceptive police practices in the investigation of criminal suspects" (2014, p. 26). In this section of the chapter, we will explore two cases where the courts had to weigh in on whether or not the level of deception and coercion used by law enforcement to secure a confession was legitimate or teetered on violating the defendants' rights.

The incident in question for the first case took place on August 13, 1973, in rural New Jersey. On this day, 17-year-old Deborah Margolin was approached by a stranger in an automobile who said that one of her family's heifers was loose at the foot of their driveway. She left alone in the automobile to go investigate, and she never returned home. Later that day, her father found her mutilated body face-down in a nearby creek. The victim's brothers provided a description of the man's clothing and car to law enforcement, and they later identified Miller as the suspect in question. They went to his place of work and later took Miller to the station where they read him his *Miranda* rights and received a written waiver (*Miller v. Fenton, 474 U.S. 104* (1985)).

A 58-minute-long interrogation followed where the detectives lied that Margolin was alive and could identify her attacker. Additionally, they told Miller that he could be identified as being at the Margolin home earlier that day. This information was also false because her brothers could only provide a description of the suspect's attire, build, and automobile; they did not directly identify Miller as the person that they had seen. The detectives also informed Miller that blood stains had been found on his front stoop, information which was also untrue. One last element of deception that law enforcement used throughout the course of the interrogation was that they said the criminal who committed this crime should not be punished but get help because he was sick and had mental health problems (Van Brocklin, 2014, para. 2). Miller's subsequent confession was admitted in court, and he was convicted of the murder.

Miller appealed his conviction, arguing that the confession should never have been admitted as evidence. The New Jersey Superior Court Appellate Division agreed and reversed the lower court's decision, finding that the confession was the result of compulsion, and therefore, impermissible. The New Jersey Supreme Court reversed, claiming that the "totality of all the surrounding circumstances" resulted in a proper and voluntary confession. Miller then challenged the case at the federal appellate level and both the federal district court and court of appeals refused to hear the case, citing that they would reach the same result as the lower court (*Miller v. Fenton*, 1985, para.

1). The U.S. Supreme Court, however, determined that the voluntariness of his confession was a legal question that warranted consideration pursuant to federal **habeas corpus** (a court order directing that a judge in the county or district where the prisoner is being held determine if there is a legal basis for the detention). Therefore, the Supreme Court effectively reversed the lower court's decision and remanded for further proceedings (*Miller v. Fenton, 474 U.S. 104* (1985)).

The above case illustrated that law enforcement may have gone too far in deceiving the defendant to secure his confession. The following case begs the same question. On September 21, 2008, Wilhelmina Hicks discovered her four-month-old son unresponsive and limp in his crib. When Matthew (the child) arrived to the pediatric hospital, he had symptoms of an irregular heartbeat, low blood pressure, severe dehydration, and respiratory failure. However, his physician ultimately determined that he suffered from blunt force trauma to the head and that the child had been "murdered." Local authorities were contacted, and they quickly turned their attention to the parents, primarily investigating the father, Adrian Thomas.

Law enforcement interrogated Thomas for a total of nine and a half hours, broken up into two sessions (two and then the remaining seven and a half hours) because he expressed suicidal thoughts between the sessions and was hospitalized for a short while. Over the course of the interrogation he was told that if he didn't take responsibility for the child's injury that his wife would be arrested and removed from the child's bedside (which was a lie because he was already deceased). He was told 21 times that they needed to know how the child was injured so that medical staff could save his life and 14 times that he would not be arrested. Additionally, he was told eight times that he would be going home if he cooperated with law enforcement. Ultimately, he confessed to "slamming" his son on the bed from 17 inches up and was found guilty of his son's murder (*People v. Thomas*, 22 N.Y.3d 629; 8 N.E.3d 308 [2014]). In 2009, he was sentenced to a 25-years-to-life prison term (McKinley, 2014, para. 6).

Thomas appealed his conviction to the New York State Court of Appeals, arguing that he had been unduly coerced into confessing. His lawyers argued that the string of false promises and threats caused their defendant to confess to something that he did not actually do. Furthermore, they alleged that the only reason that Thomas provided a story of "slamming" his son on the bed was because law enforcement put the idea in his head (NYS Court, 2014, para. 4). The justices sided with Thomas and reversed the lower court's order, suppressed the confession, and ordered that a new trial be set for a later date. Based on the ruling of the New York State Court State of Appeals, if Thomas were to be tried again, it would have to be done without the videotaped confession (Gavin, 2014, para. 3). Six years after his son's death, Thomas was tried a second time and found not guilty (Gardiner, 2014, para. 2).

Discussion Questions

1. Do you think that law enforcement should be allowed to use deception in order to secure a confession?

2. What are your reactions to the two cases above? Do you think that law enforcement went too far?

In the above examples, one could argue that there was a certain level of intentional deception used by law enforcement to reach their end goal. But what about those instances where law enforcement is not acting purposefully unethical but through accident or negligence they significantly impact the lives of criminal suspects? Furthermore, what if some of these criminal suspects are not even suspects at all but rather seemingly (or allegedly) innocent people swept up in faulty policy lineups? Erroneous police lineups and eyewitness misidentification will be the focus of the final topics of this section of the chapter dealing with craftiness in the context of policing.

Duke Lacrosse Rape Case

On March 13, 2006, members of the Duke Lacrosse team hired two exotic dancers to come to a party. Supposedly some of the players were upset that two African-American strippers showed up when they had specifically requested either white or Hispanic women. According to the women, they had racial slurs thrown at them and one player allegedly shook a broomstick at the women (Chang, 2014, para. 3). Within a matter of days, Crystal Magnum (a 27-year-old mother of two) came forward and said that she had been raped, sodomized, beaten, and strangled by three of the players. She was then brought into the police station to look at picture lineups. The lead detective told her to sit at the table and "look at people we have reason to believe attended the party" (Neff et al., 2006, para. 12). She was then shown 46 photos that only included players from the lacrosse team via a power point presentation where she looked at each headshot for a minute and then a blank screen in between each photograph. She identified two defendants quickly and reported 100% certainty with her decision. She also identified a third defendant with 90% certainty.

Once news of how the police conducted their lineup broke, many became critical of how the Durham Police Department ran the investigation. According to one source, the process for the police lineup was in violation of Durham PD's policy. This policy called for an independent investigator to administer the lineup (not the lead detective as had been done); the lineup should also have included five "fillers" for every suspect (Neff et al., 2006, para. 13–14). "Fillers" are described as being essential to the lineup process because they often add credibility to the witness since they have to deliberate over people who are clearly not the suspect (Weston, 2006, para. 4). As described another way by Gary Wells, president of the American Psychology-Law Society, it is like having "a multiple-choice test without any wrong answers" (Setrakian, 2006, para. 8). There were other issues aside from the shoddy police lineup that helped to poke holes in the prosecution's case, and no more than 13 months after the allegations were made, all three defendants had their charges dismissed.

Picking Cotton

The above case primarily dealt with an erroneous police lineup. In the following case, there were issues with the police lineup, but more so law enforcement procedures and the impact that they had on eyewitness misidentification. In 1984, 22-year-old Jennifer Thompson woke up to a stranger at the foot of her bed who raped her at knifepoint and threatened to kill her if she made any noise. During the ordeal, Jennifer tried to study as much as she could about the suspect so that if she lived, she could do everything in her power to help the police to catch the guy. Later that day, she went to the police station and provided details to a sketch artist. Two days later she went in and saw a photo lineup of six men (Hughes, 2014, para. 1–2). Law enforcement received an anonymous tip that Ronald Cotton looked a lot like the photo sketch they had seen on the news, and since Ronald already had a mug shot due to minor run-ins with the law, they included his photo in the lineup (Celizic, 2009, para. 9). Thompson looked at the six pictures that were laid down in front of her and quickly eliminated four of them. She then stared at the remaining two pictures for a total of four to five minutes and picked Ronald Cotton as the man who raped her. While picking Cotton, the conversation between Thompson and the detectives went like this:

> Thompson: "Yeah. This is the one. I think this is the guy."
> Detective: "You 'think' that's the guy?"

Thompson: "It's him."
  Detective: "You're sure?"
Thompson: "Positive."

She then signed and dated the back of the photo and asked them if she did ok. They replied, "You did great, Ms. Thompson" (Hughes, 2014, para. 2–8). Eleven days later, she was brought in for a physical lineup and Ronald Cotton was the only person in the group who also had their picture in the photo lineup. Thompson quickly identified Cotton and as they were leaving the room she asked the detectives how she did. They responded, "You did great, that was the guy you picked out in the photo lineup" (Eyewitness Identification, n.d.). By the time they had reached the trial, Thompson said she was 100% certain that Cotton was the man that had raped her and that nobody could tell her otherwise. Even though there was limited physical evidence linking Cotton to the crime scene or the rape itself, he was found guilty and sentenced to life in prison plus fifty-four years. The entire case was based almost exclusively off of Thompson's eyewitness identification.

Cotton tried to challenge his conviction during his time in prison, but he often was confronted by various legal roadblocks. It wasn't until nearly 10 years into his sentence that he was finally cut a break. He had heard through the grapevine in prison that another man named Bobby Poole (who was in the same prison as Cotton) had confessed to his cell mate that he was the one who actually raped Jennifer. Additionally, Cotton had been watching the OJ Simpson trial and heard about DNA testing, which was a form of forensic science that was increasingly being used by law enforcement. He confronted his lawyers with this information, and the prosecution decided to hand over all of the DNA evidence to let the defense do with it what they wanted. They ran the DNA that was collected from Thomson's rape kit and found out that the DNA matched Bobby Poole, not Ronald Cotton. Nearly 11 years after Cotton was arrested and charged with Thompson's rape he was exonerated on all of his charges and given back his freedom (Ronald Cotton, n.d., para. 1).

You could assume that this is where the story ends: Cotton is given his freedom and Thompson has to live with the guilt of knowing that she had made a terrible mistake. Interestingly enough, Thompson wanted to meet Cotton to tell him that she was sorry. Cotton agreed, and the two met up in a church that, coincidentally enough, was located in the same town where she had been raped nearly 11 years prior. After begging for his forgiveness, Thompson was shocked to hear him say that he had forgiven her years before and that she had just made an honest mistake. In the wake of this tragic accident, Thompson and Cotton wrote a book called *Picking Cotton* and have toured the country together doing appearances and giving speeches to help reform eyewitness identification policies at the local and national level. They have made it their goal to help others learn from their mistakes.

The two cases above illustrate a few of many problems that have been noted with how lineups are executed and the ways that they may accidentally or purposefully be biasing witnesses in making their decisions. In the Duke Lacrosse case, there were problems with not using fillers and also having the detective who was on the case administer the lineup. By having the lead detective administer the lineup, some inherent biases may slip in. This proved to be the case in the example of Ronald Cotton. Many of the detectives knew that Cotton was the suspect in question and through multiple layers of affirming that Thompson had done a good job and picked the right guy, they had further solidified in her memory that Cotton was the man who had raped her. Research overwhelmingly points toward the malleability of a victim's memory and how her level of confidence in her decision can be swayed or changed as time lapses from the crime. These are two problematic things that law enforcement must stay mindful of when executing a lineup.

Another issue that has been heavily debated in literature about police lineups is whether or not the photos should be presented sequentially or simultaneously to witnesses. In sequential lineups, the witness is presented the photos one at a time. In simultaneous lineups, multiple pictures are looked at side-by-side, all at once. The research is mixed, and there is no definite answer as to which is the best option; however, many note that there are tradeoffs to each approach. In the sequential approach, the witness has to deliberate over each picture as it coincides with her memory. In the simultaneous approach, the witness often deliberates as to which picture looks the most similar to the criminal (whether or not the actual suspect is in the photo lineup). However it appears as though this is a debate which will continue to thrive as there simply is "not enough evidence for the advantage of one procedure over another" (Hughes, 2014, para. 34).

Given the two stories discussed above and the expansive literature that highlights the problems with police lineups, what if any suggestions can be made to reform the way that law enforcement is administering police lineups? According to the National Academy of Sciences, there need to be more federal mandates about how police lineups should be administered. With nearly 16,000 law enforcement agencies in the U.S., there are few nationally mandated standards, which means that many states have different policies and procedures in place for administering police lineups. As such, the academy provides five suggested recommendations on how police lineups should be conducted (Sanburn, 2014, para. 9): (1) Train all officers in eyewitness identification, including education on how vision and memory works; (2) Use a **double-blind administration**, which means that those administering the lineups are not aware of the suspect's identity and that the victim knows that law enforcement does not know the identity of the suspect; (3) Develop standard instructions for witnesses on how to not bias their choices; (4) Videotape the witness identification process; (5) And last, record confidence statements with the witness at the time of identification (National Academy of Sciences, 2014, p. 5). Many agree that these recommendations would help to improve the entire eyewitness identification process.

Discussion Questions

1. If you were Ronald Cotton, do you think you could have forgiven Jennifer Thompson?

2. Which do you think is more problematic for criminal suspects: blatant cases of craftiness such as entrapment, lying, or deceit, or accidental/negligent errors like in the cases above?

Corrections

Random Drug Tests

The use of **random drug tests** (drug tests conducted without warning and/or at odd intervals) in correctional facilities are primarily seen as a mechanism to keep inmates safe, ensure certain offenders are complying with the conditions of their confinement, and help the offenders treat and rehabilitate addictive tendencies. While most people would agree that random drug tests are a necessary element within a jail or prison, some question the intent of corrections when these tests are done in a work release or community environment. Are corrections officials truly trying to help the offender successfully reintegrate back into society or are these tests simply a crafty way of returning the offender to confinement?

According to a **National Institute of Justice (NIJ)** (the research and development branch of the United States Department of Justice) study of Hawaii's HOPE program (Hawaii's Opportunity and Probation with Enforcement), random drug tests are an effective method of reducing an offender's drug recidivism and helping that individual succeed as a pro-social and contributing member of society (NIJ, 2012). Prior to implementing the HOPE program, probationers in Hawaii often received notice of a pending drug test up to a month in advance. Under the new format that emphasized swift and certain actions for failed tests, offenders were assigned a color code at their hearing and required to call the court each morning to see if their color was being tested that day. Results of the study found, when compared to an offender control group, that "Fifty-five percent [were] less likely to be arrested for a new crime. Seventy-two percent less likely to use drugs. Sixty-one percent less likely to skip appointments with their supervisory officer. Fifty-three percent less likely to have their probation revoked. As a result, HOPE probationers served or were sentenced to 48 percent fewer days, on average, than the control group" (NIJ, para. 2).

While those results are a positive indicator for the use of random drug tests, the American Civil Liberties Union (ACLU) felt these types of tests, especially when done at an offender's workplace, are unfair (ACLU, 2014). The Drug Policy Alliance (2015) agreed and in their overview of drug testing policies stated "Drug testing is also a near universal feature of the criminal justice system in the United States, with most probationers and parolees required to undergo drug testing regardless of the nature of their underlying offense or history of drug use. These drug testing policies are a huge infringement on personal privacy and have gone far beyond any reasonable mandate to improve public safety" (para. 1). They, like the ACLU, believe that corrections should be focusing on the successful reintegration of offenders back into society and remove antiquated policies that are rooted in "conjecture and fear" (para. 1).

Perhaps one of the more controversial issues regarding the use of random drug tests is the affect these tests, and their potential for false positive results, can have on pregnant mothers and their unborn children. A 2001 U.S. Supreme Court decision made it illegal to drug test pregnant women without consent if the results of those tests could lead to criminal charges (Brown, 2014). The question arises, however, concerning the rights of pregnant probationers or parolees and their ability to consent. In addition, there is the distinct possibility that a false positive result from a random drug test that does not lead to further charges or revocation could lead to an investigation by child protective services and subsequent loss of parental rights upon birth. Confounding the matter even more was the recent Alabama Supreme Court decision in *Ex Parte Hicks* that said in no uncertain terms that "there is no exception from prosecution for pregnant women who use controlled substances that are prescribed by physicians" (The Drug Policy Alliance, 2014, para. 3). Again, prisoner advocates question the true intent of correctional officials with respect to random drug tests and the effectiveness on enforcement and reintegration that these procedures offer to offenders and society.

Discussion Question

1. What do you believe the true intent of random drug tests are when used by correctional officials on offenders under correctional supervision?

2. Should pregnant offenders be given special rights regarding the implementation of random drug tests and the use of their results?

3. With respect to random drug tests, which do you feel is more important — offender rights or public safety?

Inmate Segregation

Inmate segregation and solitary confinement are often used as synonymous terms that are interchangeable in their meaning. While it is true that solitary confinement is a form of inmate segregation, inmate segregation, as a general term, is not synonymous with solitary confinement. According to the National Commission on Correctional Health Care (2015), **inmate segregation** refers to those inmates who "are isolated from the general population and who receive services and activities apart from other inmates" (para. 1). Depending on the type and term of segregation, inmates may be overseen by correctional officials and medical staff or simply left to the protection and oversight of facility officers.

While long-term inmate segregation and its negative effects are discussed in other sections of this text, the use of **holding cells** (temporary inmate or arrestee housing) as a crafty way of inmate manipulation is a controversial technique that is rarely discussed. From an architectural standpoint, holding cells are typically temporary housing locations within a lockdown facility that are designed to hold one or more inmates, are usually indoors, have a toilet/sink combination, have a bench, and are enclosed (Cisco-Eagle, 2015).

The use of holding cells and the intent behind placing inmates within their confines has been the focus of a number of high-profile cases in recent years. Perhaps the most notable of these incidents is the case of Sandra Bland, a 28-year-old African-American female who was arrested in Waller County, Texas, after she was accused of assaulting a police officer during a traffic stop (Sanchez, 2015). According to Waller County Sheriff R. Glenn Smith, Bland was combative during the arrest, as evidenced by her kicking at the arresting officer and speaking to him in vulgar language. Upon her arrival at the county jail, Bland mentioned to a correctional officer during her intake process that she had attempted to commit suicide in the past. Jail intake forms listed the cause of her past suicidal thoughts as the loss of a baby and listed her method of trying to kill herself as overdose of pills (Schuppe, 2015). Because of this information and concerns over her safety, Bland was placed in a holding cell pending further investigation and diagnosis of any possible mental health issues. A few days later, Sandra Bland reportedly committed suicide by strangling herself with a garbage bag in her cell.

Bland's supporters, however, challenged the sheriff's statements and believe Sandra was placed in a holding cell because she was a black female and not out of a desire to oversee her safety or diagnose any possible mental health issues (Pandit, 2015). In essence, she was placed in that particular location because of not only who she was, but to also teach her a lesson. Some in the community echoed a distrust of law enforcement and correctional officials and challenged the reason for Bland's placement. Still others took on an even more sinister, conspiracy theory approach, stating that they believed Bland was already dead in her booking photo (Dart & Swaine, 2015). Of particular concern for many who question the events that occurred during Bland's three-day stay at the county jail is the personal history of Sheriff Smith. Smith, who used to be the police chief of Hempstead, Texas, until he was removed from office due to allegations of police misconduct, was, according to some, a racist with anger management issues (Blidner, 2015). Was placement in a holding cell truly in Bland's best interests or should she have been placed in a location where others, including inmates, officers, and medical staff, were better able to monitor and care for her?

Discussion Questions

1. In your opinion, should holding cells be banned for arrestees or inmates who have or are displaying disruptive or combative behavior?

2. Should correctional officials explore better housing options for inmates other than holding cells?

3. Do you believe correctional officials placed Sandra Bland in a holding cell as a form of punishment?

Body Scanners

As arrestees, inmates, and others continue to find more creative ways of sneaking contraband into jails and prisons, correctional officials are turning to innovative methods to help deter such actions. One such technique is a piece of technology used in many airports across the nation—**body scanners** (technology that allows the operator to screen persons without making physical contact or asking the individual to remove their clothes). The procedure is not without controversy, however, and many feel the use of scanners by correctional officials is nothing more than a creative method of gathering information on offenders, visitors, and others that may be legally questionable.

Take for example the Salt Lake County Metro Jail, located in Salt Lake County, Utah. Correctional officials there believe body scanners allow them to thoroughly search inmates without invasive techniques, such as body cavity searches (Cutler, 2014). Scanners are not used on arrestees who are simply processed and released, nor on facility visitors.

Another agency exploring the use of body scanners is the Alachua County Sheriff's Office in Alachua County, Florida. According to Captain Jeff Ciotier, the jail's security operations division commander, "Security is enhanced by ensuring tools and/or weapons are not introduced into the facility by prisoners/inmates" (Alcantara, 2013, para. 5). Traditionally, if the officers in the Alachua County Jail suspected an inmate or arrestee was concealing contraband inside of their body, multiple officers could take up to fifteen minutes strip searching the individual and even then, there was no guarantee the item(s) would be found. Now, with body scanning technology, offenders can be screened in seconds, and items that are located on or in an individual's body can be easily detected.

Not everyone, however, feels the use of body scanning technology in jails or prisons is a good idea. In fact, some argue using the technology is a waste of time and money, and may scan and store data about an individual that could be illegal. For instance, a team of researchers from the University of California at San Diego, the University of Michigan, and Johns Hopkins University found they could easily circumvent the scanners used by the **Transportation Security Administration (TSA)** (a U.S. government agency designed to protect the country's transportation systems) and smuggle guns, knives, and explosives past the scan (Groppe, 2014). Unfortunately, many of the scanners being used by correctional facilities across the United States are the same TSA scanners that were removed from airports over security concerns.

In addition to smuggling concerns, the technology used by TSA produced near-nude images of those being scanned (Accardo & Chaudhry, 2014). Jail officials, however, are not as concerned about these privacy issues as those involved in airport security due to the reduced expectation of privacy within a lock-down correctional facility. Jail administrators did, however, acknowledge those issues will be much more prevalent if and when body scanners are used on visitors or guests entering a facility.

In the end, the debate on the viability and use of body scanners within jails or prisons is still ongoing. Both officers and administrators acknowledge that body scanners are just one type of technology used to identify contraband and were never meant as a replacement for diligent and personal security reviews. For many, a body scanner is nothing more than an additional tool in the tool chest when it comes to jail and prison security.

Discussion Questions

1. Is the use of body scanners by correctional officials too invasive, even for those in lockdown facilities with dramatically reduced expectations of privacy?

2. Given how easy it was for researchers to circumvent scanning results, could the use of body scanners in jails and prisons give officers and administrators a false sense of security?

3. What limits, if any, would you place on the use of body scanners within correctional facilities?

Global Positioning Systems

Finding new and innovative ways to hold offenders accountable, while at the same time maintaining public safety through monitoring and supervision, has been at the forefront of the American criminal justice system for some time. A favorite technology among correctional and court officials, that is now being challenged in a number of court cases, is the use of the **Global Positioning System (GPS)** (satellite-based monitoring and navigation technology). Traditionally used for high-risk offenders and sex offenders, GPS monitoring has been expanded and used in conjunction with the criminal justice system's desire to offer a greater number of alternative sanctions for individuals' violations of criminal law. As with any type of technology, especially those used for tracking or monitoring purposes, concerns over the violation of an offender's constitutional rights are ever present.

Take, for example, the case of Dennis A. Wilson, a pre-trial offender being charged with driving without a license, resisting arrest, and threatening a law enforcement officer. In question were the actions of probation officials when they shared Wilson's location data with police when they wanted to question him about a shooting near his home (Allen, 2015). Once Wilson's location was identified and the car he was a passenger in was pulled over, an officer approached the vehicle to question him. The driver of the vehicle, Angelo West, pulled a gun and shot the officer in the face. During an ensuing gunfight between West and other officers on the scene, West was killed and Wilson, who was not involved in either the shooting or gunfight, was taken into custody. At his hearing, Wilson's lawyer argued that probation officials had no right to share his location with law enforcement, stating, "My client has a private interest in his position even though he's enrolled in a GPS-monitoring program" (Manning, 2015, para. 11).

In a similar case, Torrey Dale Grady, a federal inmate convicted of being a repeat sex offender, also argued that collecting data about his location was illegal. While previous court cases focused on the use of GPS monitoring by law enforcement, Grady argued in a petition to the U.S. Supreme Court that forcing him to wear an ankle bracelet linked to satellite technology while on parole (that allowed corrections officials to know his exact whereabouts at any given time) was a violation of his Fourth Amendment right against an unreasonable search (Vaas, 2015). He felt that as long as the government, in this case, corrections, was gathering information about his location, that the acquisition of such data constituted a search and as such, was illegal to do without a warrant.

In March 2015, after hearing both sides, the Court unanimously sided with Grady and agreed that forcing him to wear a GPS tracker while on parole was a form of an illegal search and as such, a violation of his Fourth Amendment rights. In their decision, the Justices referenced two previous cases heard before the Court, "In 2012, it [the Court] ruled that placing a GPS tracker on a suspect's car, without a warrant, counted as an unreasonable search. The following year, it [the Court] said that using drug-sniffing dogs around a suspect's front porch—without a warrant and without their consent—was also unreasonable, as it trespassed onto a person's property to gain information about them" (Meyer, 2015, para. 8).

The recent ruling by the U.S. Supreme Court may well have far-reaching implications regarding the use of GPS technology and the monitoring and supervision of offenders. Even more problematic, however, is the affect this decision may have on the use of GPS monitoring as an alternative sanction. In response to the Court's decision, agencies may now react by eliminating the opportunity for **high-risk offenders** (criminals convicted of heinous offences such as murder, rape, and robbery) to serve their sentences and attend treatment outside of jail and prison walls. Only time will tell.

Discussion Questions

1. In your opinion, do individuals who agree to participate in GPS monitoring programs completely give up all rights to privacy regarding their locations?

2. If correctional officials use GPS monitoring, but do not archive the offender's location data, does their real-time use of the offender's location constitute a search?

3. Should correction agencies go back to older forms of electronic monitoring where officers were made aware of offender breaches of a specified electronic barrier, but were not given real-time location data?

Drug Dogs

As correctional facilities across the U.S. try to find innovative and effective methods of controlling and finding contraband, many institutions are implementing the use of **drug dogs** (canines specially trained to find illegal narcotics). Common breeds for drug dogs include German shepherds, Belgian malinois, and Dutch shepherds. Along with locating illegal narcotics within correctional facilities, drug dogs can also be trained to find other types of contraband that might constitute a security threat, such as illegal mobile phones (Warren, 2015).

While on the surface, the use of drug dogs might seem like a very positive blend of officer intuition and the canine's unique sense of smell, but for many, including the American Civil Liberties Union (ACLU), the use of drug dogs, especially with respect to staff and visitors, is troubling. According to the ACLU, a plaintiff in a lawsuit against the Massachusetts Department of Corrections, "Although DOC [Department of Corrections] is properly concerned about the presence of drugs inside the prisons, intrusive searches by dogs that may terrify children and be regarded as a significant invasion of privacy will inevitably reduce the numbers of visits and make it more difficult for those who do come to have a normal meeting with their loved ones" (Andersen, 2014, para. 3).

Jean Trounstine, a prison activist, agrees with the ACLU. According to Trounstine, when she questioned the Massachusetts DOC about research supporting the use of drug dogs as screening mechanisms for jail/prison visitors and staff, the agency couldn't provide any (Trounstine, 2013). She went on to cite an unnamed study from Australia that claimed "Without secrecy ... searches are not as effective, and secrecy is nearly impossible. Searches slow down as soon as dogs are present, and instead of acting as a deterrent, the dogs act as signals that searches are in process" (para. 2). Both Trounstine and the ACLU question the true intent of using drug dogs to search visitors and staff, and wonder if there aren't ulterior motives behind their actions.

In response to various concerns regarding the use of drug dogs and any possible adverse reactions or interactions with the animals, some agencies, such as the California Department of Corrections and Rehabilitation, are moving away from traditional drug dogs to passive or friendlier breeds, such as Labrador retrievers and German short-hair pointers. While maintaining their need to screen visitors and staff for security reasons, the department feels the use of dogs that appear to be less intimidating will lower the stress of those being searched and improve the visitors' experience (Thompson, 2014). Wayne Conrad, a retired dog handler for the California Department of Corrections and Rehabilitation disagreed with the need to change the breed to reduce the intimidation factor of the current drug dogs, stating, "Two of the (new) German shorthaired pointers are larger than any dog we have right now. They're more intimidating than most of the (malinois) that we have, so it didn't make any sense" (Warren, 2015, para. 14).

Discussion Questions

1. Do you feel the use of prison drug dogs to search visitors and staff is a violation of their Fourth Amendment right against an illegal search?

2. In your opinion, are corrections agencies actually using drug dogs as a law enforcement tool, instead of a screening mechanism?

3. Is the breed of dog used to screen visitors and staff an important part of the debate over their use?

Officer Corruption

While inmates are often the center of attention when it comes to contraband and other illicit activity within a lockdown facility, there are unfortunately times when it is the officers who are the culprits. Drug smuggling, illegal cell phones, and even officer prostitutes are just some of the nefarious activities corrections officers have committed and for which they have been found guilty. The crafty ways these illegal activities have occurred pale only in comparison to the damage the officers' actions have done to the profession of corrections.

One high-profile case of officer corruption occurred at New York City's Rikers Island in 2014. Seven corrections officers were charged with a variety of offences ranging from smuggling drugs to assaults on inmates and even **falsifying records** (a type of white-collar crime that involves changing an official document to deceive one or more people) (NBC News, 2014). According to prosecutors, "Correction Officers Steven Dominguez and Divine Rahming boasted of sneaking cocaine and oxycodone into Rikers five times in the past few months. They also offered to use their 'badge and gun' as protection for drug dealing outside the jail" (Smith, 2014, para. 7).

In another case out of Rikers Island, officer turned criminal turned inmate turned author Gary Heyward ran a big drug smuggling and prostitution business out of his unit at the facility. In a book written by Heyward, he detailed the life of a criminal who was employed as a corrections officer. According to the former officer, "He would strap bags of tobacco to his body underneath his uniform to work and would sell $2 worth for around $200. For $500 he would also deliver burner phones to an inmate and would set higher prices for more specific orders — such as liquor, coke, cooch [female sex organ] and, in one instance, red velvet cupcakes" (Robinson, 2015, para. 7 & 8). Heyward's life of craftiness and corruption expanded when he was approached by a female corrections officer who asked if he would provide protection for her and two other female officers while they sold sex to inmates. "Heyward called the jailhouse sex workers 'copstitutes' — law enforcement officers who turned tricks. His illicit hustle behind bars earned him so much cash, his city job was merely icing on the cake" (Connelly, 2015, para. 2). Unfortunately for Heyward, his life of crime ended when he was arrested on multiple counts of corruption and sentenced to two years in prison. An interesting twist to Gary Heyward's story, however, is that after all of the corruption, the multiple violations of his oath as an officer, and his time spent in prison for crimes committed while working as a corrections officer for New York City, he is now employed, once again, by the city of New York and his promoting his book that details his life of crime, corruption, and dishonor (Washington, 2013).

Discussion Questions

1. Like drug dealers outside of prison, should correctional employees who profit from selling drugs inside a correctional facility face the possibility of having their homes and cars confiscated if a connection can be made between their illegal profits and the purchase of these items?

2. In your opinion, when a corrections officer sneaks contraband into a facility, what is damaged more, the image of the profession or the public trust?

Officers and Contraband

Contraband within a correctional facility is an ever-present and growing problem worldwide. For example, the New Zealand Department of Corrections saw a 61% increase in contraband system-wide between the years 2010 and 2016 (Department of Corrections, 2018). Items typically referred to as contraband include drugs, **drug paraphernalia** (implements used to ingest illegal drugs), weapons, alcohol, tattoo equipment, money, and tobacco. Historically, blame for the introduction of contraband into a correctional facility has been placed on visitors, primarily the offender's family and friends. New evidence, however, places culpability for these occurrences squarely on the shoulders of correctional officers and staff.

During a 2018 study by the Prison Policy Initiative, researchers found that sheriff departments routinely claimed that getting rid of in-person visits, in favor of **video visits** (monitors that allow for inmates to visit family and friends without having to take the offender out of their housing unit), would make their facilities safer and reduce the occurrences of contraband being introduced into their facilities (Renaud, 2018). Prison Policy Initiative officials claimed that a review of news stories addressing arrests for introducing contraband inside of jails and prisons during 2018 clearly showed that almost all of the contraband coming into jails did so because of correctional staff. Their research showed that in that year alone, "20 jail staff members in 12 separate county jails were arrested, indicted, or convicted on charges of bringing in or planning to bring in contraband" (Renaud, 2018, para. 4).

While the methodology of this study is questionable, news articles do seem to show the possibility of this growing and disturbing trend. For example, three correctional officers were recently arrested in the state of New York for accepting bribes to traffic drugs and other contraband inside a private correctional facility. Officers Jermaine Harmon, Khari Faison, and Compton Richmond were all charged with bringing drugs, cell phones, and other contraband inside a correctional facility. The private jail, located in Queens, New York, also houses federal inmates for the **United States Marshals Service** (the oldest law enforcement agency in the United States), so their charges will be heard in federal, not state court (U.S. Department of Justice, 2020). According to Special Agent in Charge Guido Modano, "The public relies on Correctional Officers to maintain order and uphold the law. Instead, these three Correctional Officers allegedly accepted bribes for smuggling drugs and cell phones into the jail, endangering their fellow Correctional Officers, staff, inmates and the public, and also jeopardizing the security of the jail facility" (para. 3). If convicted of all charges, each offender is facing up to 20 years in prison.

In another disturbing case, three Baltimore corrections officers were indicted for their role in an alleged racketeering case that involved smuggling contraband into downtown Baltimore's Chesapeake Detention Facility. Officers Darren Parker, Andre Davis, and Talaia Youngblood were charged with sneaking drugs, tobacco, and cell phones into the facility, beginning as early as 2016 (Gessler, 2020). The indictment claims the three offenders used clothing, bags, and food containers to hide the illegal items as they passed through security check points. Once inside, they would leave the contraband in predetermined locations throughout the facility for inmates to pick up and distribute. If convicted, all three offenders could face up to 20 in prison.

Discussion Questions

1. In your opinion, should correctional officers receive harsher sentences for introducing contraband to a correctional facility than their civilian counterparts?

2. Should some types of contraband, such as illegal drugs, carry a harsher sentence than other types of contraband, such as tobacco?

3. If you were the sheriff of a local jail, what steps would you take to catch officers and staff introducing contraband into your facility?

Breaking into Jail

While most people are either trying to break out of or just stay out of jail, there are some individuals who have actually been caught trying to break in. One such case involved 24-year-old Patrick Rempe of Indian River County, Florida. Rempe, feeling a little blue over the Christmas holiday and missing his friends, who were locked up in the county jail, decided it was time for him to visit his buddies. Instead of waiting for normal visiting hours, however, Rempe, who claimed his was high on **flakka** (a synthetic drug), got into his car, crashed into the front door of the facility, barely missing a sheriff's deputy, and then attempted to climb a fence to get in (Duchon, 2015). Unfortunately for him, facility officers quickly responded and charged Patrick with "aggravated assault on a law enforcement officer, battery on a law enforcement officer, three counts of felony criminal mischief, leaving the scene of a crash with property damage and driving under the influence" (Moye, 2015, para. 8). To make matters worse, Rempe will most likely have to pay for the damages to the facility's fence, estimated at $5,000. To compound matters, even if he had gotten over the first fence, he would have then had to climb an interior fence and find a way to get past the locked door of the building that housed his friends.

Another bizarre case involved Monique Armstrong of Mesa, Colorado. Distraught that her 18-year-old brother was being incarcerated on suspicion of driving the wrong way, possession of drug paraphernalia, and driving under the influence of drugs, Monique felt she needed to take matters into her own hands. The 22-year-old sister decided her brother should not spend another moment in jail and actually called 911 to tell officers she was going to the Mesa County Jail to get her brother out (Greenwood, 2014). After setting off the facility's perimeter alarms, Armstrong was found entrapped in the chain-link fence and razor wire. Once officers assisted her out of the fence and into the jail, Monique decided to break the smash-proof **jail pod** (a housing unit inside a jail) windows in an attempt to free her brother (who was nowhere near her unit). Unfortunately for Ms. Armstrong, she was charged with suspicion of theft and first-degree criminal trespass, and her brother was released on bond five hours after her arrest.

Finally, in true *Shawshank Redemption* fashion, 25-year-old Sylvester Jiles didn't enjoy life after prison and just wanted to go back and hang out with his friends. After three days of freedom, Jiles, who was convicted of manslaughter, walked up to correctional officers at the Brevard County Detention Center in Florida and asked to be let back in because he claimed he was afraid the family of the victim might try to harm him (Wright, 2010). Confused at his request, the officers turned him away and told him to file a police report. That didn't deter Sylvester, however, who proceeded to climb the center's 12-foot exterior fence, eventually getting caught in its razor wire. After being rescued by the facility's officers and given medical treatment for his cuts and bruises, Jiles got his wish and was booked back into the jail for trespassing on jail property and resisting an officer (MSNBC Staff, 2010). At his new court hearing reality began to sink in, and Sylvester lashed out at the presiding judge. After being led out of the courtroom, Jiles received 15 additional years behind bars for his new offenses and for violating his probation. Once he had calmed down, Sylvester apologized to the judge and said "I'm not going against your sentence, sir. You say 15 years. It is what it is" (para. 6).

Discussion Questions

1. Should inmates who fear for their safety upon release from jail or prison be allowed to stay within the jail or prison?

2. Should someone charged with attempting to break into a correctional facility be punished in the same manner as someone who attempted to break out?

3. If you were in charge of a local jail or prison, how concerned would you be with someone attempting to break into your facility?

Chapter Key Terms

Nolo contendere
Remanded
Cross complaint
Habeas corpus
Double-blind administration
Random drug tests
National Institute of Justice
Inmate segregation
Holding cells
Body scanners
Transportation Security Administration

Global Positioning System
High-risk offenders
Drug dogs
Falsifying records
Drug paraphernalia
Video visits
United States Marshals Service
Flakka
Jail pod

References

Accardo, J., & Chaudhry, M. A. (2014). Radiation exposure and privacy concerns surrounding full-body scanners in airports. *Journal of Radiation Research and Applied Sciences*, 7(2), 198–200.

Ackerman, M. (2014, May 8). Sheriff's department sued by school district after autistic boy arrested in drug sting. *The Fix*. http://www.thefix.com/content/sheriffs-department-sued-school-district-after-autistic-boy-arrested-drug-sting.

Alcantara, C. (2013, January). Body scanner gives jail inside view of criminals. https://jailtraining.org/body-scanner-gives-fl-jail-inside-view-of-criminals/ (site last visited on April 23, 2021).

Allen, E. (2015). GPS led police to vehicle involved in officer shooting. *The Boston Globe*. www.bostonglobe.com.

American Civil Liberties Union (ACLU). (2014). Privacy in America: Workplace drug testing. www.aclu.org.

Anderson, N. (2013, October 13). Entrapped! When Craigslist predator stings go too far. Ars Technica. http://arstechnica.com/tech-policy/2013/10/entrapped-when-craigslist-predator-stings-go-too-far/.

Andersen, T. (2014, January). Lawsuit objects to prison visit searches. *The Boston Globe*. www.bostonglobe.com.

Blidner, R. (2015, August). Texas sheriff tells pastor keeping vigil for Sandra Bland she runs "church of satan." *New York Daily News*. www.nydailynews.com.

Brown, E. N. (2014, May). Pregnant women increasingly face criminal prosecution for positive drug tests. Reason. www.reason.com.

Celizic, M. (2009, March 10). She sent him to jail for rape; now they're friends. Today. https://www.today.com/news/she-sent-him-jail-rape-now-theyre-friends-1C9016956.

Chang, L. (2014). The Duke Lacrosse rape scandal was 8 years ago, so where are they now? Bustle. http://www.bustle.com/articles/26053-the-duke-lacrosse-rape-scandal-was-8-years-ago-so-where-are-the-accused-now.

Cisco-Eagle. (2015). Prisoner holding cell. www.cisco-eagle.com.

Connelly, S. (2015, March). Ex-Rikers guard, who served time for selling drugs to inmates, also pimped out female officers as 'copstitutes': Book. *New York Daily News*. www.nydailynews.com.

Cook, J. (2011). How the weirdos behind 'To Catch a Predator' blew $1.2 million. Gawker. http://gawker.com/5789577/how-the-weirdos-behind-to-catch-a-predator-blew-12-million.

Cutler, A. (2014, September). Salt Lake County inmates to face full body scanners. Fox 13 News. www.fox13now.com.

Dart, T., & Swaine, J. (2015, July). Sandra Bland: Suspicion and mistrust flourish amid official inconsistencies. *The Guardian*. www.theguardian.com.

Department of Corrections. (2018). Contraband in prisons. New Zealand. https://www.corrections.govt.nz/resources/statistics/contraband_in_prisons.

Downs, D. (2014). Drug cops sting autistic boy; school sues. *East Bay Express*. http://www.eastbayexpress.com/LegalizationNation/archives/2014/05/06/drug-cops-sting-autistic-boy-school-sues.

Duchon, R. (2015, December 16). Man high on "Flakka" rams car into county jail, spits on deputy. NBC News. https://www.nbcnews.com/news/us-news/man-high-flakka-rams-car-county-jail-spits-deputy-n481536.

The Drug Policy Alliance. (2014). Alabama Supreme Court rules that women can be charged with chemical endangerment if they become pregnant and use a controlled substance. www.drugpolicy.org.

The Drug Policy Alliance. (2015). Drug testing policies. www.drugpolicy.org.

Eyewitness Identification-Getting it Right (n.d.). Innocence Project. http://www.innocenceproject.org/causes-wrongful-conviction/eyewitness-misidentification.

Farberov, S. (2013, July). Woman who hid loaded gun inside genitals (and bags of meth in her butt) sentenced to 25 years in prison. *Daily Mail*.www.dailymail.co.uk.

Garcia, A. (2013, September). Oklahoma inmate caught "keistering" a loaded gun into jail. Raw Story. www.rawstory.com.

Gardiner, B. (2014). Stunning 'not guilty': Adrian Thomas acquitted of killing infant son six years ago at second trial. *Times Union*. https://www.timesunion.com/local/article/Adrian-Thomas-found-not-guilty-in-son-s-death-5548244.php.

Gavin, R. (2014). Court: Police 'cajoled' murder confession. *Times Union*. http://blog.timesunion.com/crime/court-of-appeals-reverses-adrian-thomas-murder-conviction/14344/.

Gennette v. State, 124 So. 3d 273 (Fla. Dist. Ct. App. 2013).

Gessler, P. (2020, October 21). 9 indicted, including 3 correctional officers, after allegedly smuggling contraband into Baltimore jail. CBS Baltimore. https://baltimore.cbslocal.com/2020/10/21/9-indicted-including-correctional-officers-after-allegedly-smuggling-contraband-into-baltimore-jail/.

Giang, V. (2012, July). Inmate talks to us over an illegal cell phone about working the jailhouse black market. Business Insider.www.businessinsider.com.

Greenwood, M. (2014, May 1). Colorado woman braves razor wire to free brother from jail, ends up arrested as he is released. *New York Daily News*.

https://www.nydailynews.com/news/national/colorado-woman-braves -razor-wire-free-brother-jail-ends-arrested-article-1.1775196.

Groppe, M. (2014, October). Full-body scanners used for local inmates may be flawed. *Lansing State Journal*. www.lansingstatejournal.com.

Hughes, V. (2014). Why police lineups will never be perfect. *The Atlantic*. http://www.theatlantic.com/technology/archive/2014/10/the-evolving -science-of-police-lineups/381046/.

Lewis, J. (2012). Man arrested in Clay County sting found dead in home. ABC First Coast News. http://www.firstcoastnews.com/news/article/251005/3/ Man-Arrested-in-Clay-County-Sting-Found-Dead-in-Home.

Mahoney, A. (2013). Cops are pretending to be high schoolers ... obligatory *21 Jump Street* reference? Law Street Media. https://legacy.lawstreetmedia. com/news/cops-are-pretending-to-be-high-schoolers-obligatory-21-jump -street-reference/.

Man facing child solicitation charges found dead in Collier. (2013). NBC2 News. http://www.nbc-2.com/story/22056832/body-found-near-collier -hazmat-scene#.VVD94Y4YF2D.

Manning, A. (2015, April). Are police violating privacy with GPS tracking? www.boston.com.

Manuel-Logan, R. (2013, July). Oklahoma woman who hid loaded gun in vagina gets 25 years. NewsOne. www.newsone.com.

McCluskey, B. (2013, September). Derringer stashed in inmate's rectum brings new meaning to the term "pocket pistol." www.guns.com.

McKinley, J. (2014). Court weighs police role in coercing confessions. *The New York Times*. http://www.nytimes.com/2014/01/15/nyregion/court-weighs -police-role-in-coercing-confessions.html?_r=0.

Meyer, R. (2015, March). U.S. Supreme Court: GPS trackers are a form of search and seizure. *The Atlantic*. www.theatlantic.com.

Miles, K. (2013). Cops pretend to be 11th graders, then arrest 25 students. Huffington Post. http://www.huffingtonpost.com/2013/12/13/cops -arrest-25-students-drug-sting_n_4442172.html?utm_hp_ref=college&ir= College.

Miller v. Fenton, *474 U.S. 104* (1985).

Miller v. Fenton (1985). Justia: US Supreme Court. https://supreme.justia.com/ cases/federal/us/474/104/.

Moran, L. (2013, September). Man jailed in Oklahoma caught with loaded pistol in his backside. *New York Daily News*. www.nydailynews.com.

Moye, D. (2015, December 17). Florida man arrested for attempting to break into jail. Huffington Post. https://www.huffpost.com/entry/florida-man -arrested-for-attempting-to-break-into-jail_n_5671cce6e4b0688701dbfd9b.

MSNBC Staff. (2010, March 23). Man gets 15 years after trying to break jail. NBC News. https://www.nbcnews.com/id/wbna36000255.

National Academy of Sciences. (2014). *Identifying the culprit: Assessing eyewitness identification.* http://www.nap.edu/openbook.php?record_id=188 91&page=R1.

National Commission on Correctional Health Care. (2015). Segregated inmates. www.ncchc.org.

National Institute of Justice (NIJ). (2012, February). HOPE program evaluation. www.nij.gov.

NBC News. (2014, June). Investigators sweep Rikers Island in probe of guards for alleged smuggling. NBC News. www.nbcnews.com.

Neff, J., Biesecker, M., & Khana, S. (2006). Police and prosecutor under scrutiny in lacrosse case. *The Times-News.* https://news.google.com/newspapers? nid=1665&dat=20060429&id=czEaAAAAIBAJ&sjid=XyUEAAAAIBAJ& pg=7022,5979415&hl=en.

Pandit, E. (2015, August). Inside the struggle for justice at the Texas jailhouse where Sandra Bland died. AlterNet.www.alternet.org.

People v. Thomas, 22 N.Y.3d 629; 8 N.E.3d 308 (2014).

Pransky, N. (2014). ACLU leader wants federal review of Polk sex stings. https://www.news-press.com/story/news/investigations/2014/08/12/aclu -leader-wants-federal-review-of-judd-sex-stings/13914073/.

Pransky, N. (2015). How law enforcement turns law-abiding men into sexual predators. https://www.wtsp.com/article/news/investigations/how-law -enforcement-turns-law-abiding-men-into-sexual-predators/67-236499 759.

Renaud, J. (2018). Who's really bringing contraband into jails? Our 2018 survey confirms it's staff, not visitors. Prison Policy Initiative. https://www.prison policy.org/blog/2018/12/06/jail-contraband/.

Robinson, W. (2015, March). Ex-Rikers Island guard, who served time for smuggling drugs and tobacco to inmates, also pimped out female officers as 'copstitutes' to prisoners and jail bosses. *The Daily Mail.* www.daily mail.co.uk.

Ronald Cotton. (n.d.). Innocence Project. http://www.innocenceproject.org/ cases-false-imprisonment/ronald-cotton.

Rubin Erdely, S. (2014). The entrapment of Jesse Snodgrass. *Rolling Stone.* http://www.rollingstone.com/culture/news/the-entrapment-of-jesse-snod grass-20140226.

Sanburn, J. (2014). Behind the messy science of police lineups. *Time.* http:// time.com/3461043/police-lineups-eyewitness-science/.

Sanchez, R. (2015, July). Who was Sandra Bland? CNN. www.cnn.com.

Schuppe. J. (2015, July). The death of Sandra Bland: What we know so far. NBC News.www.nbcnews.com.

Setrakian, L. (2006). Police report sheds new light on Duke case. ABC News. http://abcnews.go.com/US/story?id=1877707.

Shealy, M. (2014). The haunting of man: Lies, damn lies, and police interrogations. *University of Miami Race & Social Justice Law Review*, 4, 21–71.

Smith, G. (2014, July). Rikers Island correction officers charged with smuggling cocaine, oxycodone. *New York Daily News*. www.nydailynews.com.

The Smoking Gun. (2011, March). Man "keistered" cell phone, MP3 player, headphones, cash, pot into California jail. www.thesmokinggun.com.

Snodgrass, D. (2014). School district sues police, claims our autistic son was victim of unconstitutional entrapment. Daily Kos. http://www.dailykos. com/story/2014/05/05/1296673/-School-District-Sues-Police-Claims-Our -Autistic-Son-Was-Victim-of-Unconstitutional-Entrapment#.

Thompson, D. (2014, September). Correction: California prisons-drug screening. *The San Diego Union-Tribune*.www.sandiegouniontribune.com.

Trounstine, J. (2013). Prison visitors sniffed by drug detection dogs: This isn't a fix. www.jeantrounstine.com.

Twenty-five men arrested during undercover child sex sting (with names, mugshots) (2011). http://www.northescambia.com/2011/06/breaking-two -dozen-men-arrested-during-child-sex-sting.

U.S. Department of Justice. (2020, March 5). Three correction officers arrested for taking bribes to smuggle drugs and other contraband into private jail. U.S. Attorney's Office, Southern District of New York. https://www.justice. gov/usao-sdny/pr/three-correction-officers-arrested-taking-bribes-smuggle -drugs-and-other-contraband.

Vaas, L. (2015, April). GPS tracking counts as a "search," says US Supreme Court. Naked Security by Sophos. www.nakedsecurity.sophos.com.

Van Brocklin, V. (2014). Case law on police deception. PoliceOne. http://www. policeone.com/legal/articles/6909121-Case-law-on-police-deception/.

Virtanen, M. (2014, February 20). NYS Court of Appeals overturns Adrian Thomas' murder conviction. The Associated Press. http://www.troyrecord. com/general-news/20140220/nys-court-of-appeals-overturns-adrian-thomas -murder-conviction.

Warren, G. (2015, March). Veteran prison dog handler resigns over new drug search program. ABC10 News.www.abc10.com.

Washington, G. (2013, November). The officer. National Public Radio. www. npr.org.

Weston, V. (2006). Lax case shines light on police lineup process. *Duke Chronicle*. http://www.dukechronicle.com/articles/2006/04/26/lax-case-shines-light-police-lineup-process#.VVVrbo4YF2C.

Winkler, A. (2014). Police entrap autistic teenager in drug sting. Reason. http://reason.com/blog/2014/03/12/police-entrap-autistic-teenager.

Wright, T. (2010, March 23). Man gets 15 years for breaking into prison. NBC Miami. https://www.nbcmiami.com/news/local/man-gets-15-years-for-breaking-back-into-jail/1851784/.

Chapter Nine

Favoritism

> All animals are equal, but some animals are more equal than others.
> — George Orwell, *Animal Farm* (1945)

Like a parent, the government is expected to refrain from **favoritism**. The Constitution requires government actors to treat all people equally without regard to race, ethnicity, or sex. Inscribed over the entrance to the Supreme Court building in Washington, D.C., are the words "Equal Justice Under Law" which echoes similar language in the Fourteenth Amendment's **Equal Protection Clause** ("nor shall any State ... deny to any person within its jurisdiction the equal protection of the laws") codifying the prohibition against government favoritism. This prohibition against favoritism is most famously explored in cases such as *Brown v. Board of Education* and *Cooper v. Aaron*, which struck down racial segregation in schools.

Criminal Law and Courts

Favoritism in the criminal justice system is most serious when the state criminalizes an action by one person while permitting other persons to perform that same act without penalty. This is particularly unfair when those singled out are discriminated against for a permanent, immutable characteristic that is largely (or entirely) outside of their own control, such as race, gender, etc. Since the end of World War II in 1945, the Supreme Court has taken a dim view of laws that treat people of one race differently than those of another.

Discrimination on other grounds, though, has been more difficult for the Court to address, as we shall see in several of the cases in this chapter. Even discrimination on the basis of race has been sufficiently contentious to serve as grounds for three of the cases in this chapter.

Craig v. Boren
429 U.S. 190 (1976)

The Court turned its attention to criminal justice and the issue of gender discrimination in our first case in this chapter. The Court considered an Oklahoma statute that treated men and women differently in terms of purchasing alcoholic beverages. At the time, men between the ages of 18 and 21 years were prohibited from purchasing 3.2% beer in Oklahoma, while women in that same age range were free to purchase such beer.

Prior to this case the Court had considered laws discriminating on the basis of race under the **strict scrutiny standard**. To find a law that discriminated on the basis of race to be constitutional under this standard, the state would have to justify the law as advancing not just any government interest, but *a compelling state interest*. In other words, the government would need to demonstrate a very important reason to treat people differently based on race. Additionally, the law would have to be *narrowly tailored* to advance that compelling state interest without any less restrictive alternatives to achieve that interest. The government could not use race if it could achieve its very important purpose in a different way without using race. It was unclear, however, what level of judicial scrutiny the Court should use when evaluating statutes such as the one at issue in the *Craig v. Boren* case, which treated people differently because of their gender.

The Court held that the Oklahoma statute violated the Equal Protection Clause of the Fourteenth Amendment. In doing so the Court adopted a new level of judicial scrutiny for gender-based discrimination. This new standard was not as difficult to satisfy as the strict scrutiny standard but was not as forgiving or as easy to satisfy as the **rational basis standard** favored by the dissenters in the *Craig v. Boren* case. The rational basis standard is the easiest judicial scrutiny test to satisfy and is satisfied whenever the government can articulate a legitimate government interest supporting the regulation. This is the standard which we will see applied in the *Plyer v. Doe, City of Cleburne,* and *Romer v. Evans* cases discussed later in this chapter.

This new **intermediate scrutiny standard** adopted in *Craig v. Boren* required that laws that discriminate on the basis of gender "must serve *impor-*

tant governmental objectives and must be *substantially related* to achievement of those objectives" in order to pass judicial scrutiny and be ruled constitutional (emphasis added). In other words, the government needed a good reason to discriminate on the basis of gender (i.e., "important governmental objective"), but not as critically important a reason as required by the strict scrutiny standard (i.e., "compelling state interest"). The connection between the government objective and the regulation was also allowed to be slightly looser ("substantially related" vs. "narrowly tailored").

The state of Oklahoma passed the first part of the new intermediate scrutiny test. Oklahoma certainly had an important government interest in promoting traffic safety, and particularly in preventing DUI accidents and fatalities. The problem was the connection between the gender category in the statute and the state's traffic safety objective. While Oklahoma attempted to justify its gender discrimination against young males on the basis of improving traffic safety, the Supreme Court found that the objective (traffic safety) and the regulation (which addressed only young males) were not sufficiently connected. The state of Oklahoma presented statistics to show that males were more dangerous due to increased rates of drinking and driving, but the Court held these statistics "cannot support the conclusion that the gender-based distinction closely serves to achieve that objective." Even though DUI arrests of 18-to-20-year-old males "substantially exceeded" female arrests for that same age group, and that males were overrepresented among those killed or injured in automobile accidents, these statistical findings were not sufficient, according to the Court, to justify the state's discrimination on the basis of gender.

The basic fact was that DUI arrest rates for both young women (.18% of females in the age group) and young men (2% of males in the age group) were both quite low, although there was a statistically significant gender disparity. "While such a disparity is not trivial in a statistical sense, it hardly can form the basis for employment of a gender line as a classifying device." In short, the connection between the gender category and the state's objective has to be quite close, and not even modest statistical evidence will be enough to justify the connection under the Equal Protection Clause. The Court went on to note that previous cases had rejected the use of gender as a reason to treat people differently in statutes when there was a greater connection to an important government interest than was presented by Oklahoma. It is interesting that *Craig v. Boren*, one of the first cases to address gender discrimination and apply the new intermediate scrutiny standard, was a case that found that the state government had discriminated against males, not females.

Discussion Questions

1. How much difference between the sexes should the state be required to show before being able to treat men and women differently? For example, should the government be able to prohibit topless women, but not topless men, in public?

2. Should it be any easier for the government to discriminate on the basis of gender than on the basis of race? Do you agree with the Court's creation of the new intermediate scrutiny standard?

Michael M. v. Superior Court of Sonoma County
450 U.S. 464 (1981)

Within a few years of *Craig v. Boren*, the Court was asked to address whether or not gender differences could ever legitimately form the basis for the state treating people differently in criminal law. Was any statute that treated people differently on the basis of sex necessarily unconstitutional favoritism, or were there some justifiable reasons to treat people of different genders differently? In the *Michael M* case, the state of California made statutory rape a crime for males but did not make similarly situated females criminally liable. The state of California's theory for treating females more favorably was based on the fact that females were already disproportionally subjected to serious consequences (such as risk of pregnancy and associated medical risks, etc.) as a result of under-age sex.

The biological fact that only women become pregnant, coupled with cultural and economic realities concerning employment and the educational consequences of teenage pregnancy, led the state to argue that its differential treatment of the sexes was justified. The U.S. Supreme Court agreed: "[T]he Equal Protection Clause does not demand that a statute necessarily apply equally to all persons or require things which are different in fact to be treated in law as though they were the same." The Court noted that it would uphold statutes where the gender classification realistically reflects the fact the sexes are not similarly situated in certain circumstances. The Supreme Court observed: "Only women may become pregnant, and they suffer disproportionately the profound physical, emotional, and psychological consequences of sexual activity. The statute at issue here protects women from sexual intercourse at an age when those consequences are particularly severe." The Court went on to note that virtually all the significant harmful consequences of teenage pregnancy fall on the young female, and therefore the California Legislature acted well within its authority when it elected to punish the only participant who, biologically and culturally, suffers few of the consequences of his conduct.

The Court also noted California's concern that criminalizing female conduct would dissuade females from coming forward to report illegal sexual activity. While the dissenters took issue with California's concern as a justification for treating males and females differently, the majority found that these types of issues should properly be left with state legislatures to consider. The concurring opinion by Justice Stewart went on to say more specifically that a pregnant, unmarried female confronts "problems more numerous and more severe" than those faced by her male partner. "She alone endures the medical risks of pregnancy or abortion" while suffering disproportionately "the social, educational, and emotional consequences of pregnancy." While quite similar to the majority's statement above, these comments recognize there are medical risks of pregnancy that a male simply does not face at all, and some risk of ongoing harms, like those stemming from missed educational opportunities, that may endure long after the pregnancy itself.

Discussion Questions

1. Do you think the majority was correct? Are there sometimes good enough reasons to treat males and females differently? Are the concerns around pregnancy sufficient to do that here?

2. Have times changed sufficiently since this case was decided in 1976 (less societal and employment discrimination against pregnant women) that these types of government discrimination based on gender should no longer be allowed under the Equal Protection Clause?

McCleskey v. Kemp

481 U.S. 279 (1987)

In the *McCleskey* case the issue was one of racial discrimination. Instead of a state statute specifically treating people differently, as seen in the previous cases in this chapter, here McClesky claimed the death penalty was administered and applied in a way that treated African Americans less favorably due to their race. Evidence presented by his defense teams showed that defendants who killed white victims were more likely to receive the death penalty.

Warren McCleskey, who was African American, was convicted of killing an off-duty white police officer during a robbery in Georgia in the 1970s. Mc-Cleskey's lawyers argued that how the death penalty was administered in the state of Georgia discriminated on the basis of race, thus violating the Equal Protection Clause. Specifically, McClesky relied upon a statistical study conducted by three professors, including David C. Baldus of the University of Iowa College of Law. The study became known as the Baldus study. It examined more than 2000 murder cases in Georgia during the 1970s. The study determined that defendants who killed African Americans were less likely to receive the death penalty than those who killed whites.

> [D]efendants charged with killing white persons receive the death penalty in 11% of the cases, but defendants charged with killing blacks receive the death penalty in only 1% of the cases.... [T]he death penalty was assessed in 22% of the cases involving black defendants and white victims; 8% of the cases involving white defendants and white victims; 1% of the cases involving black defendants and black victims; and 3% of the cases involving white defendants and black victims.

In large part, this seemed to be due to decisions made by prosecutors, who were much more likely to seek the death penalty in cases involving black defendants and white victims versus other types of cases. Defendants charged with killing white victims were 4.3 times as likely to receive a death sentence as defendants charged with killing blacks.

Despite the statistical evidence that the death penalty was administered and applied differently, based particularly on the race of the victims, the Supreme Court still upheld the death penalty for McCleskey. It did so by rejecting statistical evidence (showing that the entire system in Georgia included racial discrimination) as sufficient to demonstrate racial prejudice in McCleskey's individual case. The Court focused instead on the lack of evidence of any racial discrimination specifically in McCleskey's case. The Supreme Court's precedent held that proving an equal protection violation requires proving purposeful discrimination. McCleskey was required to prove that the decision-makers in his specific case acted with discriminatory purpose. McCleskey offered "no evidence specific to his own case that would support an inference that racial considerations played a part in his sentence. Instead, he [relied] solely on the Baldus study."

The Court was concerned that if such statistical evidence were accepted, it would impact not only McCleskey's case but all capital punishment cases across the state of Georgia. While the Court had accepted statistical evidence to help prove racial discrimination in a few other types of cases, the Court found that the use of social science data was inappropriate in capital sentencing decisions because neither the prosecutor, nor especially the jury, would be in a position to rebut or refute claims of racially prejudiced decision making in individual cases. Capital sentencing decisions were fundamentally different from other types of cases where the Supreme Court had relied upon statistical evidence. The difference stemmed from the uniqueness of each capital -sentencing decision:

> Most importantly, each particular decision to impose the death penalty is made by a petit jury selected from a properly constituted venire. Each jury is unique in its composition, and the Constitution requires that its decision rest on consideration of innumerable factors that vary according to the characteristics of the individual defendant and the facts of the particular capital offense.

The Court also noted that prosecutors have traditionally enjoyed wide discretion to make charging decisions and sentencing recommendations, and this discretion would be undermined if prosecutors were required to defend their decisions to seek the death penalty "often years after they were made." Implementation of capital punishment laws requires a healthy dose of discretion. "Because discretion is essential to the criminal justice process, we would demand exceptionally clear proof before we would infer that the discretion has been abused." The majority held that the Baldus study was "clearly insufficient" to support an inference that any of the decision-makers in McCleskey's case acted with discriminatory purpose.

This was a closely contested case, with the Court divided 5 to 4. The dissenters were upset that the majority did not give more credence to the statistical evidence contained in the Baldus study. The dissenters focused on the fact the defendants charged with killing white victims in Georgia were 4.3 times more likely to be sentenced to death than defendants charged with killing black victims. Justice Brennan, writing for the dissenters, specifically noted that "there was a significant chance that race would play a prominent role in determining if [McClesky] lived or died." The dissenters argued that it was this risk that was the critical consideration. The dissenters noted that in previous cases, "the Court [had] been concerned with the *risk* of the imposition of an arbitrary sentence, rather than the proven fact of one." The dissenters argued that the focus on risk "acknowledges the difficulty of divining the jury's motivation in an individual case" and thus is more appropriate than a legal standard that requires specific proof of racial discrimination in an individual case.

Discussion Questions

1. Was the Court correct to require McCleskey to prove racism affected decision making in McCleskey's individual case, instead of allowing social science data to show there is a problem with the system as a whole?

2. Should discriminatory impact be treated the same as discriminatory intent?

Discrimination against Other Groups

The Equal Protection Clause not only protects against discrimination on the basis of race and gender but protects against discrimination on the basis of other characteristics as well, even if to a lesser degree. Our next case presents a situation where the criminal justice system is permitted to discriminate against noncitizens in hiring, but other parts of the government are limited in how they may discriminate against noncitizens when licensing officials.

Bernal v. Fainter
467 U.S. 216 (1984)

Mr. Bernal was a Mexican citizen who moved to the United States in 1961. He began to work for a rural legal aid group in Texas, helping migrant farmworkers. To further assist farmworkers with legal matters, he attempted to become a **notary public** in Texas. A notary public has a government license to verify (i.e., notarize) signatures, helping prove the person signing legal documents is who he or she claims to be. Unfortunately for Mr. Bernal and his farm worker clients, a Texas statute prohibited noncitizens from serving as notary publics. Since Mr. Bernal was a Mexican, not American, citizen, he was ineligible to become a notary public under the state statute.

Mr. Bernal challenged the Texas statute in federal district court. The district court ruled in his favor, finding the Texas statute violated the Equal Protection Clause of the Fourteenth Amendment. However, the Fifth Circuit Court of Appeals reversed and upheld the Texas statute. At that point, Mr. Bernal took his case to the United States Supreme Court.

The Supreme Court noted that generally, "a state law that discriminates on the basis of alienage can be sustained only if it can withstand strict judicial scrutiny." However, there is a **political function exception** that covers regulations for government officials administering policies associated with democratic government. When the exception applies, states are permitted to discriminate on the basis of citizenship and prohibit noncitizens from performing certain jobs. The Court held the exception did not apply to the Texas notary public statute because none of the activities that Mr. Bernal engaged in directly impacted representative democracy. The Court noted that "Texas notaries are not invested with policymaking responsibility or broad discretion." The Court struck down the Texas notary public law by relying on previous **precedents** (earlier court cases considering the same or similar legal issues), which had struck down similar state laws excluding noncitizens from working as attorneys and civil engineers. Yet the Court recognized it had previously upheld state laws preventing noncitizens from serving as schoolteachers, as well as police and probation officers since people performing these jobs routinely exercise discretion in applying government policies. Indeed, law enforcement and corrections officers "routinely exercise the State's monopoly of legitimate coercive force."

So, while the Court has allowed states to sometimes play favorites on the basis of citizenship, the Court's decision in *Bernal v. Fainter* can be seen as limiting the legal exception which allows states to play favorites. Why are attorneys and notary publics more protected against discrimination by application of strict scrutiny to enforce the Equal Protection Clause, whereas laws prohibiting noncitizens from working as teachers were scrutinized under a lower standard? This is because, according to the Court, teachers "present materials that educate youth respecting the information and values necessary for the maintenance of a democratic political system." Teachers and law enforcement work directly for the government, have some control over how government chooses to implement its laws, and have direct authority over other individuals. Notary publics, and even attorneys, do not handle matters of state policy but instead have duties which are essentially clerical and ministerial and cannot give orders. Thus, whether governments can discriminate on the basis of citizenship in restricting noncitizens from certain jobs, without violating the Equal Protection Clause, depends on the type of job and type of duties performed.

Discussion Questions

1. Do you agree there should be a political function exception, where the government can show favoritism toward citizens for certain jobs?

2. Do you find the Court's treatment of police, probation officers, and teachers on the one hand, compared to attorneys and notary publics on the other, to be a defensible distinction?

Plyler v. Doe
457 U.S. 202 (1982)

The issue in *Plyler v. Doe* concerns government discrimination on the basis of illegal immigration status. While unsanctioned entry into the United States is a crime, the Supreme Court was forced to confront whether Texas, and its local subdivisions such as school districts, may refuse to provide elementary and secondary education to the children of illegal immigrants (who are thus illegal immigrants themselves).

In May 1979, the Texas Legislature decided to withhold state school funding from students who were not legally admitted into the United States. Local school districts were also authorized to deny enrollment to children not legally admitted to the United States. Texas argued that it was entitled to defend its state treasury (and local school district budgets) by not paying for students illegally in the country. When the case was tried in federal district court, the court recognized that increases in immigration of Mexican nationals to the United States created problems for Texas schools, which were exacerbated by the special education needs of many immigrant Mexican children. However, the district court struck down the Texas statute denying education to undocumented children on the basis that it violated the Equal Protection Clause of the Fourteenth Amendment. The district court reasoned that undocumented children denied an education will be unconstitutionally "disadvantaged as a result of poverty, lack of English-speaking ability, and undeniable racial prejudices, [and] will become permanently locked into the lowest socio-economic class."

The Supreme Court agreed with the district court. The Supreme Court noted that immigrants, even immigrants whose presence in this country violates criminal statutes, have long been recognized as "persons" for purposes of the Fourteenth Amendment's Equal Protection Clause, which reads: "nor shall any State … deny to any *person* within its jurisdiction the equal protection of the laws." The Court reasoned that a person's initial illegal entry into a state, although a criminal act and grounds for expulsion, does not negate the simple fact that a person's presence within the state's territorial perimeter makes a person subject to the jurisdiction of the state. "[U]ntil he leaves the jurisdiction — either voluntarily, or involuntarily in accordance with the Constitution and laws of the United States — he is entitled to the equal protection of the laws that a State may choose to establish." Therefore, even immigrants whose presence in the U.S. is illegal still have some protections under the Equal Protection Clause.

The Court then turned to basic principles of favoritism. While the Equal Protection Clause directs that all persons similarly circumstanced be treated alike, it does not require things which are different in fact or opinion to be treated in law as though they were the same. The Court thus recognized that persuasive arguments support Texas and its policy to discriminate against and withhold benefits from those whose presence within the United States illegally is the result of their own illegal conduct. However, children are different. The parents have the ability to conform their conduct to the law and societal norms, and could presumably remove themselves from Texas pursuant to the law, but children can affect neither their parents' conduct nor their own status or presence in the state. "[L]egislation directing the onus of a parent's misconduct against his children does not comport with fundamental conceptions of justice."

The Court then went on to discuss the many ways in which denial of education harmed children. Denial of education forecloses the very means by which the immigrant group as a whole might raise its level of esteem in which it is held by the majority. Yet this consideration of public policy paled in comparison to the immediate impact on individual children. Education allows an individual to be self-reliant and self-sufficient. The inability to read and write will handicap a child each and every day of his or her life. "The inestimable toll of that deprivation on the social, economic, intellectual, and psychological well-being of the individual, and the obstacle it poses to individual achievement, make it most difficult to reconcile the cost or the principle of a status-based denial of basic education with the framework of equality embodied in the Equal Protection Clause."

The Court acknowledged that undocumented aliens are not a **suspect class** (a suspect class is a group of people, like African Americans or women, who are protected against government favoritism by strict or intermediate judicial scrutiny, as we saw in the first several cases of this chapter). Since undocumented status is not a suspect class, the government need only satisfy the rational basis test, and show a legitimate reason for treating undocumented immigrants differently. Moreover, the Court also acknowledged that education is not a fundamental right (i.e., there is no constitutional right to receive an education from the government). Nevertheless, the Court found the Texas statute "imposes a lifetime hardship on a discrete class of children not accountable for their disabling status." The denial of basic education, the Court found, will deny children the ability to grow up and live within the structure of our civic institutions and will foreclose any realistic possibility they will contribute in even the smallest way to the progress of our nation. Thus, in light of these substantial costs, the discrimination by the Texas Legislature against children of illegal immigrants could "hardly be considered rational unless it furthers some substantial goal of the state." In other words, for the statute to pass the rational basis test, Texas needed to identify a legitimate goal that the statute accomplished.

Turning to the goals Texas advanced for its law, the Court found the justifications and reasons for enacting the law to be inadequate. The Court identified three potential state interests that arguably supported the denial of educational benefits to children. First, while a state may seek to protect itself from an influx of illegal immigrants, the Court found the statute did not provide an effective method of dealing with the urgent demographic and economic problems surrounding illegal immigration. "We think it clear that charging tuition to undocumented children constitutes a ludicrously ineffectual attempt to stem the tide of illegal immigration, at least when compared with the alternative of prohibiting the employment of illegal aliens."

Second, Texas argued that excluding undocumented children from education was justified because of the special burdens they impose on the state's ability to provide high-quality public education. The Court found there was no evidentiary support provided by the state to support its claim that exclusion of undocumented children is likely to improve the overall quality of education in the state. In terms of educational costs and needs, undocumented children are "basically indistinguishable" from children whose families have moved to the country legally.

Third, Texas argued that undocumented children are appropriately singled out because their unlawful presence makes them less likely to remain within the state and thus to utilize their educational attainments within the state. Yet, a state has no assurance that any child will employ the education provided by the state within the state's borders. Nevertheless, it was clear many students would remain indefinitely and become lawful residents or citizens. "It is difficult to understand precisely what the State hopes to achieve by promoting the creation and perpetuation of a subclass of illiterates within our boundaries, surely adding to the problems and costs of unemployment, welfare, and crime." Hence the Court recognized that preventing future crime was a reason to require states to provide education to undocumented children today.

The Court concluded by finding that whatever savings might be achieved by denying such children an education, these cost savings are "wholly insubstantial in light of the costs involved to the children, the State, and the Nation." Since Texas had no substantial state interest in denying educational benefits to children, the Court found the state had violated the Equal Protection Clause under the lowest level of judicial scrutiny (rational basis scrutiny). The Court ordered Texas to provide funding to local school districts for undocumented children and require local school districts to admit children of illegal immigrants.

Four justices on the Court dissented, noting, "The Constitution does not constitute us as 'Platonic Guardians' nor does it vest in this Court the authority to strike down laws because they do not meet our standards of desirable social policy, 'wisdom' or 'common sense.' We trespass on the assigned functions of the political branches under our structure of limited and separated powers when we assume a policymaking role." The dissenters rejected the idea that the Court should try to provide "effective leadership" to fix serious national problems simply because the elected branches of government have failed to do so. The Equal Protection Clause simply does not make illegal aliens a suspect class, nor does it preclude legislators from classifying people on the basis of factors and characteristics over which they may have little control, such as ill-health, need for public assistance, or place of residence. Furthermore, the dissenters pointed out that the federal government had seen fit to exclude illegal aliens from numerous social programs including food stamps, old-age assistance, aid to families with dependent children, aid to the blind and permanently disabled, as well as Medicare, and these exclusions tend to support the rationality of excluding undocumented children from such programs to help "preserve the state's finite revenues for the benefit of lawful residents."

Discussion Questions

1. Do you agree with how the Court rejected each of the three state interests Texas offered to justify its law? What if Texas was not allowed by Congress to pass its own employer verification law, should it then be allowed to require undocumented children to pay tuition to attend public elementary and secondary schools?

2. Should elected legislatures or unelected judges decide whether the cost savings from denying education to undocumented children (as well as other policy benefits) is "wholly insubstantial in light of the costs involved to the children, the State, and the Nation"?

City of Cleburne v. Cleburne Living Center
473 U.S. 432 (1985)

In 1980 the Cleburne Living Center sought to establish a group home for the intellectually disabled in the city of Cleburne, Texas. The problem was that establishing such a home in the residential area where the home was proposed violated the city's zoning ordinances. While zoning ordinances are not exactly criminal laws, they are closely related. They are similar to criminal laws in that zoning ordinances typically prohibit certain behavior and provide for penalties for failing to comply with the restriction. On the other hand, unlike criminal law, these **civil penalties** are typically fines, or injunctions which a judge orders to prevent that behavior, instead of jail sentences or probation.

The City of Cleburne's zoning ordinance allowed many group homes to locate in residential neighborhoods. This included group homes such as apartment houses, boarding houses, fraternity or sorority houses, hospitals, and nursing homes, but not group homes for "the insane or feebleminded or alcoholics or drug addicts." The federal district court considering the case upheld the ordinance, which discriminated against the intellectually disabled, as constitutional. The district court concluded that no fundamental right was implicated and that intellectual disability did not constitute a suspect class under the Constitution, which would elevate the level of judicial scrutiny. This meant that the lowest level judicial scrutiny, the rational basis test, was used by the district court to evaluate the ordinance's constitutionality. Under this lowest standard of judicial review, the district court deemed the ordinance rationally related to the city's legitimate interests in the safety and fears of residents in the adjoining neighborhood.

The Fifth Circuit Court of Appeals reversed, finding that intellectual disability constituted a quasi-suspect classification (like gender), which required the application of intermediate level judicial scrutiny. The Fifth Circuit justified its application of intermediate scrutiny due to the history of "unfair and often grotesque mistreatment" of the intellectually disabled, and the fact that discrimination against the intellectually disabled was likely to reflect deep-seated prejudice. Additionally, the intellectually disabled lacked political power, and intellectual disability is an immutable characteristic.

The Supreme Court took the case but agreed with neither the district court nor the Fifth Circuit. While the Equal Protection Clause of the Fourteenth Amendment is "essentially a direction that all persons similarly situated should be treated alike," the Court acknowledged that "the general rule is that legislation is presumed to be valid and will be sustained if the classification drawn by the statute is rationally related to a legitimate state interest." This last sentence captures the essence of the rational basis test. The Court held that the rational basis standard, not the intermediate scrutiny standard, applied by the Fifth Circuit, was the appropriate test in this case. Classifications of the basis of intellectual disability are different from classifications based on race, alienage, or national origin.

The Court found that classifications like race are so likely tied to prejudice that they should be subjected to strict scrutiny. On the other hand, there are many legitimate, non-prejudicial reasons to treat the intellectually disabled differently. The intellectually disabled have a reduced ability to cope with and function in the everyday world, and they may require special care for their benefit. "How this large and diversified group is to be treated under the law is a difficult and often a technical matter, very much a task for legislators guided by qualified professionals and not by the perhaps ill-informed opinions of the judiciary." The Court was reluctant to second-guess all statutes where the intellectually disabled are treated differently by applying intermediate scrutiny. The Court was also concerned that if it did apply intermediate scrutiny for the intellectually disabled, it would likely have to do so for other groups. It would be difficult to distinguish other groups with immutable disabilities and who have also suffered prejudice from portions of the public. Such other groups that might also demand intermediate scrutiny included the aging, the disabled, the mentally ill, and the infirm. Therefore, the Court rejected applying intermediate scrutiny (requiring a regulation be substantially related to an important government interest) and instead applied the basic-level rational basis test (a regulation need only be rationally related to a legitimate government interest).

The Court concluded that the City of Cleburne's zoning ordinance treating the intellectually disabled differently did not pass rational basis scrutiny. The ordinance was constitutionally flawed because "the State may not rely on a classification whose relationship to an assertive goal is so attenuated as to render the distinction arbitrary or irrational." Although the city council had been concerned with the negative attitude of the majority of property owners located near the proposed facility, that was not a legitimate reason to discriminate even under the rational basis test. The Court held that mere negative attitudes or fear were not a permissible basis for treating a home for the intellectually disabled differently than apartment houses, nursing homes, and other group homes allowed by the city in residential districts under the zoning ordinance. Thus, we see the Court applying the Equal Protection Clause of the Fourteenth Amendment, even when using its lowest level of judicial scrutiny, to strike down ordinances that discriminate if the only basis for treating people differently is fear or other illegitimate government interests.

Discussion Questions

1. Do you think this same standard should also apply to halfway houses or other residential facilities that help juveniles or non-violent adult offenders reintegrate into the community? What about homes for violent offenders?

2. If the case could be simply distilled down to the proposition that "prejudice is not rational," what kinds of reasons to treat people differently are legitimate? If community fear is not legitimate, what about studies showing elevated crime rates or lower property values?

Marriage and Intimacy

Issues surrounding marriage and sexual intimacy have been some of the most difficult issues in the criminal law. As society has changed, government regulations have become less severe, moving from criminal punishments to lack of official government recognition and denial of protection from discrimination. Yet, the same issues of government favoritism, and identifying which groups are deserving of which level of protection, remain through these cases.

Loving v. Virginia
388 U.S. 1 (1967)

The state of Virginia had criminalized interracial marriage for most of its history. Mildred Jeter, a black woman, and Richard Loving, a white man, were married in the District of Columbia, even though they were residents of Virginia. Shortly after their return to Virginia after their marriage, they were charged and pleaded guilty to violating Virginia's ban on interracial marriages. As part of their plea agreement the trial judge sentenced them to one year in jail, but the judge suspended the sentence upon the condition that they exile themselves from Virginia for a period of 25 years. Several years after the plea agreement, the Lovings filed a motion to vacate the judgment in their criminal case. They argued that Virginia's ban on interracial marriage violated the Fourteenth Amendment. The Virginia state courts refused to allow the Lovings' convictions to be vacated, and the case was appealed to the U.S. Supreme Court. At the time, in 1967, sixteen states still prohibited interracial marriages.

Virginia argued before the Court that since the statute applied to both blacks and whites equally (both blacks and whites were barred from marrying under the law) that its statute was racially neutral and constitutional. The Supreme Court rejected this argument, recognizing that Virginia's law still categorized (and punished) people on the basis of their race. It also rejected Virginia's argument that the 39th Congress, which had proposed the Fourteenth Amendment for ratification, had contemplated state bans on interracial marriage. The Court found that the original meaning and anticipated application of the Fourteenth Amendment by the 39th Congress did not control the contemporary interpretation of its provisions. The Court thus showed its willingness to recognize and correct historical mistakes.

The Court applied the strict scrutiny standard since Virginia's statute discriminated on the basis of race. The Court found there "is patently no legitimate overriding purpose independent of **invidious** racial discrimination which justifies this classification." The Court used the term invidious to explain that Virginia's law was based only on ill will and animosity toward blacks, and by extension, interracial marriage. There was no compelling state interest to support the law (as required by strict scrutiny) since there was no legitimate interest whatsoever to support the law. With very few exceptions, racial categories in the law cannot be justified (although we will see one such exception discussed in the *Grutter v. Bollinger* case at the end of this chapter). The Court thus struck down the Virginia ban on interracial marriage as violating the Equal Protection Clause of the Fourteenth Amendment.

In addition to violating the Equal Protection Clause, the Court also found the Virginia statute violated the Due Process Clause of the Fourteenth Amendment, which protects fundamental rights from invasion by the state. Some of these fundamental rights are found in the Bill of Rights (such as freedom of speech discussed in Chapter 1). Others, like the right to privacy (also discussed in Chapter 1), or the right to marriage, are not explicitly written anywhere in the Constitution. This will be an important distinction, as we shall see when we examine the *Obergefell v. Hodges* case later in this chapter. The Court stated in *Loving*,

> Marriage is one of the basic civil rights of man fundamental to our very existence and survival. To deny this fundamental freedom on so unsupportable a basis as the racial classifications embodied in these statutes, classifications so directly subversive of the principle of equality at the heart of the Fourteenth Amendment, is surely to deprive all the State's citizens of liberty without due process of law.

Thus, the prohibition against unjustified government favoritism is not limited exclusively to the Equal Protection Clause, but is a fundamental principle embedded in the Constitution, and finds its expression in various clauses of the Constitution.

Discussion Questions

1. Does it bother you that the Court consciously changed the interpretation of the Constitution when the 16 states with bans on interracial marriage would have been more than sufficient to block a constitutional amendment? Is it the proper role of the Court to fix historical mistakes the democratic process cannot easily fix?

2. As much sympathy as you might have for the Lovings, should all defendants who have pled guilty be able to withdraw their guilty pleas and convictions whenever the Court recognizes a new constitutional interpretation?

While our next case concerning favoritism might not immediately appear to be related to criminal justice issues, it addresses issues surrounding employment discrimination that could easily apply to the hiring of law enforcement and corrections officers, as well as other criminal justice staff throughout many state and local agencies.

Romer v. Evans
517 U.S. 620 (1996)

In *Romer v. Evans* the state of Colorado sought to overrule several municipal ordinances that had been adopted to protect individuals from employment and housing discrimination because of their sexual orientation. In 1992, the people of Colorado passed an amendment to the Colorado Constitution, known as Amendment 2. The state constitutional amendment prohibited all legislative, executive, or judicial action at any level of state or local government designed to protect people from discrimination on the basis of their sexual orientation. This was in response to cities like Aspen, Boulder, and Denver who had passed, by city ordinance, protections against discrimination on the basis of sexual orientation for people working and living in their cities. The campaign for Amendment 2 characterized the city ordinances as special treatment for homosexuals. The Supreme Court of Colorado ruled Amendment 2 must be judged using strict scrutiny. The case was sent back down to the trial court to apply the strict scrutiny standard and then worked its way backed up through the appellate process. When the case reached the U.S. Supreme Court, however, the Court applied only a rational basis level of judicial scrutiny. Yet, as in *City of Cleburne*, the state law here, Amendment 2, was struck down as violating the Equal Protection Clause of the Fourteenth Amendment.

The Supreme Court was concerned that Amendment 2 put homosexuals in a solitary class with respect to relations in both the private and governmental spheres. "The amendment withdraws from homosexuals, but no others, specific legal protection from the injuries caused by discrimination, and it forbids reinstatement of these laws and policies." Homosexuals as a group were targeted specifically for legal disadvantages in Colorado, even though the supporters of Amendment 2 had argued that all they were trying to do was prevent local governments from extending special protected status to homosexuals.

The Court noted that state and local governments have not limited **anti-discrimination laws** (which prohibit discrimination in employment, housing, and accommodations) only to groups that have been given the protection of heightened judicial scrutiny under the Equal Protection Clause by the Supreme Court. The Supreme Court has applied heightened judicial scrutiny under the Constitution to groups on the basis of race, sex, ancestry, as well as to children born to single or unmarried parents. States and local governments are free to protect additional groups using state statutes and local ordinances to prohibit discrimination on the basis of age, military status, pregnancy, parenthood, custody of a minor child, political affiliation, physical or mental disability, sexual orientation, etc. In other words, these groups are not required to be protected against discrimination by the U.S. Constitution, but state and local governments have the option to protect them. The problem comes when state governments stop local governments from passing such anti-discrimination laws (at least on the basis of sexual orientation):

> Amendment 2 bars homosexuals from securing protection against the injuries that these public accommodations laws address. That in itself is a severe consequence, but there is more. Amendment 2, in addition, nullifies specific legal protections [created under local city ordinances] for this targeted class in all transactions in housing, sale of real estate, insurance, health and welfare services, private education, and employment."

The Court acknowledged that "the Fourteenth Amendment's promise that no person shall be denied the equal protection of the laws must coexist with the practical necessity that most legislation classifies for one purpose or another, with resulting disadvantage to various groups or persons." For certain groups like race, gender, or ancestry (i.e., suspect classes), the Court scrutinizes these laws closely to limit these disadvantages and often strikes down the laws. But for other groups, such as those identified by age or by sexual orientation, the Court traditionally has only applied the rational basis standard of scrutiny. That means the Court only looks to whether there is a legitimate government purpose that is rationally connected to the regulation.

Here the Court found there was no legitimate government interest in repealing all of the local ordinances protecting sexual orientation, so Amendment 2 failed rational basis scrutiny. The Court found that Amendment 2's sheer breadth "is so discontinuous with the reasons offered for it that the amendment seems inexplicable by anything but animus toward the class it affects; it lacks a rational relationship to legitimate state interests." The Court went on to say that laws such as Amendment 2 can only cause the courts to infer they were passed because of animosity toward homosexuals. Amendment 2, which makes a general announcement that gays and lesbians should not have any particular protections from the law, "inflicts on them immediate, continuing, and real injuries that outrun and belie any legitimate justifications that may be claimed for it." In short, Amendment 2 violates the Equal Protection Clause because it fails to bear a rational relationship to a legitimate government purpose.

The Court will expand the constitutional rights for homosexuals in the next case of *Obergefell v. Hodges.* After *Obergefell,* homosexuals have at least the constitutional right to same-sex marriage, and *Obergefell* suggests that government itself cannot discriminate against homosexuals on the basis of their sexual orientation. One of the next major debates in the country, however, is likely to concern proposals for federal and state statutes, as well as local ordinances, that protect homosexuals from discrimination from private employers and other citizens in the private sphere (i.e., laws barring discrimination against homosexuals in private employment, housing, and accommodations) as we explored in *Elane Photography v. Willock* in Chapter 1. So, one should not read the next case of *Obergefell v. Hodges* as superseding and replacing *Romer,* but rather as specifically addressing state government discrimination on the basis of sexual orientation. For what state governments must not do in regulating discrimination in the private sphere by private citizens, those are issues that will still be controlled by *Romer v. Evans,* which teaches that states may not place blanket limits on the kinds of legal protections cities and counties may establish for homosexuals. State legislatures might not be required to pass antidiscrimination laws to protect homosexuals because of *Romer v. Evans,* but state legislatures probably cannot repeal local anti-discrimination laws either unless they prevent local governments from passing anti-discrimination ordinances for all groups.

Discussion Questions

1. Should laws passed by the voters of a state be entitled to extra deference by judges since the people of that state have spoken through direct democracy, or is this a reason to apply a little extra judicial scrutiny?

2. What kinds of groups should be protected by anti-discrimination laws? Would there ever be a reason to be less protective of any groups seeking employment for criminal justice positions (such as an anti-discrimination law protecting former felons)?

Our next case also does not have immediately obvious connections to criminal justice, but it does directly impact the criminal justice system. Specifically, marriage laws control the admission of evidence in criminal trials. As we shall see in Chapter 13, the spousal privilege can prevent a person in a formal marriage (but not merely cohabitating partners) from testifying against his or her spouse. This case might also have implications for Court precedents prohibiting discrimination during jury selection, which currently protect defendants and jurors from discrimination on the basis of race, gender, and ethnicity.

Obergefell v. Hodges

576 U.S. 644 (2015)

In *Obergefell v. Hodges* the Court again confronted the issue of sexual orientation, this time in the context of state laws refusing to issue marriage licenses to same-sex couples and refusing to recognize out-of-state marriages between same-sex couples. James Obergefell had met John Arthur two decades before the case began, but after John was diagnosed with ALS (amyotrophic lateral sclerosis) the couple resolved to formalize their commitment. By the time of the marriage, John's condition had deteriorated to the point where he could no longer travel normally, so the wedding took place on the tarmac inside the medical transport plane which had carried John from their home in Ohio to Maryland, where same-sex marriage was then legal. Three months after their marriage John passed away, but the state of Ohio refused to list James as the surviving spouse on John's death certificate. James sued, seeking to force Ohio to recognize their marriage, and end a legal rejection James deemed would be "hurtful for the rest of time." The Supreme Court ultimately took James's case, along with the cases of two other same-sex couples, and ruled that states must both license same-sex marriages as well as recognize same-sex marriages performed in other states.

Unlike the preceding cases in this chapter, the Court justified this result primarily upon the authority of the Due Process Clause in the Fourteenth Amendment, as well as upon the rejection of favoritism contained in the Equal Protection Clause. The narrow five-member majority ruled, in an opinion written by Justice Kennedy (the same justice who authored the *Romer v. Evans* decision), that states could not discriminate against same-sex couples because the right to marry is a fundamental right, with ancient origins. "[T]he Court has long held the right to marry is protected by the Constitution," Justice Kennedy wrote, citing back to the *Loving v. Virginia* case.

While the majority decision acknowledged that its precedents, such as *Loving*, had only been previously applied to opposite-sex partners, Justice Kennedy identified four principles drawn from the rationale of previous opinions which required that the scope of the fundamental right to marry must be expanded to include same-sex couples. First, "the right to personal choice regarding marriage is inherent in the concept of individual autonomy." This concept was implicit in the *Loving* decision, but in recognizing the autonomy of couples to commit to one another, it does not matter whether the choice to commit is between an interracial couple or between a same-sex couple. Second, Justice Kennedy noted that marriage is a two-person union of incomparable importance to the committed individuals forming the union, a concept recognized in cases like *Griswold v. Connecticut* (discussed earlier in Chapter 5), which recognized the right of married couples to use contraception. The *Griswold* case described marriage as "an association for as noble a purpose as any involved in our prior decisions." Here Justice Kennedy also looked to *Lawrence v. Texas* (also discussed earlier in Chapter 5, and again later in Chapter 15), which established that "same-sex couples have the same right as opposite-sex couples to enjoy intimate association." This quote directly captures the idea that government cannot play favorites based on the sexual orientation of the couples concerned, neither in the area of criminal law nor in terms of family and domestic-relations laws, such as a marriage.

As a third point in favor of its holding in *Obergefell*, the Court reasoned that the right to marry safeguards children and families, not merely the rights of couples, drawing upon earlier decisions recognizing related rights of childrearing, procreation, and the right to direct the education of children. The government's decision to play favorites in terms of the kinds of couples allowed to marry causes the children of the excluded couples to "suffer the stigma of knowing their families are somehow lesser." This stigma, and associated material costs of uncertainty, serves to "harm and humiliate the children of same-sex couples." Fourth, the right to marriage is recognition of marriage as "a keystone of our social order." To help support that order, state governments created a "constellation of benefits" linked to marriage, which the state was denying to same-sex couples, "lock[ing] them out of a central institution of the Nation's society." Thus, the Court proceeded through a Due Process Clause analysis to reach its conclusion, but much of the reasoning employed by Justice Kennedy in his majority opinion speaks to the concept of unjustified favoritism. Indeed, Kennedy rejects favoritism by government for certain couples: "[S]ame sex couples seek in marriage *the same legal treatment* as opposite-sex couples, and it would disparage their choices and diminish their personhood to deny them this right" (emphasis added).

Justice Kennedy goes on to argue this result, and condemnation of favoritism in the realm of marriage, is dictated both under the Due Process Clause as well as under the Equal Protection Clause, and that these clauses are "connected in a profound way" and although not always coextensive, may in some instances (such as the decision to marry) be instructive as to the meaning and reach of the other. "[T]he marriage laws [in question in *Obergefell*] are in essence unequal: same-sex couples are denied all the benefits afforded to opposite-sex couples and are barred from exercising a fundamental right." Justice's Kennedy's repeated assertion that all same-sex couples seek is "equal dignity in the eyes of the law" is simply another way of saying that the Constitution rejects unjustified government favoritism of one group over another.

Discussion Questions

1. What level of judicial scrutiny do you think the Court will now apply in evaluating the constitutionality of laws that might discriminate on the basis of sexual orientation?

2. Law enforcement and corrections officers are called upon to enforce laws that an officer might disagree with personally. Would you feel comfortable arresting or incarcerating local officials (such as Kim Davis, the county clerk in Kentucky) who have refused to issue same-sex marriage licenses?

Exceptions

Of course, in rejecting favoritism, the Court does not require that each person be treated exactly the same in every context, or that government must always be blind to differences between persons. This concept is further illustrated in the next case.

Grutter v. Bollinger
539 U.S. 306 (2003)

In 1996, Barbara Grutter, who is a white Michigan resident, applied to attend the University of Michigan Law School. Her qualifications included a 3.8 grade point average and a 161 LSAT (Law School Admissions Test) score. Good scores, to be sure, but not a lock for admission into one of the top 10 law schools in the country. Barbara was first waitlisted and then ultimately denied admission. Indeed, the median LSAT score for the entering law school classes at the University of Michigan in recent years has been nearly a 170 with a median undergraduate GPA of over 3.75.

Barbara sued the University of Michigan Law School because of its admissions policies. The law school sought a mix of students with varying backgrounds and experiences. The law school had a diversity objective, which sought to "achieve that diversity which has the potential to enrich everyone's education and thus make a law school class stronger than the sum of its parts." To do so, the law school admissions system required admissions officials to evaluate each application based on all the information in the student's file and look past merely their undergraduate grade point average and LSAT scores to include race as one element in the admissions process.

At trial in federal district court the director of admissions for the University of Michigan Law School testified that while he did not direct his staff to admit a particular percentage or number of minority students, he did want to ensure that a critical mass of underrepresented minority students would be admitted so as to realize the educational benefits of a diverse student body. Other testimony from officials of the law school stressed that the term "critical mass" meant enough underrepresented minority students so that minority students would feel comfortable participating in class and not feel isolated or feel like spokespersons for their race. The race of applicants must be considered because, according to the Law School, a critical mass of underrepresented minority students could not be enrolled if admissions decisions were based primarily on undergraduate GPA and LSAT scores. This meant that for some students race might not play any part at all in their admission (especially if they had high scores), but for other students their race might be a "determinative" factor in the decision to admit or not admit. Since the University of Michigan is a state-run law school, its admissions policies, like any government regulations, must comply with the Equal Protection Clause of the Fourteenth Amendment. Since its admissions policy took race into consideration, how race was used in the admissions policy was subjected to strict scrutiny.

The University of Michigan Law School's admissions policy considered a variety of types of diversity. Yet the policy reaffirmed the law school's longstanding commitment to one particular type of diversity: "racial and ethnic diversity with special reference to the inclusion of students from groups which have been historically discriminated against, like African-Americans, Hispanics, and Native Americans." Testimony from one of the faculty members who helped develop the law school's admissions policy explained that this language did not purport to remedy past discrimination but rather to bring to the law school students who might have a perspective different than for members of groups that had not been the subject of historical discrimination. When asked to explain why the policy excluded other groups that had experienced historical discrimination, such as Asians and Jews, this professor explained such groups were not mentioned specifically in the policy because individuals of these groups were already admitted to the law school in significant numbers. The University of Michigan Law School's admissions policy resulted in 35% of underrepresented minority applicants being admitted in 2000, but if race were not allowed as an admissions factor, only 10% of these underrepresented minority applicants would have been admitted. This would have changed the demographics of the incoming law school class from 14.5% underrepresented minority students to only 4% underrepresented minority students.

The federal district court held that the law school's admissions policy violated the Equal Protection Clause. The district court applied strict scrutiny and found the law school's asserted interest in assembling a diverse student body was not a compelling state interest, and even if it were a compelling state interest, the admissions policy was not narrowly tailored to further that interest. The Sixth Circuit Court of Appeals reversed. The Sixth Circuit decided that the U.S. Supreme Court had binding precedent that recognized diversity as a compelling state interest. The Supreme Court agreed to hear the case to resolve the conflict amongst lower federal courts over whether diversity constituted a compelling state interest for purposes of applying strict scrutiny in higher education admissions programs.

The Supreme Court in *Grutter* examined its previous precedents, specifically a concurring opinion written by Justice Powell in *Regents of University of California v. Bakke*. In *Bakke*, Justice Powell had rejected the use of race in admis-

sions to reduce the historic deficit of traditionally disfavored minorities and rejected the use of race in remedying past societal discrimination. Such use of
race in admissions would effectively punish innocent third-parties "who bear
no responsibility" for whatever harm previous discrimination against minorities
might have caused previously. This use of race is known as **reverse discrimination**—preferring one race of applicants to offset or remedy discrimination
in prior years. It can only be done when the specific agency or government
entity had discriminated in the past, not when there was merely general societal
discrimination against a particular race or ethnic group. Even an interest in increasing the number of underrepresented minority professionals who might
serve in underrepresented communities was suspect, according to Justice Powell,
because the programs of admissions were not closely connected to placing underrepresented professionals in those communities.

Justice Powell in *Bakke* had approved the use of race as advancing only one
compelling state interest, the attainment of a diverse student body. It was this
justification that the Court in *Grutter* reaffirmed: institutions of higher education have "a compelling interest in attaining a diverse student body." Thus,
according to the Court, universities should be given a fair amount of
educational discretion to select those students who the university believes "will
contribute the most to the robust exchange of ideas." This includes considering
the race and prior legacy of historical discrimination targeted at certain groups
in admissions policies in order to help promote cross-racial understanding
and break down racial stereotypes in the classroom.

The Court found that the University of Michigan Law School's admissions
policy enabled students to better understand persons of different races. Such
benefits are important and laudable objectives, making classroom discussion
"livelier, more spirited, and simply more enlightening and interesting when
students have the greatest possible variety of backgrounds." Student body diversity also promotes learning outcomes and better prepares students for an
increasingly diverse workforce and society, better preparing students to be
professionals. The Court made conspicuous reliance upon the fact that race-
conscious admissions policies were not only permissible for law schools but
for the military service academies and other universities as well. Specifically,
the Court noted that "the military cannot achieve an officer corps that is *both*
highly qualified *and* racially diverse unless the service academies and the ROTC
use limited race-conscious recruiting and admissions policies" (emphasis in
original). Even the federal government weighed in, filing an **amicus brief** in
support of the University of Michigan. Amicus briefs are filed by governments,
legal interest groups, and law professors who have an interest in the policies
a precedent might set but who are not actual parties to the case. The Bush Ad-

ministration argued in its amicus brief that "ensuring that public institutions are open and available to all segments of American society, including people of all races and ethnicities, represents a paramount government objective."

The Court then turned its attention more specifically back to law schools by recognizing that law schools, especially highly ranked law schools, "represent the training ground for a large number of our Nation's leaders." A handful of highly selective law schools at that point in 2003 "account[ed] for 25 of the 100 United States senators, 74 United States Court of Appeals judges, and nearly 200 of the more than 600 United States District Court judges." The very legitimacy of the entire political system was at stake, according to the Court, and recognizing racial diversity as grounds for admission to institutions of higher education was necessary so the path to leadership in this country was "visibly open to talented and qualified individuals of every race and ethnicity."

The Court held racial diversity in higher education was a compelling state interest, but that was not the end of the case. Recall that strict scrutiny requires not only a compelling state interest, but a government regulation must also be narrowly tailored to achieve that interest without any less restrictive alternatives. So, it was understandable that the Court, in evaluating the race-conscious admissions policy, would caution the states: "[W]hen drawing racial distinctions is permissible to further a compelling state interest, government is still constrained in how it may pursue that end: The means chosen to accomplish the government's asserted purpose must be specifically and narrowly framed to accomplish that purpose." The Court reminded universities that race needs to be used in a flexible, nonmechanical way to achieve student diversity, and "universities cannot establish quotas for members of certain racial groups or put members of those groups on separate admissions tracks." Quotas would flunk the narrowly tailored requirement in the strict scrutiny test.

The University of Michigan Law School admissions policy was found not to constitute a racial quota since there was no fixed number or proportion of opportunities reserved exclusively for certain minority groups. A program is not a quota merely because it uses race as a "plus" factor or gives race a greater weight than some other factors when striving to achieve student body diversity. Instead, the law school engaged in "a highly individualized, holistic review of each applicant's file, giving serious consideration to all the ways an applicant might contribute to a diverse educational environment." There were no mechanical, predetermined diversity bonuses based on race or ethnicity as there were in admissions programs the Court struck down as unconstitutional on the same day it decided the *Grutter* case.

Furthermore, the Court held that narrow tailoring does not require exhaustion of every conceivable race-neutral alternative, but only a "serious, good faith consideration of workable race-neutral alternatives that will achieve the diversity the university seeks." The Court found that the law school's race-conscious admissions program did not unduly harm nonminority applicants, like Barbara Grutter. Yet the Court acknowledged that:

> [R]ace conscious admissions programs must be limited in time. This requirement reflects that racial classifications, however compelling their goals, are potentially so dangerous that they may be employed no more broadly than the interest demands. Enshrining a permanent justification for racial preferences would offend this fundamental equal protection principle.
>
> … We take the Law School at its word that it would like nothing better than to find a race-neutral admissions formula and will terminate its race-conscious admissions program as soon as practicable. It has been 25 years since Justice Powell first approved the use of race to further an interest in student body diversity in the context of public higher education. Since that time, the number of minority applicants with high grades and test scores has indeed increased. We expect that 25 years from now, the use of racial preferences will no longer be necessary to further the interest approved today.

Thus, the Court restrained the use of government favoritism, even for the most important reasons, to a limited period of time. Since the Court's 2003 decision in *Grutter,* much of the remaining time for race-conscious admissions programs has presumably passed, and some states like Michigan have entirely outlawed the use of race in admissions by voter referendum, while other states like Colorado have voted to retain its use. The Court continues to hear cases concerning race in education, and some commentators have suggested that it may call a halt to the use of race-conscious admissions before the year 2028. Nevertheless, such a critical issue to the criminal justice system as how some of its most important players, lawyers and judges, are initially selected and trained remains an area where race can legitimately be considered in a manner consistent with the Equal Protection Clause.

Discussion Questions

1. Would you vote to retain the use of race-conscious admissions programs in higher education — why or why not?

2. If diversity in the classroom is of critical importance, how might you encourage it without considering race? Do you think it is especially

important that minority defendants have defense attorneys who are minorities, or is it enough that their defense attorneys attended schools with diverse classrooms?

Chapter Key Terms

Favoritism
Equal Protection Clause
Strict scrutiny standard
Rational basis standard
Intermediate scrutiny stan-
dard
Notary public
Political function exception

Civil penalties
Precedents
Suspect class
Invidious
Anti-discrimination laws
Reverse discrimination
Amicus brief

Chapter Ten

Favoritism in Law Enforcement and Corrections

Profiling undermines public safety and strains police-community trust. When law enforcement officers target residents based on race, religion or national origin rather than behavior, crime-fighting is less effective and community distrust of police grows.

—Ranjana Natarajan

Law Enforcement

As the previous chapter demonstrated, the criminal justice system should ensure that everyone is given equal protection of the law. This means that law enforcement and the corrections system should try to steer clear of bias and not provide preferential treatment for one group over another. While there are many examples of how law enforcement could use bias to shape their decisions regarding the treatment of various groups, we will explore the topics of race, ethnicity, and sexual orientation/identity below.

One could argue that the opposite of favoritism is discrimination. There is perhaps no more poignant an example of where law enforcement is challenged for using discriminatory practices than that of racial profiling. Racial profiling is often described as law enforcement targeting individuals based on their race; however, it encompasses a broader range of personal characteristics (i.e., race, ethnicity, national origin, and religion) that law enforcement uses to help them when determining who to stop, detail, and/or question (Leadership Conference on Civil and Human Rights, 2011, p. 7). Although racial profiling is banned among federal law enforcement agencies, data indicates that it is a practice that is still being used at the state and local level. Currently, 20 states' laws do not explicitly ban the use of racial profiling, and of those that have some semblance of racial profiling laws on the books (30), a small fraction require that data be collected and/or disseminated as public information (Born suspect, 2014, p. 1).

While we know it happens and there is general consensus regarding the public's disapproval of it, it is hard to decouple human bias from the practice of policing (Natarajan, 2014, para. 1–2). The majority of officers have good intentions and do not purposefully try to discriminate against particular groups. However, it is not to say that there are never instances where law enforcement and other entities of the criminal justice system use someone's characteristics to shape their decisions. The two cases below will call into question whether law enforcement, and the broader criminal justice system, used the defendant's race to shape their actions.

KFC Robber

Lenell Geter was a man that many individuals described as reliable, upstanding, and a hard worker. So was it possible that he could have been a gainfully employed black engineer who also did armed robberies in his spare time? Not to mention, was it possible that Lenell Geter snuck out from work midday to go commit a robbery of a Kentucky Fried Chicken in a neighboring town? On the surface, many would argue that it seems highly unlikely. However, the prosecution persuaded a jury enough to convict a completely innocent man of a crime that he did not commit.

Geter was an engineer at E-Systems military and electronics research center in Greenville, Texas. It was no secret that this Texas town was predominately white. In fact, at one point in time, there was even a road sign announcing it as having "The Blackest Land—The Whitest People" (Levine, 1992, p. 137). Perhaps that is why Geter was targeted as the robber; he was one of a few black men in the town. However, was it a mistake or was it racial bias by the prosecution and jurors? As we'll see from our discussion below, many argue that it was the latter due to the prosecution ignoring evidence that would have proven Geter's innocence and focusing rather on information that proved his guilt.

The armed robbery in question happened on August 21, 1983, at 3:20 pm in Balch Springs, Texas (CBS News Video, 1983). There had been a string of robberies at other restaurants in and around the Greenville area, so law enforcement drew on the public to help them with any information that could be of assistance to law enforcement. Because there were employees of the restaurant who came into direct contact with the suspect, the authorities were able to advertise a sketch drawing through various media outlets. This led one elderly woman to notify the local police department that she had noticed a black man (Geter) who frequently hung around a nearby park (which she said "upset" her) so she provided them with his license plate number (McBride, 1987, p. 9). Police began following Geter around to keep an eye on his activities, and shortly thereafter, five employees from the KFC robbery identified him from a lineup. The prosecution felt as though they had the right guy even though they produced no physical evidence linking Geter to the crime (Levine, 1992, p. 137). Beyond the issues noted above, there were a total of nine coworkers who provided an **alibi** for Geter, stating that they either saw him and/or spoke with him at work on the day the robbery occurred. Furthermore, his supervisor testified that he had given Geter a task at 1:00 pm and that his work was completed and submit by 4:00 pm. The defense claimed that this proves there was no way that Geter could have made the 50-minute drive from his work to Balch Springs to commit the robbery and then back to work to complete his work (CBS News Video, 1983). Regardless of the alibi from coworkers and the absence of any evidence tying Geter to the crime, the all-white jury found him guilty and sentenced him to life imprisonment (due to the prosecution charging him with the string of robberies, not just the KFC case in question) (Fishleder, 1984, para. 3).

Geter maintained his innocence throughout the entire trial and refused to plea bargain. Even after he was sent to prison, he continued to profess his innocence, and due to the national attention that his case received, he was contacted and interviewed by *60 Minutes* to share his story. This perhaps helped to save Geter's life because in the documentary, Morley Safer interviewed all parties involved with this case. It is through his interviews that we learned there were three coworkers who were never questioned by law enforcement or the prosecution/defense, and they could place Geter at work 20 minutes before and 60 minutes after the robbery (Stowers, 2001, para. 12). It was argued that this would have proven his innocence because there was no way his coworkers could have seen him at work so close to the time of the robbery if you factored in the nearly two-hour round-trip driving time it would have taken for him to get to and from Balch Springs. Additionally, law enforcement started receiving tips that another man by the name of Mason (who had been arrested in the past for a series of holdups in the Dallas area) could perhaps be the one committing the robberies. His physical description and facial features fit the profile of the suspect, and he had been seen carrying around a blue athletic bag like the one that had been used in the robberies. When law enforcement apprehended Mason, he had the bag in question in his possession, as well as a long-barreled revolver. Both of the items matched descriptions provided by the eyewitnesses. Law enforcement brought in the original five eyewitnesses and four of the five who initially identified Geter now identified Mason as the man who robbed the KFC (Levine, 1992, p. 138).

When the prosecution caught wind of this news, they decided to dismiss all of the charges against Geter. Sixteen months after he was sent to prison, he was exonerated on all charges and let go. Prosecutors said that the entire ordeal was the result of mistaken identity; however, Geter's lawyers argued that there was ill intent behind the actions of those trying to prove his guilt. Rather, they claimed that "shoddy police work, overzealous prosecutors and racism in the small, predominately white Texas town" were to blame (McCartney, 1984, p. 9, para. 6). After he got his freedom back, Geter claimed that he had forgiven those who had falsely convicted him, yet he was still upset enough to file a lawsuit against the prosecutors and police. While he filed a $28 million dollar suite alleging a violation of his Civil Rights, he settled with the city of Greenville, TX for $50,000 dollars (City officials settle, 1990, para. 1). As for Mason, he staunchly defended his innocence and claimed that they were just trying to find a scapegoat to take the fall for the burglaries.

Discussion Questions

1. Were there any sections of the story where you felt as though the police and prosecutors were acting discriminatorily?

2. If you were Geter, do you think you would have also filed a civil suit or just let the issue go?

Sitting While Black

On January 31, 2014, Chris Lollie was sitting in the First National Bank Building in the downtown St. Paul skywalk when he was confronted by a security guard who asked him to leave. He said he was sitting there waiting to pick up his two children from New Horizon Academy and that they would be out soon (Hayden, 2014, para. 1). Although this information is not documented anywhere in newspaper reports, a video shows Lollie being confronted by the bank's security guard on two separate occasions and being asked to move along even though there was also one white patron sitting in the bank during the entire event (Yuen, 2014). After about two minutes of sitting at the entrance of the bank, Lollie starts to leave when he is confronted by three St. Paul police officers. He starts recording the incident on his cell phone and there is also hallway surveillance recording the incident.

He is first confronted by a female officer who asks him to identify himself. He responds that he does not have to identify himself because he's not broken any laws and that since there was no sign saying that he couldn't sit there (in a spot that is technically public space), he sat there. The officers said that they wanted to figure out what the problem was back at the bank, to which Lollie responded, "The problem is I'm Black" (Garcia, 2014, para. 10). A male officer then enters the scene and the video shows him trying to grab Lollie's arm. The conversation then continues:

> Lollie: "I've got to get my kids [pulls away his arm]. Please don't touch me!"
>
> Male officer: "You're going to jail, then."
>
> Lollie: "I'm not doing anything wrong. Come on brother, this is assault."
>
> Male officer: "I'm not your brother. Put your hands behind your back; otherwise it's going to get ugly."
>
> Lollie: "I haven't done anything wrong! Can somebody please help me?! That's my kids right there! My kids are right there!"

At that point, you can hear the taser being used and the male officer again commanding him to get his arms behind his back. Lollie then says that he hasn't done anything wrong and that he's a working man just trying to take care of his kids, "And you tase me. For what? I don't have any weapons" (Crockett, 2014, para. 15–30). Lollie was arrested on charges of trespassing, disorderly conduct, and obstructing legal processes.

After the event, Lollie posted his video to YouTube, and the St. Paul Police Department quickly received flack for how the event was handled. The police chief defended his officers' actions, but the mayor called for an independent panel to review the event. The Police Civilian Internal Affairs Review Commission consisted of five community members and two police officers (Yuen, 2014, para. 10). They watched the videos numerous times over and reviewed all of the documentation and ultimately exonerated the officers on any allegations of improper procedures and excessive use of force. In the aftermath of the decision, a local NAACP leader stated that he wasn't surprised because "The citizen review board is just another arm of the police department" (Yuen, 2014, para. 17).

Lollie had the charges against him dropped, but he still felt as though the City of St. Paul should be held accountable for its actions. He claimed that the event was not only traumatic to him, but also to his children. Even though neither of his children witnessed the event, classmates in his daughter's class did. Lollie said that his daughter suffers harassment from her peers and that she developed a fear of police which causes her to have nightmares. He filed a lawsuit seeking $500,000 in punitive and **compensatory damages** (money awarded in a civil suit to reimburse a person for loses or injury they suffered as a result of the unlawful conduct of another) claiming that his Fourteenth Amendment rights were violated and that the police falsified reports against him. Additionally, the suit claimed that the officers used excessive force and detained Lollie without a "reasonable, articulable suspicion" (Xiong, 2014, para. 2). While the specific details surrounding the proceedings of the trial have never been released, it was disclosed that the city of St. Paul agreed to pay $100,000 to settle with Mr. Lollie (Ibrahim, 2016, para. 1).

Discussion Questions

1. Do you think that Lollie should have just identified himself or do you support him resisting the officer's inquiries because he felt as though he had done nothing wrong?

2. Given the limited information that you know about this case, do you feel as though Lollie was unfairly targeted for being a young Black male?

Show Me Your Papers

In 2010, Arizona passed one of the most controversial anti-immigration laws to date, titled SB1070. Frustrated with federal immigration laws and the number of undocumented immigrants in the state of Arizona, SB1070 specified four key pieces (among others) of legislation relating to undocumented immigrants:

1. Section 2(B), which is known as the "show me your papers" clause, requires police officers to check the immigration status of anyone they have detained or arrested.
2. Section 3 would make it a crime to be in Arizona without valid immigration papers.
3. Section 5(C) would make it a crime to apply for a job without valid immigration papers.

4. Section 6 would allow a police officer to arrest someone if they believed that the individual has committed a crime (at some point in time) that could result in their deportation. Additionally, this arrest can be made without a warrant (Howe, 2012, para. 4).

The U.S. district court weighed in on the constitutionality of these sections of SB1070 and ruled that three of the four provisions were unconstitutional (Kunichoff, 2012, para. 1). The U.S. Supreme Court agreed with the lower court's decision and struck down Sections 3, 5(C), and 6 because they were all **preempted** (trumped or something else takes precedent) by federal immigration laws, but determined that Section 2(B) could remain.

While many opponents of SB1070 argued this was a victory due to some of the stricter provisions being overruled, others noted that the most contentions section of SB1070 was left intact. "Show me your papers" will require "that police, while enforcing other laws, question the immigration status of those suspected of being in the country illegally" (Arizona immigration law, 2014, para. 6). Therefore, someone stopped for a traffic stop can be held for a reasonable amount of time to determine their immigration status. Additionally, if someone has broken a state, county, or local law and the officers have "reasonable suspicion" that the individual is here illegally, law enforcement is required to contact Immigration and Customs Enforcement (ICE) (Kunichoff, 2012, para. 9).[1] The strongest argument against the "show me your papers" provision was that it invites racial profiling against Latinos and anyone who law enforcement deems to be foreign (Arizona's SB 1070, n.d., para. 3).

SB1070 quickly garnered a lot of public attention, and while there had been previous cases challenging the legality of "show me your papers," nobody had challenged the constitutionality of enforcing the law. This was the case until Maria del Rasario Cortes was pulled over in September 2012 for driving with a cracked windshield (Kowalski, 2014, para. 1). She was approached by Deputy Chad Ladosky and asked for her license, identification papers, and if she had a visa. Cortes provided her name to the deputy and informed him that she had already applied for a **U-Visa**, which grants citizenship and working rights to victims of domestic violence. She explained to Deputy Ladosky that she was cooperating with law enforcement to prosecute her abuser and that she could show him the U-Visa documents in her glove box. He allegedly replied that he wasn't interested in seeing it, and shortly thereafter, Deputy Kristina Stolz arrived on the scene (Vargas-Cooper, 2014, para. 1–3). She patted down Cortes,

---

1. One key exception to Section 2(B) is if enforcing it would interfere with an investigation or if someone is either the victim or witness of a crime (Kunichoff, 2012, para. 10).

put her in handcuffs, and put her in the back of her squad car. Cortes was then driven 13 miles away to a U.S. Customs and Border Patrol office and detained for five days. According to Cortes, nobody communicated with her about what was happening during this time, and she was worried about what would happen to her three children.

The ACLU of Phoenix filed a lawsuit in federal court arguing that Cortes' Fourth Amendment rights had been violated due to her being subject to an unreasonable seizure. According to her lawyer,

> At no time during the stop did these Defendants have either probable cause or reasonable suspicion that Ms. Cortes was involved in criminal activity and at no time was Ms. Cortes told that she was under arrest for any reason. At no time during the stop did Ms. Cortes believe that she was free to leave the scene (Vargas-Cooper, 2014, para. 7).

Additional information about how the two deputies handled Cortes was also uncovered through the lawsuit. For example, it was only when they arrived at Border Patrol that Cortes was written a traffic citation for her windshield, lack of license, and failure to provide proof of insurance. This contradicted with Deputy Lakosky's report of the incident because he stated that she was "cited and released." There was no mention of arresting, handcuffing, or transporting her to Border Patrol.

Pinal County Sheriff Paul Babeu defended his two deputies and argued that they took appropriate actions and did what is required of them by law (i.e., Section 2(B) of SB1070). Cortes' legal team disagreed and was seeking punitive damages for her constitutional rights being violated. Eventually the parties settled for $25,000. In follow-up interviews with Sheriff Babeu he explained that he settled with the plaintiff to avoid the money it would cost to litigate the dispute and that he likely saved hundreds of thousands of dollars in the process (Macias, 2014, para. 6).

Discussion Questions

1. Do you feel as though SB1070 unfairly targets ethnic minority groups like Latinos/as?

2. Do you think that the deputies in the above story handled their interaction with Cortes appropriately? What suggestions do you have if you feel as though they could have handled the issue differently?

Calling the Cops on the Cops

"People have a clear constitutional and civic duty to report crimes they witness to the police. But what happens when the police are the ones committing the crime" (Morales, 2010, para. 1)? On March 13, 2009, a gay tourist (Harold Strickland), who used to live in the area, was walking along South Beach in Miami Beach, Florida, talking to his sister on the telephone when he witnessed two individuals chase another man (Oscar Mendoza) through a parking lot and start beating him while yelling homosexual slurs. He hung up with his sister and immediately called the Miami Beach Police Department to report the incident. The dispatcher asked if he could get closer to identify a license plate number on the car they were standing by, but Strickland told them that there was no license plate number. He then noticed that the two individuals beating the man were wearing walkie-talkies and had handcuffs and guns; he quickly deduced that they were undercover officers (Morales, 2010, para. 17).

As Strickland got closer, the two undercover officers noticed his presence and asked him what he was doing there. The call was quickly disconnected, and Strickland reports being shoved to the ground and also hearing the officers use anti-gay epithets while they tied his hands behind his back. Allegedly, one of the undercover officers said, "We know what you're doing here. We're sick of all the fucking fags in the neighborhood" (Garcia, 2010, para. 4). Strickland explained to the officers why he called 911 and that he intended to report them. Allegedly one officer taunted him to go ahead and do so because they make "guys like him disappear every day" (Morales, 2010, para. 5).

There were discrepancies between the two officers' stories and those of Strickland and Mendoza. According to police reports, Officers Hazzie and Forte thought that Mendoza was trying to break into cars outside the park and that Strickland was his accomplice. Strickland stated that he was walking across from the parking lot on the beach when he saw the scuffle (his sister corroborated his story) while Mendoza said that he was searching for his dog's collar in the parking lot (Smiley, 2012, para. 9–10). Ultimately, both men were charged with loitering and prowling. Later, these charges were dropped due to there being no evidence to substantiate them.

Strickland, along with the ACLU of Florida, filed a lawsuit against the City of Miami Beach claiming that his rights had been violated under federal and state law (American Civil Liberties Union of Florida, 2010, para. 4). The lawsuit referenced numerous problems with how the Miami Beach PD handled the issue, but highlighted two issues they felt were more systemic and long-standing within the agency. One problem they noted were the numerous reports of gay men in and around the Flamingo Park area complaining they had been harassed by law enforcement. A second issue they noted was the re-taliation that citizens reported when they brought forth misconduct allegations (*On Top* Magazine Staff, 2011, para. 3). Eventually, the city settled the suit with Strickland and paid him $75,000 (SFGN Staff, 2011, para. 3). Officers Hazzi and Forte were fired due to an internal investigation showing that they acted unethically and falsified information to cover up their behavior. Additionally, the Miami Beach PD beefed up their policies regarding the reporting of mis-conduct and also implemented more training for officers about harassment of the LGBTQ community. In the wake of the settlement, Strickland reported that he was pleased with the outcome, but felt as though it was sad that it took him going through the ordeal he did to draw attention to a well-known problem in the Flamingo Park area. He hoped that the new changes being made within the Miami Beach PD mean that nobody else will ever have to go through what he did (Williams, 2011, para. 9).

Discussion Questions

1. Do you feel as though the settlement they reached with Strickland and the changes that the Miami Beach PD made were enough? Do you have suggestions for how they should have better handled the issue?

2. If there have been numerous reports of public sex among gay males, do you think that law enforcement should be allowed to profile indi-viduals based on their sexual orientation?

Use Your Own Bathroom

The above case provided an example of discrimination against a certain group for their sexual preference, while the following case discusses discrimination against a certain group for their **gender identity**. Brenda Wernikoff was born a male (Bruce), but began identifying as a woman in her mid-50s. She had been staying at a homeless shelter in Boston because she no longer felt comfortable living in her uncle's house after she underwent her gender identity change. Al-though the homeless shelter's policy is to allow transgender people to use whatever bathroom they feel is appropriate (following the Boston Public Health Commission's policies), one of the staff called the police because Brenda was in the women's bathroom and it made other residents uncomfortable. A female officer showed up and confronted Brenda, asking her to leave the bathroom. In the police reports, the officer wrote that "said male stepped in officers' face and started pointing his finger in officer's face" (Cramer, 2013, para. 26). Brenda was arrested on disorderly conduct charges and taken to the police station.

It is at this point that the story allegedly takes a turn for the worse. Brenda reports that at every stage of the handcuffing, transporting, and booking process she felt humiliated. Even though she asked to be referred to as Brenda, the officers that she interacted with continued to call her Bruce and use the pronoun he when referring to her. She then claims that she was forced to strip and jump up and down to make her breasts jiggle all while being mocked by the officers (St. Amand, 2013, para. 4). The officers in question obviously refuted these charges, and Brenda eventually sued and settled with the city for $20,000. She was also awarded $10,000 from the shelter for the undue hardship that they caused her for not following their own policies regarding inclusivity and non-discriminatory treatment (Cramer, 2013, para. 10).

In response to how the case was handled, the Boston Police Department acknowledged that they had acted inappropriately and outside of both their own, as well as the city of Boston's guidelines regarding sexual orientation and gender identity. The city of Boston has an ordinance that gives people the right to use restroom facilities based on their gender identity and the city failed to train its officers on this ordinance (Transgender Woman Settles, 2013, para. 3). In an effort to learn from their mistakes, the Boston Police Department reached out to the Massachusetts Transgender Political Coalition to receive training and rewrite policies for dealing with transgender people. Among the suggestions made were to train officers to address transgender people by their adopted or legally changed name, as well as have two officers of the gender requested by the suspect administer pat downs and searches (St. Amand, 2013, para. 5–6).

In the above example, it appears as though Boston has learned from this experience and has taken active steps to move forward. However, there continue to be huge discrepancies from city to city and state to state regarding gender identity issues. Currently, only 13 states protect transgender people from discrimination based on gender identity in public accommodations. While this seems like a step in the right direction for proponents of these laws, they are still critical that the definition of "public accommodation" differs from state to state and there are no federal laws put in place to oversee these practices (Bennett-Smith, 2013, p. 8). Additionally, many more states recognize and provide protections against discrimination in employment, housing, and public accommodations based on one's sexual orientation, but states are still lagging behind in recognizing gender identity (i.e., transgender people) as a protected status (ACLU, Non-Discrimination Laws, n.d., interactive map). According to Ilona Turner, director of the Transgender Law Center in San Francisco, "Transgender people have the same needs and deserve the same access to public stores and facilities as others … they need to go to the bathroom like everyone else" (Chapple, 2013, para. 14).

Discussion Questions

1. If you could suggest one federal mandate that law enforcement should follow when dealing with transgender suspects, what would it be?

2. What is your personal opinion about the above case? Should transgender individuals be allowed to use their restroom of choice?

Corrections

School-to-Prison Pipeline

While school disciplinary policies might not immediately strike one as obviously connected to corrections, there is actually a close link between the educational policies impacting teenagers at school and the corrections system. The **school-to-prison pipeline** is a concept based on the observation that what happens in school (increasingly in recent years) does not stay in school. Schools are often outsourcing what once were internal disciplinary matters to the criminal justice system. If a referral is made to an actor in the criminal justice system, such referrals may contribute to establishing a juvenile and/or criminal record for that student. Since school disciplinary policies suffer from disproportionate racial impacts, this raises concerns that improper government favoritism is also tainting the school-to-prison pipeline through disproportionate referrals into the criminal justice system.

In 2014, the U.S. Departments of Education and Justice jointly set guidelines for school discipline (Deeney, 2014, para. 2). The civil rights arms of both of these departments are heavily involved in helping schools avoid racially discriminatory disciplinary practices. The Department of Education has been collecting civil rights data since 1968 which reveals that, "Although African-American students represent 15% of students [in the study], they make up 35% of students suspended once, 44% of those suspended more than once, and 36% of students expelled" (Deeney, 2014, para. 3). The Department of Education study goes on to note that over half of students who are involved in school-related arrests, or referred to law enforcement, are Hispanic or African-American. So while school suspensions themselves involve educational policy, if schools instead (or additionally) choose to make calls to law enforcement or juvenile probation officers, then that choice implicates the larger criminal justice system.

Part of the problem is the widespread adoption of **zero-tolerance policies**, which "presume all explanations for infractions as small as being late to school are [illegitimate] excuses and there's no such thing as mitigating circumstances" (Deeney, 2014, para. 1). Such policies impact poor black and Latino students disproportionately, since in reality their socio-economic circumstances often do cause difficulties for the students themselves, or their parents/guardians, which interfere with 100% compliance.

Zero-tolerance policies were created to address concerns about crime in schools and the need to teach accountability and maintain order. The government's interests in accomplishing the goals behind these policies are important, but the execution of zero-tolerance policies often leads to harsh consequences and punishments. Zero-tolerance polices might even be counterproductive and prevent the government from achieving the goals of accountability and order, if they dishearten students, delay a student's studies or deny a student's access to services, and place students right back in the family, home, and street environments that are contributing to the problem(s) in the first place. For instance, zero-tolerance attendance policies might on their face only seem to concern the educational system—but if school absences are also being reported to juvenile probation officers, this concerns the corrections system as well. In addition, zero-tolerance suspensions or expulsions might also contribute to preventing students from graduating (a risk factor for later incarceration), as well as placing a student in violation of the terms of their juvenile probation if they have already entered the corrections system.

The new set of guidelines (adopted by the Departments of Education and Justice) seeks to show that order can be maintained by substituting a new set of principles for zero-tolerance policies. The Department of Education's Guiding Principles "mention **restorative practices** no less than nine times" (Deeney, 2014, para. 5). Restorative practices draw upon the larger restorative justice movement in the criminal justice system, which seeks to resolve conflict between victims and offenders through mediation, "non-punitive conflict resolution," peer support, and communication between victims, perpetrators, and facilitators. Instead of the immediate, unwavering, harsh punishment that zero-tolerance polices require (even for minor offenses) in an effort to deter future misbehavior, the restorative practices approach is dedicated to amends-making, apologies, restitution, and instilling in perpetrators a deeper insight and appreciation for the harms they have caused others.

A notorious North Philadelphia junior high school known as the "Jones Jail" was reorganized as the Memphis Street Academy and adopted a restorative practices approach. It saw the number of violent incidents drop 90% in a single year (Deeney, 2014, para. 7). Many observers were skeptical of such results, but corroborating support has come from the local police department. The police department no longer needs to send the 11 patrol officers they once assigned to the school on a daily basis to stand watch at the end of the school day.

Discussion Questions

1. Are there any policies that should remain as zero-tolerance policies? Which ones? Why?

2. Zero-tolerance policies have a disproportionate impact on racial and ethnic minorities. Is this reason enough to eliminate them, or must the existence of effective alternative policies be demonstrated first?

Private Probation Officers as Debt Collectors

The shooting of Michael Brown, an unarmed black teenager, in Ferguson, Missouri, on August 9, 2014, may ultimately have profound effects on the municipal court and probation systems surrounding Ferguson. The governor of Missouri formed a commission to come up with proposals to address the underlying causes of anger and despair in communities like Ferguson that contributed to the unrest following the shooting of Michael Brown. The 198-page report developed by that commission was released in September 2015.

The commission's findings were wide ranging. It validated what we saw in the previous section, noting that in Missouri 14.3% of black elementary students were suspended at least once during a recent school year compared with 1.8% of white students (Davey, 2015b, para. 3). It also found that Black motorists "were 75% more likely to be pulled over for traffic stops in Missouri than whites" (Davey, 2015b, para. 3). Both findings suggested that government favoritism, intentional and unintentional, was driving dissatisfaction and unrest and needed to be corrected if the community was to heal.

The commission listed 47 priorities for reform, including increasing the minimum wage, expanding eligibility for Medicaid, and "consolidating the patchwork of 60 police forces and 81 municipal courts" covering the St. Louis area and its suburbs (Davey, 2015b, para. 2). The highly fractured institutional situation made it difficult for defendants to satisfy their financial obligations from fines and court costs across jurisdictions and also to hold municipal officials accountable. Yet most of the commission's proposals faced a daunting prospect in the state legislature, and in the initial legislative session after the commission's report bills requiring body cameras for police officers and modifications to the state rules on lethal force failed to pass.

One reform item did pass the Missouri Legislature, however, and that was a limitation on how much revenue municipalities can keep from traffic fines (Davey, 2015b, para. 15). The situation in Missouri illustrates a nationwide problem where probation officers' duties and debt collection collide. This is especially troubling in a context where the criminal justice system is providing revenue for over-stretched municipalities. Traffic citations and fines can provide a major source of revenue for small cities and suburbs. Some cities, like Ferguson, have been aggressive in seeking those funds. "In 2013, Ferguson … had the highest number of arrest warrants — often served by municipal courts when someone fails to appear in court [or fails to pay their fines] — in the state relative to its size: 1,500 warrants per 1,000 people" (Davey, 2015a, para. 14). Government discrimination (e.g., in the form of disproportionate traffic stops), combined with the rise of private probation companies, has created a perfect storm where financial incentives encourage the abuse of the tools of the criminal justice system in order to collect sums of money off those least able to pay.

The appeal of **private probation** is that municipalities can outsource the enforcement of municipal court orders and the collecting of court costs and fines, often with the threat of jail time looming over the mostly unemployed and indigent who are required to pay the fines. "More than 1,000 low-level courts across the US rely on the so-called 'offender funded' probation model, signing contracts with for-profit companies that oversee probation requirements like monitoring, drug tests and fine collection" (Gambino, 2014, para. 6). Yet one report notes that, at least in the St. Louis area, "the greater the minority population of the city, the greater percentage of its [municipal] revenue stream comes from fines" (Pishko, 2015, para. 13).

Aside from traffic fines where municipalities might make money, there is also a great deal of money at stake in low-level crimes like public drunkenness. It might cost as much as $50 a day to house a misdemeanor offender in jail. The cost savings for states and localities for placing that person on probation instead are huge, since probationers might cost the system only $1.25 per day, and even less if private companies hired to monitor those on probation seek to collect the costs (Gambino, 2014, para. 8). Yet the private probation companies collecting the fees stand to make large sums of money from the payment plans they set up for probationers. For instance, in one case the probationer was set on a payment plan to make monthly payments of $145, but each installment included $40 that went to the probation company (Picchi, 2015, para. 8).

Local governments are now implicated in systems of favoritism where those able to pay their fines and court costs upfront pay the face value of the fines and costs, whereas the poor must pay through installment plans and the total cost for them might be twice as much as the face value of fines and tickets (Picchi, 2015, para. 13). Not only are there the obvious concerns with favoritism by the government treating those with low income unfairly, there is also a racial component. "These practices disproportionally impact minorities, who end up paying more money in total—and represent a greater percent of the jail population—than non-minorities" (Pishko, 2015, para. 8).

In a recent report compiled by Human Rights Watch, the for-profit probation model is described as designed "to prey on poor misdemeanor offenders, ensnaring them in debt and threatening imprisonment if financial obligations are not met" (Hsieh, 2014, para. 2). In one case documented by Human Rights Watch in Georgia, a resident was jailed for failing to pay more than $1,000 in accumulated fees and costs stemming from his original crime of stealing a two-dollar can of beer (Hsieh, 2014, para. 3). "Poorer offenders stay on probation longer and end up paying significantly more, due to supervision fees levied by private firms" (Hsieh, 2014, para. 7).

Human Rights Watch also found that the private probation companies make a lot of money in the process of supervising probation, finding that companies in Georgia made nearly $40 million in fees in just one year (Gambino, 2014, para. 10). The big problem is that many of those least able to pay are placed on probation in the first place precisely because they are not able to pay. They have outstanding court costs and fines, and the court places them on probation to require them to make payment arrangements (Gambino, 2014, para. 14). The incentives become truly distorted when probation companies offer their employees financial bonuses based on the amount of fees they collect. The incentive is high to use aggressive squeeze tactics to pressure probationers, and in some cases their family members, to pay the fines. When probationers fail to pay the court-ordered fines, as well as the company fees, "the companies can, and do, push law-enforcement to arrest them. That leaves probationers with a stark choice: pay up or be locked up" (Gambino, 2014, para. 17).

It is true that the Supreme Court has struck down debtors' prisons as unconstitutional, and also outlawed imprisonment for simple inability to pay fines. Nevertheless, "[p]eople are incarcerated across the country without any judicial inquiry as to their ability to pay" (Pishko, 2015, para. 7). The private probation companies operate "as debt collectors with handcuffs" and with little oversight (Pishko, 2015, para. 8). There is little incentive, and thus little attempt is made, for the criminal justice system to sort out those who are genuinely unable to pay and those who simply do not want to. Probation revocation hearings may only last a matter of minutes, and few offenders are offered legal representation at such hearings to make the case that they are unable to pay.

Since local courts often have parts of their budgets funded by these fees, local courts are incentivized to accept the fines collected from the private companies and turn a blind eye to the collection practices employed. Even though the Supreme Court has struck down practices where judges are paid a percentage of fines imposed or where police officers are paid upon the number of tickets they write, municipal court systems (and sometimes the municipalities themselves) remain dependent on the fees and revenues generated by these private probation companies that collect fees from probationers.

Jailing probationers for inability to pay can have drastic consequences. Several people who were locked up for inability to pay fines in Jennings, Missouri, attempted suicide. Two died (Pishko, 2015, para. 13). People can also lose their jobs and income while locked up for an inability to pay. In a 2015 case out of Alabama, the plaintiff was incarcerated because she was unemployed and could not pay the fixed bond amount. The U.S. Department of Justice filed a statement of interest and argued "any bail or bond scheme that mandates payment of pre-fixed amounts for different offenses in order to gain pretrial release, without any regard for indigence, not only violates the 14th Amendment's Equal Protection Clause, but also constitutes bad public policy" (Pishko, 2015, para. 15). The case was settled later that year, and in affirming the settlement the federal district court observed:

> Criminal defendants, presumed innocent, must not be confined in jail merely because they are poor. Justice that is blind to poverty and indiscriminately forces defendants to pay for their physical liberty is no justice at all. By enacting a new policy that takes account of the circumstances of those who come before its courts, the Clanton Municipal Court has made marked strides in improving the quality of justice it delivers (*Jones v City of Clanton*, M.D. Ala. 2015).

Discussion Questions

1. What kind of oversight of private probation companies might be warranted?

2. Should the amount of extra fees and payments to private probation companies be fixed as a proportion of the face value of court-ordered fines? What downsides to such a policy might exist?

Powder vs. Crack Cocaine Sentencing

Disproportionate impacts upon race do not occur only in school disciplinary and probation cases. Much more serious sentencing and corrections policies can have a disproportionate impact on the basis of race as well. One area where this has been clearly evident is the disparity built into federal sentencing law concerning the amount of powder cocaine versus crack cocaine one must possess before triggering a mandatory minimum sentence.

From the mid-1980s until 2010, crack cocaine users possessing only 5 grams of crack cocaine were charged with a felony under federal law, requiring a five-year mandatory minimum sentence in prison, even for first-time offenders. This was despite the fact that "no other first-time simple possession drug offense required jail time, nor a mandatory minimum sentence." (ATTN: Staff, 2015, para. 7). For sake of comparison, 5 grams is approximately the weight of two pennies. However, in order to get the same sentence, those convicted of possessing cocaine powder were required to be caught with 500 grams of cocaine powder, a disparity of 100 to 1 (Graves, 2010, para. 3). This despite the fact that "[e]ven the U.S. Sentencing Commission, a federal agency, found that crack cocaine is not appreciably different from powder cocaine, either in its chemical composition or the physical reactions of its users" (ATTN: Staff, 2015, para. 3). Likewise a first-time offender with 50 grams of crack was required to be sentenced to at least ten years in prison, whereas someone possessing powder cocaine would need five kilograms to receive that mandatory minimum sentence (ATTN: Staff, 2015, para. 6).

For years it has been understood that the crack vs. powder cocaine sentencing disparity has a disproportionate impact on African-Americans. Representative Keith Ellison spent 16 years as a trial lawyer dealing with hundreds of cocaine cases before entering Congress. He was part of the movement to get the 100-to-1 disparity reduced. He noted that "Basically whites use cocaine, blacks use crack ... or are arrested with it. It's not even use, actually. Blacks don't use that much crack but ... [are] disproportionately more likely to be arrested with it" (Graves, 2010, para. 3). Ellison would show up to criminal court to see whites getting probation and blacks getting ten years in prison for basically possessing the same substance, one in powder form, one as crack. Crack is cheaper and less pure, so it is predominately found in low-income communities (ATTN: Staff, 2015, para. 5). Surveys of drug users show that all racial groups in the country use crack cocaine at a rate of between .5% and 1.6% of the population. Yet "77% of all people arrested for crack cocaine were black" (Graves, 2010, para. 6).

The reason for this sentencing disparity reaches back, in part, to college sports. Len Bias was a college basketball star playing for the University of Maryland when in 1986 he died as a result of a cocaine overdose (Graves, 2010, para. 8). His overdose was initially blamed on crack cocaine (although this later turned out not to be true — it was actually powder cocaine that Bias used). In the fear and outrage by the public that followed the death of Bias, in the context of the larger War on Drugs, Congress took drastic steps and implemented harsh mandatory minimum sentences treating powder and crack cocaine differently.

By 2010 Congressman Ellison and others were dismayed at the destruction caused, not just by crack cocaine, but by the harsh sentences imposed by the criminal justice system stemming from fears over crack cocaine: "the reality is that it's just that we've incarcerated a whole generation of black urban youth." Representative Ellison pointed out that the reforms passed by Congress in 2010 did not allow anybody to get out of prison. Rather "you're going to get a sentence that is at least similar, at least more similar, to what people who deal powder cocaine get" (Graves, 2010, para. 14).

The U.S. Sentencing Commission reported that over 70,000 crack cocaine offenders have been sentenced in federal court since 1996. This means over 5,500 crack offenders sentenced each year, of which almost 2,000 receive a five-year mandatory minimum sentence, and around 2,700 receive a ten-year mandatory minimum. The reforms passed by Congress in 2010 expected to "impact almost 3,000 crack offenders each year and reduce crack sentences by 27 months on average" (Graves, 2010, para. 12). It was projected to free up over 1,500 prison beds and save $42 million over five years.

While the savings are real, a substantial sentencing favoritism remains. The 100-to-1 disparity was not eliminated, rather it was merely reduced to an 18-to-1 disparity. Instead of 5 grams of crack cocaine equaling 500 grams of powder cocaine, now 28 grams of crack cocaine equal 500 grams of powder cocaine (Graves, 2010, para. 3). Congressman Ellison says the reason is racism: "Even though white people sell drugs all the time, people ... just don't think of them as doing that. I mean that's what racism's about: it's an unrealistic and inflated sense of guilt associated with people of color and an unrealistic inflated sense of innocence associated with people who are white. And they think they're fairer, nicer, kinder.... Whereas they look at somebody who's black and say: Crook! Send him away!" (Graves, 2010, para. 5).

The reform legislation, The Fair Sentencing Act of 2010, did not make the sentencing reductions explicitly retroactive. Thus there are "thousands of federal inmates still serving time under sentences that would not have been imposed under the new law. Most are black" (Greenhouse, 2014, para. 2). Various courts considered whether the law should be interpreted as retroactive. One panel of the United States Court of Appeals for the Sixth Circuit held that:

"The discriminatory nature of prior crack sentences is no longer a point of legitimate debate [and applying the old law] would perpetuate proven racial discrimination and thereby violate equal protection" (Greenhouse, 2014, para. 9). Nevertheless, the full Sixth Circuit overturned the panel's decision on a vote of 10 to 7 and decided to follow all of the other U.S. Courts of Appeals (who have considered the issue) to rule against the retroactivity of the Fair Sentencing Act (Greenhouse, 2014, para. 10).

This led to political pressure being placed upon President Obama to commute sentences through the use of the **presidential pardon power**, for those with excessively long drug sentences. The president has full discretion to either fully pardon someone, in which case their conviction is wiped from their record, or to simply commute (i.e., reduce) the sentence and order an inmate released from prison while preserving the conviction. In fact, President Obama in July 2015 did commute the sentences of 46 drug offenders, the largest single-day group of commutations since the 1960s under President Lyndon B. Johnson (Davis and Harris, 2015, para. 4).

President Obama's commutations, however, did not stem the calls for further commutations and additional congressional reforms to address mandatory minimum sentences for nonviolent drug offenders. While these are laudatory goals, the fact remains that "White Americans are more likely than black Americans to have used most kinds of illegal drugs.... Yet blacks are far more likely to go to prison for drug offenses" (ATTN: Staff, 2015, para. 18). In fact, blacks are arrested three times as frequently as whites, and blacks make up nearly half of all state prison drug offender populations despite being only 14% of the total U.S. population (ATTN: Staff, 2015, para. 18). This government favoritism is allowed because the sentencing laws do not explicitly categorize based upon race, but rather have a known disproportionate effect on African Americans.

Discussion Questions

1. Should laws with a racially disproportionate impact be treated the same as discrimination explicitly on the basis of race? Why or why not?

2. What might be the best way to address this situation — endorse the new status quo, pass further legislation, allow courts to address the situation, or rely upon presidential commutations (where the president's advisors can assess rehabilitation during incarceration)?

Racial Segregation in Prison

Racial segregation in prisons would seem to be something deep in America's past, but that is not true. Until recently, the state of California continued to maintain racial segregation in its prisons, albeit to address security concerns from prison gangs, which are often organized upon racial lines. In 2013, it was reported that inmates across California had colored signs hanging above their cell doors: "blue for black inmates, white for white, red, green or pink for Hispanic, yellow for everyone else" (Thompson, 2013, para. 1). This system allowed corrections officials, when there was prison violence, to restrict all prisoners of that same race from the yard and/or certain areas to prevent further violence. The official justification for the color coding system was "to prevent race-based victimization, reduce race-based violence, and prevent theft and assaults" (Thompson, 2013, para. 5).

Several lawsuits were filed in response to such policies in California. It is a critical issue: "Nearly half the 1,445 security-based lockdowns [in California] between January 2010 and November 2012 affected specific racial or ethnic groups" (Thompson, 2013, para. 9). The basic problem is determining who is a member of a prison gang, and who might merely seek out protection from members of their own race or ethnicity during a fight. Yet other alternatives to racial categories do exist. A program adopted at Pelican Bay State Prison (in response to a lawsuit) begin assessing risks posed by individual inmates in order to determine restrictions upon inmates. The program proved successful, and violence dropped as a result of the new policy (Thompson, 2013, para. 28). The Supreme Court has condemned the use of race as a proxy for gang membership and violence (Thompson, 2013, para. 28).

Yet court intervention has sometimes been criticized as "engaging in unreasonable meddling in a situation they know nothing about and cannot really appreciate" (Walsh, 2014, para. 1). Bob Walsh, a former California Department of Corrections officer, noted that prison inmate gangs "have a very strong tendency to be racially focused." Walsh reports, based on his experience as a line officer, a sergeant, and a lieutenant, that "with very, very few exceptions, inmates refuse to share a cell with an inmate not of his racial group" (Walsh, 2014, para. 4). Attempts to impose racial desegregation in prisons meet with resistance to staff from inmates, as well as fights between inmates. When desegregation is imposed fights frequently break out between inmates "if for no other reason than they believe they will be punished by their groups if they do not fight" (Walsh, 2014, para. 8). Walsh opines that the system of race/gang-based segregated housing could be overcome, but only with extensive support and willingness to deal with consequences and costs "much, much higher than the courts and other outside critics believe it will be" (Walsh, 2014, para. 12).

In 2014 California officials did agree to end racially segregated prison housing policies. In the settlement agreement, reached as a result of a lawsuit, the state agreed that future lockdowns may not be imposed or lifted based on race or ethnicity (California prisons agree, 2014, para. 3). Instead lockdowns will be targeted at affected areas of the prison, or inmates suspected of association with a particular incident, or the gangs involved. "The agreement with attorneys representing inmates came after the U.S. Justice Department said in a non-binding court filing last year that the old policy violated the 14th Amendment that requires equal protection under the law." (California prisons agree, 2014, para. 6).

News reporting of the settlement in some sources seemed to be optimistic that "the state has agreed to switch to a system that determines prisoner by prisoner who is to be locked down" (St. John, 2014, para. 9). The actual language of the settlement agreement, however, suggested lockdowns or other modifications may still be imposed "on all inmates, and lifted from all inmates ... in an affected area" (*Mitchell v. Cate*, 2014, para. 15). While individualized review of inmates might be the goal, it seems the California Department of Corrections reserves the right to substitute lockdowns based on wings, floors, or units, instead of upon race.

Discussion Questions

1. How might costs go up, as Walsh warns, by California's transition to its new policy?

2. What other challenges might you foresee in ending all consideration of race in California's correctional programs?

Chapter Key Terms

Alibi

Compensatory damages

Preempted

U-Visa

Gender identity

Trespassing

School-to-prison pipeline

Zero-tolerance policies

Restorative practices

Private probation

Presidential pardon power

References

American Civil Liberties Union (ACLU). (n.d.). ACLU non-discrimination laws: State by state information map. https://www.aclu.org/map/non-discrimination-laws-state-state-information-map?redirect=maps/non-discrimination-laws-state-state-information-map.

American Civil Liberties Union (ACLU). (n.d.). Arizona's SB 1070. Deactivated link (retrieved 2015). https://www.aclu.org/feature/arizonas-sb-1070.

American Civil Liberties Union of Florida (ACLUFL). (2010, February 3). ACLU gives notice of intent to sue Miami Beach for unlawful arrest of gay men and individuals who report police misconduct. https://aclufl.org/2010/02/03/aclu-gives-notice-of-intent-to-sue-miami-beach-for-unlawful-arrest-of-gay-men-and-individuals-who-report-police-misconduct/.

Associated Press in Greenville (1990, November 2). City officials settle $28 million Civil Rights suit for $50,000. https://apnews.com/article/ad60a6c478c155a78aee2c2bd94cccfe.

Associated Press in Phoenix. (2014, September 26). Arizona immigration law faces lawsuit by Mexican woman over 'illegal' arrest. The Guardian. http://www.theguardian.com/world/2014/sep/26/arizona-immigration-law-challenge-lawsuit-illegal-arrest.

ATTN: Staff. (2015, September 9). Here are the sentencing disparities between crack and cocaine. http://www.attn.com/stories/3095/war-on-drugs-crack-cocaine.

Bennett-Smith, M. (2013, April 15). Ally Robledo, transgender woman, cited for trespassing after using women's bathroom in Idaho. Huffington Post. http://www.huffingtonpost.com/2013/04/15/ally-robledo-transgender-trespassing-grils-bathroom-idaho_n_3086988.html.

California prisons agree to end race-based lockup policy. (2014, October 23). CBS News. https://www.cbsnews.com/news/california-prisons-agree-to-end-race-based-lockup-policy/.

CBS News Video. (1983). Lenell Geter's in jail. http://www.cbsnews.com/videos/lenell-geters-in-jail/.

Chapple, R. (2013). Transgender woman charged with trespassing, banned from Idaho supermarket for using women's bathroom. New York Daily News. http://www.nydailynews.com/news/national/transgender-woman-banned-idaho-store-women-restroom-article-1.1315827.

Cramer, M. (2013). Transgender woman settles lawsuit with Boston over treatment during 2010 arrest. http://www.boston.com/news/local/massachusetts/2013/02/05/transgender-woman-settles-lawsuit-with-boston-over-treatment-during-arrest/jldg4ZWAzhEU5srQSiYANI/story.html.

Crockett, S. A. (2014). Watch: Police defend arrest of black man reportedly tased in front of his kids. The Root. https://www.theroot.com/watch-poli ce-defend-arrest-of-black-man-reportedly-tas-1790876896.

Davey, M. (2015a). Ferguson one of 2 Missouri suburbs sued over gantlet of traffic fines and jail. *The New York Times*. http://www.nytimes.com/2015/ 02/09/us/ferguson-one-of-2-missouri-suburbs-sued-over-gantlet-of-traffic -fines-and-jail.html.

Davey, M. (2015b). Panel studying racial divide in Missouri presents a blunt picture of inequity. *The New York Times*. http://www.nytimes.com/2015/09/ 14/us/panel-studying-racial-divide-in-missouri-presents-a-blunt-picture -of-inequity.html.

Davis, J. and Harris, G. (2015). Obama commutes sentences for 46 drug offenders. *The New York Times*. https://www.nytimes.com/2015/07/14/us/ obama-commutes-sentences-for-46-drug-offenders.html.

Deeney, J. (2014). How to discipline students without turning school into a prison. *The Atlantic*. http://www.theatlantic.com/education/archive/2014/01/how -to-discipline-students-without-turning-school-into-a-prison/282944/.

Fishleder, P. (1984). Follow-up on the news; Lenell Geter. *The New York Times*. http://www.nytimes.com/1984/08/19/nyregion/follow-up-on-the-news -lenell-geter.html.

Ford, Z. (2013). Idaho transgender woman charged with trespassing for using grocery store restroom. ThinkProgress. http://thinkprogress.org/lgbt/2013/ 04/15/1864641/transgender-trespassing/.

Gambino, L. (2014). Thrown in jail for being poor: The booming for-profit probation industry. The Guardian. http://www.theguardian.com/money/ 2014/mar/02/poor-for-profit-probation-prison-georgia.

Garcia, A. (2014). Sitting while Black in Minnesota: Cops tase man for not stating his name. Raw Story. http://www.rawstory.com/2014/08/sitting -while-black-in-minnesota-cops-tase-man-for-not-stating-his-name/.

Garcia, M. (2010). Greetings from Miami Beach Fla. The Advocate. http:// www.advocate.com/news/daily-news/2010/02/04/miami-beach-sued-wrong ful-arrest-officers-reassigned.

Graves, L. (2010). Crack-powder sentencing disparity: Whites get probation, Blacks get a decade behind bars. Huffington Post. http://www.huffington post.com/2010/08/02/crack-powder-sentencing-d_n_667317.html.

Greenhouse, L. (2014). Crack cocaine limbo. *The New York Times*. http://www. nytimes.com/2014/01/06/opinion/greenhouse-crack-cocaine-limbo.html.

Hayden, J. (2014). St. Paul police violently arrest a black man for sitting on bench, waiting for his children. Daily Kos. http://www.dailykos.com/story/

2014/08/28/1325409/-St-Paul-police-violently-arrest-a-black-man-for
-sitting-on-bench-waiting-for-his-children-VIDEO.

Howe, A. (2012). S.B. 1070: In plain English. SCOTUSblog. http://www.scotus
blog.com/2012/06/s-b-1070-in-plain-english/.

Hsieh, S. (2014, February 6). Skip meals or go to jail? The Nation. http://www.
thenation.com/article/skip-meals-or-go-jail-how-profit-probation-industry
-preys-poor/.

Ibrahim, M. M. (2016). St. Paul pays $100k to settle skyway stun gun arrest.
Minnesota Public Radio. https://www.mprnews.org/story/2016/02/18/st
-paul-pays-lollie-100k-settle-skyway-taser-arrest.

Jones v City of Clanton, M.D. Ala. 2015 (No. 2:15-cv-00034-MHT-WC).

Kowalski, D. (2014). U-Visa holder sues Pinal County (AZ) sheriffs for
unlawful arrest. LexisNexis Legal News Room. http://www.lexisnexis.com/
legalnewsroom/immigration/b/outsidenews/archive/2014/09/26/u-visa
-holder-sues-pinal-county-az-sheriffs-for-unlawful-arrest.aspx.

Kunichoff, Y. (2012). "Show me your papers" provision goes into law in Arizona. *Truthout*. http://www.truthout.org/news/item/11649-show-me-your
-papers-provision-goes-into-law-in-arizona.

The Leadership Conference on Civil and Human Rights. (2011, March). *Restor-
ing a national consensus: The need to end racial profiling in America*.
https://www.blackradionetwork.com/images/userfiles/racial_profiling2011.
pdf?phpMyAdmin=d8afc5c6e9b6ffb205b5fe3c0c1273fa.

Levine, J. P. (1992) *Juries and politics*. Brooks/Cole Publishing Company.

Macias, A. (2014). ACLU defendant receives settlement from Pinal County
Sheriff's Department. http://kjzz.org/content/80555/aclu-defendant
-receives-settlement-pinal-county-sheriffs-department.

McBride, J. (1987). Conviction of Lenell Geter. *The Washington Post*. https://
www.washingtonpost.com/archive/lifestyle/1987/02/03/convictions-of
-lenell-geter/b5d47/ca1-448e-443e-8414-63ccaa862104/.

McCartney, S. (1984, March 23). Cleared of robbery charge, Lenell Geter begins
new life. *The Dispatch*. https://news.google.com/newspapers?nid=1734&
dat=19840323&id=_-YbAAAAIBAJ&sjid=i1IEAAAAIBAJ&pg=4733,924
4845&hl=en.

Mitchell v. Cate, 2:08-CV-01196-TLN-EFB (E.D. Cal. Oct. 7, 2015), Stipulated
Settlement.

Morales, E. (2010). After anti-gay incident, all eyes on Miami Beach Police.
American Civil Liberties Union. https://www.aclu.org/blog/speakeasy/
after-anti-gay-incident-all-eyes-miami-beach-police?redirect=blog/lgbt
-rights/after-anti-gay-incident-all-eyes-miami-beach-police.

Natarajan, R. (2014). Racial profiling has destroyed public trust in police. Cops are exploiting our weak laws against it. *Washington Post*. http://www. washingtonpost.com/posteverything/wp/2014/12/15/racial-profiling-has -destroyed-public-trust-in-police-cops-are-exploiting-our-weak-laws-against -it/.

National Association for the Advancement of Colored People (NAACP). (2014). *Born suspect: Stop-and-frisk abuses and the continued fight to end racial profiling in America*. https://www.naacp.org/criminal-justice-issues/racial profiling/.

On Top Magazine Staff. (2011, August 2). Miami Beach pays Harold Strickland $75,000; Fires officers for targeting gay men. *On Top*. http://www.ontop mag.com/article.aspx?id=9101&MediaType=1&Category=26.

Picchi, A. (2015). Towns start pulling back on private probation firms. CBS News. http://www.cbsnews.com/news/towns-start-pulling-back-on-pri vate-probation-firms/.

Pishko, J. (2015). Locked up for being poor. *The Atlantic*. http://www.theatl-antic.com/national/archive/2015/02/locked-up-for-being-poor/386069/.

SFGN Staff. (2011). ACLU of Florida reaches settlement in unlawful arrest of man reporting police misconduct in Miami Beach. South Florida Gay News. http://southfloridagaynews.com/Local/aclu-of-florida-reaches -settlement-in-unlawful-arrest-of-man-reporting-police-misconduct-in -miami-beach.html.

Smiley, D. (2012). Miami Beach cop fired in gay bashing case to get his job back. *Miami Herald*. http://www.miamiherald.com/incoming/article1945160.html.

St. Amand, J. (2013). Boston Police Department adopt transgender inclusive policy. http://www.edgeboston.com/news/national/news/145726/boston_ police_department_adopt_transgender_inclusive_policy.

St. John, P. (2014). California prisons end race based policy for inmate violence. *Los Angeles Times*. http://www.latimes.com/local/lanow/la-me-ln-california -prisons-race-policy-inmate-violence-20141023-story.html.

Stowers, C. (2001, November 15). The way of the gun. *The Dallas Observer*. http://www.dallasobserver.com/news/the-way-of-the-gun-6391064.

Thompson, C. (2013). Are California prisons punishing inmates based on race? ProPublica. http://www.propublica.org/article/are-california-prisons -punishing-inmates-based-on-race.

Transgender woman settles lawsuit with city of Boston. (2013). National Lawyers Guild, National Police Accountability Project. http://www.nlg -npap.org/news/transgender-woman-settles-lawsuit-city-boston.

Vargas-Cooper, N. (2014, September 26). Insane traffic stop tests 'show me your papers' law. The Intercept. https://firstlook.org/theintercept/2014/

09/26/woman-held-detention-five-days-first-lawsuit-filed-arizona-show -papers-law/.

Walsh, B. (2014, August 26). Why racial segregation in prisons isn't about race. Corrections1. http://www.correctionsone.com/bob-walsh/articles/74977 11-Why-racial-segregation-in-prisons-isnt-about-race/.

Williams, S. (2011). ACLU settles Miami wrongful arrest suit. Care2. http:// www.care2.com/causes/aclu-settles-miami-wrongful-arrest-suit.html.

Xiong, C. (2014, November 14). Man arrested in downtown St. Paul skyway sues police, city. Star Tribune. http://www.startribune.com/man-arrested -in-st-paul-skyway-sues-3-police-officers-city/282658401/.

Yuen, L. (2014). Panel clears cops in St. Paul skyway stun gun arrest; lawsuit expected. Minnesota Public Radio. http://www.mprnews.org/story/2014/ 11/14/lollie-lawsuit.

Chapter Eleven

Cruelty

> The ultimate tragedy is not the oppression and cruelty by the bad people but the silence over that by the good people.
>
> —Martin Luther King, Jr.

The Constitution teaches us the value of avoiding cruelty by prohibiting modes of punishment that are barbaric, including executions that are unnecessarily torturous, sentences that are disproportionately long, and conditions of confinement that inflict injury or death. In other words, this area of law teaches us the necessity of humaneness in our pursuit of justice. The first group of cases in this chapter will look at the origins and development of the Cruel and Unusual Punishment Clause in the Eighth Amendment. Then we will address issues surrounding how best to carry out the death penalty. Next we will look at the problem of disproportionate sentences, before finally turning to cases governing conditions of confinement.

Evolving Standards of Decency

Perhaps the most cited case in Eighth Amendment jurisprudence is the following case. It acknowledges that the definition of what is "cruel" and "unusual" is not permanently fixed, but rather evolves as society's understanding of those terms shifts.

Trop v. Dulles

356 U.S. 86 (1958)

Albert Trop was a native-born American citizen who served in the Army during World War II. He was stationed in French Morocco. One day in 1944, while serving time in the stockade for disciplinary matters, he escaped and left the Army base. The next day, however, without funds, food, or means of transportation, Trop climbed aboard a passing Army truck and turned himself in. Nevertheless, Trop was court-martialed for wartime desertion, sentenced to three years hard labor, and dishonorably discharged.

That might have been the end of the story, but in 1952, after Trop returned home to the United States, he applied for a passport. Trop's passport application was denied on the basis of a congressional statute which stripped Trop of his citizenship because of his wartime desertion. The congressional statute had roots back to a Civil War statute stripping a deserting soldier of his "rights of citizenship." The meaning of this phrase in the Civil War statute was not clear. Perhaps it had been meant to strip the right to vote or hold political office, as was similarly done with section 3 of the Fourteenth Amendment to many Confederate soldiers who had previously taken an oath to support the U.S. Constitution. Yet, before World War II, Congress had clarified that not only were the rights of citizenship to be removed, but that a person was to be **denationalized** (a person's entire nationality and citizenship were to be revoked) for wartime desertion. This left Trop stateless, as a person without a country (at least for legal purposes), even though he was living in the United States.

The Court held that "denationalization as a punishment is barred by the Eighth Amendment" even though it involves no physical mistreatment or torture. The Court traced the history and purpose of the Eighth Amendment's Cruel and Unusual Punishment Clause. The Court noted that the phrase "no cruel and unusual punishments" in our Constitution was taken verbatim from the English Bill of Rights of 1689, and the principal it represents can be traced back to the Magna Carta, which was first adopted in 1215. Governments have the power to punish, but the Eighth Amendment requires that this power be exercised within civilized limits.

The Court acknowledged that the phrase "cruel and unusual punishments" is not precise. More importantly, the Court held that the meaning of those words is not static. The words are not limited in their meaning to what was meant in 1689 when they were written into the English Bill of Rights, nor what they met in 1791 when the Eighth Amendment was ratified. Rather "the Amendment must draw its meaning from the **evolving standards of decency** that mark the progress of a maturing society." This quote is perhaps the most famous and often used quote in the Court's Eighth Amendment cases. The Court is not locked in to any one particular interpretation for all time; they can adjust the application of the Cruel and Unusual Punishment Clause to fit new situations and punishments like that in Trop's case.

Even having accepted an adaptable legal standard, the constitutionality of Trop's punishment presented a difficult question for the Court, dividing it 5 to 4. Chief Justice Earl Warren, writing for four justices, acknowledged the dissent's point that "Since wartime desertion is punishable by death, there can be no argument that the penalty of denationalization is excessive in relation to the gravity of the crime." Indeed, it was especially difficult to object given the fact, as Justice Brennan in his concurring opinion pointed out, that deserters such as Trop might live out their lives with only minor inconvenience, working, marrying, raising a family, and "generally experience[ing] a satisfactorily happy life" despite being stripped of their citizenship. Nevertheless, five justices voted that Congress could not strip citizens of their citizenship as punishment.

Chief Justice Warren explained that Congress might constitutionally apply capital punishment to wartime deserters, "[b]ut it is equally plain that the existence of the death penalty is not a license to the government to devise any punishment short of death within the limit of its imagination." Justice Brennan added that denaturalization as a punishment is the very antithesis of rehabilitation, and instead of assisting the offender to return to full membership in society, "it excommunicates him and makes him, literally, an outcast."

Justice Brennan admitted that Trop's desertion constituted a refusal to perform "one of the highest duties of American citizenship — the bearing of arms in time of a desperate national peril." He further admitted there is a "certain rough justice" in concluding that "he who refuses to act as an American should no longer be an American." Yet, in Brennan's view Congress's response to strip citizenship was "naked vengeance" and thus "beyond the power of Congress to enact." Chief Justice Warren was a bit more philosophical stating that denationalization is "more primitive than torture" as it strips the individual of his political existence and his status in the national and international political community: "in short, the [defendant] has lost the right to have rights."

Discussion Questions

1. Might there be crimes so heinous or treasonous (such as the Boston Marathon or Oklahoma City bombing were) that full revocation of

citizenship should be allowed? Why is removing citizenship viewed as crueler than life in prison (or even execution)?

2. Many states strip felons of the right to vote, and the Fourteenth Amendment still bars holding office to anyone rebelling against the United States who has previously taken an oath to support the U.S. Constitution. How many citizenship rights might be removed before violating the spirit of the holding in *Trop v. Dulles*?

In our next case we will directly confront the question of whether the death penalty constitutes cruel and unusual punishment. Aside from a few cases in the 1970s, like *Furman v Georgia*, 408 U.S. 238 (1972) (which held that how the death penalty was then administered was arbitrary and capricious), the Court has consistently answered that question "no," but for several decades now there have been dissenting voices on the Court.

Baze v. Rees
553 U.S. 35 (2008)

Ralph Baze objected to the means by which Kentucky proposed to execute him. At the time, Kentucky used lethal injection to implement capital punishment, and specifically a three-drug protocol used by 35 other states and the federal government. Attorneys for Baze acknowledged that, if conducted properly, Kentucky's system for execution would be carried out without undue pain. Baze had concerns about whether Kentucky's protocol would be carried out properly. Of particular concern was whether they would verify that he was asleep after giving him the first drug before they administered the second and third drugs that would actually kill him.

Kentucky used three drugs to perform executions in 2008. The first drug, sodium thiopental (also known as Pentothal), is designed to induce a deep, coma-like unconsciousness. If used correctly, this will prevent pain. The problem is the second and third drug will cause pain if the first drug is not administered properly. The second drug is pancuronium bromide (also known as Pavulon), which both inhibits muscle movements (including preventing convulsions and seizures which can be misperceived as signs of consciousness or distress) and also stops breathing, and the third drug is potassium chloride, which causes the heart to stop beating.

To consider Baze's claim, the Court first examined the history of the death penalty in the United States. The Court noted that by the middle of the nineteenth century hanging was the nearly universal form of execution in the United States. Beginning in the late 1800s, electrocution was proposed as an alternative to hanging. By 1915, twelve states had adopted electrocution, and by the middle of the twentieth century it was the method most widely used for capital punishment. Then in 1977, Oklahoma adopted lethal injection, and over the next couple decades virtually every state followed that example. By the time Baze brought his case to the Supreme Court in 2008, thirty-six states used lethal injection as the exclusive or primary method for administering the death penalty.

Throughout this history, with cases specifically addressing the constitutionality of the firing squad in 1879, electrocution in 1890, and other means of execution in the twentieth century, the Court observed that it had "never invalidated a State's chosen procedure for carrying out a sentence of death as the infliction of cruel and unusual punishment." On the other hand, it was clear that a state is not free to simply adopt any means of execution it might prefer. Despite inheriting the phrase "nor cruel and unusual punishments inflicted" from England, the Court made clear that traditional English penalties such as burning or disemboweling alive are unconstitutional, where the deliberate infliction of pain for the sake of pain through torture was added to the penalty.

One consistent characteristic of Supreme Court opinions in this area is that the Court is very divided on such issues. The justices tend to write many opinions for each case, sometimes without any opinion gaining a majority of five votes. In Baze's case the nine justices wrote six separate opinions. Adding these opinions together, there were five justices supporting Kentucky's method of imposing the death penalty — finding that Kentucky had taken adequate steps and established adequate procedures to prevent unnecessary infliction of pain. Two justices had serious concerns about the death penalty in general, but found that Baze had not proven that Kentucky's method was unconstitutional. The remaining two justices objected to Kentucky's use of these methods.

Chief Justice John Roberts wrote for the three swing-vote justices (himself, Alito, and Kennedy) in the middle of the Court. The chief justice wrote that "simply because an execution method may result in pain, either by accident or as an inescapable consequence of death, does not establish the sort of objectively intolerable risk of harm that qualifies as cruel and unusual." A prisoner cannot challenge a state's method of execution merely by showing a slightly or marginally safer alternative might be available. This would transform the Court into a medical board of inquiry to determine execution best practices, which in turn would "embroil the courts in ongoing scientific controversies beyond their expertise, and would substantially intrude on the role of state legislatures in implementing their execution procedures." However, the chief justice allowed if a state refused to adopt an alternative which would "significantly reduce a substantial risk of severe pain," that would be considered cruel and unusual punishment.

The chief justice detailed all the steps that Kentucky took to make sure that the first drug will be properly administered so as to prevent pain to the condemned prisoners. Baze argued the most humane option would simply be a massive overdose of the first drug, but the Court ruled that Baze failed to prove that eliminating the second drug, or even both the second and third drugs, was necessary. The chief justice said "it is important to reemphasize that a proper dose of [sodium] thiopental obviates the concern that a prisoner will not be sufficiently sedated. All the experts who testified at trial agreed on this point." Acknowledging that reasonable people of good faith disagree on the morality and efficacy of capital punishment, and many who oppose capital punishment would never find any method of execution acceptable, the chief justice concluded "Kentucky has adopted a method of execution believed to be the most humane available, one it shares with 35 other states." Kentucky uses a method that Baze and his attorneys acknowledged would, if administered as intended, result in a painless death. The chief justice found it unnecessary to intervene because while methods of execution had been frequently challenged in the Court, the Court had rejected those challenges, and society had nonetheless steadily moved to more humane methods of administering capital punishment. "The firing squad, hanging, the electric chair, and the gas chamber have each in turn given way to more humane methods, culminating in today's consensus on lethal injection."

Discussion Questions

1. Do you agree with Baze that it would be better to just give the first drug that causes a prisoner to go into a deep sleep? Does the state have any interest (such as making the execution go more quickly) in also giving the drugs that paralyze muscles and stop the heart?

2. Does it follow that if the death penalty is constitutional, there must be a constitutional means to carry it out?

By 2015, the controversy over lethal injection had come full circle as the state of Oklahoma, who had initially adopted lethal injection, was called before the Supreme Court to defend its current practices. What was different about this case than the previous case? Oklahoma had been forced to substitute a new drug into its three-drug protocol because protests and political pressure in Europe had forced drug manufacturers to stop providing the first drug in the lethal injection protocol for states to use in executions. This case will be explored in greater detail below.

Glossip v. Gross

576 U.S. ___, 135 S. Ct. 2726 (2015)

Richard Glossip, who had been sentenced to death in Oklahoma, argued that the state's use of midazolam as the first drug in its three-drug protocol (substituted for the now unavailable sodium thiopental) failed to render a person unable to feel pain. Justice Alito wrote an opinion that garnered a true majority of the justices on the court. The Court noted that "because some risk of pain is inherent in any method of execution, we have held that the Constitution does not require the avoidance of all risk of pain." The Court recognized that if the Eighth Amendment required the elimination of all risk of pain, this would effectively outlaw the death penalty altogether.

In 2011, the company that manufactured sodium thiopental stopped marketing the drug entirely. States then sought an alternative to the first drug used for lethal injection which put a condemned prisoner to sleep. By 2012, all 43 executions carried out that year in the United States used pentobarbital as a replacement to sodium thiopental. Then that drug also became unavailable. So Oklahoma, beginning in 2014, substituted midazolam for the first drug in its three-drug protocol.

Oklahoma's first use of midazolam was a disaster. The condemned prisoner, Clayton Lockett, regained consciousness partway through the execution and began to move and speak. Witnesses reported Lockett cursing and saying, "something is wrong ... the drugs aren't working." An investigation revealed that the IV was improperly inserted into Lockett's leg and therefore the midazolam, instead of entering Lockett's bloodstream, had leaked into the tissue surrounding the IV entry point. While prison officials attempted to halt Lockett's execution after he regained consciousness, Lockett died about 10 minutes later.

Following the investigation into Lockett's execution, Oklahoma revamped its lethal injection protocol, including increasing the dose of midazolam and instituting new safeguards to verify a prisoner was unconscious prior to administering the second and third drugs. Prior to the Court hearing Glossip's case, Oklahoma used its new protocol to successfully execute another prisoner.

The Court looked back to the *Baze* case as precedent and reaffirmed that "prisoners cannot successfully challenge a method of execution unless they establish that the method presents a risk that is 'sure or very likely to cause serious illness and needless suffering.'" Prisoners must instead identify an alternative that is "feasible, readily implemented, and in fact significantly reduces a substantial risk of severe pain." In short, the Eighth Amendment requires a prisoner to establish the existence of a known and available alternative with significantly less risk.

The Court determined that Glossip could not offer as a safer alternative more effective drugs that are now unavailable to Oklahoma. The Court then anticipated the next logical move by death penalty opponents, which would be to pressure drug manufacturers to stop producing or providing this newest drug, midazolam. The Court suggested that it would be constitutionally acceptable to return to one of the other methods of execution if the latest drug became unavailable as well. The Court, addressing arguments made by the dissenters, specifically declined to overrule its previous decisions upholding the firing squad, electric chair, and gas chamber.

The Court also addressed the trial court's factual findings regarding midazolam. The Court reviewed those findings under a **clear error standard** (under this standard an appellate court is not allowed to overturn a trial court's findings of fact merely because it would have decided the facts differently). "The District Court did not commit clear error when it found that midazolam is highly likely to render a person unable to feel pain during an execution." The Court noted that aside from Lockett's botched execution, 12 other executions had been conducted using midazolam and they appeared to have been conducted without any significant problems. Furthermore, Lockett was given only 100 mg of midazolam, while Oklahoma's new protocol required five times that dose of midazolam. The Court ended with an interestingly harsh criticism of its dissenting colleague's viewpoints: "Finally, we find it appropriate to respond to the principal dissent's groundless suggestion that our decision is tantamount to allowing prisoners to be 'drawn and quartered, slowly tortured to death, or actually burned at the stake.' That is simply not true, and the principal dissent's resort to this outlandish rhetoric reveals the weakness of its legal arguments."

Feelings were obviously running high on the Court about this controversial topic. Two justices wrote a concurring opinion solely to attack the dissenting justices' arguments. Justice Scalia wrote: "It is impossible to hold unconstitutional that which the Constitution explicitly contemplates." He cited the **Fifth Amendment** as explicitly providing that no person shall be held to answer for a capital crime without an indictment by a grand jury and that no person shall be deprived of life without due process of law. If the Fifth Amendment expressly addresses capital punishment, how can the Eighth Amendment be interpreted to prohibit it? Justice Scalia argued that historically the Eighth Amendment was understood to prohibit only punishments that added terror, pain, or disgrace to a capital sentence. He characterized Justice Breyer's dissent as containing "gobbledy-gook" for saying that the death penalty is cruel because it is unreliable, when in Justice Scalia's view it is the convictions and not the punishments that are unreliable. He also criticizes Justice Breyer's argument that the major alternative to capital punishment, life in prison without the possibility of parole, sufficiently incapacitates dangerous defendants. Justice Scalia noted that one of the additional defendants in the case (besides Glossip who was named in the title of the case) was already in prison when he committed the murder that landed him on death row. Justice Scalia concluded by saying:

> We federal judges live in a world apart from the vast majority of Americans. After work, we retire to homes in placid suburbia or to high-rise co-ops with guards at the door. We are not confronted with the threat of violence that is ever present in many Americans' everyday lives. The suggestion that the incremental deterrent effect of capital punishment does not seem "significant" reflects, it seems to me, a let-them-eat-cake obliviousness to the needs of others. Let the People decide how much incremental deterrence is appropriate.

The target of all this rancor by Justice Scalia was Justice Breyer's dissenting opinion which asks for a full briefing of the more basic question of whether the death penalty violates the Constitution. It seems clear that the dissenters are preparing for a reconsideration of the constitutionality of capital punishment in this country. Justice Breyer identified three fundamental constitutional defects with capital punishment as currently practiced in this country: "(1) serious unreliability, (2) arbitrariness in application, and (3) unconscionably long delays that undermine the death penalty's penological purpose." This leads to a fourth problem, the fact that most places within the United States have abandoned its use (counting counties that actually sentence defendants to death, as opposed to the number of states that authorize it).

Justice Breyer's opinion skipped over the issues surrounding the three-drug protocol and focused on how the death penalty itself is administered and assigned. Justice Breyer quoted Justice Potter Stewart writing over 40 years before in the *Furman v. Georgia* case as stating "the Eighth and Fourteenth Amendments cannot tolerate the infliction of a sentence of death under legal systems that permit this unique penalty to be so wantonly and so freakishly imposed." Justice Breyer noted that "in 2012, just 59 counties (fewer than 2% of all counties in the country) accounted for *all* death sentences imposed nationwide."

Justice Sotomayor wrote the dissent directly addressing the majority's view on the Oklahoma three-drug protocol, and her opinion was no less passionate. She argued the majority opinion leaves petitioners "exposed to what may well be the chemical equivalent of being burned at the stake." A return to the firing squad might be "significantly more reliable" and even constitutional, but since only Utah has used this method of execution since the 1920s it "could be seen as a devolution to a more primitive era." Yet, a return to the firing squad, with all the blood and violence to the prisoner's body that comes with it, "may be vastly preferable to an excruciatingly painful death hidden behind a veneer of medication."

The Court is sure to return to addressing the issues of cruelty concerning the death penalty in upcoming cases.

Discussion Questions

1. Do you agree the Court should place the burden on the prisoner to show an available option that is more humane? How much deference should be shown to state legislatures and state corrections departments?

2. How would you feel if your state moved to adopt the firing squad as an alternative to lethal injection? Would it matter if condemned prisoners were allowed to choose in each state between the firing squad and lethal injection?

Disproportionate Sentences

Cruelty is not just about physical pain. As we saw in *Trop v. Dulles* it is also about undue harshness. Our next case illustrates that prison sentences can simply become too long for the crimes the defendant has committed.

Solem v. Helm

463 U.S. 277 (1983)

Jerry Helm committed a string of non-violent felonies during the 1960s and 1970s in South Dakota while he was suffering with alcohol problems. By 1975, Helm had several third-degree burglary convictions as well as convictions for obtaining money under false pretenses, grand larceny, and a third-offense DWI. Finally, in 1979, Helm was again arrested for writing a bad check in the amount of $100. While normally this offense, on its own, would carry a maximum sentence for five years in prison and a $5,000 fine, because of Helm's previous convictions the maximum penalty was life in prison without the possibility of parole. That is the sentence the trial court imposed, explaining to Helm "I think you certainly earned this sentence, and certainly proven that you're an habitual criminal, and the record would indicate you are beyond rehabilitation and the only prudent thing to do is to lock you up for the rest of your natural life, so you won't have further victims of your crimes.... You'll have plenty of time to think this one over."

The issue facing the Court was whether the Eighth Amendment prohibits a life sentence without possibility of parole for a seventh nonviolent felony. The Court traced the history of the principle against disproportionately long sentences. The Court looked all the way back to Magna Carta, adopted originally in 1215, which contained three prohibitions against excessive punishments. English law continued to raise barriers to disproportionate senses, included in the 1689 English Bill of Rights, with language familiar to us today: "excessive Baile ought not to be required nor excessive Fines imposed nor cruel and usual Punishments inflicted." The Framers of the Eighth Amendment adopted its language directly from the English Bill of Rights.

As early as 1910 the U.S. Supreme Court recognized the principle that "punishment for crime should be graduated and proportioned to offense." In the years leading up to Helm's case the Court struck down capital punishment in certain instances by applying the principle of proportionality. For instance, the Court struck down the death penalty for felony murder when the defendant did not take a life or intend that lethal force be used. Likewise, the Court has held that the death penalty is grossly disproportionate and excessive punishment for rape.

Long prison sentences were similarly limited by the proportionality requirements of the Eighth Amendment. The Court noted that even "a single day in prison may be unconstitutional in some circumstances." The Court ruled that lower courts, when applying a proportionality analysis, should look to (1) the gravity of the offense and the harshness of the penalty; (2) the sentences imposed on other criminals in the same jurisdiction; and (3) sentences imposed for commission of the same crime in other jurisdictions. Applying these standards to Helm, the Court noted that Helm's crime was "one of the most passive felonies a person could commit." There was neither violence nor threat of violence directed to any person, and the $100 value of the bad check issued by Helms was a fairly small amount. Moreover, while a state is justified in punishing a recidivist more severely than a first offender, Helm's prior offenses, while felonies, were all relatively minor felonies.

The Court went on to observe that no one in South Dakota, other than Helm, had ever been given the maximum sentence of life in prison without the possibility of parole on the basis of comparable crimes. Instead, Helm was being treated in the same manner as, or more severely than, criminals in South Dakota who had committed far more serious crimes. Furthermore, compared to other jurisdictions, it appeared that "Helm was treated more severely than he would have been in any other State."

In previous cases the Court had upheld a life sentence for several non-violent felonies, but in those cases the defendant was eligible for parole in as little as 10 to 12 years. Helm was not eligible for parole under South Dakota law — his only opportunity for release was the mere possibility of **executive clemency** (his sentence being commuted by the governor, or the governor granting a pardon, both of which are wholly discretionary decisions and infrequently granted). The Court concluded that Helms's sentence was "significantly disproportionate to his crime, and is therefore prohibited by the Eighth Amendment."

Four justices dissented, objecting that "this type of proportionality review has been carried out only in a very limited category of cases, and never before in a case involving solely a sentence of imprisonment." The dissenters argued that previous precedent had rejected distinctions between violent and nonviolent offenses. The dissenters also objected to comparing sentences a defendant would receive in different states. "Stealing a horse in Texas may have different consequences and warrant different punishment than stealing a horse in Rhode Island or Washington, D.C." The dissenters were particularly concerned that once the Eighth Amendment was used to strike down sentences outside of the death penalty context that the standards applied by justices would be merely subjective. In other words, justices would not be applying the law, but simply applying their own personal preferences as to which sentences constituted cruelty. "It is indeed a curious business for this Court to so far intrude into the administration of criminal justice to say that a state legislature is barred by the Constitution from identifying its habitual criminals and removing them from the streets. Surely seven felony convictions warrant the conclusion that respondent is incorrigible."

Discussion Questions

1. Do you agree with the Court that Helm's felonies were relatively minor? Does the public deserve to be protected from habitual offenders

with third-offense DWIs, even if the most recent crime is only a $100 bad check (especially if, as with Helm, alcohol-related circumstances contributed to the latest bad check)?

2. While stealing a horse in Texas may be different than stealing a horse elsewhere, is writing a $100 bad check the same everywhere? What kinds of crimes might state legislatures have more discretion to treat harshly?

Ewing v. California
538 U.S. 11 (2003)

The Court wrestled again with disproportionality and recidivism statutes in the case of *Ewing v. California*. Gary Ewing, in 2000, while on parole from a nine-year prison term, walked into the pro shop at a golf course in Los Angeles and walked out with three golf clubs, worth nearly $1,200, concealed in his pants leg. Under California law this was felony grand theft. The larger problem for Ewing, however, was that he had a long criminal history.

Ewing had prior convictions in 1984 for theft, in 1988 for felony grand theft auto, in 1990 for petty theft, in 1992 for battery and theft, and in 1993 for burglary, possessing drug paraphernalia, appropriating lost property, unlawfully possessing a firearm, and trespassing. These convictions all lead to short jail sentences and/or probation. Then, in October and November of 1993, Ewing committed three additional burglaries and one robbery, for which he was sentenced to nearly ten years in prison. However, Ewing was paroled in 1999. So, when Ewing was caught with the golf clubs in 2000 he was charged under California's three strikes law.

The Court explained that California's **three strikes law** (an anti-recidivism statute providing a severe, even life sentence, for a third felony) reflected a nationwide shift in sentencing policy towards incapacitating and deterring repeat offenders who threatened public safety. California's law was adopted partially in response to the 1993 kidnapping and killing of 12-year-old Polly Klaas. Polly's murderer had a long criminal history, including two prior kidnapping convictions. Her murderer served only half of his most recent sentence and would have been in prison on the day Polly was killed if he had served his full sentence. Following Polly Klaas's murder, California joined a wave of states enacting three strikes laws. Three strikes laws vary across the country but share the common goal of providing lengthy prison terms for habitual felons.

Gary Ewing was sentenced under California's three strikes law, and because of his prior violent felonies he was sentenced to a term of 25 years to life in prison. The Court noted that in previous cases it had held that it did not violate the Eighth Amendment for a state to sentence a three-time offender to life in prison *with* the possibility of parole. Yet in *Solem*, as seen above, the Court held that a life sentence *without* possibility of parole for a seventh non-violent felony did violate the Eighth Amendment. The eligibility for parole was a key consideration. So was Ewing's sentence, which did provide a possibility of parole after many years of prison, unconstitutional?

The Court pointed out that Ewing's claim, that a 25-year-to-life sentence for "shoplifting three golf clubs" was unconstitutionally disproportionate, painted an incomplete picture of the legal issue. His offense was not merely shoplifting three golf clubs. Rather it was more properly characterized as "stealing nearly $1,200 worth of merchandise after previously having been convicted of at least two violent or serious felonies." While critics might doubt the three strikes law's wisdom, cost efficiency, and effectiveness, the Court argued this criticism was appropriately directed not at the courts, but at the legislature, which has the primary responsibility for making policy choices for criminal sentencing. "We do not sit as a 'superlegislature' to second-guess these policy choices." Instead the Court saw its role merely as determining whether California has a reasonable basis for believing that dramatically enhanced sentences for habitual felons advance the goals of its criminal justice system. The constitutional issue does not go to the wisdom of the law, but only to whether the sentence is "grossly disproportionate" to his offense.

In evaluating the seriousness of Ewing's offense the Court looked not only at his current felony, but also to his long history of felony recidivism. "Any other approach would fail to accord proper deference to the policy judgments that find expression in the legislature's choice of sanctions." The Court argued that states are permitted to deal more harshly with those "who by repeated criminal acts have shown that they are simply incapable of conforming to the norms of society." The Court found this case was different from the situation in *Solem* and held that Ewing's sentence of 25 years to life in prison (with the possibility of parole after 25 years) was not grossly disproportionate, and therefore the sentence did not violate the Eighth Amendment's prohibition on cruel and unusual punishments.

The dissenting justices objected that the Court should have focused more closely on the length of time Ewing would actually spend in prison. In the past the Court had upheld recidivism statutes where the defendant was likely to be paroled in 10 to 12 years, but struck down statutes where the defendant was likely to spend the rest of his life in prison. Ewing was likely to spend at least

25 years in prison before parole. While this was not formally a life sentence without the possibility of parole, for Ewing, who was 38 and was seriously ill at the time of his sentencing, serving at least 25 years meant that he was likely to die in prison.

The dissenters also noted that from the end of World War II until 1994, the most someone like Ewing could have received in California for grand theft was 10 years in prison, and they would most likely serve less than four years of that sentence. Under the U.S. federal sentencing guidelines, most recidivist sentences would not exceed 18 months in prison, and the federal sentencing guidelines imposed only 10 years of prison time even for the worst kinds of recidivists.

Discussion Questions

1. Is the possibility of parole the appropriate constitutional standard, or should the actual time spent in prison (as the dissenters argue) determine whether a sentence is grossly disproportionate?

2. Should a functional life sentence (i.e., inmate likely to die in prison before parole) be considered the same as a formal sentence of life in prison without the possibility of parole? Would this give an unfair advantage to older defendants?

Most recently the Court turned to the specific issue of disproportionality of sentences in juvenile cases. That is the issue in our next case.

Miller v. Alabama

567 U.S. 460 (2012)

Evan Miller was raised by a mother who suffered from alcoholism and drug addiction and a step-father who abused him. By the time he was 14 years old, Evan had attempted suicide four times. One day when Evan was 14 years old, a neighbor, Cole Cannon, came over to Evan's home to make a drug deal with Evan's mother. Evan and a friend, Colby, then left with Cole to go to his trailer to smoke marijuana and play drinking games.

When Cole passed out, Evan grabbed his wallet and took the $300 inside. Evan attempted to replace the wallet back in Cole's pocket, but Cole woke up and grabbed Evan by the throat. Colby then struck Cole with a baseball bat and Evan, once released, took the baseball bat and beat Cole senseless. Then Evan took a sheet, placed it over Cole's head, said, "I am God, I've come to take your life" and delivered a final blow. Evan and Colby then lit the trailer on fire to cover up the evidence of the crime. Cole eventually died from his injuries and smoke inhalation.

Evan was charged as an adult and convicted of committing murder in the course of arson. That crime, in Alabama, carried a mandatory minimum punishment of life in prison without the possibility of parole. The trial judge therefore had no discretion to impose a different punishment, or even to consider Evans's youth and other characteristics in sentencing him.

The Court considered whether Evan's punishment was excessive under the Eighth Amendment's Cruel and Unusual Punishment Clause. The Court explained that the Eighth Amendment "guarantees individuals the right not to be subjected to excessive sanctions" and that right "flows from the basic precept of justice the punishment for crime should be graduated and proportioned to both the offender and the offense." Then, quoting *Trop v. Dulles*, the Court further explained it views that concept "less through a historical prism than according to 'the evolving standards of decency that mark the progress of a maturing society.'"

The Court explained that two lines of cases converge in the *Miller* case. The first line of cases had barred the death penalty for certain types of crimes, such as rape, and certain categories of individuals, like the developmentally disabled and juvenile defendants. The second line of cases had barred mandatory imposition of capital punishment, requiring sentencing judges (and juries) to consider the individual characteristics of the defendant and the details of the defendant's offense. Evan's sentence violated principles established in both lines of cases.

As to the first line of cases the Court had held that "children are constitutionally different from adults for purposes of sentencing." This is because juveniles have diminished culpability and greater prospects for rehabilitation and are therefore less deserving of the most severe punishments. Juveniles lack maturity and have an underdeveloped sense of responsibility which leads to recklessness, impulsivity, and heedless risk-taking. Juveniles are also more vulnerable to outside negative influences and peer pressure. These observations are based not only on common sense and "what any parent knows," but also recent scientific research in psychology and brain development. While this first line of previous cases had mostly dealt with the death penalty, it was also true of life-in-prison sentences. The Court stated, "Life without parole forswears altogether the rehabilitative ideal [and it] reflects an irrevocable judgment about an offender's value and place in society, at odds with a child's capacity for change." The Court also noted that life sentences are especially harsh punishments for juveniles because juveniles almost inevitably serve more years and a greater percentage of his or her life in prison than an adult offender.

The Court then examined its second line of precedents, which had held that individualized sentencing was required when imposing the death penalty. Mandatory death sentences are flawed because they give no consideration to the character and record of the individual offender and exclude from consideration the possibility of mitigating factors. Likewise mandatory life sentences for juveniles are flawed when sentencing judges are not permitted to consider a juvenile's individual situation. Especially important here was the fact that under Alabama's sentencing scheme a judge would have no ability to consider the mitigating qualities of youth. "[Y]outh is more than a chronological fact. It is a time of immaturity, irresponsibility, impetuousness, and recklessness." The Court looked to precedent, where it had invalidated a death sentence because the trial judge did not consider evidence of the juvenile's neglectful and violent family background, including his mother's drug abuse, father's physical abuse, and his own emotional disturbance. The trial judge sentencing Evan was prevented from considering similar evidence of Evan's upbringing by Alabama's mandatory sentencing scheme.

Having examined the principles in both lines of cases, and considered their application to juveniles like Evan, the Court held "the Eighth Amendment forbids a sentencing scheme that mandates life in prison without possibility of parole for juvenile offenders." The Court went on to clarify that this did not guarantee that every juvenile convicted of murder would gain eventual freedom. A sentencing judge may still impose a life sentence for juveniles, but must take into account how children are different and how those differences might justify a sentence other than life in prison.

The Court was again divided in this case. The dissenters took issue with the majority opinion claiming authority to reform the criminal justice system for juveniles. "Determining the appropriate sentence for a teenager convicted of murder presents grave and challenging questions of morality and social policy. Our role, however, is to apply the law, not to answer such questions." The dissenters noted that this punishment could not fairly be characterized as "unusual" under the Eighth Amendment's Cruel and Unusual Punishment Clause because over 2,500 prisoners were then serving life sentences without parole for murders they committed before the age of 18.

Accepting the majority's position that society's views may evolve, the dissenters argued that society's views have evolved in the opposite direction from what the majority suggested: "For most of the 20th century, American sentencing practices emphasized rehabilitation of the offender and the availability of parole. But by the 1980's, outcry against repeat offenders, broad dissatisfaction with the rehabilitative model, and other factors led many legislatures to reduce or eliminate the possibility of parole, imposing longer sentences in order to punish criminals and prevent them from committing more crimes." The dissenters pointed out that statutes establishing life without parole sentences became more common in the past quarter century, and most states have changed their laws relatively recently to expose teenage murderers to such sentences.

The dissenters went on to disagree that there was any way to draw meaningful lines in these types of cases. The dissenters noted that the majority had already declared that discretionary life without parole sentences for juveniles should be "uncommon," which has the same meaning as "unusual." The dissent characterized the majority as doing nothing other than inviting appellate judges to overturn sentences imposed by juries and trial judges. "If that invitation is widely accepted and such sentences for juvenile offenders do in fact become 'uncommon,' the Court will have bootstrapped its way to declaring that the Eighth Amendment absolutely prohibits them."

Discussion Questions

1. Do you agree with the reasoning in the majority or dissenting opinions? Which arguments are most persuasive? Least persuasive?

2. Are judges or state legislators better able to discern whether juveniles have diminished culpability?

The court deciding the next case decided to wait for the *Miller* precedent before rendering its decision. The cases are similar, but distinctly different in that *Miller*'s holding was based on the excessiveness of *mandatory* life without the possibility of parole for a juvenile, whereas the discretionary sentence imposed below was recommended by a jury.

State v. Houston

353 P.3d 55 (Utah 2015)

In 2006, Cameron Houston was seventeen and a half years old. He was living at a residential treatment facility for juvenile sex offenders due to two prior guilty pleas of sexual assault against family members. Houston had experienced a difficult childhood, including physical, verbal, and sexual abuse, and had a deformity in his ear since birth making it difficult for him to learn to speak. His parents had divorced, and at age eight, he attempted suicide and was diagnosed with severe depression.

In February, during a winter snowstorm, a twenty-two year old college student and staff member at the facility, Raechale Elton, drove Houston the few blocks to his independent living home associated with the facility. She went into his residence to sign him into the logbook. As she did so he attacked her from behind and raped her. She fought and screamed so Houston stabbed her repeatedly, slit her throat, and admitted later to attempting to remove her trachea to halt her screaming. Houston was charged with aggravated sexual assault, rape, and aggravated murder.

In exchange for the promise of dropping all of the charges but aggravated murder, Houston recounted the entirety of the events to detectives showing no emotion or remorse. A five-day sentencing hearing for Houston was held before a jury, which by a vote of 11–1 sentenced Houston to life imprisonment without the possibility of parole (LWOP). Houston challenged his LWOP sentence under both the Eighth Amendment and the Utah Constitution.

The Utah Supreme Court affirmed Houston's sentence, ruling that as a discretionary sentence it aligned with the *Miller v. Alabama* precedent. Houston's sentencing jury was required to review any mitigating factors presented and then decide the best sentence for Houston. The Utah Supreme Court focused on the idea that the Supreme Court did not categorically bar the imposition of LWOP sentences for juveniles in *Miller* and while rare, there are "appropriate occasions" for the imposition of such a harsh penalty as LWOP. The Utah Supreme Court observed that under the then-applicable Utah statute there was a presumptive sentence of twenty years, and LWOP for juveniles could be imposed only if ten or more jurors agreed it was appropriate under the circumstances.

The Utah Supreme Court also grappled with the constitutionality of Houston's sentence under the almost identical cruel and unusual punishment clause of the Utah Constitution. States are free to recognize constitutional rights that are broader and more expansive than the federal constitutional rights on the basis of their state constitutional provisions. Houston argued the Utah Supreme

Court should embrace a more protective interpretation of its state provisions, but the Utah Supreme Court ultimately ruled Houston's LWOP sentence was proportional to the crime and was in violation of neither the Eighth Amendment nor Article I, Section 9 of the Utah Constitution. The Utah Supreme Court emphasized it was not the only state supreme court to reach such a conclusion and explained that a large majority of the states authorized the imposition of LWOP sentences for juveniles convicted of murder prior to the *Miller* decision. Since thirty-nine states permitted juvenile LWOP sentences as of 2010, while only six jurisdictions affirmatively prohibited them, the Utah Supreme Court reasoned that societal consensus had not moved to a categorical constitutional prohibition on LWOP sentences for juveniles convicted of homicide.

Justice Durham dissented on state constitutional grounds. She argued Supreme Court precedent recognized that juveniles are irresponsible, immature, vulnerable to negative influences, and less able to remove themselves from dangerous situations. Juveniles collectively tend to age out of offending, and it is difficult to make reliable predictions at sentencing as to which perpetrators will be able to reform and rehabilitate versus those that cannot. She noted the United States is the only country that allows juvenile LWOP. "Both the extreme infrequency of a juvenile LWOP sentence in Utah and global rejection of permanent incarceration for crimes committed before adulthood confirm my independent assessment that juvenile LWOP is cruel and unusual under the Utah Constitution."

Interestingly, the Utah Legislature repealed its statute permitting juvenile LWOP following the *Houston* case. It did so only prospectively, however, leaving Houston's sentence in place. Houston's ultimate fate remains unresolved as he continues to contest his sentence in federal court. It is worth noting that while a couple of states have struck down juvenile LWOP sentences under their state constitutions, and other state legislatures have joined the Utah Legislature in statutory repeals, many states continue to impose juvenile LWOP sentences.[1]

---

1. See Denniston & Binning, (2019), "The Role of State Constitutionalism in Determining Juvenile Life Sentences, 17 Geo. J.L. & Pub. Pol'y 599.

Discussion Questions

1. Are sentencing judges making decisions soon after offenses, or parole boards making decisions well after offenses, better suited to deciding whether an offender should spend their life behind bars?

2. Should courts consider international law and norms when interpreting constitutional rights?

Conditions of Confinement

Finally, the Eighth Amendment is violated not only by certain types of punishments or the length of certain punishments, but also by the conditions in which someone is confined. Our next case demonstrates that corrections officials are limited in the types of tools they may use to punish prisoners for failing to comply with orders given by staff.

Hope v. Pelzer

536 U.S. 730 (2002)

Larry Hope was a prisoner at Limestone Prison in Alabama. In May 1995, Hope was working on a chain gang near the interstate highway when he got into an argument with another inmate. Both men were returned to the prison and handcuffed to a "hitching post." Hope spent two hours chained to the post, and on that occasion he was offered drinking water and a bathroom break every 15 minutes, with his responses to these offers recorded in an activity log. Hope was only slightly taller than the hitching post so that his arms had to be held above shoulder height during that time, which caused discomfort, and in trying to move his arms to relieve that discomfort the handcuffs cut into his wrists.

In June 1995, Hope was again shackled to the hitching post after an exchange of vulgar remarks with a guard at the chain-gang worksite led to a wrestling match between Hope and the guard. Four other guards intervened. Hope was subdued, transported back to the prison, and shackled to the hitching post, where he remained for approximately seven hours. Hope was required to remove his shirt prior to being shackled to the post, so he spent all day shirtless in the sun while it burned his skin. On this occasion Hope was given water only once or twice and no bathroom breaks. At one point a guard taunted

Hope by bringing some water for some dogs, but the guard then purposefully knocked the water cooler over in front of Hope, spilling the water onto the ground.

The Court found that the use of the hitching post for punitive purposes in prison violated the Eighth Amendment. The Court noted that the "unnecessary and wanton infliction of pain constitutes cruel and unusual punishment" and that among unnecessary wanton inflictions of pain are those totally without penological justification. The Court did not completely outlaw any use of the hitching post or otherwise shackling prisoners to bars in prison. Rather the Court made a point of distinguishing a situation where such methods were used in an emergency, or even used in a situation to encourage compliance with orders given by guards. The constitutional problem occurred when the hitching post was used after the fact to punish a prisoner for an infraction. Such use of the hitching post violated the Eighth Amendment.

By the time Hope was attached to the hitching post he had already been transported back to the prison. "Despite the clear lack of an emergency situation, the [guards] knowingly subjected him to a substantial risk of physical harm, to unnecessary pain caused by the handcuffs and the restricted position of confinement for a seven-hour period, to unnecessary exposure to the heat of the sun, to prolonged thirst and taunting, and to a deprivation of bathroom breaks that created a risk of particular discomfort and humiliation." The Court noted that prior lower court decisions had placed the guards on notice that their conduct was unconstitutional here. The Court looked to an earlier Eleventh Circuit case which had found that guards might use temporary denial of drinking water to encourage prisoners to comply with the rules and to do the work required. Once the prisoner complied, the prisoner would receive water like everyone else. This was acceptable so long as the method of coercion did not place the prisoner's health at risk. Yet, denial of water as punishment, once the prisoner was back in the prison and "after he terminates his resistance to authority" would violate the Constitution.

The Court contrasted Hope's situation with that in the Eleventh Circuit case: "Hope was not restrained at the worksite until he was willing to return to work. Rather, he was removed back to the prison and placed under conditions that threatened his health." Indeed, the Court noted that the Alabama Department of Corrections seemed to recognize the potential problems with using hitching posts when it promulgated regulations concerning these types of situations back in 1993. The regulations authorized the use of the hitching post when an inmate refused to work or was otherwise disruptive to the work squad. In that event, however, an activity log should be completed for each inmate detailing his responses to offers of water and bathroom breaks every 15 minutes. No such log was completed for Hope during his seven-hour shackling in June 1995.

Additionally, the U.S. Department of Justice (DOJ) had investigated the use of the hitching post by the Alabama Department of Corrections (ADOC) prior to this case. "Among other findings, the DOJ report noted that ADOC's officers consistently failed to comply with the policy of immediately releasing any inmate from the hitching post who agrees to return to work." The DOJ found that the hitching post was being used systematically as improper punishment for relatively trivial offenses and not to accomplish any legitimate penological goals.

Discussion Questions

1. Compare the hitching post to some of the equipment available to corrections officials as described in the next chapter. Might the hitching post be preferable, at least in the context of encouraging work or compliance with demands?

2. Why is the hitching post different from administrative segregation for punishment? If seven hours on the hitching post is unconstitutional as punishment, why is 20 years in administrative segregation constitutional? Does the difference turn on physical versus psychological suffering? Should it?

So far we have looked at intentional punishments and acts done intentionally to prisoners. In the following case we will consider whether unintentional conduct that is dangerous to the health of inmates can rise to the level of an Eighth Amendment violation.

Brown v. Plata

563 U.S. 493 (2011)

There was no one prisoner who was the focus of the *Brown v. Plata* case. Rather the case was a consolidation of two **class-action lawsuits** (a case collecting a group of similarly situated plaintiffs with common legal claims) brought on behalf of prisoners in California based on medical injuries and neglect stemming from severe prison overcrowding. The first lawsuit was filed in 1990 (over 20 years before the Supreme Court finally ruled) on behalf of a class of seriously mentally ill prisoners housed in California prisons. The district court hearing that case found that California prisons had failed to implement necessary suicide prevention procedures, due largely to severe understaffing. "In 2006, the suicide rate in California's prisons was nearly 80% higher than the national average for prison populations." Mentally ill inmates languished for months, or even years, without access to necessary mental health care. A **special master** (an expert designated by a court to investigate, collect evidence, and/or supervise the implementation of court orders) was appointed by the federal district court to oversee reforms in California prisons related to mental health treatment. In 2007, after twelve years of work, the special master reported that despite the district court's orders attempting to impose reforms, the quality of mental health care in California prisons was deteriorating, not improving.

In the second lawsuit, a class of state prisoners with serious medical conditions filed suit. This lawsuit began in 2001. The district court in that case found that "the California prison medical care system is broken beyond repair, resulting in an unconscionable degree of suffering and death." Many inmates had died from excessively delayed treatment. One analysis suggested over 60 inmates per year were dying in the California prison system from preventable or possibly preventable causes, or in other words at a rate of one preventable death every five to six days. California prisons "were unable to retain sufficient numbers of competent medical staff and would hire any doctor who had a license, a pulse, and a pair of shoes." Overcrowding increased the spread of infectious disease, contributed to prison violence, and increased reliance on prison lockdowns which further inhibited the delivery of medical care. "Everyday ... California prison wardens and healthcare managers make the difficult decisions as to which of the class action [court orders] they will fail to comply with because of staff shortages and patient loads."

The district courts making these factual findings, however, were not authorized to order the release of prisoners to address the underlying problem of prison overcrowding. They had, instead, appointed special masters to oversee the prisons and had ordered the implementation of medical and mental health care programs, but these remedies did not seem to help the problem. Therefore, the attorneys for the prisoners asked to convene a special three-judge court which would have the authority, under congressional statutes, to order the release of prisoners.

The three-judge court heard 14 days of testimony and issued a 184-page opinion which included extensive factual findings. The three-judge court ordered California to reduce its prison population to 137.5% of design capacity within two years (from nearly double the number of prisoners the prisons were designed to hold). That meant, without any increased capacity due to new construction, the three-judge court was ordering California to reduce its prison population by up to 46,000 prisoners. Not surprisingly, the state of California appealed this decision to the Supreme Court, based on concerns of releasing prisoners who might return to the street and commit further crimes.

The Court began its consideration by reviewing applicable Eighth Amendment principles. "Prisoners retain the essence of human dignity inherent in all persons.... The basic concept underlying the Eighth Amendment is nothing less than the dignity of man." The Court went on to recognize that a prison's failure to provide food and health care for inmates may produce physical torture or a lingering death. "A prison that deprives prisoners of basic sustenance, including adequate medical care, is incompatible with the concept of human dignity and has no place in civilized society."

The Court acknowledged that before the three-judge court may order a prisoner release, congressional statutes require that the district courts must first have entered an order for less intrusive relief and given the state a reasonable time to comply and improve the prison conditions. The three-judge court must then find by "clear and convincing evidence" that crowding is the primary cause of the violation of the Eighth Amendment and that no other relief will remedy the Eighth Amendment violation. The three-judge court must further find that an order releasing prisoners is "narrowly drawn, extends no further than necessary…, and is the least intrusive means necessary to correct the violation of the Federal right."

The Court noted that plenty of time had passed since the entry of the remedial orders by the district courts in the two class-action cases combined within the case of *Brown v. Plata*. The special master in the mental health case had issued over 70 orders directed at achieving a remedy through construction, hiring, and procedural reforms. "Having engaged in remedial efforts for 5 years [in one case] and 12 [in the other], the District Courts were not required to wait to see whether their more recent efforts would yield equal disappointment."

The Court also noted that the three-judge court had found that "at the time of trial, vacancy rates for medical and mental health staff ranged as high as 20% for surgeons, 25% for physicians, 39% for nurse practitioners, and 54.1% for psychiatrists." Filling these positions would still be inadequate because these numbers reflected budgeted positions (positions the state had authorized). According to expert medical testimony, even if all vacancies for authorized positions were completely filled this would not handle the level of need given the current overcrowded conditions. Even in the newer and more modern prisons the clinic space designed and provided, according to the find-ings of one of the special masters, was only half what was necessary for the op-eration of the prisons. "Staff operate out of converted storage rooms, closets, bathrooms, shower rooms, and visiting centers." These makeshift facilities im-peded effective delivery of healthcare, placed the safety of medical staff at risk, and compounded the difficulty of hiring additional staff. Space was not only short for staff, but prisoners awaiting care as well. Mentally ill prisoners were housed in administrative segregation while awaiting mental-health treatment beds. Some mental health prisoners were kept in segregation six months or more awaiting treatment.

A medical expert described living quarters, including converted gymnasiums which might hold up to 200 prisoners (and where up to 54 prisoners might share access to a single toilet), as "breeding grounds for disease." Worse, the overcrowding caused prisons to increasingly rely upon lockdowns to maintain order. In 2006, prison officials instituted 449 lockdowns, with the average lock-down lasting 12 days, and twenty lockdowns lasted 60 days or longer. During lockdowns prisoners require escorts to go to medical facilities, or medical staff must travel to meet the inmate, which further burdens overworked staff.

The Court approved the three-judge court's findings that overcrowding was the primary cause of the constitutional violations. Corrections officials from all over the country testified before the three-judge court and concluded over-crowding was the root of the problem. The former head of corrections in Texas described conditions in California prisons as "appalling, inhumane, and un-acceptable" and "in more than 35 years of prison work experience, I have never seen anything like it."

The Court acknowledged that Congress intended for prisoner release orders to be a remedy of last resort, but it did not forbid such measures altogether: "While prison caps must be the remedy of last resort, a court still retains the power to order this remedy despite its intrusive nature and harmful conse-quences to the public if, but only if, it is truly necessary to prevent an actual violation of a prisoner's federal rights." The Court recognized that there was simply no other alternative to prisoner releases in this situation. Hiring addi-tional staff was not a sufficient remedy. For years, California had been unable to fill positions necessary to provide adequate medical and mental health care. Moreover, overcrowding itself causes violence and other negative conditions that made it difficult to hire and retain staff. Even if the additional staff could be found, hired, and retained, there was insufficient space for this additional staff to work.

The Court did allow that the state might comply with the prison population limit by transferring prisoners to county facilities or facilities in other states, or by constructing new facilities to raise the prison system's design capacity. Realistically, however, there was no possibility that California would be able to construct enough prisons to build itself out of the crisis that it had created.

Finally, the Court addressed two of the more controversial aspects of this case. The Court acknowledged that the prisoners who were most likely to benefit from the order reducing the prison population, were prisoners that typically did not have serious medical conditions or mental illness. The prisoners least in need of care were the ones more likely to be released under the order. The Court nevertheless concluded that the population limit ordered did not fail simply because it had positive effects beyond the groups of prisoners bringing the lawsuits. The Court also acknowledged the danger of placing criminals back into the community, but cited testimony from expert witnesses explaining that statistical evidence showed prison populations could be lowered without adversely affecting public safety.

Discussion Questions

1. The dissenters think judges have little experience to oversee prisons (and dictate the number of medical staff, beds, etc.). Should prison overcrowding cases be appealed to a board of corrections officials across the country instead of judges?

2. How long should state prisons have to remedy structural deficiencies that lead (even if indirectly) to prisoner deaths?

Chapter Key Terms

Denationalized
Evolving standards of decency
Clear error standard
Fifth Amendment

Executive clemency
Three strikes law
Class-action lawsuits
Special masters

Chapter Twelve

Cruelty in Law Enforcement and Corrections

Rodney King's case was a symbol of police abuse. I remember before the tape of Rodney King, we talk[ed] about police abuse [but] people thought we were making it up.

— Al Sharpton

It is my personal conclusion that, under any common meaning of the term, CIA detainees were tortured. I also believe that the conditions of confinement and the use of authorized and unauthorized interrogation and conditioning techniques were cruel, inhuman, and degrading.

— Sen. Dianne Feinstein

Law Enforcement

In many instances, criminal suspects need to be punished and held accountable. However, the ways in which the criminal justice system apprehends and administers that punishment is to be free from cruelty and brutality. In the following section, we will first explore two instances where you could argue that the method through which law enforcement (in the first case) and agents working on behalf of the government (in the second case) were trying to reach their end goal teetered on the edge of treating suspects in a cruel and inhumane way. The second half of the section on policing will then transition to a discussion of what excessive force is and some examples of its use in contemporary policing.

Multiple Anal Probes

On January 2, 2013, David Eckert was pulled over in a Walmart parking lot in Deming, New Mexico, for going through a stop sign too quickly. He was asked to get out of his car and although he was standing upright, the officers said that it appeared as though he was holding his legs together and clenching his butt cheeks (Staley, 2013, para. 5). According to officers on the scene, Eckert seemed suspicious due to his clenching so they ran a drug-sniffing dog around the perimeter of his car. It alerted to drugs on the passenger side of his car, but after officers searched his vehicle, no drugs were found. Officers obtained a search warrant to search his anal cavity and what followed was a 14-hour-long series of invasive searches (David Eckert appears, 2013, para. 2).

He was taken in handcuffs to a nearby hospital emergency room, and the doctor on staff was asked to conduct a forcible search of his rectum. Dr. Adam Ash refused because he felt as though it was not the right thing to do since it was not medically necessary. Eckert allegedly protested the search that was about to happen (and all of the ones that followed) and asked if he could make a phone call. He was denied the phone call because he was not technically under arrest. The officers then drove him to an emergency room that was 50 miles away, and Eckert was then subjected to multiple anal cavity searches by finger, enemas, x-rays, and a colonoscopy (Kristof, 2014, para. 4–6). First, Eckert's abdomen was x-rayed and no drugs were found. He was then subjected to two searches of his anus with a doctor's finger and again, no drugs were found. Next, Eckert was given an enema, and he was forced to defecate in front of doctors and police officers. This happened three times total. Each time, they searched through his stool and found no narcotics. After undergoing one more x-ray, Eckert was sedated and had a colonoscopy performed where they inserted a camera into his anus and they searched his rectum, colon, and large intestines. Neither of these final two searches showed any drugs in his anal cavity or intestinal tract (Howerton, 2013, para. 12). In total then, Eckert underwent two x-rays, three anal searches with a doctor's finger, three enemas, and a colonoscopy. And if the nature of the searches that he underwent were not egregious enough, Eckert was billed about $6,000 for the medical services that he received (which he never consented to).

Along with his lawyers, Eckert filed a lawsuit against Hidalgo County and the City of Deming alleging that his rights had been violated. They also challenged the validity of the search warrant that law enforcement secured to execute the cavity searches as well as his being denied the ability to make a telephone call when he requested it (Contreras, 2014, para. 5). According to Eckert's lawyers, there were three problems with the search warrant: (1) it did not specify how the cavity search would be executed, (2) the warrant was valid only in Luna County but he was taken to nearby Grant County after the first doctor refused to do the search, and (3) the warrant had expired by three hours when the final procedure (colonoscopy) was performed (News Corp Australia Network, 2013, para. 9). Additionally, his lawyers challenged the basis for the search warrant since it claimed that Eckert was known to insert drugs into his anal cavity because he had been caught by law enforcement doing so in the past. While he has a long history of drug-related charges, none of them dealt with smuggling or transporting of drugs in his rectum (Howerton, 2013, para. 13–17). Eckert settled with Hidalgo County for $650,000 dollars and the City of Deming for $950,000 dollars ($1.6 million total). He attempted to file civil lawsuits against the district attorney who signed the search warrant and the doctors who performed the probes; however, all of these cases were dismissed with prejudice (essentially meaning that no future actions or lawsuits stemming from this issue will be permitted) (McClintic, 2016, para. 1). Eckert said that he "felt very helpless and alone on that night" but that he feels as though some justice has been served. Mainly, he hopes that getting his story out will prevent others from being treated the same way that he was (Goldstein, 2014, para. 8).

Discussion Questions

1. Do you feel as though law enforcement needs verbal consent from a criminal suspect to subject them to an anal cavity search?

2. Was there a tipping point where you feel as though the extent of the anal searches went too far, or are you in favor of how law enforcement handled the situation?

Terrorist Interrogations

In March 2004, a CIA informant ("Asset Y") disclosed that Janat Gul was planning with senior al-Qaeda leaders to conduct attacks in the United States just prior to the 2004 presidential election in November. From the beginning, some CIA operatives expressed reservations with the reliability of the information, concerned that it was vague and provided them with little actionable intelligence. Gul was captured three months later, and the CIA sought and received approval from National Security Advisor Condoleezza Rice, Vice President Dick Cheney, and Attorney General John Ashcroft to use the CIA's **enhanced interrogation techniques** (approved interrogation techniques that do not violate local and international standards of humane treatment) against Gul (Roston, 2014, para. 6). The document positioned Gul as "one of the most senior radical Islamic facilitators in Pakistan" and that getting information from him was vital to saving American lives (Senate Select Committee, 2012, p. 345).

They began the interrogation process (i.e., sleep deprivation, being slapped/hit, standing for long periods of time, etc.) with Gul in July 2004. By August, the CIA detention team wrote to headquarters that they did not believe he was withholding vital information and that they were going to proceed with caution. A short while later, they reported back to CIA headquarters that Gul was starting to become disoriented and hallucinate (he reported seeing his wife and children in the mirror and hearing their voices in the white noise) and that he asked to die or be killed. Additionally, they noted that the interrogation techniques appeared not to be working because Gul did not disclose anything about the pre-election plot. CIA headquarters demanded that the interrogations continue, and Gul was then subjected to a 47-hour session of standing sleep deprivation where he wore nothing other than a diaper (Ferner & Sheppard, 2014, para. 29).

By September, the CIA started to receive information from other interrogation suspects that Asset Y's information may have been bogus. Upon further investigation, Asset Y admitted that he had fabricated the story and that Gul had nothing to do with the pre-election attack. Even though the CIA knew the informant's information to be falsified, they still held steadfast to the idea that Gal "was one of the highest-ranking facilitators in Pakistan with long-standing access to senior leaders in al-[Qaeda]" (Senate Select Committee, 2012, p. 348). Those involved with detaining and interrogating Gal disagreed and stated that he was not the man that he was made out to be and that "we do a disservice to ourselves, the mission and even [Janat Gul] by allowing misperceptions of this man to persist" (Senate Select Committee, 2012, p. 349). While one could only hope that cases like Janat Gul's were isolated incidents, a report of the CIA's own internal accounting estimated that at least 26 people were wrongfully detained out of the 119 that they held during the years of the report (Ackerman, 2014, para. 25).

Gul was subjected to one of the CIA's post-9/11 detention and interrogation programs. Obviously, these programs have divided people, as some praise the practice because they help ensure Americans' safety while others condemn the techniques used to interrogate known and alleged terrorist suspects. In a 2014 report released by the Senate Intelligence Committee summarizing the CIA torture programs, numerous failures were noted such as the programs being mismanaged and the abuses being more widespread than initially believed (Watkins & Grim, 2014, para. 4). For example, the enhanced interrogation techniques often included sleep deprivation, facial holds/slaps, stress positions (sometimes for multiple days), standing sleep deprivation, nudity, water dousing, water boarding, blind folding, and threatening suspects with power tools. Additionally, the report noted more than one instance where a suspect's life was threatened and/or their family members were threatened with sexual assault or death if the suspect did not disclose information (Wing, 2014, para. 39). In other documented cases, some detainees were subjected to rectal feedings where they would have liquids or pureed food inserted through their rectum. There was often no medical need to do this, but rather the interrogators reported that it was one way to get "total control over the detainee" (Senate Select Committee, 2012, p. 82). In one of the more severe cases discussed, an "uncooperative" suspect was found dead in his cell from hypothermia because he was only wearing a sweatshirt and was forced to sit on a cold concrete floor without pants after undergoing a cold shower and other torture techniques. Supposedly no CIA officials were disciplined after his death, and the practice of stripping detainees nude was still used widely even after the hypothermia incident.

In the wake of this report, CIA Director (at the time) George Tenet stood behind the effectiveness of these programs and their use of enhanced interrogation techniques. He argued that these facilities were necessary to get intelligence that could be used to save American lives. However, public support started to wane as more newspaper stories publicized the extent of the torture and the shortcomings of these programs at apprehending known terrorist suspects. Criticisms even started coming in from the American correctional system. Individuals from the Federal Bureau of Prisons toured the Cobalt facility (which is said to house medium-level detainees) and said that they had "never been in a facility where individuals were so sensory deprived" and that one detainee there "literally looked like a dog who had been kenneled" (Ackerman, 2014, para. 13). While these enhanced interrogation techniques were something approved under the Bush Administration, President Obama signed an executive order in January 2009 that prohibits the CIA from holding detainees for anything other than short-term or transitory purposes. Additionally, the enhanced interrogation techniques were no longer acceptable and the interrogation techniques used had to align with the Army field manual. One could assume that this means that the U.S. now detains and interrogates alleged and known terrorist suspects in more humane ways than what occurred in the wake of 9/11. However, we only know what the government wants us to know, a fact which became evident with the release of the report on the CIA's Detention and Interrogation Program. The document is 9,400 pages long, and the president showed only 6,000 of those pages to classified governmental groups and only 525 heavily blacked out pages were released to the public (Ackerman, 2014, para. 16).

Discussion Questions

1. Do you support or oppose the practice of torturing alleged/known terrorist suspects?

2. Do you think that the CIA investigators who tortured the man that died from hypothermia should be held criminally responsible for his death?

Cleveland Police and Excessive Force

Up to this point in the textbook, we have covered many cases where we could question the tactics used by law enforcement to execute their goals. Examples include allegations of police misconduct, corruption, racial profiling, and excessive force. In these previous examples, often times we were talking about a few "bad apples" among a department, and only in select cases of misconduct and corruption did we discuss transgressions committed among an entire department (see Chapter 4). In the following example, we will discuss a police department that was cited by the U.S. Department of Justice for engaging in numerous unethical abuses of power. You could even argue that these examples fall under the scope of cruelty since they were tactics that were deemed to be unnecessarily used.

The Department of Justice conducted an independent review of the practices used by the Cleveland Police Department (CPD) between the years 2010 and 2013 after receiving allegations that CPD officers used excessive force and that the department failed to hold its officers accountable. During the course of their review, the Department of Justice examined documents that covered reports of officers using deadly and **less lethal force** (a level of force applied which is commonly understood to have less potential for causing death or serious injury than conventional, more lethal police tactics, although death or serious injury can still result from these practices); CPD procedures and training materials; witness interviews; officers and supervisor interviews; and interviews with other various stakeholders throughout the community. The results were rather alarming and showed that officers (1) used unnecessary and excessive deadly force (including shootings and head strikes with weapons), (2) used unnecessary, excessive, or retaliatory use of less lethal force (including tasers, chemical sprays and fists), (3) used force against the mentally ill or those in crisis, and (4) used dangerous tactics that placed officers and civilians at unnecessary risk. In summarizing the key findings, the reported noted that they have reason to believe that the CPD "engages in a pattern or practice of the use of excessive force in violation of the Fourth Amendment of the United States Constitution" (U.S. Department of Justice, 2014, p. 1). Furthermore, the report noted that the allegations of excessive force are due to structural deficiencies that stem from supervisors' unwillingness to discipline wrongdoers. For example, only 51 of the nearly 1,500 sworn officers were disciplined over a three-year period for their connection with an excessive force allegation. Additionally, there were only six occasions where officers were suspended for improper use of force (Shoichet, 2015, para. 11–12).

A few notorious cases which made the news were discussed throughout the report. For example, in one case which will be discussed in greater detail below, more than 100 officers chased down and ultimately killed two suspects who had done nothing wrong. In another case, officers chased down a suspect, and then when he was subdued and in handcuffs, kicked him in the head numerous times, causing serious damage. Another case discussed how a man who was in distress and having seizures on the sidewalk was tasered by officers while he was strapped to the gurney in the back of the ambulance. Officers said that he made threats about wanting to beat the officers up so they were trying to further subdue him. And in a last blow to the CPD, an officer punched a 13-year-old boy in the face until his nose bled in retaliation for the boy kicking an officer's car door and the officer's leg (Shoichet, 2015, para. 7–18).

The first case discussed above was perhaps the most damning to the CPD and was described as something that "carved a deep schism into the community" and uprooted citizen trust in the police (Caniglia, 2014a, para. 1). On November 29, 2012, two individuals by the name of Timothy Russell (driver) and Malissa Williams (passenger) drove by the Cuyahoga County Courthouse when officers reported hearing what sounded like gunshots being fired. Officers quickly pursued the suspects, and the chase escalated very quickly. It was reported that more than 100 officers in 62 police cars chased the suspects for approximately 25 minutes at speeds of 100 miles per hour (Caniglia, 2014b, para. 5). During the chase, there were reports of radio transmissions that stated the suspects may be armed and firing from the car. When the chase ended outside of the city in a school parking lot, the suspects' car was surrounded by officers. The following details are fuzzy, but law enforcement reported hearing gunshots from the car (which later were proven to be gunshots coming from other officers) so 13 officers returned fire, shooting a total of 137 times. Each suspect suffered more than 20 gunshot wounds and was pronounced dead at the scene. Investigations of the crime scene showed that neither suspect was armed and that there were no bullet casings in the car. It was later determined that the "gunshot" sound heard outside of the courthouse was likely their engine back-firing (Buduson, 2014, para. 20).

In the wake of the event, the CPD launched a full investigation and, in a rare twist of fate, six of the officers were indicted on criminal charges. Officer Michael Brelo was indicted on two counts of manslaughter and relieved of duty for firing 49 of the 137 shots (15 at close range while on the hood of the car). The remaining five individuals were supervisors who were charged with **dereliction of duty** for their failure to control the chase, which put both the public and officers involved in danger (Buduson, 2014, para. 2–8). Additionally, on the one-year anniversary of the shooting, the families of Russell and Williams filed a wrongful death lawsuit claiming the use of excessive force. The city agreed to pay $1.5 million to each of the families. In a released statement, the city asserted that the settlement does not acknowledge liability, but rather was reached to avoid a lengthy and costly litigation process (Caniglia, 2014b, para. 3).

The above cases and the results of the reports left the CPD with a tarnished record. The report showed that not only does the department fail to hold its officers accountable, but it often attempts to cast accused officers in the best possible light. According to the CPD, they started making remedial changes based on the findings from the report, but others acknowledged that more needed to be done. As such, the city and Department of Justice entered into a consent decree which called for independent monitors to supervise the progress being made. The police chief of Cleveland stated that he was committed to improving his department and that they will work hard to make the department better and regain the public's trust (Shoichet, 2015, para. 29–33).

Discussion Questions

1. If you had the authority to punish officers who used excessive force, what punishment do you think would be appropriate?

2. Law enforcement has to resort to force at times to fulfill their duties while maintaining public safety. At what point do you think the amount of force being used becomes excessive? Can you provide some examples to illustrate your point?

Rodney King

Simply uttering Rodney King's name can evoke negative emotions of anger and distrust among American citizens about the profession of policing. Many view his name as synonymous with police brutality, excessive force, and racial injustice. It is likely that the public would never have known about what happened to Rodney King on that fateful night back in 1991 had it not been for a bystander who decided to record the incident from his apartment balcony. On the evening of March 3, 1991, Rodney King and two passengers led the Los Angeles Police Department (LAPD) on a nearly eight-mile-long high-speed chase throughout the greater Los Angeles area (Gray, 2015, para. 1). Rodney King was a parolee who was driving while intoxicated and perhaps this knowledge fueled his decision to try to evade the police. When King finally pulled over, he was surrounded by 27 officers, and while his two passengers quietly allowed themselves to be handcuffed, King resisted. Four of the officers surrounded King and one officer used his taser on King two separate times. The officers argued that this had little impact on subduing Rodney, which influenced their decision to resort to using their batons. During the 81-second video, the four officers are seen delivering over 56 blows to King's head, neck, and extremities (Cops on trial, 1994).

To the layperson watching the video, it seemed like a clear case of police brutality. People argued that there were numerous instances where you can see King stumbling on the ground, and at no time does he seem to be charging at the officers. Furthermore, some argued that this video tape was just the culmination of police-citizen interactions that had been strained for years and fueled by racial tensions and allegations of police using excessive force. Citizens of Los Angeles thought it would be a fairly open-and-shut case in that the film spoke for itself: the officers were using excessive force. Ten days after the incident occurred, the four officers (Powell, Wind, Briseno, and Koon [the supervising officer on scene]) were indicted on charges of assault with a deadly weapon and excessive use of force by a police officer (Rodney King biography, 2015, p. 1–3). The defense claimed that the officers would not get a fair trial or an impartial jury if the case stayed within the jurisdiction where the incident occurred. Therefore, they were granted a change of venue and the trial took place in a nearby suburb called Simi Valley with an all-White jury. During the trial, the defense tried to put the jurors in the shoes of the officers that night by portraying them as reacting out of fear since nothing seemed to take King down. The prosecution, on the other hand, played up the extent of the beating, highlighting the number of blows and ways in which they were delivered. The jury deliberated, decided that none of the officers were guilty, and acquitted them on all of the charges.

The verdict sent a shockwave throughout the City of Los Angeles as many believed that there had been a huge miscarriage of justice. Shortly after the verdict was read, the city erupted into violence. What followed is one of the most violent and destructive riots in the history of the United States. The riots lasted approximately four days, and it is estimated that there were over $1 billion dollars in damages, more than 50 people killed, 2,000 people injured, and over 6,000 people arrested for rioting, looting, and arson (Sastry and Bates, 2017, para. 27–30).

Unlike many cases of excessive force that we have previously discussed throughout the textbook, those in positions of authority thought the officers were in the wrong. The then police chief (Daryl Gates) felt as though the force that was used was excessive, and the mayor at the time (Tom Bradley) said that he disagreed with the verdict that the jury had reached. Many different governmental agencies started their own independent investigations, which led President George H.W. Bush to call for the U.S. Department of Justice to bring federal charges against the officers. Two of the four officers (Powell and Koon) were found guilty and sentenced to 30 months in a federal prison camp (Cops on trial, 1994). King then filed a lawsuit against the City of Los Angeles and settled for $1.8 million dollars to compensate for his loss of earnings, medical bills, and for the pain and suffering that the event caused him (Mydans, 1994, para. 1).

Discussion Questions

1. Google the Rodney King video before responding to this question. Do you think that the officers engaged in excessive force? Would you define this as police brutality?

2. Why do you think that citizens of Los Angeles resorted to rioting? Could you see yourself ever taking part in a riot?

Freddie Gray

For those who have been paying attention to the media of late, it likely comes as little surprise to say that the profession of policing could use an image overhaul. The public's trust in the police is waning due to so many sensationalized cases where there have been confrontations between an African American male and the police that ends badly (e.g., Michael Brown, Eric Gardner, Walter Scott, George Floyd). Furthermore, many argue that these confrontations are motivated by race and that the officer in question resorted to excessive or deadly force simply because the suspect in question was Black. The above case of Rodney King provides a good example of this. Many argue that Rodney King was racially profiled and that the officers resorted to the level of violence that they did because they were acting on stereotypes about African American criminals. In a similar vein, many argue that race was the underlying factor that led officers to resort to excessive or deadly force in the cases listed above. In what follows, we will explore the case of Freddie Gray in more detail to see what events may have ultimately led to his death.

On April 12, 2015, Freddie Gray was stopped by police in a high-crime area of Baltimore simply because he ran away from them. He was not accused of doing anything wrong or breaking the law, but as the police report noted, he fled when he noticed their presence. The officers then patted him down and discovered that he had a switchblade clipped to the inside of his pant leg. A bystander recorded law enforcement arresting Gray and putting him into the back of their transportation wagon, which would take him to the police station. The recording shows Gray complaining that he is unable to breathe, and it appears as though law enforcement is helping to support his weight as he walks/ is dragged into the back of the van. Forty-four minutes later when he arrives at the station he is unconscious and not breathing (Blum, 2015, para. 4–8). Gray was quickly transported to a local hospital, where he slipped into a coma, was resuscitated, underwent surgery, and died seven days later. Gray's spine was severed nearly 80 percent and that this is an injury which is common among the elderly who fall or individuals who have been in a car accident (Gorta, 2015, para. 4–5). Autopsy reports showed that Gray suffered a single "high-energy injury" which was mostly likely caused by sudden deceleration or acceleration of the van and the state medical examiner's office ruled it as a homicide rather than an accident due to the officer's negligence to follow safety procedures (Fenton, 2015, para. 1–2).

As was the case with the Rodney King incident, people argued that Gray had been racially profiled and that the police used excessive force. Like in LA, citizens of Baltimore revolted and there was a far less violent and shorter lived series of riots that broke out in the greater Baltimore area. The protests were said to start peacefully but eventually got violent and resulted in many arrests and officer injuries (Map: Riots, 2015). Whereas the riots of LA were in response to the acquittal of the four officers who beat Rodney, protestors in Baltimore rioted because they were demanding answers. How and when was Gray injured? Why was he not given medical attention sooner when he requested it? And why was he not wearing a seat-belt in the back of the van (Hermann & Wiggins, 2015, para. 2)?

Some reports argue that the answer lies in **"rough rides"** which is a practice where law enforcement tries to cause injury or pain to a suspect in the back of a transport van. One report which focused exclusively on Baltimore found that there had been numerous lawsuits brought against the police department for the injuries that suspects incurred after riding in the back of the van. There were two separate incidents of a suspect being taken into custody and arriving at the station with spinal injuries: one was a quadriplegic who later died from pneumonia and the other survived but is currently paralyzed from the neck down (Donovan & Puente, 2015, p. 14–19). These were just two of the more sensationalized cases discussed in this report, but interviews with law enforcement who had to testify in court corroborate that this is a practice which may be more common than we would like to think.

District Attorney Marilyn J. Mosby pressed charges against the six officers involved in Gray's arrest, and they were later indicted by a grand jury on a series of charges. The officer driving the van faced the most serious charge of second-degree depraved-heart murder, which carries a penalty of up to 30 years, while three other officers face charges of manslaughter, which carries a penalty of up to 10 years. All six officers were indicted on charges of second-degree assault, which carries a penalty of up to 10 years as well (Pérez-Pena, 2015, para. 10–12). Mosby also tried charging all of the officers with false imprisonment, claiming that it was not illegal for him to carry the switchblade, but those charges were dropped for three of the officers.

Officer Porter was one of the first officers tried, and his case resulted in a mistrial (Hung jury in first, 2015, para. 1). In subsequent trials, two other officers wound up with acquittals on all of the charges. Then, in a rather controversial and contested move, District Attorney Marilyn J. Mosby dropped the three remaining state cases. Currently, all six officers are back at work, albeit in non-patrol capacities (Dedaj, 2017, para 4–11).

Discussion Questions

1. Not putting Gray's seat belt on is a violation of protocol. Do you think this information should weigh heavily on the outcome of the trial and the officers' levels of culpability?

2. Do you think that the charges being filed against the officers are excessive or warranted given the situation?

Corrections

The Death Penalty and Lethal Injection

Perhaps no other issue in corrections causes as much concern over the topic of cruelty as does the implementation of the death penalty. It should be remembered, however, that the courts hand down the penalty of death, and the method by which the execution is carried out is determined by the legislative branch of the government, overseen by the medical community. Corrections is simply the branch of our criminal justice system given the unfortunate task of carrying out the orders of the court.

Throughout the history of the United States, various methods of **execution** (the taking of a human life by legal means) have been used and discarded due to public concern over the cruel nature of the techniques. According to Debbie Siegelbaum of BBC News (2014), the most common methods of execution in the United States over the last 100 years have been (in order of number of executions): (1) electrocution, (2) hanging, (3) lethal injection, (4) gas chamber, and (5) firing squad. Of these, the method with the greatest percentage of "**botched**" (departing from legal protocols that result in a prolonged or painful death) executions is lethal injection (7.1%), while the firing squad has had none. Siegelbaum went on to say that "eight US states allow electrocution, three allow the gas chamber, another three allow hanging, [and] two allow the firing squad" (para. 15).

In recent years, the controversy over the death penalty in general, and lethal injection in particular, has been fueled by a number of high-profile death cases in which the offender appeared to suffer throughout the procedure. During one instance, Joseph Rudolph Wood III, a man convicted of killing his girlfriend and her father in 1989, is said to have taken almost two hours to die once the procedure began. Wood's execution started at 1:57 pm and at around 2:05 pm, he was said to have started gasping. Then, according to some witnesses, "Wood turned his head and looked curiously at the 20 or so witnesses in the room. He found the family of his victims, the sisters and brother-in-law of Debra Dietz, the estranged girlfriend he killed, along with her father, Eugene, in Tucson in 1989. He grinned, seemed to laugh at them and jerked his head back to look at the ceiling" (Kiefer, 2014, para. 9). Stephanie Grishman, a witness for the Arizona Attorney General's Office said, "There was no gasping of air. There was snoring. He just laid there. It was quite peaceful" (Pearce et al., 2014, para. 14).

Others, however, had a different account of Wood's execution. Cassandra Stubbs, the director of the American Civil Liberties Union's Capital

Punishment Project believed "Joseph Wood suffered cruel and unusual punishment when he was apparently left conscious long after the drugs were administered. According to his emergency papers filed by his attorneys, he was choking and snorting over an hour into the process" (Koplowitz, 2014, para. 3). In response, Arizona Governor Jan Brewer replied, "One thing is certain, however, inmate Wood died in a lawful manner, and by eyewitness and medical accounts he did not suffer. This is in stark comparison to the gruesome, vicious suffering that he inflicted on his two victims — and the lifetime of suffering he has caused their family" (Pearce et al., 2014, para. 7).

Another high-profile case was the execution of Ohio inmate Dennis McGuire. McGuire, convicted of murdering Joy Stewart and her unborn child in 1989, was the first in Ohio to receive an untested two-drug cocktail used for lethal injections. A witness to the execution, Father Lawrence Hummer, shared a description of McGuire's final moments, "Over those 11 minutes or more he was fighting for breath, and I could see both of his fists were clenched the entire time. His gasps could be heard through the glass wall that separated us. Towards the end, the gasping faded into small puffs of his mouth. It was much like a fish lying along the shore puffing for that one gasp of air that would allow it to breathe. Time dragged on and I was helpless to do anything, sitting helplessly by as he struggled for breath" (Hummer, 2014, para. 12). Hummer went on to say, "I've seen people die many times before: in nursing homes, families I've known, my own mother. In most settings I've found death to be a very peaceful experience. But this was something else" (para. 7).

The Ohio Department of Corrections, however, emphatically believes the procedure was both constitutional and humane. The fact that the drug combination was untested in death sentence executions was irrelevant because an independent report came to the conclusion that McGuire was never in any distress or pain. According to the report, "An anesthesiologist reviewed the accounts of witnesses and prison employees and McGuire's medical records, and the state ultimately determined the execution did not violate the constitutional protection against cruel and unusual punishment" (Connor, 2014, para. 5).

In the end, death penalty executions are emotional, as well as legal issues. There will always be two opposing views on the constitutionality of such actions (even the U.S. Supreme Court has wavered in its position), and people will always wonder about the effects of governmental actions on the offender at the time of their death. While many methods of execution may not be unusual, the question still remains — are they cruel?

Discussion Questions

1. Knowing that executions must meet both criteria to be unconstitutional, do you believe death sentences are a cruel and unusual punishment?

2. Addressing both types of deterrence, do you feel executions are a deterrent to crime?

3. Do you feel there is a humane method to execute a human being?

Tasers

The use of **tasers** (an electrical weapon that causes temporary paralysis) inside America's correctional facilities has long been a point of contention among prisoner rights advocates. Corrections officials feel the device is a necessary tool when inmates become physically aggressive towards officers and staff. Opponents, however, feel tasers are used more as a punishment for non-compliance and as such, are cruel implements of revenge.

Take, for example, a recent incident at the Fairfax County Jail in Fairfax, Virginia. Natasha McKenna, a mentally ill woman with a history of violence against officers, was arrested on a felony warrant for assaulting an Alexandria law enforcement officer (Jackman & Jouvenal, 2015). Because she was arrested by Fairfax police for an Alexandria warrant, Fairfax County could not transport McKenna to a nearby mental health facility. After numerous requests by Fairfax County to Alexandria to transfer custody, the decision was made by Fairfax County to go ahead and move McKenna. Alexandria's correctional facility was made aware of the pending transfer.

While removing McKenna from her cell at the Fairfax County facility, the inmate became violent and aggressive with officers. Due to her actions, the jail's **Emergency Response Team** (specially trained officers who deal with aggressive inmates and or high-risk transfers) was called, and the officers attempted to place the inmate in a restraint chair for her safety and the safety of the officers. It was during this move to the restraint chair that some claim McKenna was tasered four times to gain her compliance (Jackman, 2015). Video of the move, however, clearly showed officers using minimal force against the inmate during the 17 minutes they were trying to get her under control, and officers could be repeatedly heard telling her to "stop resisting" and "hold still" (Carey & Culver, 2015, para. 2). Unfortunately, sometime during the transfer McKenna's heart stopped beating, and after being rushed to a local hospital, she ultimately died.

The jail in Denver, Colorado, has also had its share of controversies surrounding the questionable use of tasers by facility officers. According to Noelle Phillips, a reporter for *The Denver Post*, the Denver Sheriff's Department could very well be in violation of federal guidelines regarding use-of-force. During her investigation, Phillips (2014) found "Denver Sheriff Department deputies often rely on their Tasers to inflict pain to force inmates, some of whom are mentally ill, to comply with orders, *The Denver Post* found in a review of the 14 Taser cases so far this year. It's a practice that goes against federal guidelines for stun guns and can be in violation of the department's own use-of-force policy" (para. 3).

Of particular concern was the incident involving inmate Isaiah Moreno. Moreno, in jail for suspicion of first-degree murder, was on **suicide watch** (a condition where an inmate has threatened to or tried to harm him/herself and is being intensely supervised by correctional staff) and began banging his head against the jail cell wall. After refusing officers' orders to stop, a number of Denver sheriff's deputies entered the cell to get Moreno to comply for his own safety (Joseph & Mitchell, 2014). Of the officers entering the cell, two displayed drawn tasers pointed at the inmate. After seeing the deputies enter, Moreno sat on the cell bench, but continued to disregard the officers' commands. At that point, Sergeant Ned St. Germain, a 20-year veteran and the officer in charge, gave the order for the two deputies with tasers to fire (Greene, 2014). Moreno fell to the floor and was eventually placed in a restraint chair.

Discussion Questions

1. In your opinion, are tasers, by their very nature, cruel and unusual punishment?

2. Should the use of tasers be allowed against someone with a diagnosed mental illness?

3. At what point does a taser move from being a safety and security instrument to a punishment tool?

Restraint Chairs

As America's jails and prisons continue to struggle with ways to manage mentally ill, addicted, and violent inmates, one particular instrument has come under attack as a cruel and punitive tool — the **restraint chair** (a device where an individual is strapped to a portable chair for their own safety and the safety of correctional staff and is unable to move their arms, legs, and torso). Restraint chairs are typically used when inmates or arrestees become aggressive or violent to the point where they may potentially harm themselves or others. In an effort to regain control of the offender, correctional officials will strap the individual into the chair, immobilizing the torso, arms, and legs, while at the same time giving the offender full use of head and respiratory functions.

While use of a restraint chair is designed to safely immobilize a person, correctional personnel must still be cautious in its use. According to Lorry Schoenly, a correctional nurse with 30 years of experience, "Staff must be observant for physical injury during the initial and ongoing periods of confinement in a restraint chair. Prolonged fighting against the restraint can lead to muscle breakdown which then can progress to kidney damage as the byproduct of muscle breakdown — myoglobin — concentrates in the blood. The inmate may easily become dehydrated and prone to blood clots in the legs and lungs. Lack of physical movement over time can lead to skin breakdown, urinary tract infection and nerve damage" (Schoenly, 2014, para. 4). Unfortunately, a device designed for safety and security has also been linked to charges of cruel and inhumane treatment.

One such incident involved 19-year-old Daniel Linsinbigler who was being detained in Florida's Clay County Jail for non-violent misdemeanor charges related to a potential psychotic episode. According to officers' reports, a little over week into his incarceration, Linsinbigler became agitated to the point where officers became concerned for his safety (Treen, 2014). While removing him from his cell, officers used **pepper spray** (an aerosol irritant used against combative or violent individuals) on the inmate to gain control of him while Linsinbigler was placed into a restraint chair. After being secured, the inmate continued to struggle and appeared to be having a reaction to the pepper spray. With his chest, arms, and legs strapped to the chair, Linsinbigler continued to try to move and repeatedly told officers he couldn't breathe (Schindler, 2014). Linsinbigler eventually died in the restraint chair, and even though his death was ruled a homicide by the local coroner, no charges were filed against the officers. In a statement to the press after an initial investigation, Sheriff Rick Beseler said "The Clay County Sheriff's Office would like to express its deepest condolences to the Linsinbigler family as the loss of life under any circumstances is tragic. However, the State Attorney's Office has ruled that there was no criminal conduct on behalf of any member of the Clay County Sheriff's Office. The responses of agency members to the resistance offered by Mr. Linsinbigler were lawful and within the scope of their duties" (Cravey, 2013, para. 2). Linsinbigler's family, however, disagreed and filed suit, eventually agreeing to a $2.2 million dollar settlement with the county (Mealey, 2014).

Another high-profile case involved Southwest Missouri man Richard Watson, who was brought to the Jasper County Jail in Missouri after his mother found him sleeping in her garage (Alder, 2014). A lawsuit, filed by the offender's mother, claimed that Watson had been placed in the chair for 21 hours and during that time, he was denied food, water, and proper medication. The Jasper County sheriff, however, denied such claims and said Watson was placed into the chair for his own safety and well-being after he broke a window in the jail with his head. Sheriff Randee Kaiser went on to say that "[D]uring the entire course of time ... we acted in a way that we felt was appropriate. We cared for him in a way that we thought was the best way" (Davis, 2015, para. 14).

Discussion Questions

1. In your opinion, is it acceptable to use restraint chairs on inmates who are or may be mentally ill?

2. Should a doctor or nurse be required to authorize the use of a restraint chair on an inmate or arrestee prior to their placement in the device?

3. At what point does a restraint chair become a punitive action, instead of a safety and control instrument?

Stun Cuffs

As controversial as tasers are, another control device might be seen as even more cruel to inmates and arrestees. **Stun cuffs** (a wireless electronic control system worn on the ankle or wrists) are often used on high-risk inmates during transportation, court appearances, facility movements, and interviews. Myers Enterprise, Inc., makers of the Stun Cuff, tout the device as a way to surreptitiously control an individual who might pose a threat of escape or injury to others. According to the company's website, "They are out of control! During trial prisoner shackling has been found unconstitutional for fear prisoners may appear guilty before a jury. On the other hand, you can't allow a murder suspect freedom in the courts, filled with innocent bystanders where they may attempt to break free. All too frequently we hear disturbing reports of prisoner escapes. Whether taking a prisoner for a doctor visit, transporting them for trial, interrogations or dealing with a prisoner that is under the influence. They must be controlled."

One agency using the technology is the Buchanan County Sheriff's Department in Missouri. According to Captain Jody Hovey, "It's a very effective tool. It affects the muscles of the body and it doesn't really affect anything else. Everybody thinks it affects your heart and all this. It doesn't. What it does really it just sends a charge through the body that locks up your muscles" (Fox2Now, 2013, para. 3). The stun cuffs, however, are not cheap. Two of the new devices cost the department approximately $2,200.

Correctional deputies are even using the device in courtrooms when requested by the presiding judge. For example, a Maryland judge ordered Jeffrey Matthew Shiflett to wear stun cuffs in her courtroom after Shiflett screamed at her and attempted to enter the judge's chambers (Neil, 2014a). Shiflett refused to put the device on, and his attorney argued the stun cuffs could potentially interfere with his client's ability to actively participate in his own defense out of fear of being shocked. Judge Ruth Ann Jakubowski disagreed with that premise, stating with reference to the device, "It would only be utilized if he becomes violent or starts acting out" (Neil, 2014a, para. 6).

Prisoner rights groups, however, feel use of the stun cuffs are paramount to institutionalized **torture** (inflicting severe pain on an individual as a punishment or as a form of pleasure for the person inflicting the pain) that is both cruel and demeaning. In fact, those opposing the use of stun cuffs will often point to online videos of officers subjecting themselves to the device at corrections trade shows. These videos frequently show officers laughing and making fun of the individual testing the stun cuffs. One anti-stun cuff activist said, "A Missouri sheriff's department tested a similar device from a different manufacturer in 2013. They too found it extremely amusing to debilitate colleagues with painful shocks. Lots of young men would react similarly, hence my reluctance to let them put devices they approach with jocularity rather than seriousness on people that they disdain. I am hardly alone in finding stun-cuffs creepy and suggestive of evil — for goodness sakes, Darth Vader seems to have pioneered their use on the Death Star" (Friedersdorf, 2015, para. 5 & 6).

In some cases, the law also appears to agree with those who are against the use of stun cuffs. A Maryland circuit court judge, Robert Nalley, was removed from the bench for ordering the court's deputy to "shock a 'rude' and 'nonresponsive' pro se defendant who wouldn't stop talking" (Neil, 2014b, para.

3). According to court records, Delvon King was accused of weapons charges and believed in an ideology that does not recognize the court's authority. King refused numerous requests and orders from the judge to stop talking and after repeated interruptions, Judge Nalley told the deputy to shock King. After a complaint by the defendant's attorney was filed with the state, a judicial spokesman said the Court of Appeals had voted to remove Nalley from the bench. In a separate investigation of the incident that found a dissenting view, "The Charles County sheriff's office also released its report on the incident, in which a deputy delivered a five-second jolt of electricity to defendant Delvon King. The report did not find wrongdoing by Nalley or the officer who activated the device" (Duncan, 2014, para. 3).

Discussion Questions

1. Do you feel stun cuffs are similar to tasers in terms of either effectiveness or cruelty?

2. Given the possibility that stun cuffs may inhibit a defendant's willingness to participate in his or her own defense, should they be allowed in the courtroom?

3. In your opinion, did Judge Nalley use the stun cuffs to control an unruly offender or to punish the offender for not following his orders?

Shackling Pregnant Offenders

Addressing the safety and security concerns surrounding pregnant offenders, while at the same time ensuring the needs and well-being of the individual and her child, have been a conundrum faced by correctional officials for some time. On one hand, inmates and arrestees within a correctional facility who are combative or in some way a security threat must be managed and controlled. A time tested and accepted method of managing these types of individuals is **shackling** (the use of restraints on a person's wrist, ankle, around the belly, or a combination of) them with handcuffs and **belly chains** (a restraint system placed around the waist of an offender that limits arm movement). On the other hand, however, combative or threatening inmates who are also pregnant present a unique set of challenges for those overseeing their care.

According to those in the nursing professions, shackling a pregnant offender is cruel, inhumane, and is considered a human rights violation by the United Nations and Amnesty International (Ferszt, 2012). The American College of Obstetricians and Gynecologists agrees, stating "[p]hysical restraints have interfered with the ability of physicians to safely practice medicine by reducing their ability to assess and evaluate the physical condition of the mother and the fetus, and have similarly made the labor and delivery process more difficult than it needs to be; thus, overall putting the health and lives of the women and unborn children at risk" (Clarke, 2013, para. 6). For many, the use of restraints of pregnant offenders is nothing more than a throwback to the Middle Ages.

In response, many states across the United States, including New York, have passed laws against shackling pregnant inmates during and after labor. Unfortunately, while these laws may be on the books, they are rarely enforced. According to Tamar Kraft-Stolar, "We interviewed actually 27 women who had given birth after the 2009 law went into effect and 23 of those 27 women had been shackled at some point in violation of the law" (Gebreyes, 2015, para. 4). In response to the perceived barbaric practice, New York State legislators passed new and more stringent anti-shackling legislation that protects pregnant inmates from being shackled at any time during their pregnancy and up to eight weeks after they have given birth (Correctional Association of New York, 2015). Thompson (2015) of The Intercept thinks this is a move in the right direction because "Shackling causes physical and psychological pain. It heightens the risk of blood clots and limits the mobility that someone needs for a safe pregnancy and safe delivery. It can cause fetal death. Shackling can also cause pulled groin muscles and the separation of pubic bones. And because of the potential for injury, many states have restricted the practice" (paras. 6 & 7).

Not everyone, however, believes inmates should be free of shackles while pregnant, during labor, or postpartum, and many agencies still use the restraints for safety and security reasons. In fact, according to the American Civil Liberties Union (2015a), 33 states across the nation still allow pregnant offenders to be shackled. One such location is Maricopa County, Arizona, which employs the use of "soft restraints" on pregnant inmates while they are in wheelchairs or beds. While the agency did not fully address their policies regarding the treatment of pregnant inmates, Deputy Chief John J. Macintyre explained that "soft restraints" are "the use of handcuffs or ankle cuffs with pregnant women, rather that leg irons or waist chains" (Costantini, 2012, para. 12).

Discussion Questions

1. In your opinion, should agencies be allowed to shackle pregnant inmates?

2. When a pregnant offender has been transported to a hospital to give birth, should the shackles be removed if requested by medical staff?

3. Do you see a difference between "soft restraints" and traditional forms of shackling?

Incarcerating Offenders during the COVID-19 Pandemic

COVID-19 (a respiratory illness caused by the SARS-CoV-2 virus) has not only disrupted services and institutions worldwide, but the coronavirus has especially plagued the corrections professionals and those they serve. According to an article by Hawks and colleagues, (2020), the first diagnosed case of a COVID-19-positive inmate occurred at New York's Riker's Island in mid-March 2020. Within two weeks, that number had increased to more than 200 offenders. Across America's jails and prisons, confined living areas, poor ventilation, the inability to social distance, and an overwhelmed medical system have made correctional facilities prime breeding grounds for the highly infectious disease. As a result, politicians and offenders' rights groups began to request and then demand that non-violent offenders, both convicted and awaiting trial, be released from incarceration.

In response, the state of New Jersey has ordered the release of more than 2,000 inmates from its prison system in an attempt to curb the virus and its spread (Wong, 2020). In signing S2519, Governor Phil Murphy said "prisoners in New Jersey can get their sentences reduced by as many as eight months for every month spent behind bars during the pandemic. People serving time for murder or sexual assault, sex offenders and inmates in federal prisons and county jails are not eligible" (para. 6). In addition, "the law requires prisons to release inmates regardless of whether they tested positive for coronavirus" (para. 7).

The state of New Jersey, however, is not alone. In California, officials from the Department of Corrections and Rehabilitation have said more than 8,400 of its inmates have been diagnosed with COVID-19 and of those, 51 have died (Associated Press, 2020). Among state prison employees, almost 2,000 have been infected, and eight have died. In an effort to slow the spread of the virus within its facilities and among its inmates and correctional staff, up to 17,600 inmates may be released early. This move, however, may place an undue burden on **probation officers** (those who oversee offenders on probation) as they scramble to find appropriate housing, transportation, and other services for those inmates being released.

Local law enforcement, while understanding of the challenges being faced by the state's correctional system, are concerned at the number and types of prisoners who may be released. Eric Nunez, president of the California Police Chiefs Association, said he understands the urgency of reducing the prison population but is alarmed by the release of some violent criminals "without a consideration for the larger impact on public safety." (Associated Press, 2020, para. 15). He went on to say that "the chiefs want to work with prison officials on improving the decision-making process." (para. 15).

Not everyone, however, was happy about the early release of offenders from America's jails and prisons. Victims' rights groups were asking how the early releases could be viewed as fair to the offenders' victims and their families. According to Californians for Safety and Justice, "two victims' families are furious after they weren't told these violent offenders have been released. One inmate excessively harassed his ex-wife and threw a **molotov cocktail** [a crude incendiary device] at her while she was sleeping. Another woman is now walking free after she shot a man and drove for hours as he bled to death in the trunk of her car" (Perlman, 2020, para. 9). California has even released two inmates sentenced to life in prison. For many, this leaves the question: "What about the victims?"

Discussion Questions

1. In your opinion, who should society focus on protecting first during the COVID-19 pandemic: the offenders or the victims?

2. What would you do to slow the spread of COVID-19 in America's jails and prisons?

3. Do you believe correctional officers and staff should receive hazardous duty pay during the COVID-19 pandemic?

Baby Shark

The hit video "Baby Shark" has taken the world by storm. Now the most watched YouTube video of all time with over 7.04 billion views, the catchy children's rhyme from the South Korean company Pinkfong is a favorite of adults and children alike (Savage, 2020). In fact, if you played the video that many times continuously, it would stream non-stop for 30,187 years!

Not everyone, however, is a fan of Baby Shark. Two Oklahoma City correctional officers, Christian Miles and Greg Butler Jr., have been charged with **cruelty** (callous indifference to the suffering of others) to prisoners for allegedly forcing inmates to listen to the tune over and over again for hours at a time. Their supervisor, Lt. Christopher Hendershott has also been charged for allowing the Baby Shark marathon to occur (MSN News, 2020). District Attorney David Prater's investigation found that at least four inmates "were forced to stand the entire time, hands cuffed behind them and secured to the wall" while the song was played on a repeating loop (Clay, 2020, para. 2). According to Prater, "It was unfortunate that I could not find a felony statute to fit this fact scenario. I would have preferred filing a felony on this behavior" (para. 5).

Miles and Butler, on the other hand, told investigators the use of "Baby Shark" was originally designed to serve as a method to correct an inmate's undesirable behavior. Using the facility's **attorney booth** (a location where attorneys meet with inmates to discuss legal issues), offenders were brought in to teach them a lesson and get them back on track. Both officers felt discipline at the jail was lacking and playing the child's rhyme might encourage inmates to stop acting like children and start following the facility's rules. The official report also said Lt. Hendershott was aware of how the inmates were being treated but took no action to either stop the abuse or discipline the officers. As a result, Miles and Butler believed their actions were justified and acceptable.

District Attorney Prater, however, disagreed and said use of the song and the conditions the inmates had to endure while it played placed undue emotional stress on offenders who might have already been suffering from physical and **emotional stress** (experiencing a negative affect that includes cardiovascular and hormonal changes) due to their confinement. Using jail video surveillance recordings, his investigators found that some inmates were subjected to the song and abusive conditions for as long as two hours. During the investigation, "Additional incidents were brought to light following staff interviews but were unable to be substantiated with video evidence and victims to support the claims" (Clay, 2020, para. 16).

In the end, Sheriff P. D. Taylor, who oversaw jail operations while the inmates were being abused, lost his authority over the jail. Lt. Hendershott retired during the course of the investigation. Miles and Butler were originally suspended and relieved of any contact with inmates. During the internal investigation, however, both officers resigned from the agency. Their misdemeanor charges of cruelty to a prisoner are still pending and at this time, it is unknown whether the inmates who were tortured during the "Baby Shark" marathons will file suit for their alleged abuses. For those who might be considering similar behavior modification techniques, one journalist had the following recommendation: don't don't don't don't don't don't (Lapin, 2020).

Discussion Questions

1. If the inmates had not been shackled to a wall for hours, would simply playing "Baby Shark" be considered a form of abuse?

2. Would playing a loop of popular children's songs be abusive in a correctional environment?

3. In your opinion, what is the primary punishment a jail or prison should inflict on offenders?

Chapter Key Terms

Enhanced interrogation
   techniques
Less lethal force
Dereliction of duty
"Rough rides"
Execution
"Botched"
Tasers
Emergency Response Team
Suicide watch
Restraint chair
Pepper spray

Stun cuffs
Torture
Shackling
Belly chains
Mitigating factor
COVID-19
Probation Officers
Molotov cocktail
Cruelty
Attorney booth
Emotional stress

References

Ackerman, S. (2014). Shocking cases in CIA report reveal an American torture program in disarray. The Guardian. http://www.theguardian.com/us-news/2014/dec/09/cia-report-torture-program-disarray.

Alder, P. (2014). Southwest Missouri man spends more than 20 hours in restraint chair and dies. www.ky3.com.

American Civil Liberties Union (ACLU). (2015). State standards for pregnancy-related health care and abortion for women in prison. www.aclu.org.

Associated Press. (2020, August 6). 17,600 CA inmates may be released early due to COVID-19, officials say. ABC30 News. https://abc30.com/california-prisons-coronavirus-updates-state-prison-inmates-released/6357785/.

Blum, B. (2015). Will we ever see justice for Freddie Gray? Huffington Post. http://www.huffingtonpost.com/bill-blum/will-we-ever-see-justice-_b_7429388.html.

Buduson, S. (2014). 6 Cleveland police officers indicted by grand jury in 2012 deadly chase, shooting. ABC News 5 Cleveland. http://www.news5cleveland.com/news/local-news/oh-cuyahoga/cleveland-police-officers-face-criminal-charges-in-2012-deadly-chase-shooting.

Caniglia, J. (2014a). Cleveland police chase and shooting grand jury: Patrolman and 5 supervisors are indicted. http://www.cleveland.com/court-justice/index.ssf/2014/05/cleveland_police_chase_and_sho.html.

Caniglia, J. (2014b). Judge approves settlement reached with families of Timothy Russell, Malissa Williams over deadly police chase and shooting. http://www.cleveland.com/court-justice/index.ssf/2014/11/judge_approves_settlement_reac.html.

Carey, J., & Culver, D. (2015, September). Inside the cell: Authorities release video of confrontation with Natasha McKenna. NBC News.www.nbcwashington.com

Clarke, J. G. (2013). Shackling and separation: Motherhood in prison. *AMA Journal of Ethics, 15*(9), 779–785.

Clay, N. (2020, October 6). Oklahoma jail workers charged after forcing inmates to listen to "Baby Shark" on loop, probe shows. *USA Today.* https://www.usatoday.com/story/news/nation/2020/10/06/oklahoma-county-jail-inmates-forced-listen-baby-shark-loop/3636063001/.

Connor, T. (2014, April). Ohio says controversial execution of Dennis McGuire was "humane." NBC News. www.nbcnews.com.

Contreras, R. (2014). David Eckert, N.M. man given enemas over non-existent drugs, settles suit with city and county. Huffington Post. http://www.

huffingtonpost.com/2014/01/16/david-eckert-enemas-anal-probe-lawsuit_ n_4610493.html.

Cops on trial. (1994, May 18).*American Justice* documentary. A&E.

Correctional Association of New York. (2015, June). CA applauds swift passage of new improved anti-shackling bill by NYs legislature. www.correctional association.org.

Costantini, C. (2012, October). Should a woman be shackled while giving birth? Most states think so. ABC News. www.abcnews.go.com.

Cravey, E. (2013, August). Inmate death ruled homicide in state report. *Clay Today*. www.claytodayonline.com.

David Eckert appears to clench his buttocks; Cops order enemas, colonoscopy, x-ray for non-existent drugs. (2013). Huffington Post. http://www. huffingtonpost.com/2013/11/05/david-eckert-enema-colonoscopy-drugs -traffic-stop_n_4218320.html.

Davis, L. (2015, January). Questioning the use of restraint chairs by law enforcement. Modus Vivendi. www.modvive.com.

Death Penalty Information Center. (2011, February). The execution of juveniles in the U.S. www.deathpenaltyinfo.org.

Dedaj, P. (2017, December 1). Six officers acquitted in Freddie Gray case now back at work. Fox News. https://www.foxnews.com/us/six-officers-acquit ted-in-freddie-gray-case-now-back-at-work.

Donovan, D., & Puente, M. (2015). Freddie Gray not the first to come out of Baltimore police van with serious injuries. *Baltimore Sun*. http://www. baltimoresun.com/news/maryland/baltimore-city/bs-md-gray-rough-rides -20150423-story.html#page=1.

Duncan, I. (2014, September). Top court bans shocking judge from hearing cases. *Baltimore Sun*. www.baltimoresun.com.

Fenton, J. (2014, June). Autopsy of Freddie Gray shows 'high-energy' impact. *The Baltimore Sun*. https://www.baltimoresun.com/news/crime/bs-md -ci-freddie-gray-autopsy-20150623-story.html.

Ferner, M., & Sheppard, K. (2014). What the CIA said it learned through torture, but didn't. Huffington Post. http://www.huffingtonpost.com/2014/ 12/09/cia-torture-effectiveness_n_6297720.html.

Ferszt, G. G. (2012, December). From our readers: Negative effects of shackling pregnant incarcerated women. My American Nurse. https://www.my americannurse.com/from-our-readersnegative-effects-of-shackling-pregnant- incarcerated-women/#:~:text=Pregnant%20women%20who%20are%20 incarcerated,substance%20abuse%2C%20and%20domestic%20violence.

Fox2Now. (2013, September). Stun-cuffs now shocking inmates at one Missouri jail. www.fox2now.com.

Friedersdorf, C. (2015, June). The 80,000-volt handcuffs that let cops shock prisoners. *The Atlantic*. www.theatlantic.com.

Gebreyes, R. (2015, March). Prisons are illegally shackling pregnant women while in labor. Huffington Post. www.huffingtonpost.com/.

Goldstein, S. (2014). New Mexico man settles for $1.6M after he was anally probed 8 times during traffic stop. *New York Daily News*. http://www.ny dailynews.com/news/national/n-m-man-settles-1-6-million-anally-probed-8-times-routine-traffic-stop-article-1.1582589.

Gorta, W. (2015, April 19). Freddie Gray dies after spine injured in police custody: Lawyer. NBC News. http://www.nbcnews.com/news/us-news/ healthy-baltimore-man-dies-after-being-restrained-police-n344506.

Graham, D. (2015). The mysterious death of Freddie Gray. *The Atlantic*. http:// www.theatlantic.com/politics/archive/2015/04/the-mysterious-death-of -freddie-gray/391119/.

Gray, M. (2015). The L.A. riots: 15 years after Rodney King. *Time*. http:// content.time.com/time/specials/2007/la_riot/article/0,28804,1614117_161 4084_1614831,00.html.

Greene, S. (2014, July). Troubling new video shows excessive force was ordered at Denver jail. *The Colorado Independent*. www.coloradoindependent.com.

Hawks, L., Woolhandler, S., & McCormick, D. (2020). COVID-19 in prisons and jails in the United States. *JAMA, 180*(8), 1041–1042.

Hermann, P., & Wiggins, O. (2015). Baltimore police cite missteps in arrest of Freddie Gray; Hogan asks for calm. *The Washington Post*. http://www. washingtonpost.com/local/md-politics/baltimore-mayor-clergy-ask-public -for-calm-during-gray-demonstrations/2015/04/24/0f961d14-ea9e-11e4 -aae1-d642717d8afa_story.html.

Howerton, J. (2013). We uncovered a major claim by the cops in the New Mexico anal probe case when we went digging through the arrest affidavit. The Blaze. http://www.theblaze.com/stories/2013/11/07/new-details-emerge -about-new-mexico-man-at-center-of-police-departments-anal-probing -controversy/.

Hummer, L. (2014, January). I witnessed Ohio's execution of Dennis McGuire. What I saw was inhumane. *The Guardian*. www.theguardian.com.

Hung jury in first Freddie Gray trial. (2015, December 16). Freddie Gray verdict: Mistrial declared over Officer William Porter. CBS News and Associated Press.

Jackman, T. (2015, April). The death of Natasha McKenna in the Fairfax jail: The rest of the story. *The Washington Post*. www.washingtonpost.com.

Jackman, T., & Jouvenal, J. (2015, April). Fairfax jail inmate in taser death was shackled. *The Washington Post*. www.washingtonpost.com.

Joseph, J., & Mitchell, D. (2014, July). New videos show alleged cases of excessive force at Denver jail. Fox 31 News. www.kdvr.com.

Kiefer, M. (2014, July). Reporter describes gruesome scene of Ariz. execution. USA Today. from: www.usatoday.com.

Koplowitz, H. (2014, July). Arizona botched execution: Joseph Rudolph Wood III dies 2 hours after lethal injection. *International Business Times*. www.ibtimes.com.

Kristof, N. (2014). 3 enemas later, still no drugs. *The New York Times*. http://www.nytimes.com/2014/01/26/opinion/sunday/kristof-3-enemas-later-still-no-drugs.html?_r=3.

Lapin, T. (2020, October 6). Playing "Baby Shark" on repeat officially deemed a form of torture. *New York Post*. https://nypost.com/2020/10/06/playing-baby-shark-on-repeat-officially-deemed-a-form-of-torture/.

Maps: Riots in Baltimore. (2015). *The Washington Post*. http://www.washingtonpost.com/graphics/local/baltimore-riots/.

McClintic, S. (2016, September). Anal cavity search case dropped by plaintiff. *Silver City Daily Press*. https://www.scdailypress.com/2016/09/16/anal-cavity-search-case-dropped-by-plaintiff/.

Mealey, J. (2014, November). Clay County to settle family's lawsuit for $2.2 million. News 4 Jax. www.news4jax.com.

MSN News. (2020, October 7). Prison guard charged with playing Baby Shark. MSN News. https://www.msn.com/en-us/news/crime/prison-guards-charged-with-playing-baby-shark/ar-BB19NvPp.

Mydans, S. (1994, April 20). Rodney King is awarded $3.8 million. *The New York Times*. http://www.nytimes.com/1994/04/20/us/rodney-king-is-awarded-3.8-million.html.

Myers Enterprise, Inc. (n.d.). Sun-Cuff by Myers Enterises, Inc.: Non-Lethal Wireless Prisoner Control Devices. www.stun-cuff.com.

Neil, M. (2014a, September 17). Murder defendant refuses judge's order to wear Stun Cuff at trial, misses opening statements. *ABA Journal*. www.abajournal.com.

Neil, M. (2014b, September). Judge who ordered deputy to shock 'rude' pro se defendant has been taken off bench. *ABA Journal*. www.abajournal.com.

News Corp Australia Network. (2013, November 6). Cops in Deming, New Mexico probe driver David Eckert who failed to stop at sign. http://www.news.com.au/world/cops-in-deming-new-mexico-probe-driver-david-eckert-who-failed-to-stop-at-sign/story-fndir2ev-1226753844828.

Pearce, M., Carcamo, C., & Srikrishnan, M. (2014, July). Arizona killer takes 2 hours to die, fueling lethal-injection debate. *Los Angeles Times*. www.latimes.com.

Pérez-Pen a, R. (2015). Six Baltimore officers indicted in death of Freddie Gray. *The New York Times*. http://www.nytimes.com/2015/05/22/us/six-baltimore-officers-indicted-in-death-of-freddie-gray.html?_r=2.

Perlman, M. (2020, July 30). District attorney says victims are not being heard ahead of convicted inmates' early release. CBS Sacramento. https://sacramento.cbslocal.com/2020/07/30/district-attorney-victims-not-heard-convicted-inmates-release/.

Phillips, N. (2014, November). Denver jail's Taser use at odds with federal guidelines, Post finds. *Denver Post*. www.denverpost.com.

Rodney King biography. (2015). http://www.biography.com/people/rodney-king-9542141#synopsis.

Roper v. Simmons, 543 U.S. 551 (2005).

Roston, A. (2014). Report reveals brutal CIA interrogation based on bogus intel. BuzzFeed. http://www.buzzfeed.com/aramroston/cia-interrogation-based-on-bogus-intel#.hwagmY89N.

Sastry, A. & Grigsby Bates, K. (2017, April). When LA erupted in anger: A look back at the Rodney King riots. *NPR*. https://www.npr.org/2017/04/26/524744989/when-la-erupted-in-anger-a-look-back-at-the-rodney-king-riots.

Savage, M. (2020, November 2). Baby Shark becomes YouTube's most-watched video of all time. BBC News. https://news.yahoo.com/baby-shark-becomes-youtubes-most-153022122.html.

Schindler, A. (2014, June). Death of a Clay County teen while in police custody raises new concerns about the safe use of restraint chairs. ABC First Coast News. www.firstcoastnews.com.

Schoenly, L. (2014, March). Use restraint when using restraint chairs. Corrections1. www.correctionsone.com.

Senate Select Committee on Intelligence: Committee Study of the Central Intelligence Agency's Detention and Interrogation Program. (2012). http://www.intelligence.senate.gov/study2014/sscistudy1.pdf.

Shoichet, C. (2015). Justice Dept.: Cleveland police has pattern of excessive force. CNN. http://www.cnn.com/2014/12/04/us/cleveland-justice-department-police-excessive-force/.

Siegelbaum, D. (2014, August 1). America's "inexorably" botched executions. BBC. www.bbc.com.

Staley, J. (2013). Federal lawsuit claims anal probe was unethically conducted by NM police, doctors. *Las Cruces Sun News*. http://www.lcsun-news.com/las_cruces-news/ci_24461411/lordsburg-n-m-mans-federal-lawsuit-claims-police.

Taylor, M. (2012, June 17). Rodney King case changed perceptions of police brutality. ABC News. https://abcnews.go.com/US/rodney-king-case-changed-perceptions-police-brutality/story?id=16589385.

Thompson, J. (2015, February). New York is illegally shackling pregnant incarcerated women. The Intercept. www.theintercept.com.

Treen, D. (2014, April). Clay investigation clears officers in the death of 19-year-old inmate last year. www.jacksonville.com.

U.S. Department of Justice. (2014, December 4). Investigation of the Cleveland Division of Police. DOJ Civil Rights Division and United States Attorney's Office Northern District of Ohio. https://s3.amazonaws.com/s3.document cloud.org/documents/1375134/cleveland-division-of-police-findings-letter. pdf.

Watkins, A., & Grim, R. (2014). Senate report says torture program was more gruesome, widespread than CIA claimed. Huffington Post. http://www. huffingtonpost.com/2014/12/09/senate-cia-report_n_6270138.html?utm_ hp_ref=politics.

Wing, N. (2014). Here are the most horrific details from the senate torture report. Huffington Post. http://www.huffingtonpost.com/2014/12/09/senate-torture-report-details_n_6295396.html?utm_hp_ref=politics.

Wong, W. (2020, November 4). More than 2,000 New Jersey inmates released to slow spread of coronavirus in prisons. NBC News. https://www.nbc news.com/news/us-news/more-2-000-new-jersey-inmates-released-slow-spread-coronavirus-n1246388.

Chapter Thirteen

Subservience

> I want no more of these deferences to authority.... I want to encourage in the young men the spirit that does not know what it is to feel that it stands in the presence of superiors.... There is no week nor day nor hour when tyranny may not enter upon this country, if the people lose their supreme confidence in themselves, and lose their roughness and spirit of defiance.
>
> — Walt Whitman

The Framers of the Constitution had a healthy dislike for and distrust of authority. **Subservience** to government was seen as a vice rather than a virtue. The Framers thus included many constraints in the Constitution limiting the means government may use to command compliance with the wishes of law enforcement and the manner in which courts may adjudicate criminal cases. We will begin with a discussion of the limits on subservience at home and on the street, then turn to issues concerning subservience before and during trial, including a look specifically at jury deliberations and how jurors are instructed regarding finding proof of a crime "beyond a reasonable doubt."

At Home and on the Street

Perhaps the most famous limit on subservience to government authority is the right to keep and bear arms found in the Second Amendment. While law enforcement officers generally have a monopoly on the use of force to ensure compliance with the law, the right of self-defense by individuals is also jealously guarded in the political arena, and recently by the courts.

The Second Amendment was a response to historical concerns, particularly in England, of the government disarming citizens to help prevent violent uprisings and revolutions, and then ruling the disarmed populations in a heavy-handed way. Like all amendments, the Second Amendment does not explain or define itself. Yet, perhaps more than other amendments in the Bill of Rights, the Second Amendment is ambiguous about who and what it is meant to protect. Unlike other amendments, the **Second Amendment** begins with preamble-like language concerning the need to maintain militias: "A well-regulated Militia, being necessary to the security of a free State." Only after this introductory language does the Second Amendment proceed to state, "the right of the people to keep and bear Arms, shall not be infringed."

As the scope and content of other provisions in the Bill of Rights were being firmly established by the Court during the twentieth century, the Second Amendment was mostly ignored. The Second Amendment was interpreted as a collective right of the people, exercised through modern militias like the National Guard. The Court, for many years, refused to recognize a personal right to possess firearms, which would shield individuals from government regulations limiting, or even prohibiting, gun ownership.

D.C. v. Heller
554 U.S. 570 (2008)

Dick Heller was a police officer living in the District of Columbia, which had effectively banned handgun possession. Heller wanted to keep his handgun at home, when off duty, for self-defense. The district court rejected Heller's claim that the Second Amendment protected a right to keep a handgun at home. Many judges at the time accepted that the Second Amendment only protected firearm possession in connection with militia service and could not be invoked by individuals.

In a case that changed decades of constitutional interpretation, the U.S. Supreme Court reexamined the Second Amendment, both its militia clause and the clause protecting the right of the people to keep and bear arms. The Court focused on the text and history of the Second Amendment, as well as how analogous state constitutional provisions had been interpreted before the twentieth century. First, the Court noted there are other constitutional provisions in the Bill of Rights protecting the "right of the people" (including the First and Fourth Amendments, and a very similar phrase in the Ninth Amendment). Each of these other amendments had been interpreted to protect individual rights, not merely the rights of a collection of people in a group like a militia.

The Court then examined the historical meaning of "keep and bear arms" and concluded the phrase simply meant "possessing" and "carrying" weapons, but did not require that the possessing and carrying be in a militia context. Third, the Court looked to analogous state constitutional provisions and state supreme court decisions holding that the right to bear arms was for individual self-defense, as well as for organizing a militia. Fourth, the Court noted that the Second Amendment did not create or grant the right to bear arms, but rather codified a pre-existing and ancient right passed down from English history. The right to have arms had been specifically listed in the English Bill of Rights of 1689, and this right clearly applied to individuals and was otherwise recognized as a fundamental individual right by English legal scholars. Turning to the post-ratification history of the Second Amendment, the Court noted that it had "found only one early-19th century commentator who clearly conditioned the right to keep and bear arms upon service in the militia — and he recognized that the prevailing view was to the contrary." Thus, the true historical meaning of the Second Amendment included an individual right.

Much of what had shaped the twentieth-century understanding of the Second Amendment was the U.S. Supreme Court case of *United States v. Miller*, 307 U.S. 174 (1939). The *Miller* case upheld a federal ban on sawed-off shotguns because they were not connected to militia use. However, *Miller* is a poor precedent. The defendants' attorneys did not show up to argue their Second Amendment claim. The attorneys did not file a written legal brief or make an appearance during oral arguments, and the history of the Second Amendment was barely examined during the case. Thus, the Court in *Heller* said: "*Miller* [appropriately] stands only for the proposition that the Second Amendment right ... extends only to certain types of weapons."

The Court concluded its decision in *Heller* with a consideration of the political arguments concerning gun violence and reasonable restrictions on gun use to prevent that violence. The majority rejected the dissent's interest-balancing approach, seeking to balance an individual's right to guns against the government's interest in preventing gun violence. While declining to explicitly establish the appropriate level of judicial scrutiny lower courts should use to evaluate gun regulations in future cases, the majority noted, "the enshrinement of constitutional rights necessarily takes certain policy choices off the table. These include the absolute prohibition of handguns held and used for self-defense in the home."

On the other hand, the majority did allow that government regulations barring felons and the mentally ill from gun possession were constitutional. Furthermore, individuals do not have a constitutional right to own tanks and bazookas, or even machine guns and sawed-off shotguns. Governments may place certain buildings, such as schools and government buildings, off-limits to guns if they choose to do so. Like the First Amendment, the Second Amendment has some exceptions (e.g., recall that obscenity is not protected by the First Amendment—see Chapter 1). While the Court did not spell out every possible limit on the Second Amendment in *Heller*, some historically recognized gun regulations, which most states have adopted, are likely to be upheld in future cases.

The Court struck down the District of Columbia handgun ban as violating Heller's right to possess a handgun in his home for self-defense. In doing so the Court rejected a subservient attitude to government authority, specifically the need for citizens in their homes to give up their weapons and yield to a government monopoly on the use of force. Defense of the individual in the home, at least, cannot be made subservient to the judgment of the state that handguns are a source of preventable gun violence. Individual security in the home cannot be made subservient to political judgments concerning collective security. It remains to be seen whether gun restrictions outside the home, in public spaces, or in automobiles will be determined to require excessive subservience to the state.

Discussion Questions

1. What limits on the right to keep and bear arms do you think should be constitutionally permitted? Should it extend to public spaces and automobiles?

2. Thinking back to Chapter 11, where we discussed several standards of judicial scrutiny (e.g., strict, intermediate, or rational basis), which do you think is most appropriate for evaluating Second Amendment claims? Would you apply different standards for different types of gun regulations?

While the Second Amendment is an obvious limit upon subservience, other provisions in the Constitution also protect Americans against subservience to their own government. One of these protections is the First Amendment. While we have already examined several First Amendment cases in Chapter 1 regarding another principle, tolerance, there are some aspects of the First

Amendment which protect against subservience as well. Protection of the rights of persons to use cameras, video recorders, and now smartphones to record the activities of police officers can be seen as a restriction on subservience. Of course, there is no explicit protection in the Constitution for such recordings, given that recording video was completely unknown to the Framers. Nevertheless, courts have found that such rights exist within the First Amendment, as we will see in the next case.

Glik v. Cunniffe
655 F.3d 78 (1st Cir. 2011)

Simon Glik used his cell phone's digital video camera to film several officers arresting another young man on the Boston Common. On October 1, 2007, Glik saw three police officers arresting a young man and heard another bystander say, "you are hurting him, stop." Glik pulled out his cell phone, and from about 10 feet away began filming what he was witnessing.

Glik's actions did not go unnoticed by law enforcement. An officer informed Glik, "I think you have taken enough pictures," to which Glik responded, "I am recording this, I saw you punch him." Officers then asked Glik if he was also recording audio. When Glik confirmed that he was recording audio, officers arrested Glik for violating Massachusetts's wiretapping statute. Glik's attempt to hold officers accountable for employing possibly excessive force led him to be arrested himself.

The prosecution of Glik did not go well for the arresting officers. In addition to being charged with violating the wiretapping statute, Glik was also charged with disturbing the peace and aiding in the escape of a prisoner. This last charge was voluntarily dismissed by the prosecution as groundless, and the other charges were resolved in Glik's favor by the Boston Municipal Court (since Glik was openly, not secretly, recording the officers). It seems clear the officers were merely retaliating against Glik for his audacity to record them performing their jobs.

This did not end the legal proceedings. When Glik's internal affairs complaint with the Boston Police Department went nowhere, Glik filed a federal civil rights lawsuit, also known as a **§ 1983 claim**, against the city of Boston under 42 U.S.C. § 1983 seeking monetary damages for the violation of his constitutional rights. After a hearing in federal district court on the officers' claims of **qualified immunity**, the district court held they were not entitled to immunity (and thus protected from legal judgment and requirement to pay damages) because Glik had a firmly established First Amendment right to record the activities of police officers in a public place.

On appeal, in order to win his lawsuit, the First Circuit Court of Appeals said that Glik had to prove the police officers had fair warning that their conduct was unconstitutional. So, was there a constitutionally protected right to videotape police officers carrying out their duties in public? The First Circuit held, "basic First Amendment principles, along with case law from this and other circuits, answer that question unambiguously in the affirmative." Yet how is this so given that Glik was not speaking, and he was not a journalist recording a news story? The First Circuit quoted the Supreme Court (in a different setting) as saying, "the First Amendment goes beyond protection of the press and the self-expression of individuals to prohibit government from limiting the stock of information from which members of the public may draw." This includes a right to gather news from any lawful source. Gathering information in a form that can be readily disseminated to others "serves a cardinal First Amendment interest in protecting and promoting the free discussion of government affairs."

The First Circuit then looked back through its own precedents. The First Circuit had previously held that a local journalist could bring a § 1983 claim against local officials for being arrested for filming public officials outside of a public meeting. Turning to the facts surrounding Glik's arrest, the First Circuit stated, "[i]t is of no significance that the present case [unlike its previous precedents] involves a private individual, and not a reporter, gathering information about public officials." The First Amendment right to gather news is, as the U.S. Supreme Court has often noted, "not one that inures solely to the benefit of the news media; rather, the public's right of access to information is coextensive with that of the press."

The First Circuit went on to recognize that the widespread availability of electronic devices today means that many current-events images and information come from bystanders with a smartphone. Indeed, news stories might as easily come from a blogger as a major newspaper. Yet, the First Circuit cautioned that the right to film officers was not without limits. The right to film is subject to **reasonable time, place, and manner restrictions** like other aspects of the First Amendment. The First Circuit noted, however, the Glik was filming police officers in the Boston Common, the oldest city park in the United States, and "the apotheosis of a public forum." Glik filmed the officers from a distance and did not speak or interfere with them in any way except to answer their questions directed at him. According to the First Circuit, "Such peaceful recording of an arrest in a public space that does not interfere with the police officers' performance of their duties is not reasonably subject to limitation."

One question still remained: was the First Amendment right to film officers clearly established at the time of Glik's arrest so that officers did not have qualified immunity? The First Circuit answered that the right was virtually self-evident. The First Circuit's previous decisions were short, but that brevity "implicitly speaks to the fundamental and virtually self-evident nature of the First Amendment protections in this area." The officers had fair warning that their conduct was unconstitutional and therefore not immune from Glik's civil lawsuit.

This does not completely resolve the larger issue of filming police officers across the United States, however, because the First Circuit's jurisdiction technically only covers a small geographical area in the Northeast. The Supreme Court has never specifically addressed this issue. Police officers around the country continue to take offense at being filmed in performance of their official duties. As we shall see in the next chapter, in 2012 the Department of Justice moved to intervene in a similar civil lawsuit, demonstrating that the U.S. government under the Obama Administration believed there was a firmly established First Amendment right to film police officers, and it encouraged local police departments to develop policies to protect that right (*Sharp v. Baltimore City Police*, CA 11-2888 (D. MD, Jan. 10, 2012), DOJ Statement of Interest).

Nevertheless, the issue remains open despite efforts to have agencies clarify their policies and provide training for their officers. As recently as March 2021 the Tenth Circuit ruled that, "Irrespective of whether the officers [in a 2014 incident in Denver] subjectively knew from their training that Mr. Frasier possessed a First Amendment right to record them performing their official duties in public spaces, this right (which we assume to exist) was not clearly established law in August 2014 when the allegedly retaliated against Mr. Frasier for recording them. Accordingly, Mr. Frasier has not shouldered his burden on the second prong of the qualified-immunity standard (the clearly-established-law prong)...." *Frasier v Evans*, 992 F.3d 1003, 1023 (10th Cir. 2021). While the Tenth Circuit assumed there was a right to record, it also said in a footnote that "We do not consider, nor opine on, whether Mr. Frasier actually had a First Amendment right to record the police performing their official duties in public spaces." *Id.* at 1020 n.4. The need for the Supreme Court to resolve this divide between the lower courts is underlined by the critical role of bystander video footage in holding law enforcement accountable (the virtue in contrast to the sin of subservience), such as in the murder conviction for former police officer Derek Chauvin for killing George Floyd in Minneapolis in May 2020.

Discussion Questions

1. Can you think of any problems with recognizing a constitutional right to film police officers? Is it any different than requiring police officers to wear body cameras?

2. Would it be beneficial to resolve these questions through a robust internal affairs investigation by the police department or citizen review board, rather than through civil lawsuits payable by money damages (which are often paid by taxpayers)?

Before and during Trial

While the constitutional protections against subservience at home and on the street are relatively new and developing, protections against subservience before and during trial are more firmly established. The two constitutional rights we will look at for rights before trial (the right to counsel found in *Gideon v. Wainwright*) and during trial (the right to confrontation found in *Crawford v. Washington*) help protect against the government riding roughshod over defendants.

The right to counsel found in *Gideon v. Wainwright* is not exactly new, but the scope of the right has vastly expanded during the last 100 years. The right "to have the assistance of counsel for his defense" are the words appearing in the Sixth Amendment. On its face the right to counsel, therefore, seems firmly grounded in historical tradition. That, however, oversimplifies the situation. The Sixth Amendment was adopted to reform the English criminal system, which had prohibited attorneys from appearing in court to represent their clients (in England, for most crimes, defendants could only seek legal advice outside of court). For the first 150 years and more of the American Republic, the Sixth Amendment was interpreted in federal criminal trials to provide a right to bring an attorney into court with you at your own expense. Attorneys were not provided to defendants by the government, however, except under special circumstances.

Up until the 1930s, state governments were completely free to decide for themselves when to provide attorneys for defendants. Many states by tradition (and sometimes by state constitutional provision or statute) provided attorneys for defendants in death penalty cases when defendants could not afford them. Otherwise, defendants were on their own to either pay for an attorney or, more likely in many cases, represent themselves during a criminal trial.

Then in 1932, as a result of the famous Scottsboro Boys case (*Powell v. Alabama*), the U.S. Supreme Court interpreted the Due Process Clause of the Fourteenth Amendment as requiring states to provide attorneys to indigent defendants in certain cases, such as when the defendant was illiterate or facing capital punishment charges. In the Scottsboro Boys case, the state of Alabama tried and convicted several African American youths for the then-capital crime of rape, within days of their arrest. Alabama did not allow these defendants time to secure their own attorneys and prepare a defense, or provide them effective representation at state expense. The trial judge initially, and confusingly, appointed all of the members of the local bar to collectively represent the defendants. No attorney in this racially charged environment was willing to take sole responsibility for their defense since the defendants were accused of raping a white woman. While the Scottsboro Boys were found to be entitled to an attorney, following *Powell v. Alabama* there was only a limited right to an attorney at government expense.

Then six years after *Powell v. Alabama*, the Supreme Court interpreted the Sixth Amendment to require the federal government to provide attorneys for indigent defendants in federal criminal trials. Yet in 1942, the Supreme Court declined, in the case of *Betts v. Brady*, to make this requirement binding upon the states. This was prior to the era of **selective incorporation**, when the Court began to read provisions in the Bill of Rights into the Fourteenth Amendment's Due Process Clause so as to apply these rights against the states and local governments. The situation into the 1960s was that most defendants were on their own to find and pay for an attorney (or they could represent themselves).

Gideon v. Wainwright
372 U.S. 335 (1963)

Clarence Gideon was accused of breaking and entering into a pool hall while intending to steal something, a felony under Florida law. Not being able to afford an attorney for himself, Gideon asked the trial court to appoint an attorney for him at state expense. The trial court denied Gideon's request, noting that Florida law only provided for appointed counsel when a defendant was charged with a capital offense. In a famous moment in legal history, after unsuccessfully defending himself and being convicted, Gideon handwrote a petition appealing to the Supreme Court. The Court had been looking for a case in which to reconsider its *Betts v. Brady* precedent, which had held that states were only obligated to provide counsel in special circumstances such as death penalty cases. The Court agreed to hear Gideon's appeal and appointed him an attorney to argue on his behalf before the Supreme Court.

After considering the arguments of Gideon's appellate counsel, the Court reversed its *Betts v. Brady* precedent. While in *Betts* the Court had decided the right to counsel was not a fundamental right, the Court in *Gideon* concluded that it had made a mistake. Upon further consideration, the Court decided the right to counsel was indeed fundamental, thus incorporated into the Fourteenth Amendment's Due Process Clause, and therefore binding upon the states and local governments. Furthermore, the right to counsel incorporated into the Due Process Clause was the same as the broad federal version that the Court had recently clarified as required by the Sixth Amendment.

States now had to provide legal counsel at government expense when a felony defendant could not afford one (which was later expanded to any criminal defendant facing jail or prison time). In support of its decision, the Court looked back to its previous precedent in *Powell v. Alabama*. In one of the more famous quotations in legal history, the Supreme Court in *Gideon* quoted from its opinion in *Powell v. Alabama*:

> The right to be heard would be, in many cases, of little avail if it did not comprehend the right to be heard by counsel. Even the intelligent and educated layman has small and sometimes no skill in the science of law. If charged with crime, he is incapable, generally, of determining for himself whether the indictment is good or bad. He is unfamiliar with the rules of evidence. Left without the aid of counsel he may be put on trial without a proper charge, and convicted upon incompetent evidence, or evidence irrelevant to the issue or otherwise inadmissible. He lacks both the skill and knowledge adequately to prepare his defense, even though he have a perfect one. He requires the guiding hand of counsel at every step in the proceedings against him. Without it, though he be not guilty, he faces the danger of conviction because he does not know how to establish his innocence.

In *Gideon* the Court acknowledged that a defendant representing himself was at a distinct disadvantage when facing a legally trained and experienced prosecutor. "That government hires lawyers to prosecute, and defendants who have the money hire lawyers to defend, are the strongest indications of the widespread belief that lawyers in criminal courts are necessities, not luxuries." The failure of state and local governments to provide attorneys for indigent defendants created the likelihood that innocent defendants would be railroaded because of their ignorance rather than tried based on their guilt or innocence. "[A]ny person haled into court, who is too poor to hire a lawyer, cannot be assured a fair trial unless counsel is provided for him. This seems to us to be an obvious truth." Without attorneys provided by the state for those who could not afford one, the entire legal process would be tainted, and vastly overmatched defendants would be forced into subservience to the state.

Discussion Questions

1. Now that the government is required to pay for attorneys for indigent defendants, does it have little incentive to regulate caseloads for defense attorneys? Does the government achieve subservience by overloading defense attorneys for the indigent?

2. Some states require indigent defendants to pay back a portion of their attorney's fee if they are able to. Would you vote for such a law in your state?

Concerns about subservience during the criminal trial process are not limited to defendants having assistance of counsel to allow them to identify defenses, object to inadmissible evidence, and have some opportunity to effectively dispute the charges brought by a government which typically enjoys considerably more investigatory resources. The Constitution is also concerned with the tactics that governments are allowed to use during the trial to obtain a conviction. Specifically, the Confrontation Clause of the Sixth Amendment limits the types of out-of-court statements (hearsay) that the state may rely upon to demonstrate a defendant's guilt.

The Confrontation Clause was adopted to address a particular concern of the Framers. The Framers' concern was exemplified in a famous case concerning Sir Walter Raleigh. Raleigh was an English nobleman who in 1603 was accused of treason. His case became famous, even infamous, because of the way that his trial was conducted. Raleigh was not convicted in the way familiar to us, where witnesses testify from the witness stand in open court. Rather the government proceeded against Raleigh on the basis of out-of-court statements, and the main witness against Raleigh did not appear during the trial. Despite Raleigh's pleas to face his accuser, he was convicted and executed. Raleigh believed that if his accuser had to make the accusation of treason "to his face" in open court, his accuser would refuse, or his accuser would admit under questioning (cross-examination) that his statement incriminating Raleigh was a lie. Sir Walter Raleigh's case helped motivate the Framers almost 200 years later to include in the Sixth Amendment the **Confrontation Clause**, stating that defendants have the right "to be confronted with the witnesses against him." That leads to the question in our next case: What does the Confrontation Clause mean today in a world with frequent police interrogations?

Crawford v. Washington
541 U.S. 36 (2004)

Michael Crawford stabbed Kenneth Lee in August 1999 in an altercation following an allegation that Lee had raped Crawford's wife. Crawford was subsequently convicted of assault and attempted murder despite Crawford's claim of self-defense. Crawford was upset that his wife's statement to police officers was allowed in as evidence at trial. The prosecution used these out-of-court statements (hearsay) to help defeat Crawford's claim of self-defense. His wife, Sylvia, was not allowed to testify at Crawford's trial, because of the **spousal privilege**. The spousal privilege, like the attorney-client privilege, is a rule of evidence that keeps certain information from being admissible in court. In the case of the spousal privilege, information told to a spouse, or sometimes witnessed by a spouse, is kept out of court. Ironically, however, while Sylvia could not testify in court, the judge found that her statements to law enforcement officers outside of court were admissible as (1) not covered by the spousal privilege and (2) even though out-of-court statements are generally excluded as hearsay, Sylvia's out-of-court statements satisfied an exception to the hearsay rule and were reliable.

So, what does this case have to do with concerns about excessive subservience to government? Crawford claimed that allowing his wife's out-of-court statements into court violated his Sixth Amendment rights under the Confrontation Clause to confront her in court. Specifically, because she was not allowed to testify, he was not allowed to cross-examine her (question her) regarding her out-of-court statements. Crawford's version of events "asserts that Lee may have had something in his hand when he stabbed him; but Sylvia's version has Lee grabbing for something only after he has been stabbed." Without cross-examination Crawford argued that there was no way to bring out to the jury whether his wife had made the statements under duress or improper coercion during the police interrogation.

When the government procures out-of-court statements by police interrogation, and then attempts to bring those out-of-court statements into court to prove the defendant was guilty without giving the defendant an opportunity for cross-examination, the government creates the same issue of subservience to government as Sir Walter Raleigh had faced. The Confrontation Clause prohibits this tactic. Defendants have a right to require witnesses to testify in open court, to cross-examine those witnesses, and not be convicted on the basis of out-of-court statements collected by the government.

Why is cross-examination so important? The Court, in its *Crawford* opinion, drew upon the views of early American legal scholars who demanded the addition of a Bill of Rights to the original Constitution: "Nothing can be more essential than a cross-examination of witnesses, and generally before the triers of the facts in question. Written evidence is almost useless; it must be frequently [obtained without the defendant present], and but very seldom leads to the proper discovery of truth." Thus, the Court concluded that the principal evil for which the Confrontation Clause was drafted was the European mode of criminal procedure, and particularly its use of out-of-court examinations and interrogations as evidence against the accused. Out-of-court examinations and interrogations might sometimes be admissible evidence under modern hearsay rules in civil cases, but the Framers certainly would not have approved such methods for use in criminal trials.

It was not sufficient, according to the Court, to leave up to the trial judge the question of whether the out-of-court statements were sufficiently reliable to be admitted. The reliability of out-of-court statements should not be the test. Rather reliability must be established in a very specific manner, through cross-examination. The Court clarified that "[the Confrontation Clause] commands, not that evidence be reliable, but that reliability be assessed in a particular manner: by testing in the crucible of cross-examination. The Clause thus reflects a judgment, not only about the desirability of reliable evidence (a point on which there could be a little dissent), but about how reliability can best be determined."

The Court noted its previous precedents did not provide the lower courts proper directions on how to assess reliability, but the problem was deeper than that. "The unpardonable vice [of the earlier precedent], however, is not its unpredictability, but its demonstrated capacity to admit core testimonial statements that the Confrontation Clause plainly meant to exclude." The concurring opinion went on to point out that Sylvia made her statements while in police custody and while she was a potential suspect in the case herself. Sylvia was told that whether she would be released "depends on how the investigation continues." Her statements were made in response often to leading questions from police detectives. The trial court found, perhaps surprisingly, that the law enforcement officers were "neutral to her and not someone who would be inclined to advance her interests and shade her version of the truth unfavorably toward her husband." The motivation of the officers was not the only problem. The concurring opinion noted, "Even if the court's assessment of the officer's motives was accurate, it says nothing about Sylvia's perception of her situation. Only cross-examination could reveal that."

Yet, the reliability of Sylvia's statements was not the Court's greatest concern. The core of the majority's concern was actually about excessive subservience, especially to judges. The Framers were loath to leave too much discretion in judicial hands, as noted by the majority opinion: "Vague standards are manipulable, and, while that might be a small concern in run-of-the-mill assault prosecutions like this one, the Framers had an eye toward politically charged cases like Raleigh's—great state trials where the impartiality of even those at the highest levels of the judiciary might not be so clear." Thus, at its essence, concerns about excessive subservience to government turn upon the lack of trust in government (even a lack of trust in supposedly neutral judges) to apply the law fairly to all persons, especially when the case is high profile or great political pressure is placed upon decision-makers.

Discussion Questions

1. What has been your experience: are there some things people will say about you behind your back, but not to your face? Would you want to be convicted of a crime for things people would not say to your face?

2. What kinds of out-of-court statements should be excepted from the rule of the *Crawford* case? 911 phone calls? What if the statement is made to someone other than a police officer or agent of the government?

Jury Deliberations

So far we have looked at excessive government subservience at home and in the street, as well as in legal proceedings leading up to and during the criminal trial. Now the question turns to who should decide whether or not someone is guilty of a crime. Must government always turn this decision over to non-government actors? The Sixth Amendment, on its face, appears to require jury trials, but as discussed above concerning the right to counsel, most of the rights in the Sixth Amendment did not apply to the states before the 1960s. When the Court finally addressed the issue of whether to incorporate the right to jury trial in 1968 in the case of *Duncan v. Louisiana*, the opinion was a tour de force concerning the need to check against excessive subservience to government.

Duncan v. Louisiana
391 U.S. 145 (1968)

Gary Duncan was convicted in Louisiana state court of simple battery, a misdemeanor, punishable by a maximum of two years in prison and a $300 fine. The charges arose from a racially charged incident, where Duncan tried to intervene to head off a confrontation between his black cousins and some white youths during the 1960s. For his trouble he was accused of striking one of the white juveniles and convicted.

Duncan's trial was held in front of a judge, not a jury. Duncan requested a jury, but his request ran into several roadblocks. The Supreme Court had previously said numerous times that the right to jury trial was not a fundamental right, thus it had declined to incorporate it into the Fourteenth Amendment's Due Process Clause. Louisiana denied Duncan a jury trial on the grounds that their state constitution required a jury trial only in capital punishment cases or where imprisonment at hard labor might be imposed.

The Supreme Court held that the Fourteenth Amendment does guarantee the Sixth Amendment right to jury trial. The Court quoted prominent eighteenth-century English jurist William Blackstone to support its decision incorporating the right to jury trial:

> Our law has therefore wisely placed this strong [barrier of trial by jury], between the liberties of the people and the prerogative of the crown. It was necessary … to vest the executive power of the laws in the prince: and yet this power might be dangerous and destructive … if exerted without check or control [as he might] imprison, dispatch, or exile any man that was obnoxious to the government, by an instant declaration that such is their will and pleasure. But the founders of the English law have, with excellent forecast, contrived that … the truth of every accusation … should afterwards be confirmed by the unanimous suffrage of twelve of his equals and neighbours, indifferently chosen and superior to all suspicion.

The Court went on to trace the history of the right to jury trial in America. As early as 1765, the Stamp Act Congress deemed "trial by jury as the inherent and invaluable right of every British subject in these colonies." The First Continental Congress would resolve in 1774 that "the respective colonies are entitled to the common law of England, and more especially to the great and inestimable privilege of being tried by [a jury of] their peers." All of the states, before and after the adoption of the Bill of Rights, had provided for a state constitutional right to trial by jury.

Nevertheless, some states, like Louisiana, had not provided a right to trial by jury for all criminal charges, but instead had carved out a group of supposedly less important cases where the right to jury was not required. Thus, in Duncan's case, the Supreme Court determined it should overturn its previous decisions declining to incorporate the right to jury trial by looking to the essential importance of this right shielding against subservience to government. "The guarantees of jury trial in the Federal and State constitutions reflect a profound judgment about the way in which law should be enforced, and justice administered. A right to jury trial is granted to criminal defendants in order to prevent oppression by the Government." It was a fear of unchecked power that led to an insistence upon community participation in the determination of guilt or innocence. Even so, this insistence on community involvement still does not cover every criminal case, as the Court carved out an exception for petty crimes where the maximum possible sentence is six months or fewer in jail. States need not provide jury trials for these petty crimes.

While Duncan's case was in some sense a case with small stakes, as Duncan only faced a maximum of two years in prison and was actually sentenced to much less, there was also a deeper, mostly unspoken concern about a specific aspect of subservience to government in this case. The Court mostly avoided discussing the underlying racial tension simmering below the surface, yet racial discrimination provided a clear backdrop to this case. The Court seemed concerned a minority defendant would be denied a fair trial before a government authority figure (in Louisiana in the racially charged context of the 1960s). This was especially true in this case, which represented a swearing match between groups of white and black witnesses. The factfinder, in this case, had to take sides as to which group was telling the truth. No forensic or other physical evidence of this alleged crime was presented as the black witnesses described Duncan as merely touching one of the white youths on the elbow, whereas the white witnesses described Duncan "slapping" the white victim.

Discussion Questions

1. Would you rather be tried before a judge or a jury? Might it depend on the type of case? How important is having some control in selecting the jury?

2. Are there some issues we should not try before juries? Can we expect juries to fairly evaluate complex scientific or expert testimony as well as judges might?

Concerns about subservience to government during jury deliberations are not limited merely to those rights explicitly stated in the Constitution. As the next case will demonstrate, some of our most prized rights are not spelled out explicitly in the Constitution. The idea that the prosecution must prove every element of the crime **beyond a reasonable doubt** is a concept familiar to most Americans. What most Americans probably do not realize, however, is that the words "beyond a reasonable doubt" do not appear anywhere in the Constitution (including the Bill of Rights). Are prosecutors then constitutionally required to meet the standard in every case, or can state legislatures relax the standard in certain situations? While this question may seem at first unusual or strange, it was a real issue concerning juvenile court during the 1960s.

Juvenile courts were originally created in the early twentieth century in order to help youth avoid some of the harshness and complexity of the adult criminal justice system. The basic idea was to allow government to intervene more easily, and have juveniles processed more quickly, so that government services and youth rehabilitation could begin in a timelier way. The New York Legislature reasoned that if juvenile court was created by statute as an alternative to the cumbersome adult criminal justice process, the legislature was free to establish new streamlined standards and procedures for the juvenile court system. One of the ways New York altered the process for juveniles was to relax the standard of proof during juvenile court proceedings. Whether New York was permitted to do this is the issue in our next case.

In re Winship
397 U.S. 358 (1970)

The case of *In re Winship* concerns a 12-year-old boy accused of entering a locker room and stealing $112 from a woman's pocketbook. We know the name of the juvenile only as Winship (hence the name of the case, *In re Winship*, which could be stated more clearly as "In the matter of Winship."). Winship was adjudicated a juvenile delinquent by the New York Family Court. Juveniles are technically "adjudicated" delinquent, instead of tried and convicted — the difference in terms was a conscious decision by the creators of juvenile courts to suggest a wholly different process than criminal court. Another difference was the kind of court hearing Winship's case. While the terms are different, and Winship was adjudicated in family court instead of criminal court, his penalties remained similar to what would be handed down in criminal court. Winship was ordered to be placed in a training school for an initial period of 18 months, but this was extendable for up to six years until Winship turned age 18. In short, Winship faced a serious sanction, but reduced procedural protections during his hearing raised issues of excessive subservience to government.

When Winship's case reached the Supreme Court, it determined that despite the absence of the words "beyond a reasonable doubt" in the Constitution, this legal standard was constitutionally required. The Court first considered the question of whether the beyond a reasonable doubt standard was generally required in criminal cases under the Due Process Clause of the Fourteenth Amendment. The Court looked to history, and its own precedents, to establish that due process required proof of guilt beyond a reasonable doubt in adult criminal court.

In reviewing the history, the Court acknowledged that, although the idea of requiring a high degree of persuasion in criminal cases was expressed from ancient times, "its crystallization into the formula 'beyond a reasonable doubt' seems to have occurred as late as 1798." A careful student of history will note that 1798 is after the drafting of the Bill of Rights and helps explain why there is no explicit mention of "beyond a reasonable doubt" in the Bill of Rights.

The Court went on to look at many of its precedents which had assumed that the reasonable doubt standard was a fundamental one required to satisfy the Fourteenth Amendment's Due Process Clause. "A society that values a good name and freedom of every individual should not condemn a man for commission of a crime when there is a reasonable doubt about his guilt." The Court asserted the "use of the reasonable doubt standard is indispensable to command the respect and confidence of the community" in the criminal justice system. The Court believed it critical that "every individual going about his ordinary daily affairs have confidence that his government cannot adjudge him guilty of a criminal offense without convincing a proper factfinder of his guilt with utmost certainty." These quotes all make the point that government power must be constrained when it comes to confining people and depriving them of their physical liberty. The alternative would place us all at the mercy of government, requiring excessive subservience.

The Court then turned its attention to the specific question of whether prosecutors in juvenile court must also satisfy the reasonable doubt standard for juvenile adjudications. The Court acknowledged that delinquency adjudication is not a criminal conviction and a "cloak of protective confidentiality" surrounds juvenile court proceedings. Nevertheless, the Court found the reasonable doubt standard was constitutionally required, even in juvenile court, because of the loss of liberty juveniles were facing. The Court rejected concerns that the reasonable doubt standard would overly formalize the juvenile court, asserting that juvenile proceedings would still remain informal, flexible, and swift. Juvenile proceedings would still permit a wide-ranging review of a child's social health history and the need for individualized treatment. In short, the Court believed that raising the legal standard for the government would not impact the state's interest in efficient and streamlined juvenile proceedings.

Two of the three dissenting justices disagreed with the Court's assumption that by raising the legal standard, the Court would not disturb the other beneficial aspects of juvenile court proceedings. Chief Justice Burger wrote in dissent that "What the juvenile court system needs is not more but less of the trappings of legal procedure and judicial formalism; the juvenile court system requires breathing room and flexibility in order to survive."

Justice Black had a much deeper concern with the majority's opinion. Justice Black wrote a dissenting opinion arguing the Court simply did not have the authority to require the reasonable doubt standard without explicit language in the Constitution. "[I]n two places the Constitution provides for trial by jury, but nowhere in that document is there any statement that conviction of crime requires proof of guilt beyond a reasonable doubt.... I believe the Court has no power to add or subtract from the procedures set forth by the Founders." Justice Black believed judges were not permitted to insert language into the Constitution on their own authority, even language as laudable and desirable as the reasonable-doubt standard: "I shall not at any time surrender my belief that [the Constitution] itself should be our guide, not our own concept of what is fair, decent, and right.... I prefer to put my faith in the words of the written Constitution itself rather than to rely on the shifting, day-to-day standards of fairness of individual judges." For Justice Black, inserting language into the Constitution requires its own form of excessive subservience by the states and their constituents to the Supreme Court.

Discussion Questions

1. Do you believe there are some rights so important that they must be read into the Constitution even if the Framers neglected to explicitly include them?

2. How might juveniles be harmed by the reasonable doubt standard? Do you think the new higher standard might change the nature of juvenile court proceedings and make it less focused on rehabilitation?

Once the Court established that the reasonable doubt standard was required for all criminal justice cases, as well as juvenile delinquency adjudications, it then had to wrestle with the question of exactly what the standard means. Certainly, the words "beyond a reasonable doubt" have some intrinsic meaning, and citizens who are asked to serve as jurors have some notion of their application by virtue of living in American society. What happens, however, when judges mistakenly instruct jurors on the meaning of the reasonable doubt standard? If the jury instruction does not do an adequate job of defining "beyond a reasonable doubt," what then should happen?

Sullivan v. Louisiana
508 U.S. 275 (1993)

John Sullivan was charged with first-degree murder in the course of committing an armed robbery at a New Orleans bar. Only one person present in the bar at the time of the robbery testified during the trial, but this person had been unable to identify Sullivan as the shooter at an earlier physical lineup. Nevertheless, at trial the witness testified she saw Sullivan holding a gun to the victim's head. During closing arguments Sullivan's attorney argued there was a reasonable doubt as to the identity of the murderer.

Despite the pleas of Sullivan's attorney, the jury found Sullivan guilty and subsequently recommended he receive the death penalty. Following the jury's suggestion, the trial court sentenced Sullivan to death. On appeal, Sullivan argued that there was a mistake in the instructions to the jury regarding the definition of "beyond a reasonable doubt." The Supreme Court of Louisiana agreed with Sullivan that the trial court made an erroneous instruction to the jury. Yet the Louisiana Supreme Court still upheld Sullivan's conviction, ruling that the erroneous instruction was harmless beyond a reasonable doubt. This is known as the **harmless error** standard — convictions will stand, despite legal errors during the trial, if the state can prove beyond a reasonable doubt the error did not make any difference to the outcome of the trial.

In reaching a decision in Sullivan's case, the U.S. Supreme Court agreed with the Louisiana Supreme Court that not all constitutional errors during a criminal trial require reversal and a new trial. Indeed, Justice Scalia, writing for a unanimous Court, noted that "most constitutional errors have been amendable to harmless-error analysis." Yet some constitutional errors, like total deprivation of the right to counsel, trial by a biased judge, and denial of the right to self-representation, always invalidate the conviction.

Do errors in instructing the jury regarding reasonable doubt always require reversal and a new trial, or may states apply the harmless error standard when the jury is erroneously instructed about reasonable doubt? The Court found that "Where the instructional error consists of a misdescription of the burden of proof, [this] vitiates *all* the jury's findings. A reviewing court can only engage in pure speculation — its view of what a reasonable jury would have done. And when it does that the wrong entity judges the defendant guilty." In effect, the judge becomes the factfinder in such situation, not the jury, and this does not comport with the right to a trial by jury. Thus, it is essential that the jury be properly instructed on the meaning of "beyond a reasonable doubt" as no fair trial, free of excessive subservience to government, can occur without a proper jury instruction on the prosecution's burden of proof.

So, to review, *In re Winship* teaches that in order to avoid excessive subservience to government the government cannot lower the standard of proof in a criminal case, or juvenile proceedings, below the reasonable doubt standard. *Sullivan v. Louisiana* teaches that if the trial judge makes a mistake regarding its reasonable doubt instructions to the jury, the state cannot fix this mistake on appeal by showing the error to be harmless by presenting overwhelming evidence of the defendant's guilt.

This leaves us with the hardest question: what exactly does "beyond a reasonable doubt" mean? The court had mostly avoided the problem of defining "beyond a reasonable doubt" in the years before, and even after *In re Winship*, generally giving states wide latitude to decide whether to define or not define the phrase "beyond a reasonable doubt." Even when states defined the phrase, the Court had not required any particular form in defining it. The Court wrestled directly with the issue of defining reasonable doubt in our next case.

Victor v. Nebraska
511 U.S. 1 (1994)

The facts of this case are irrelevant, only the nature of the instruction to the jury on reasonable doubt was at issue. The jury was instructed:

> A defendant in a criminal action is presumed to be innocent until the contrary is proved, and in case of a reasonable doubt whether his guilt is satisfactorily shown, he is entitled to a verdict of not guilty. This presumption places upon the State the burden of proving him guilty beyond a reasonable doubt. Reasonable doubt is defined as follows: It is *not a mere possible doubt*; because everything relating to human affairs, and *depending on moral evidence*, is open to some possible or

imaginary doubt. It is that state of the case which, after the entire comparison and consideration of all the evidence, leaves the minds of the jurors in that condition that they cannot say they feel an abiding conviction, *to a moral certainty,* of the truth of the charge. (Emphasis added by Supreme Court.)

Helpful, but potentially still somewhat confusing? The Supreme Court thought so too. The Supreme Court noted that this particular instruction was largely drawn from a famous jury instruction given over 150 years ago in the state of Massachusetts. Moreover, this instruction had effectively been adopted as the gold standard and used by several states for properly defining "beyond a reasonable doubt." However, for several years, judges had been concerned that some of the words in this instruction were no longer helpful to modern juries. For instance, the terms "moral evidence" and "moral certainty" as used in this instruction no longer had much meaning for the average citizen.

The Supreme Court acknowledged that "Words and phrases can change meaning over time: A passage generally understood in 1850 may be incomprehensible or confusing to a modern juror." But did this jury instruction, using the old term "moral certainty" likely so confuse this jury as to be unconstitutional? The Court stated, "The problem is … that a jury might understand the phrase to mean something less than the very high level of probability required by the Constitution in criminal cases." The Court noted this potential problem was mitigated by the fact that the jury was also instructed that it must have "an abiding conviction, to a moral certainty, of the truth of the charge." The term "abiding conviction" was sufficient to satisfy the Court that, despite its concerns over the accompanying phrase "moral certainty," the instruction given was constitutional.

The Court upheld the use of the above instruction in this case, and therefore, the defendant's conviction. Yet the Court made clear "we do not condone the use of the phrase." The Court pointed out that most definitions of reasonable doubt used by the federal courts do not contain reference to "moral certainty." "But we have no supervisory power over the state courts, and in the context of the instructions as a whole we cannot say that the use of the phrase rendered the instruction given [in this case] unconstitutional." The Court had previously identified terms like "grave uncertainty," "actual substantial doubt," and "moral certainty" as constitutionally problematic, even striking down (in an unsigned opinion) one jury instruction where all three had been used. Yet, the Court allowed the use of "moral certainty" in the jury instruction in this case, where it appeared from reading the entire jury instruction as a whole that "there is no reasonable likelihood that the jurors who determined [the defendant's] guilt applied the instructions in a way that violated the Constitution." In short, the Constitution does not necessarily require states, even when using archaic language, to change their traditional definitions of "beyond a reasonable doubt."

Justice Ginsburg, in a concurring opinion, acknowledged that defining "beyond a reasonable doubt" had proven so difficult that some judges had been admonished not to attempt the definition at all. She found this to be unhelpful. Justice Ginsburg noted that the Federal Judicial Center had proposed a definition of reasonable doubt that she found to be clear, straightforward, and accurate. That model jury instruction reads:

> The government has the burden of proving the defendant guilty beyond a reasonable doubt. Some of you may have served as jurors in civil cases, where you were told that it is only necessary to prove that a fact is more likely true than not true. In criminal cases, the government's proof must be more powerful than that. It must be beyond a reasonable doubt. Proof beyond a reasonable doubt is proof that leaves you firmly convinced of the defendant's guilt. There are very few things in this world that we know with absolute certainty, and in criminal cases the law does not require proof that overcomes every possible doubt. If, based on your consideration of the evidence, you are firmly convinced that the defendant is guilty of the crime charged, you must find him guilty. If on the other hand, you think there is a real possibility that he is not guilty, you must give him the benefit of the doubt and find him not guilty.

Justice Ginsburg identified the terms "firmly convinced" and "real possibility" as the key terms in the model instruction. The instruction endorsed by Justice Ginsburg is at present perhaps the best statement and definition of "beyond a reasonable doubt," and has been widely cited by many legal scholars and criminal justice practitioners.

Discussion Questions

1. Is there a meaningful difference between the Court requiring certain words (a model jury instruction), and the Court striking down certain words or phrases in jury instructions as unconstitutional?

2. Would Justice Ginsburg's model jury instruction help clarify the meaning of "beyond reasonable doubt" if you were sitting on a jury or would you prefer a mathematical equivalent like "you must be more than 95% certain" of the defendant's guilt?

Even the model jury instruction endorsed by Justice Ginsburg is subject to criticism, however. The use of the word "must" in the second half ("If, based on your consideration of the evidence, you are firmly convinced that the defendant is guilty of the crime charged, you *must* find him guilty.") seems to instruct the jury that they are required to follow the law as stated by the trial judge, and may not engage in jury nullification. **Jury nullification** is the practice of juries returning a not-guilty verdict even when the prosecution proves a case beyond a reasonable doubt because the jurors object to the law itself or its application to a particular defendant.

Paul Butler, a former federal prosecutor, reports that when he clerked for federal judge Mary Johnson Lowe, she refused to use the "must" language in jury instructions, such as Justice Ginsburg's model jury instruction. Instead, Judge Lowe would instruct juries, "if you find guilt beyond a reasonable doubt, you *may* convict." Paul Butler goes on, in his book *Let's Get Free: A Hip-Hop Theory of Justice*, to advocate for jury nullification in some nonviolent, minor drug-possession cases. He argues juries should use their power to block convictions in appropriate cases so as to help manage high levels of incarceration and avoid further damaging minority neighborhoods. But are juries constitutionally permitted to nullify states' laws by refusing to convict guilty defendants?

Jury nullification has a long and controversial history dating back before the United States was a country. In 1735, the famous case of John Peter Zenger provided an example of using jury nullification to resist unpopular or illegitimate laws. Zenger was charged with seditious libel for critical statements he had published about New York colonial governor, William Cosby. The trial judge found the published statements constituted libel as a matter of law and directed the jury to return a guilty verdict against Zenger. However, the jury refused to convict Zenger of the charges, in effect nullifying the libel law, at least in Zenger's case.

Other juries before the Civil War refused to convict defendants for assisting or harboring slaves in violation of the fugitive slave laws passed by Congress. In the twentieth century juries nullified charges against Prohibition-era rum-runners, Vietnam War protestors, and family members assisting terminally ill loved ones commit suicide. That juries have the power to negate laws which they feel are illegitimate, even laws passed by democratically elected legislatures, is a fact that was recognized by the United States Supreme Court in *Sparf v. United States* in 1895. On the other hand, since this is a power that can be abused by juries, the Supreme Court has refused to require lower courts to instruct juries that they have this power. For instance, the dangerous side of jury nullification is illustrated by juries who refused to convict white supremacists for lynching or otherwise committing violence against African Americans, or who refused to convict for federal civil rights violations during the 1960s. The Supreme Court of Kansas recently considered the issue of jury nullification in the context of jury instructions, as we shall see in the next case.

State v. Smith-Parker

340 P.3d 485 (Kan. 2014)

William Jerome Smith-Parker was convicted of two murders but objected to the instructions given to the jury in his trial. The jury was instructed, "if you do not have a reasonable doubt from all the evidence that the State has proven murder in the first degree ... then you *will* enter a verdict of guilty" (emphasis added). The Kansas Supreme Court found this jury instruction to be faulty. It considered whether words like "must" or "will" enter a verdict of guilty are appropriate. In a prior precedent 30 years before it had held the words "should" and "must" could be used interchangeably in criminal jury instructions. In the *Smith-Parker* case, the Kansas Supreme Court overturned that decision.

The Kansas Supreme Court noted that while it would continue to oppose instructing criminal juries regarding jury nullification, it acknowledged that juries possess the inherent power to reject the trial judge's statement of the law. The trial judge's instruction in this case, went too far because "[i]t essentially forbade the jury from exercising its power of nullification." The Kansas Supreme Court concluded that both the word "must" and the word "will" are invalid for jury instructions on reasonable doubt as they "fly too close to the sun of directing a verdict for the State. A judge cannot compel a jury to convict, even if it finds all elements proved beyond a reasonable doubt."

Discussion Questions

1. Do you think jurors should be instructed that they have the power to engage in jury nullification? Would you understand from the language of "may convict" or "should convict" that you had the power to decide whether a law was legitimately applied in a defendant's case?

2. What types of cases would be appropriate for juries to engage in jury nullification?

Chapter Key Terms

Subservience

Second Amendment

§ 1983 claim

Qualified immunity

Reasonable time, place and
   manner restrictions

Selective incorporation

Confrontation Clause

Spousal privilege

Beyond a reasonable doubt

Harmless error

Jury nullification

Chapter Fourteen

Subservience in Law Enforcement and Corrections

George Latimer: Now, I will ask you this, Lieutenant Calley: Whatever you did at My Lai on that occasion, I will ask you whether in your opinion you were acting rightly and according to your understanding of your directions and orders?

William Calley: I felt then and I still do that I acted as I was directed, and I carried out the orders that I was given, and I do not feel wrong in doing so, sir ...

— William Calley, quoted in "Lt. William Calley, Witness for the Defense"

Law Enforcement

As the previous chapter highlighted, subservience to authority is something that individuals often fear, and it is a topic that continues to be debated among the Courts. There are many points when an individual's constitutional rights butt heads with the authority that law enforcement and those in the corrections system have to carry out their duties. In the following section below, we will be exploring how law enforcement attempts to get and maintain subservience to their authority by looking at a few recent cases. After exploring the idea of "contempt of cop," we will transition to cases where an individual's First and Second Amendment rights were challenged by law enforcement. Generally, these two issues collided because individual citizens didn't see eye to eye with law enforcement: for law enforcement, they were simply performing their duties, while citizens were simply invoking their rights.

It is assumed that if you are asked to do something by law enforcement that you will willingly comply so as to not seem suspicious or to interfere with the tasks that they are trying to accomplish. However, what if you feel as though you are not in the wrong, and because you know your rights, feel as though you do not have to comply with their requests? Can non-compliance be used as a justification for you being held criminally liable? Or taken a step further, can your non-compliance be used to justify law enforcement resorting to force? Given the recent climate of police-citizen interactions, some have cleverly spun the phrase "contempt of court" to "contempt of cop" to capture these ideas. Contempt of court is the idea that an individual is disrespecting the authority of the judge and the process of the trial by being disruptive. Using a play on words, **contempt of cop** makes a similar argument about a citizen disrespecting the authority of law enforcement by not complying with their commands (Izzy, 2014, para. 1). While a number of cases could be discussed to illustrate this concept, some argue that contempt of cop is most prevalent in cases where law enforcement escalated the situation by resorting to excessive or deadly force. The two cases that will be briefly discussed here are the deaths of Eric Garner and Walter Scott.

Eric Garner

On July 17, 2014, Eric Garner was supposedly breaking up a fight on a street corner when he was confronted by law enforcement for selling untaxed cigarettes (something they had targeted him for doing in the past) (Browne Dianis, 2014, para. 3). He was surrounded by a handful of officers and a bystander recorded the entire event on his cellphone. What we can see is Garner quickly getting heated with law enforcement, asking why they always harass him for doing nothing wrong and then putting his hands up in the air to prevent them from handcuffing him. Garner refused to go down to the ground and be handcuffed, so in an effort to subdue him, Officer Daniel Pantaleo puts him in a chokehold. Garner was a large man weighing in at a little over 350 pounds and standing to a height of 6'3" (Pearson, 2014, para. 3). As Officer Pantaleo took him to the ground, you could hear Garner saying repeatedly that he couldn't breathe. He winds up dying shortly after the encounter, and while the medical examiners determined that his asthma and obesity may have played a minor role in his death, he ultimately died from compression to the neck and chest (Botelho, 2014, para. 11) as a result of the chokehold.

Many called for Pantaleo to be criminally charged; however, his supervisors stood behind his actions on that day. While the NYPD has a policy forbidding officers from using a chokehold, the New York police commissioner stated that there are no local laws that criminalize it. Furthermore, his superiors supported him by saying that it was a tragic accident and that there was no ill intent behind his actions. According to Tom Fuentes (former FBI assistant director, police officer, and current CNN law enforcement analyst), people need to put themselves in the shoes of police and think about what they would have done that day. He asks, how long can/should law enforcement wait to take action and intervene? "And, if a person does not comply, what can they do — let him go or step in, perhaps using force" (Botelho, 2014, para. 27)?

Criminal charges (which were never publicly disclosed) were filed against Officer Pantaleo, but he was never indicted. In the wake of the incident, he released a statement saying that it was never his intention to hurt Mr. Garner and that Garner's family is in his prayers. Additionally, he asked for them to accept his condolences for their loss (Celona et al., 2014, para. 5–6). When Eric's widow (Esaw) was asked if she accepted this apology, she emphatically replied, "Hell no" and that "the time for remorse was when my husband was yelling to breathe" (Burke et al., 2014, para. 1–3). And while the Garner family knew that they could not hold the officer or police department criminally responsible, they decided to sue the city for wrongful death charges (Celona et al., 2014, para. 31). A year after Mr. Garner's passing, his family reached a settlement for $5.9 million dollars with New York City. While his family is pleased with this outcome, his mother had the following words to say about the outcome of that settlement: "Don't congratulate us. This is not a victory. Victory will come when we get justice" (Haller & Pearce, 2015, para. 1–2).

Discussion Questions

1. Do you think there is any legitimacy to the concept "contempt of cop" or is it just a buzzword created for media outlets?

2. Do you think that Officer Pantaleo should have been held criminally liable for Garner's death, or did the grand jury get it right?

Walter Scott

Similar to the above case, this is an issue where an unarmed Black man is ultimately killed for his non-compliance. Whereas Garner's case took place in

New York City and on the street corner, this case dealt with a motorist who ran away from police in South Carolina. Walter Scott was pulled over on April 4, 2015, by Officer Michael Slager for having a broken taillight (Swaine, 2015, para. 8). At some point during the traffic stop, Scott fled on foot and Slager chased after him. While we may never be able to fully know the details as to why Scott ran, some speculate that he could have been fearful that he would be taken into custody over his unpaid child support (he owed over $18,000 in back payments) (Yan, 2015, para. 6). Aside from this minor transgression, Scott was said to have a clean record and no prior run-ins with the law. Eventually, Scott and Slager ended up on a sidewalk set back from the road, and it is at this point the video footage recorded by a bystander captures the last moments of Scott's life. What the video shows is Scott and Slager close to one another and then Scott breaking free and starting to run. You then see Slager pull out his gun and shoot Scott in the back while he is running away. He then walks over to Scott and puts handcuffs on him while Scott is lying face down on the ground. Officer Slager shot his weapon eight times, and Scott was struck and killed by five of the bullets.

After Slager shot Scott, he called in to dispatch and said "shots fired, and subject is down. He grabbed my taser" (Murdock, 2015, para. 3). In a story printed later that day in a local newspaper, the police released a statement saying that Officer Slager and the suspect struggled after he ran on foot from the traffic stop and that the suspect then gained control of Slager's taser in an attempt to use it against him. Officer Slager then resorted to using his service weapon to bring the suspect down (Elmore & MacDougall, 2015, para. 11–13). At this point in time, the video had not been released, and many speculated that this might be the only version of the story had the bystander's cellphone footage never been released. However, three days later the video was handed over to a news station, and it quickly went viral. While the video starts with the brief altercation between the two men, which is closely followed by the shots, you can see in the opening seconds that there is what appears to be a taser that was deployed. It looks as though it is on the ground and then after the shots are fired, you can see Slager walk over to Scott and drop something near his body. Legal analysts and police experts believe the item to be a taser which Slager may have dropped next to Scott to make it appear as though he had possession of it when the shots were fired. Some people argue that while there may be truth to Officer Slager's account about there being an altercation over the taser, that he still was more knowledgeable than Scott in how to properly use and maintain control of it. In his five-year career, Officer Slager had used his taser a total of 14 times, with six of those being within the past year (Blinder et al., 2015, para. 4–6).

Once the North Charleston Police Department caught wind of the videotape and began analyzing it for themselves, they released Officer Slager from his duties. The autopsy showed that the wounds were to Scott's back, head, and ear, and it was ruled a homicide. Slager was charged with first-degree murder, which carries a potential sentence of life in prison or death (Martinez, 2015, para. 3 & 55). He was denied bond, and although he was terminated from his position, the North Charleston PD decided to continue paying his insurance until his pregnant wife gave birth to their child. Rather than first-degree murder, Slager was found guilty of second degree murder and obstruction of justice and was sentenced to 20 years in prison (Osunsami & Shapiro, 2017, para 1).

In both cases above you could make a clear argument for these being illustrations of police using excessive or deadly force. However, these cases have been presented to illustrate the idea of subservience to authority and a criminal suspect not adhering to law enforcement's orders. In both cases, many argued that death could have been avoided had the men simply complied with the officer's requests. In the case of Garner, some argued that had he not resisted arrest and forced law enforcement to resort to using the chokehold, that he'd likely still be alive. The case of Scott is a little less clear cut since there is so much that may never be known about the alleged altercation between Officer Slager and Scott. However, in this case as with Garner's, many argued that had he not fled and simply complied with Slager's requests that he likely would still be alive to this day. The counter-argument, though, is how do you justify someone dying over resisting arrest or running from the police? Perhaps these are two examples where contempt of cop ends up violently spiraling out of control.

Discussion Questions

1. Do you think that Officer Slager was following protocol or did he too quickly resort to deadly force?

2. Given the limited information that you have about this case, what sentence do you think would be appropriate for Officer Slager?

The above cases provided a general overview of subservience to law enforcement and how things can go horribly awry when the suspect in question does not comply. The following case is less severe in nature, but nonetheless, begs the question of which should trump: a citizen's First Amendment rights or law enforcement's authority. The following case will explore a topic that is increasingly becoming common practice: video recording law enforcement while they go about their daily duties. As technology has advanced, nearly everyone has the capability to record everything and anything that they want simply with the push of a button on their cell phone. However, just because this is an option, does it mean that citizens should be able to freely and openly record law enforcement officers? The following case will explore this question in greater detail.

Video Recording the Police

In 2010, Christopher Sharp pulled out his cell phone when his friend was being arrested by law enforcement at the Preakness Stakes in Baltimore. According to Sharp, she was intoxicated and resisting arrest, but he felt compelled to record the incident since he thought that they were being too rough when they were taking her into custody. According to bystanders (and a video recording that another bystander released), she was slammed to the ground and had her head pushed into the concrete floor. In the video, you can see that she is bleeding profusely from her face while she is being handcuffed and taken away from the scene. Sharp is quickly confronted by officers demanding that he hand over the phone because it is now considered evidence. Sharp initially resisted their request, but because he was fearful that he himself would be arrested as well, he quickly handed over the video. An officer deleted all of the videos on his cell phone (including personal videos of his family) before returning it to Sharp (*Sharp v. BCPD*, 2011, para. 1–2).

In 2011, Sharp filed a complaint against the Baltimore Police Department and three unnamed officers alleging that a policy that the police department uses (General Order J-16: "Video Recording of Police Activity") violates constitutional protections that citizens have under the First, Fourth, and Fourteenth Amendments. While there were many twists and turns in the case, the parties eventually settled on a joint stipulation of dismissal (*Sharp v. Baltimore City Police*, 2011, para. 1–5). Three years after the litigation process started Sharp was awarded $250,000 in damages and attorney fees (Wenger, 2014, para. 1).

Baltimore has a long history of threatening citizens with criminal charges when they don't stop recording police activities as requested. As an example, recording bystanders have been threatened with loitering, obstruction of justice, and wiretapping charges if they are unwilling to stop recording (Fenton,

2012, para. 2). Often times these charges do not hold up because there is case law which has weighed in on the topic (i.e., *Glik v. Cunniffe* discussed in Chapter 13), stating that the First Amendment protects our rights to record audio and video of law enforcement without needing to get consent. Additionally, the First, Seventh, Ninth, and Eleventh Circuits have weighed in on this issue and unanimously recognize an individual's First Amendment right to record law enforcement while they are performing their duties (Recording police officers, 2013, para. 1–6). The only caveat to this topic is that your recording cannot hamper law enforcement performing their duties. If you were to do so, you could open yourself up to criminal charges or litigation.

Many argue that recording law enforcement while carrying out their duties is not only a right of ours that is protected but that it is a civic duty. With all of the recently documented cases of police brutality and excessive or deadly force, some argue that these recordings are necessary "to hold rogue police officers more accountable" (Butler, 2014, para. 1). Additionally, these recordings can be used to show instances where law enforcement was acting within the bounds of their responsibilities. As such, it builds in more accountability across the board, which many argue is a good thing regardless of how you slice it.

In the absence of any federal mandate and recognizing that inconsistent definitions of what First Amendment protections and recording law enforcement means from state to state, the U.S. Department of Justice (DOJ) weighed in on the issue. The statement made by the DOJ heavily discussed the case of Sharp and the Baltimore Police Department to illustrate how their written policies regarding citizens recording police activities needed to be updated. According to the DOJ, the Baltimore PD needs to better advertise that recording police is a protection that everyone (press or laymen) has under the First Amendment. Additionally, the DOJ suggested that the Baltimore PD needs to better instruct its officers to not threaten, intimidate, or prohibit an individual from recording them (Smith, 2012, pp. 2–11). And last, while the DOJ had a series of other recommendations, they suggested that the Baltimore PD publicize and then meticulously begin enforcing their revised policies. Among them was that an individual recording law enforcement activity does not constitute probable cause, and as such, cannot be used to justify an arrest. Additionally, while officers can temporarily detain a recorder if their footage is determined to be evidence, they must secure a search warrant before they can access the data on the phone (Hermann, 2012, para. 14–15).

Discussion Questions

1. How do you feel about recording police while they perform their duties? Is it too intrusive or does it provide a good "check and balance" of sorts?

2. Do you feel like the DOJ statement and resulting changes that Baltimore implemented regarding video recording police officers is going to truly change law enforcement behavior regarding this issue?

Waco Siege

In the above case, we explored the issue of a citizen's First Amendment rights butting heads with law enforcement authority. In the following case, we will be exploring how our Second Amendment rights may be challenged by a different authoritative figure: the federal government. What makes this case unique though is that many argued that it was the botched efforts by law enforcement (namely the FBI and ATF) that ultimately lead to the death of approximately 86 individuals, not the actions of those who were being targeted.

Vernon Howell (who went by the name of David Koresh) believed that he was the prophet, and he created the religious sect called the Branch Davidians, a Christian group that spawned from the Seventh Day Adventist Church (Hannaford, 2013, para. 1–3). This group was said to hold extreme views about Christianity and have an overall distrust of the government. Koresh and his followers built a compound (called "Mount Carmel") just a few miles outside of Waco, Texas, where he thought they could all live in harmony and be separated from the outside world. While a final head-count of exactly how many individuals lived on the grounds was never released, it was estimated that there were nearly a hundred men, women, and children from all over the world living at Mount Carmel and worshiping under Koresh.

The activities that occurred behind the concrete walls slowly gained attention from local law enforcement agencies in 1992 when they received a tip that the Davidians might be producing and stockpiling illegal weapons. A UPS delivery man who had reportedly made many deliveries in the past to the compound noticed what appeared to be hand grenades and black gunpowder in a damaged package that was being delivered to Koresh. The local police passed this information along to the Bureau of Alcohol, Tobacco and Firearms and a nearly year-long investigation into the activities of Koresh and others on the compound followed. It was discovered that there were large shipments of firearms made to the compound on a frequent basis and that when the driver arrived with the delivery, he was escorted to an off-site facility and paid in cash (Danforth, 2000, p. 124).

There were two additional problems that the government took issue with and eventually used as fuel to justify their storming of the compound. The first was that officials argued there were allegations of child abuse occurring and that illegal drugs were being produced (i.e., methamphetamine) on the grounds (McCurry, n.d., para. 12–13). The allegations of child abuse came from a **confidential informant** who had been kicked out of the group, so, after the fact, many challenged the validity of this information. The ATF gathered their intelligence on the drug allegations from aerial surveillance of "hot spots" and tracking incoming packages that contained chemicals commonly used to make methamphetamine. Armed with this information, the ATF requested a search warrant of the premises, based upon probable cause that the Davidians were in possession of destructive devices and other illegal weapons. Additionally, although it's never been formally released, the affidavit contained some discussion of child abuse as well as an indication that government officials were going in to arrest Koresh on a variety of federal charges. Interestingly enough, there was no mention in the affidavit about drugs or the chemicals that the feds had allegedly been tracking.

On February 28, 1993, approximately 80 agents surrounded the compound to execute the warrant. Contradictory information about exactly what occurred next has been presented through many sources, but allegedly those at the compound opened fire first. A shootout ensued, and six Davidians and four agents wound up dead. While many would assume that the initial gun battle would result in the Davidians surrendering, this was far from the case: what followed was a 51-day standoff. Those from the compound refused to come out, but eventually, Koresh let 37 people (21 of them children) leave during negotiations (Atrocity in Waco, n.d., para. 7). It was uncertain at this point whether or not those living on the compound refused to surrender or if they were being forced against their will to stay on the grounds. Regardless of the reason for their unwillingness to surrender, the ATF decided that it was best for everyone's safety to get the remaining individuals out of the building and off of the complex. On April 19, 1993, the ATF (and FBI) surrounded the complex with tanks and also used tear gas in an effort to force the occupants out. At this point, the events that transpired took a tragic turn for the worse: a fire started on the complex, and 76 individuals (mostly women and children) were unable to escape and perished in the fire. The true cause of the fire is up for debate, as the handful of survivors said that the fire was started by the feds, while the feds claim the fire was set from the inside in an effort to commit mass suicide.

Unfortunately, this is not only a tragic incident but also one which has severely tarnished the federal government and challenged the authority and decision-making ability of law enforcement. Many argued that the ATF was involved simply because the government felt threatened by Koresh and his right-winged followers. Furthermore, some argued that the ATF and FBI knew after the first encounter they were going in on shaky grounds (i.e., not enough evidence against Koresh), but that they had to stand behind the mission because they were now engaged in a standoff with the Davidians. In the aftermath of the 51-day standoff, many media outlets reported that the main reason for going into the complex was to "rescue" the children from child abuse. Critics of this argument point out two flaws here: (1) child abuse allegations usually fall under state, not federal jurisdiction, and (2) the main reason they secured the search and arrest warrant was for illegal weapons, not child abuse as the media was claiming (McCurry, n.d., para. 12–15). Many argued that this was just a public relations tactic to help the ATF and FBI "save face" when they started receiving flak for what happened.

A series of investigations followed in the wake of the event, and it slowly trickled out that there may have been some holes in the investigation. The congressional committee issued a report on August 2, 1996, that stated some of the decisions made leading up to and during the execution of the warrant were "premature, wrong, and highly irresponsible" (Danforth, 2000, p. 189). While they were willing to take ownership of these vague faults, the committee held steadfast to the idea that Koresh (not the agents) were responsible for the fire and that those from inside the compound fired on agents first (not the other way around). Additionally, they stood behind the legitimacy of the warrants by referencing all of the illegal weapons that they found in the compound after sifting through the rubble. Among them were semiautomatic firearms that had been modified into fully automatic weapons, grenades, and silencers (Peacock, 1995, para. 4). Others argue that these documents were fabricated by the FBI in an effort to cover their tracks and that those on the compound were in possession of legal firearms. These more extreme views fall under conspiracy theories that the Waco siege only happened because the government felt threatened that the Davidians were forming a militia (The guns of Waco, 1995, para. 5–6).

Lots of Americans were displeased with how the event was handled, and many considered it the sinister icing on the cake when charges were pressed against a handful of surviving Davidians. The most severe of the charges were murder and conspiracy to murder for the deaths of the four agents. All of the defendants were acquitted on these charges, but five defendants were convicted of the lesser offense of manslaughter. An additional seven defendants were charged with using or carrying a firearm during a conspiracy to murder federal officers, another for possessing a live grenade, and a final with **aiding and abetting** (also called an accessory; helping in the commission of a crime, but usually the individual is not present when the crime is committed) the illegal possession of machine guns (Danforth, 2000, pp. 181–182). The defendants received lengthy sentences ranging from five to 40 years and the convictions were challenged and affirmed by the United States Court of Appeals for the Fifth Circuit. The case eventually wound up in the hands of the U.S. Supreme Court and was remanded back to the district court. The manslaughter charges stayed, but the less severe charges that revolved around possession of illegal firearms were reduced for a majority of the defendants.

Many questioned whether or not the government should be and/or was ever held accountable for the actions that occurred during the siege at Mount Carmel. As was discussed above, many reports in the aftermath of the event pointed fault at the Davidians for initially shooting at the agents and starting the fires. Regardless of this information, approximately 100 survivors and relatives of the deceased sued the government for $675 million, alleging the use of excessive force was what caused the deaths. A five-member jury determined that agents of the ATF and FBI were not responsible for initiating the standoff or starting the fires (Jury clears US, 2000, para. 1–2). Additionally, the jury heard toxicology and autopsy reports that showed many victims died from self-inflicted wounds consistent with suicide and that the use of tear gas had no bearing on their deaths. Fire experts also testified that the three fires that broke out simultaneously could have only been started from the inside and were only further spurred by high winds that day. As such, the federal judge dismissed the **wrongful death** (when a person dies due to the negligence or misconduct of another) case, citing that neither poor planning nor negligent behavior on the part of the ATF or FBI was to blame for the events that occurred on April 19, 1993 (Judge dismisses Waco, 2000, para. 5). In the wake of the ruling, the Department of Justice released a statement saying that the "terrible tragedy was the responsibility of David Koresh and the Branch Davidians, not the federal government. We are pleased the jury affirmed that view" (Milloy, 2000, para. 3).

Even over 25 years after the incident, simply mentioning the Waco siege can stir up a lot of emotions. Many argue that regardless of what commissions or reports show, there will continue to be a number of unanswered questions about the events that transpired on those fateful days. However, in the context of this chapter, the Waco siege begs the age-old question: could things have turned out differently had the Davidians just surrendered at the first altercation? Is it possible that their non-compliance only further enraged the government, causing them to escalate the level of force that they used at the end of the 51-day standoff? Additionally, is it a possibility that the agents were overzealous in their attack on the compound because they wanted vengeance for the four deceased agents? While we will likely never know the answer, the Waco siege provides us with a good avenue through which to explore the perhaps darker side of subservience to authority.

Discussion Questions

1. Do some additional research of your own. What is your conclusion; did the government, ATF, and FBI have legitimate reason to be concerned with the Davidians?

2. Do you think that they should have pressed criminal charges against the defendants after the fact or should they have let the issue go?

Denver Jury Nullification Fliers

Events surrounding the distribution of jury nullification fliers outside a courthouse in Denver, Colorado, reveal an interesting example of excessive subservience to government. On July 27, 2015, Mark Iannicelli was arrested on charges of felony jury tampering for distributing fliers with information about jury nullification to prospective jury members in front of the Lindsey-Flanigan Courthouse in Denver. Armed with a cardboard sign proclaiming, "Juror Info" Iannicelli handed out fliers entitled "All You Need to Know About Jury Nullification." Some of Iannicelli's fliers made it into the hands of citizens arriving for jury duty that day, who were part of the prospective jury pool. Prosecutors did not look kindly on Iannicelli trying to inform the jury of their inherent powers of jury nullification. Each count of the **jury tampering** charges read: "Mark Iannicelli, with intent to influence a juror's vote, opinion, decision, and other action in a case ... unlawfully and feloniously attempted directly and indirectly to communicate with [a jury pool member], other than as part of the proceedings in the trials of the case; in violation of section 18-8-609 [of the Colorado Revised Statutes]" (*People v. Iannicelli*, No. 15CR03981, 2015).

These actions by the Denver Police Department and the Denver district attorney sparked indignation from several sources. U.S. District Court Judge William Martinez issued an order granting a **preliminary injunction** barring Denver police from enforcing the state court "plaza order," which had been adopted to control access to the outside of the Lindsey-Flanigan Courthouse in Denver before a controversial murder case. Judge Martinez's injunction allowed Iannicelli and his fellow protestors to continue distributing the jury nullification fliers. However, Judge Martinez's order did not address the underlying state criminal charges, as the Denver district attorney was not listed as a named party in the federal proceedings (*Fully Informed Jury Association v. City and County of Denver*, 2015).

The Denver Post editorial board opined "It is astonishing that Denver police would arrest someone for handing out political literature outside a courthouse. It's even more astonishing that prosecutors would charge that person with seven felony counts of jury tampering." (*Denver Post* editorial board, 2015, para. 1–2). *The Denver Post* editorial board acknowledged that "jury nullification is understandably controversial — and is especially resented by courts and prosecutors." It nevertheless opined that "[t]hose who believe the public needs to know about this possibility should have every right to publicize their views — even outside a courthouse. Maybe *especially* outside a courthouse. If not there — near the precincts of American justice were protests and leafleting of all sorts are an honorable tradition — then where?" The editorial board rejected the idea that even the targeting of potential jury pool members was a sufficient justification to bring criminal charges.

This action by Denver police and prosecutors raised two aspects of subservience: (1) freedom of speech concerns protesting the power of government, and (2) more specifically, the power of jurors to engage in jury nullification (see discussion in the previous chapter). Even the Denver city attorney, Scott Martinez (no relation to Judge Martinez), was concerned about police actions in this case, instructing officers to stop arresting people distributing pamphlets outside the courthouse (Phillips, 2015, para. 18). This action pitted the City Attorney's Office against the District Attorney's Office.

These actions by Judge Martinez, the Denver city attorney, and the largest newspaper in the state, *The Denver Post*, fell on deaf ears in the Denver District Attorney's Office, which proceeded with criminal charges against the defendants.

So where is the line between protected free speech rights and jury tampering? The Denver District Attorney's Office maintained Iannicelli crossed that line. Other courts have disagreed. Federal District Court Judge Kimba M. Wood dismissed similar charges of jury tampering against Julian P. Heicklen in New York back in 2012. She argued that the jury tampering statute only covered situations where an individual attempted to influence a juror by means of written communication made in relation to "a specific case pending before that juror" (Weiser, 2012, para. 5). Judge Wood refused to stretch the jury tampering statute to cover speech not meant to influence a juror's actions in a specific case.

In Iannicelli's case the state district court dismissed the criminal charges. However, the Denver District Attorney's Office appealed the case all the way to the Colorado Supreme Court. While acknowledging the jury tampering statute could apply to interactions with potential jurors, the Colorado Supreme Court ruled, like Judge Wood, that the jury tampering statute "is limited to those who attempt to influence a juror in a specific, identifiable case." Since the district attorney did not charge Iannicelli with such specific conduct, the district court properly dismissed the charges at issue (*People v. Iannicelli*, 449 P.3d 387, 391 [Colo. 2019]).

Discussion Questions

1. Do you think it was appropriate for the Denver district attorney to prosecute Iannicelli for jury tampering? Would it be appropriate to exclude from jury service any prospective juror that accepted a flier from Iannicelli?

2. Would it be better for judges to simply inform jurors of their power to nullify, or allow attorneys to do so, instead of having jurors rely upon pamphlets and websites?

Corrections

Defense Attorneys Are Now Social Workers

This next story is equal part courts and corrections (and to be fair a sprinkling of law enforcement). As discussed in the previous chapter, the right to counsel is one of the protections afforded by the Sixth Amendment to protect against excessive subservience to government. What appointed counsel should do on behalf of their clients, however, was mostly left unstated. The role of appointed counsel was probably assumed to be something akin to what you see lawyers doing on television: investigating cases, representing clients during hearings, cross-examining witnesses, making legal objections to the admission of evidence, etc. The reality of legal representation, however, can be very different when guilt is assumed, and the attorney is attempting to satisfy the corrections system — focusing on the consequences of a conviction.

As discussed in Chapter 10, for less serious crimes corrections officials have become collections agents. Corrections officials, and more specifically probation officers, may also be the overseers of a probationer's compliance with court-ordered drug treatment, employment requirements, and educational programs. Yet, what is the role of the defense attorney in an assembly-line version of criminal justice where most criminal defendants plead guilty and there are very few trials or contested hearings? Certainly, one answer is that this allows defense attorneys to take on a much higher caseload. But it can also lead to re-defining the very role of the criminal defense attorney and their interactions with the criminal justice system.

Every day in this country public defenders are being asked to step outside of their typical constitutional mandate and provide a wide array of social services and legal aid, making them look less like traditional defense attorneys and more like social workers (Natapoff, 2015). Brushes with the criminal justice system tend to make people poor, as the corrections portion of the criminal justice system collects fines and fees. There are other collateral consequences of convictions, such as making it difficult to hold jobs, get credit, etc., which contribute to poverty. "Public defenders must contend with their client's poverty as both cause and effect of their involvement with the criminal system" (Natapoff, 2015, p. 447). There is also an interconnection with the education system, as seen in Chapter 10, when teachers send students to police and probation officers. In such a world, the role of the criminal defense attorney shifts from that of advocate during the legal process, to guide and navigator through the social/criminal welfare system.

While traditional roles of legal counsel continue to prevail at the top of what is known as the **penal pyramid** (with a few serious violent crimes at the pinnacle, where defendants might face long terms of incarceration, and a vast base of small property and traffic offenses at the bottom, where defendants might spend little time in jail but have long and significant relations with probation officers), near the base of the pyramid the role of counsel has been transformed. For these types of cases, attorneys must increasingly deal with clients assigned to specialty courts such as drug, mental health, and veterans' courts, and their accompanying probation officers, which are providing (or at least overseeing) treatment, counseling, and moral support in lieu of traditional punishments (Natapoff, 2015, p. 448). "Probation officers have taken up residence in public schools. Infractions that once led to a trip to the principal's office and a call to a child's parents have now become the basis for criminal charges and referral to the juvenile system" (Natapoff, 2015, p. 450). In such a world, the role of the defense attorney is to help his or her client navigate that system, get treatment and take advantage of services, and otherwise improve their odds of success in probation. It is true that "[p]ublic defenders have long grappled with the noncriminal needs of their clients. They find them drug treatment programs, bus tokens, and clothing for job interviews" (Natapoff, 2015, p. 459).

But if the probation system's role is to get clients successfully treated and into paying jobs, then a defense attorney's purpose in such a world is to facilitate those goals for their client. In such a world, standard questions of guilt and innocence are not particularly central.

Rather than helping his or her client avoid conviction, now the attorney's job is increasingly handling the consequences of the plea deal. "A classic example is a lawyer representing a drug-addicted client, looking for ways to translate her client's criminal case into drug treatment. Public defenders may use competency hearings to get their clients mental health treatment" (Natapoff, 2015, p. 461). Even the Supreme Court has started to recognize that some **collateral consequences** of punishment (legal or economic consequences of a conviction which are not part of the criminal code but stem from other types of law) are so significant that criminal defense attorneys must advise clients about them. For instance, in *Padilla v. Kentucky* the Court concluded that deportation was such a significant collateral consequence that criminal defendants must be made aware of the immigration law consequences of a guilty plea (Natapoff, 2015, p. 459). "The criminalization of poverty and the vast expanse of collateral consequences—formal and informal—that attend a conviction mean that defense lawyers do not merely engage legal rules but must evaluate the impact of the criminal case on their client's life situation" (Natapoff, 2015, p. 463). Innovative public defender's offices are seeking lawyers with interdisciplinary training in such fields as social work, immigration, and mental health professions, and hiring support staff to provide GED classes, job placement, and other social services to coordinate with the demands of probation officers.

Discussion Questions

1. The changing nature of corrections is driving changes in the role of attorneys—are these changes for the better or the worse? Are attorneys or probation officers better suited to make these changes and serve their "clients" in these ways?

2. What other types of collateral consequences should defense attorneys be required to advise their clients about?

Inmates Defending Themselves

While at the bottom of the penal pyramid the traditional role for lawyers might be changing (even growing), there may be no role for lawyers at all in more serious corrections settings. David Sweat's prison disciplinary proceedings stemming from his June 2015 escape from the Clinton Correctional Facility in Dannemora, New York, illustrates this oversight concerning excessive government subservience. CNN reported that David Sweat's prison disciplinary hearing was closed to the public. Not only closed to the public, but the date and the time of the hearing was not released, and the results of the hearing itself were not released for several weeks after the hearing (Holland et al., 2015). At the hearing, David Sweat did not have an attorney. He was expected to defend himself against the charges on his own without any assistance from legal counsel.

Were such hearings of minor consequence, dealing only with matters like denial of commissary privileges or visitation, perhaps this would not be particularly troubling or raise concerns of government subservience. Yet many of these hearings are hardly of minor consequence. "Consequences like solitary confinement, which, while bad enough on its own, can also mean a lack of access to classes and other programs that might get you out sooner. And time in solitary can be a reason for parole boards to deny parole" (Roth, 2015, para. 5). In David Sweat's specific case, he faced extended solitary confinement: "It can be years and years and years. There is really no limit to how long they could sentence him to solitary," according to Karen Murtagh, executive director of Prisoners' Legal Services of New York (Holland et al., 2015, para. 14). There could also be the whole host of subsidiary deprivations that follow from being subjected to solitary confinement, including denial of phone and commissary privileges and being denied permission to receive packages. In fact, at the internal disciplinary hearing Sweat was sentenced to six years of solitary confinement (Quant, 2019). However, "Sweat is unlikely to find relief after six years: People who escape or attempt to escape are often labeled security risks and kept in 'administrative segregation' for decades or even the rest of their lives" (Quant, 2019, para 16).

What do these prison disciplinary hearings typically look like? The inmate is sitting handcuffed, while the hearing officer sits at a desk. The hearing officer will be a corrections officer, and while the hearing officer is forbidden from having had direct involvement in the underlying situation that gave rise to the hearing (so as to prevent prejudging the matter), the hearing officer often knows the other corrections officers involved. There is no presumption of innocence, and the burden of proof upon the state is quite low. If attorneys were allowed to represent the inmate, they might call to the witness stand the officer writing out the complaint and ask that officer questions, investigate the logbooks, and call other witnesses who observed the situation. Inmates, in contrast, often do not know how to do that (Roth, 2015). Inmates often do not know what to do to create a factual record (and otherwise present issues in the proper format) that will be sufficient to appeal the matter to the state corrections department or on to state court.

Discussion Questions

1. Should there be some constitutional limit to the harshness of consequences that might be imposed at a prison disciplinary proceeding without an attorney present?

2. Even if attorneys are not provided at state expense, should they be permitted? Should the hearings at least be open to the public so that the news media can perform its traditional watchdog role?

Beat Up Squads

The inmates whom David Sweat and co-conspirator, Richard Matt, left behind during their escape from Clinton Correctional Facility in Dannemora, New York, also did not fare well. Inmates there reported brutal interrogations following David Sweat's escape from the facility. Three guards, bearing no name badges, punched one inmate and slammed his head against the wall shouting questions: "Where are they going? What did you hear? How much are they paying you to keep your mouth shut?" (Schwirtz & Winerip, 2015, para. 2). That inmate also reported one of the guards put a plastic bag over his head and threatened to waterboard him.

In what has been characterized as a "campaign of retribution" in the days following David Sweat's escape from the Clinton Correctional Facility, numerous inmates reported abuses at the hands of guards, including beatings while handcuffed, being choked, slammed against cell walls, etc. (Schwirtz & Winerip, 2015, para. 4). Many inmates were transferred out of the Clinton Correctional Facility to other prisons, and others were placed in solitary confinement and stripped of privileges. More than 60 inmates filed complaints with Prisoners' Legal Services of New York, an organization that assists indigent prisoners. One inmate, who worked with David Sweat in the prison tailor shop, said guards tied a plastic bag around his neck and tightened it until he passed out (Schwirtz & Winerip, 2015, para. 13). Another inmate reported being thrown in solitary confinement for three weeks and having his belongings discarded, including family photographs and a wedding ring (Schwirtz & Winerip, 2015, para. 13).

Even that treatment was not as bad as that reported by inmates at Fishkill Correctional Facility in New York. Inmates there reported in April 2015 observing as many as 20 correctional officers, informally known as the "beat up squad," repeatedly kicking and punching Samuel Harrell, an African American inmate, while shouting racial slurs. One inmate reported that correctional officers treated Harrell "like he was a trampoline, they were jumping on him." (Winerip & Schwirtz, 2015, para. 2). Harrell was thrown down a staircase, with his body bent into an impossible position, perhaps already dead at that point. The medical examiner reported Harrell had cuts and bruises to his head and extremities, but no illicit drugs in his system as corrections officers had claimed, except for an antidepressant and tobacco. The manner of Harrell's death was listed as a homicide (Winerip & Schwirtz, 2015, para. 9).

Harrell's death was particularly despicable given that he suffered from mental illness. Harrell would "go through the house turning over family photographs for fear they were staring at him [and] he also believed the television was talking to him" (Winerip & Schwirtz, 2015, para. 14). After the beating, Harrell lay on the floor while officers periodically walked by kicking and hitting him. In July 2015 another inmate at that facility was beaten so severely he lost two front teeth and had to be hospitalized. A week later he was still covered with cuts and bruises.

Holding corrections officers accountable in New York has proven to be extremely difficult, even for the most heinous cases. Ramon Fabian, an inmate at the Ulster Correctional Facility in New York, reported that in 2014, while serving a one-year sentence for a drug conviction, he was escorted to a part of the prison out of view of the electronic surveillance cameras. Told to face the wall for a pat-down frisk, Fabian stood arms outstretched and legs spread. Fabian then "looked down and saw the toe of a boot swinging up between his legs" (Robbins, 2015, para. 3–4). After being kicked in the groin, Fabian collapsed. Unable to walk, he crawled back to his cube.

Fabian was later transported 80 miles to a hospital in Albany, where doctors performed emergency surgery to remove part of his right testicle (Robbins, 2015, para. 4). When questioned by the Department of Corrections Inspector General's Office, the offending corrections officer denied any knowledge of the incident. Ultimately Fabian was awarded $400,000 in compensatory damages as part of a default judgment by a federal district court (*Fabian v Bukowski*, N.D.N.Y 2017). Corrections officer Michael Bukowski was acquitted of criminal assault against Fabian (Schwirtz and Winerip, 2015). The New York Department of Corrections sought to fire Bukowski, but he was permitted to maintain his employment. He is not alone in retaining his position: "Since 2010, [New York] has sought to fire 30 prison guards accused of abusing inmates" but due in part to a convoluted union arbitration process "[o]fficials have prevailed only eight times" (Robbins, 2015, para. 8)

In Fabian's case, the offending corrections officer was found guilty of using excessive force by an arbitrator, who was agreed upon by the corrections department and the labor union representing the corrections officer. Nevertheless, the arbitrator reduced the penalty from dismissal to a 120-day unpaid suspension. In a rare act, corrections officials refused to follow the arbitrator's decision, leading to a lawsuit on behalf of the offending corrections officer. The state judge hearing the lawsuit agreed with the corrections department. She ruled that the 120-day suspension "shocks the judicial conscience and cannot be upheld" (Robbins, 2015, para. 41). The state court ordered a rehearing by an arbitrator, but since these records are generally confidential unless appealed to a court, we do not know what the arbitrator ultimately decided.

According to the ACLU, the United States is the only democracy in the world without an independent oversight authority to monitor prisons (Starr, 2015). While there have been some calls for states to create independent oversight boards, "there doesn't seem to be much political will to create independent oversight" of state prisons (Starr, 2015, para. 15). What independent oversight at the state level has existed has mostly been dropped in recent years. Even federal oversight of state and local corrections institutions is rare. "While it is not uncommon for the [U.S.] Department of Justice to enforce oversight of a police department, it is rare for such intervention to take place at a prison or a jail" (Starr, 2015, para. 9). The Los Angeles County Sheriff's Department seems to be one of the few examples of federal oversight of state or local corrections officials.

Discussion Questions

1. What might be ways to discourage "beat up squads"? Should corrections officials be given a zero-tolerance policy—any excessive use of force and the officer will be terminated?

2. If termination is too harsh, how about using solitary confinement for corrections officials for punishment for use of excessive force?

Chapter Key Terms

Contempt of cop

Confidential informant

Aiding and abetting

Wrongful death

Jury tampering

Preliminary injunction

Penal pyramid

Collateral consequences

References

Atrocity in Waco, Texas. (n.d.). CoverUps.com. http://www.coverups.com/great-coverups/waco-coverup.htm.

Blinder, A., Fernandez, M., & Mueller, B. (2015). Use of tasers is scrutinized after Walter Scott shooting. *The New York Times*. http://www.nytimes.com/2015/06/01/us/use-of-tasers-is-scrutinized-after-walter-scott-shooting.html.

Botelho, G. (2014). Was a New York police officer's chokehold on Eric Garner necessary? CNN. http://www.cnn.com/2014/12/04/us/eric-garner-chokehold-debate/index.html.

Browne Dianis, J. (2014). Eric Garner was killed by more than just a chokehold. MSNBC. http://www.msnbc.com/msnbc/what-killed-eric-garner.

Burke, K., Moore, T., Tracy, T., Parascandola, R., & Semanszko, C. (2014). 'The time for remorse was when my husband was yelling to breathe': Eric Garner's widow lashes out at NYPD cop who put her husband in fatal chokehold. *New York Daily News*. http://www.nydailynews.com/new-york/nypd-eric-garner-chokehold-death-not-indicted-article-1.2031841.

Butler, P. (2014). Ferguson police broke the law when they stopped civilians from videotaping them. *The Washington Post*. http://www.washingtonpost.com/posteverything/wp/2014/08/15/ferguson-police-broke-the-law-when-they-stopped-civilians-from-videotaping-them-and-theyre-just-the-latest/.

Celona, L., Conley, K., & Golding, B. (2014). Cop cleared in chokehold death of Eric Garner. *New York Post*. http://nypost.com/2014/12/03/cop-cleared-in-eric-garner-chokehold-death/.

Danforth, J. (2000). Final report to the Deputy Attorney General concerning the 1993 confrontation at the Mt. Carmel Complex. Deactivated link (retrieved 2015). http://www.waco93.com/Danforth-finalreport.pdf.

Denver Post Editorial Board. (2015). Jury nullification is not a crime, Denver. *Denver Post*. http://www.denverpost.com/editorials/ci_28662070/jury-nullification-is-not-crime-denver.

Elmore, C., & MacDougall, D. (2015). Man shot and killed by North Charleston police officer after a traffic stop; SLED investigating. *The Post and Courier*. http://www.postandcourier.com/article/20150404/PC16/150409635.

Fabian v Bukowski, N.D.N.Y 2017 (No.9:16-cv-00878-LEK-DEP).

Fenton, J. (2012). In Federal Hill, citizens allowed to record police — but then there's loitering ... *Baltimore Sun*. http://articles.baltimoresun.com/2012 -02-11/news/bal-in-federal-hill-citizens-allowed-to-record-police-but -then-theres-loitering-20120211_1_loitering-officers-police-union.

Fully Informed Jury Association v. City and County of Denver, No. 15-cv -1775-WJM-MJW, (D. Colo. Aug. 25, 2015) (order granting preliminary injunction).

The guns of Waco and Ruby Ridge. (1995). *The New York Times*. http://www. nytimes.com/1995/07/14/opinion/the-guns-of-waco-and-ruby-ridge.html.

Haller, V., & Pearce, M. (2015). Eric Garner's mother on $5.9-million settle-ment: 'Don't congratulate us.' *Los Angeles Times*. https://www.latimes.com/ nation/la-na-eric-garner-family-settlement-20150714-story.htm.

Judge dismisses Waco wrongful death lawsuit. (2000). CBC. http://www.cbc.ca/ news/world/judge-dismisses-waco-wrongful-death-lawsuit-1.235596.

Jury clears US over Waco deaths. (2000). BBC. http://news.bbc.co.uk/2/hi/ americas/834416.stm.

Hannaford, A. (2013, April 18). The standoff in Waco. *Texas Observer*. http:// www.texasobserver.org/the-standoff-in-waco/.

Hermann, P. (2012). Baltimore police told not to stop people taking photos or video of their actions. *Baltimore Sun*. http://articles.baltimoresun.com/ 2012-02-11/news/bs-md-ci-police-video-orders-20120210_1_police-offic ers-johns-hopkins-university-s-division-darrel-w-stephens.

Holland, L., Fantz, A., & Dolan, J. (2015). Escapee David Sweat to face prison discipline hearing. CNN. http://www.cnn.com/2015/07/06/us/new-york -prison-break/.

Izzy, M. (2014). "Contempt of cop" — The law of standing up to police officers. LegalMatch. http://lawblog.legalmatch.com/2014/04/09/contempt-of-cop -the-law-of-standing-up-to-police-officers/.

Lt. William Calley, Witness for the Defense. Famous American Trials. http:// law2.umkc.edu/faculty/projects/ftrials/mylai/myl_Calltest.html.

Martinez, M. (2015). South Carolina cop shoots unarmed man: A timeline. *The New York Times*. http://www.nytimes.com/2015/06/01/us/use-of -tasers-is-scrutinized-after-walter-scott-shooting.html.

McCurry, R. (n.d.) Waco, Texas: Where a part of America's heart and soul died. Island One Society. http://www.islandone.org/Politics/Waco.McCurry. html.

Milloy, R. (2000). Jury finds for U.S. in deaths at Waco. *The New York Times.* http://www.nytimes.com/2000/07/15/us/jury-finds-for-us-in-deaths-at -waco.html.

Murdock, S. (2015, April 8). Officer Michael Slager tells dispatch 'he grabbed my taser' after killing Walter Scott (AUDIO). Huffington Post. http://www. huffingtonpost.com/2015/04/08/michael-slager-audio-dispatch_n_702 8018.html.

Natapoff, A. (2015). *Gideon*'s servants and the criminalization of poverty. *Ohio State Journal of Criminal Law, 12,* 445–464.

Osunsami, S., & Shapiro, E. (2017). Ex-cop Michael Slager sentenced to 20 years for shooting death of Walter Scott. ABC News. https://abcnews. go.com/US/cop-michael-slager-faces-19-24-years-prison/ story?id=51595376.

Peacock, C. (1995). The Department of the Treasury: Memorandum to the press. Public Broadcasting Service. http://www.pbs.org/wgbh/pages/front line/waco/treasury.html.

Pearson, J. (2014, August 1). Eric Garner's death by police chokehold ruled a homicide. Huffington Post. http://www.huffingtonpost.com/2014/08/01/ eric-garner-homicide_n_5642481.html.

People v. Iannicelli, No. 15CR03981 (Denver County Court filed July 28, 2015) (Complaint and Information).

Phillips, N. (2015). Legal battle over First Amendment plays out at Denver courthouse. *Denver Post.* http://www.denverpost.com/news/ci_28735862/ legal-battle-over-first-amendment-plays-out-at-denver-courthouse.

Quandt, K. (2019, January 10). Showtime's 'Escape at Dannemora' Left Out Torture and Abuse. *The Appeal.* https://theappeal.org/showtimes-escape -at-dannemora-left-out-torture-and-abuse/.

Recording police officers and public officials. (2013). Digital Media Law Project, Berkman Center for Internet & Society. http://www.dmlp.org/legal-guide/ recording-police-officers-and-public-officials.

Robbins, T. (2015). Guarding the prison guards: New York State's troubled disciplinary system. *The New York Times.* http://www.nytimes.com/2015/ 09/28/nyregion/guarding-the-prison-guards-new-york-states-troubled -disciplinary-system.html.

Roth, A. (2015). No lawyers allowed. Life of the Law. http://www.lifeofthelaw. org/2015/07/no-lawyers-allowed/.

Schwirtz, M., & Winerip, M. (2015). After 2 killers fled, New York prisoners say, beatings were next. *The New York Times.* http://www.nytimes.com/ 2015/08/12/nyregion/after-2-killers-fled-new-york-prisoners-say-beatings -were-next.html.

Sharp v. Baltimore City Police. (2011). Civil Rights Litigation Clearinghouse, University of Michigan Law School. http://www.clearinghouse.net/detail. php?id=11963.

Sharp v. BCPD. (2011). Baltimore police delete personal videos at Preakness. American Civil Liberties Union of Maryland. http://www.aclu-md.org/ our_work/legal_cases/1.

Smith, J. (2012). Christopher Sharp v. Baltimore City Police Department, et. al. U.S. Department of Justice, Civil Rights Division. http://www.justice. gov/crt/about/spl/documents/Sharp_ltr_5-14-12.pdf.

Starr, T. J. (2015). Prison guard 'beat up' squad accused of killing inmate: Why prison abuse is so common and overlooked. AlterNet. http://www.alternet. org/print/civil-liberties/prison-guard-beat-squad-accused-killing-inmate -why-prison-abuse-so-common-and.

Steffen, J. (2015). Men accused of felony jury tampering plead not guilty in Denver. Denver Post. http://www.denverpost.com/news/ci_28789423/ men-accused-felony-jury-tampering-plead-not-guilty?

Swaine, J. (2015). Walter Scott shooting: Officer laughs about adrenaline rush in recording. The Guardian. http://www.theguardian.com/us-news/2015/ apr/12/walter-scott- shooting-officer-michael-slager-audio-recording.

Schwirtz, M. & Winerip, M. (2015, Dec. 8). Judge acquits guard in assault that maimed New York state prisoner. *The New York Times.* https://www.ny times.com/2015/12/09/nyregion/judge-acquits-guard-in-assault-that-maimed -new-york-state-prisoner.html.

Weiser, B. (2012). Jury statute not violated by protester, judge rules. *The New York Times.* http://www.nytimes.com/2012/04/20/nyregion/indictment -against-julian-heicklen-jury-nullification-advocate-is-dismissed.html.

Wenger, Y. (2014). City to pay $250,000 to man who claims police deleted video of an arrest. *Baltimore Sun.* http://articles.baltimoresun.com/2014 -03-03/news/bs-md-ci-camera-settlement-20140303_1_christopher-sharp -police-city-solicitor.

Winerip, M., & Schwirtz, M. (2015). Prison guard 'beat up squad' is blamed in New York inmate's death. *The New York Times.*http://www.nytimes. com/2015/08/19/nyregion/fishkill-prison-inmate-died-after-fight-with -officers-records-show.html.

Yan, H. (2015). Police shoot man in the back: Who was Walter Scott? CNN. http://www.cnn.com/2015/04/08/us/south-carolina-who-was-walter-scott/ index.html.

Chapter Fifteen

Botched Justice: Poorly Decided Legal Cases of the Past

"The greatest threat to liberty will come from people who claim to be acting for beneficial purposes.... The insidious threat to liberty will come from well-meaning people with zeal."
> — Dissenting opinion of Justice Louis Brandeis in
> *Olmstead v. United States*, 277 U.S. 438 (1928)

Lessons in constitutional principles come not only from cases supposedly decided correctly, but also from cases in the past that now clearly constitute bad decisions. The Supreme Court normally seems to do a good job protecting American constitutional values, but it has not always gotten its ethics right.

The cases in this chapter will not always directly involve criminal justice issues. Some of the best examples of "botched justice" involve matters of race, gender, or religion that never involved anyone being arrested for an actual crime. It would be a shame to skip over such landmark cases in a rather obsessive and misplaced attempt to limit our review to purely criminal justice matters. In any event, when it comes to botched justice, there is little air between some of the so-called "civil" cases that follow and the technically more "pure" criminal justice cases that are also presented. Botched justice is botched justice.

In reading these cases we can observe that even learned people with good intentions can get things very wrong. If nothing else, this should cause us all to pause before reflexively accepting all modern Supreme Court decisions as works of ethical flawlessness. Appellate judges, even of the Supreme Court variety, clearly make mistakes. It is a little scary, though, when they err since their bad decisions affect an entire people and help cast in cement or else help change the trajectory of present and future morals. The American Supreme Court is often described as being the most powerful court on the planet. When you are the brightest light on the highest hill, much can rightfully be expected.

The cases that follow are arranged in the order that they came into being over the course of nearly two centuries. We start with a case from the early 1800s and conclude the chapter with a case from the late 1900s. Time will tell whether cases more recent than that will eventually make it to the list of "botched justice."

Johnson v. M'Intosh
21 U.S. (8 Wheat.) 543 (1823)

In 1775, a man named Johnson bought some land in present-day Illinois from local Native Americans (the Piankeshaw) who occupied the area. After Johnson died, the land was thought to have passed to his heirs. However, in 1818 a man name M'Intosh bought the same parcel of land from the federal government. The plaintiffs (those who supposedly inherited the land from Johnson) sought in court to have the newcomer M'Intosh ejected from their land. The Johnson heirs thought that their right to the land was superior to that of M'Intosh since their ancestor bought the land from the Native Americans decades ago. M'Intosh, on the other hand, thought his claim was superior since he purchased it from the federal government and not merely from local Native Americans. The federal trial court ruled that the land now belonged to M'Intosh despite his Johnny-come-lately status. The matter eventually landed before the U.S. Supreme Court.

The decision of the Supreme Court in affirming the lower court decision was unanimous. The land belonged to the party that Congress (not the Native Americans) had sold it to. Johnson never held title to the land. He had only occupied it.

Justice Marshall wrote the opinion on behalf of the Court. He reasoned that Native Americans, as a conquered people, had no right to the land. The land belonged to those who "discovered" and conquered it, that is, to the European settlers. True, the Native Americans had sovereignty over the land prior to the arrival of the Europeans, but this sovereignty was extinguished when it passed to the European powers (in this case, the British). When the Americans achieved independence from the British in 1776, this sovereignty over the land passed from the British government to the United States government. The bottom line was that the Native Americans had no title to the land they supposedly sold to Johnson. It belonged to the Europeans and later to the American government. Since M'Intosh bought it from the rightful owner (the American federal government), his title was the legitimate one.

Marshall wrote, "While the different nations of Europe respected the right of the natives as occupants, they asserted the ultimate dominion to be in themselves, and claimed and exercised, as a consequence of this ultimate dominion, a power to grant the soil while yet in possession of the natives." Marshall wrote that even this limited right to mere occupancy could be terminated at any time by the European power that "discovered" the land. He went on to say that, "The history of America from its discovery to the present day proves, we think, the universal recognition of these principles" and that, "Thus all nations of Europe who have acquired territory on this continent have asserted in themselves and have recognized in others the exclusive right of the discoverer to appropriate the lands occupied by the Indians." Naturally (according to Justice Marshall), "The United States, then, has unequivocally acceded to that great and broad rule by which its civilized inhabitants now hold the country."

Marshall opined that "Conquest gives a title which the courts of the conqueror cannot deny, whatever the private and speculative opinions of individuals may be, respecting the original justice of the claim which has been successfully asserted.... As the white population advanced that of the Indians necessarily receded. The country in the immediate neighborhood of agriculturists became unfit for them."

Apparently, Marshall thought that since the Native Americans were not making efficient use of the land anyway (they were much more interested in hunting than in agriculture), their losing sovereignty over their occupied land was not that big a deal. In any event, the land was no longer theirs to sell to Johnson by the time 1775 rolled around. The European "discoverers" of the land had the natural right to own and govern it.

Discussion Questions

1. Should monetary reparations be made to Native Americans for the lands forcibly taken from them by white conquerors? Or, has a sort of "statute of limitations" necessarily run at this point?

2. Have European and other immigrants to America made better use of the land than did the Native Americans of long ago?

The case of *Johnson* may have posed no moral problems for Americans of the early 1800s, but American sensibilities towards Native Americans have undoubtedly changed over the many, many intervening years. The idea that Native Americans should simply have their lands stripped from them due to being conquered by a supposedly more civilized people who could make better use of the resources would strike modern sensibilities as racist and unfair. That said, *Johnson*, unlike any of the other cases that follow in this chapter, is still "good law." It's central ruling, upholding a **conquest doctrine** of sorts (that the federal government and not Native Americans possessed title to the conquered lands and that Native Americans could therefore not sell land that did not belong to them), has never been rescinded by the Supreme Court!

Another case that shows the extreme racism of its day is the *Dred Scott* decision that follows. Many scholars think that this is the *worst* decision and written opinion ever made by the U.S. Supreme Court. It is the poster child of infamous American Supreme Court cases.

Dred Scott v. Sanford
60 U.S. 393 (1857)

There is a good chance you have heard of the *Dred Scott* decision, but you perhaps are not sure why. This infamous case of the mid-1800s held that slaves are not citizens and so angered abolitionists in the north that it ultimately helped facilitate the American Civil War.

Dred Scott was an enslaved person who lived in Missouri, one of the slave states. His "owner" took him to territories that were free (today the states of Illinois and Minnesota), where he lived for an extended period of time. Eventually, Scott returned with his owner to Missouri and his owner passed away, leaving Scott and his family to his widow, Eliza Irene Sanford Emerson. She eventually transferred ownership of the family to John Sanford, her brother. Scott wanted to be free, so he sued Sanford in Missouri court claiming that he had become a free person while living in free areas of the country. Scott relied heavily on the Missouri Compromise for his argument, which authorized slavery in the southern portion of the expanding western frontier, but forbade slavery in the northern section of the frontier (Illinois and Minnesota, where Scott had been taken to live for quite some time, were both clearly in the free area).

Missouri courts ultimately held in favor of Sanford, so Scott appealed to the U.S. Supreme Court. Justice Tanney, a pro-slavery Southerner, wrote the opinion for the six-person majority. First, the majority ruled that federal courts simply had no jurisdiction over this matter. Therefore, whatever the Missouri state courts ruled remained the law. True, Scott claimed to be a citizen of Missouri while Sanford was a citizen of New York, and the U.S Constitution did give federal courts jurisdiction over a lawsuit whenever the controversy involves citizens of two different states (so-called "**diversity jurisdiction**"). But Justice Tanney argued that Dred Scott was not a citizen of any state, despite his argument that he had been emancipated by living up north. Specifically, Tanney wrote that no black person, emancipated or not, could seriously be considered a citizen of any state. Tanney believed that the framers of the Constitution never meant for black people to be perceived as citizens. Neither did the drafters of the Declaration of Independence mean to include blacks when it said, "all men are created equal." Rather, black people "were at that time considered as a subordinate and inferior class of beings, who had been subjugated by the dominant race, and whether emancipated or not, yet remained subject to their authority, and had no rights or privileges but such as those who held the power and the Government might choose to grant them."

Imagine the supposed unacceptable consequences, fretted Justice Tanney, if blacks were ever deemed by the Supreme Court to be citizens. As citizens, the Privileges and Immunities Clause of the Constitution would necessarily:

> Give to persons of the negro race, who were recognized as citizens in any one State of the Union, the right to enter every other State whenever they pleased, singly or in companies, with or without pass or passport, and without obstruction, to sojourn there as long as they pleased, to go where they pleased at every hour of the day or night without molestation ... and it would give them the full liberty of speech in public and in private upon all subjects upon which its own citizens might speak; to hold public meetings upon political affairs, and to keep and carry arms wherever they want.

Since black people, enslaved or free, could not be citizens of any state, the federal courts had no jurisdiction based on the diversity of two citizens of two different states, presenting the federal courts with a controversy. Tanney concluded that "Dred Scott was not a citizen of Missouri within the meaning of the Constitution of the United States, and not entitled to sue in its courts."

Despite having ruled that the federal courts lacked jurisdiction over the matter, Justice Tanney could not resist going on to give a ruling on the second issue: Whether the Missouri Compromise (that had kept the peace for decades over the slavery question and helped keep a civil war at bay) was even constitutional. He wrote that it was not constitutional.

Tanney said that any law passed by Congress which took a slave owner's property away from him merely because that person had moved his property (e.g., a slave) to a free territory deprived that owner of property without due process of law, in violation of the Fifth Amendment.

Discussion Questions

1. What can we learn from the *Dred Scott* case about the prevalence and depth of racism in mid-nineteenth-century America?

2. Were the framers of the Constitution indeed as racist as Justice Tanney unwittingly asserts?

3. Was Abraham Lincoln, the nineteenth century's "Great Emancipator," probably racist by today's standards?

Though Southerners loved the decision of the Court, Northerners had a different take. They saw it as a power play of a Court packed with Southerners to expand the influence of the slave states. This decision, instead of helping to settle the slavery question, simply inflamed the passions of abolitionist-minded people throughout the north.

The case that follows shows a different form of **animus** (ill will based on prejudice) towards one's fellow human beings. It involves nineteenth-century attitudes toward prison inmates. As you shall see, prison inmates were not particularly thought of as full-fledged humans deserving a guarantee of even basic human rights.

Ruffin v. Commonwealth
62 Va. 21 Gratt. 790 (1871)

Woody Ruffin was a convict serving his sentence in the Virginia State Penitentiary in the mid- to late-1800s. While he was a prisoner, he was hired out by the prison to work on the Chesapeake and Ohio Railroad. His work site was in the county of Bath, in a different part of the state than that of where the prison was located. While working for the railroad, Ruffin was being overseen by a private security guard employed by the railroad under an agreement with the prison. Ruffin allegedly murdered the guard in an attempt to escape, but Ruffin's plan ultimately failed, and he was apprehended and charged with the murder.

State law at the time provided that any prison inmate charged with a new felony while yet serving his sentence would be tried by a jury in the circuit court of the city of Richmond, regardless of where the offense may have actually occurred. The Richmond jury found Ruffin guilty of the murder of the guard.

Ruffin appealed, claiming that the original Bill of Rights, which was incorporated into and adopted by the Virginia State Constitution, guaranteed "that in all capital or criminal prosecutions, a man hath a right to a speedy trial by an impartial jury of his vicinage." Ruffin argued that he should have been tried in the county of Bath (not Richmond) because that is where the alleged murder took place, and that would have been the correct "vicinage." In the alternative, Ruffin argued that at a minimum, a jury composed of people from Bath should have been assembled and sent to Richmond for his trial.

Ruffin was aware that the Virginia Legislature earlier had passed a statute that designated the circuit court of the city of Richmond to "have jurisdiction of all criminal proceedings against convicts in the penitentiary." But he said that a state constitution always trumped a mere state statute.

The Virginia Supreme Court heard the appeal and found no error regarding the venue in which the trial had been conducted. It said that constitutional principles, like the one cited by Ruffin, must be given a "reasonable rather than a literal construction." It noted that the Bill of Rights does not apply to prison inmates, but only to free people. It went on to say that, with regards to any prison inmate,

> For the time being, during his term of service in the penitentiary, he is in a state of penal servitude to the State. He has, as a consequence of his crime, not only forfeited his liberty, but all his personal rights except those which the law in its humanity accords to him. He is for the time being the slave of the State. He is civiliter mortus; and his estate, if any, is administered like that of a dead man. The bill of rights is a declaration of general principles to govern a society of freemen, and not of convicted felons and men civilly dead. Such men have rights it is true, such as the law in its benignity accords to them, but not the rights of freemen. They are the slaves of the State undergoing punishment for heinous crimes committed against the laws of the land. While in this state of penal servitude, they must be subject to the regulations of the institution of which they are inmates, and the laws of the State to whom their service is due in expiation of their crimes.

The court reasoned that since the state constitution does not apply to him, it is within the power of the state, through its legislature, to decide the manner of his trial including, if it so wishes, to designate as a matter of convenience which court will have special jurisdiction to hear his trial. If the state wishes, out of convenience, to designate the city of Richmond where the penitentiary is situated to be the place for the trial, it is within its right to do so.

The fact that the prisoner was in the county of Bath when he committed the murder didn't mean he was not an inmate of the state prison in Richmond. He was still "bound by the regulations of that institution, as if he had been locked within one of its cells. These laws and regulations attach to the person of the convict wherever he may be ... as certainly and tenaciously as the ball and chain which he drags after him." If a prisoner commits a crime, either in the prison itself or while on an outside work assignment in another county, he still can be tried in Richmond as the state legislature so wishes. Slaves of the state apparently only have such rights as the state (through its legislature) wishes to give them, and none other.

Discussion Questions

1. What is it about the term "slave of the state" that is so offensive?

2. Why can't we always trust legislatures and governors to ensure that prisoners are being treated fairly? What makes judges so different?

3. What are some of the basic human rights that prisoners should have despite the crimes they have done?

This idea that prison inmates are nothing more than **slaves of the state**, with no constitutional rights whatsoever, became known as the "**hands off doctrine.**" Courts simply took a "hands off" approach whenever prisoners complained about conditions of confinement or any other alleged violations of their human rights. As the opinion above indicates, courts considered prison inmates to be **civilly dead** and without any constitutional rights whatsoever.

This sad state of affairs existed as late as the mid-twentieth century, when the U.S. Supreme Court formally put an end to the "hands off doctrine" and clearly held that even inmates have some constitutional rights. In the case of *Wolf v. McDonnell*, 418 U.S. 539, 555–56 (1974), the Court ruled that "There is no Iron Curtain between the Constitution and the prisons of this country." Many specific prisoner rights cases are now part of our constitutional law cannon.

So far, we have seen cases that illustrate injustices towards people due to their race or their status as inmates. You knew a case on gender had to be coming. The next case deals with gender discrimination. This case should be of particular interest to women considering attending law school or some other professional or graduate program.

Bradwell v. Illinois
83 U.S. 130 (1873)

Myra Bradwell, an Illinois resident of the 1870s, wanted to be admitted to the state bar so she could practice law. Bradwell met all of the qualifications in terms of learning and moral fitness. Nevertheless, the Illinois Supreme Court denied her application merely because she was a woman. The court opined that the common law of England, which formed the basis of Illinois law, forbade women from practicing law. Indeed, female lawyers were unheard of going as far back into English history as anyone could tell. It continued by saying that "The proposition that a woman should enter the courts of Westminster Hall in that capacity, or as a barrister, would have created hardly less astonishment than one that she should ascend the bench of bishops, or be elected to a seat in the House of Commons." Illinois's highest court concluded that "God designed the sexes to occupy different spheres of action, and that it belonged to men to make, apply, and execute the laws, was regarded as an almost axiomatic truth." Given all of this, it could never have been the intention of the Illinois Legislature to allow women to be admitted to the state bar.

The case next wound up on appeal before the U.S. Supreme Court. There, the attorney representing Mrs. Bradwell pointed out that the Fourteenth Amendment provided that, "No State shall make or enforce any law which shall abridge the privileges or immunities of citizens of the United States...." He said that among the "privileges" of American citizenship that Illinois had to honor was the right to practice any lawful profession of one's choice, including the practice of law.

The U.S. Supreme Court (with one dissenter) disagreed. Writing for the majority, and without giving much analysis, Justice Miller wrote that, "We agree with [Bradwell's attorney] that there are privileges and immunities belonging to citizens of the United States.... But the right to admission to practice in the courts of a State is not one of them." Justice Miller pointed out that, "The opinion just delivered in the Slaughter-House Cases renders elaborate argument in the present case unnecessary" and that, "It is unnecessary to repeat the argument on which the judgment of those cases is founded. It is sufficient to say they are conclusive of the present case."

Justice Miller thus provided a rather summary dismissal of Mrs. Bradwell's case based on an apparent narrow interpretation of the Constitution's Privileges or Immunities Clause. But, the really interesting position was not the main opinion, but rather the concurring one written by Justice Bradley (who was joined in his separate, concurring opinion by two other justices). Apparently, these three justices, while agreeing with the result, wanted to put forth a clearer vision of why they believed women should not be admitted to the bar. It is this concurring opinion, rather than the main opinion, that has become the more famous (or infamous).

Justice Bradley began by writing, "I concur … but not for the reasons specified." He continued,

> The civil law, as well as nature herself, has always recognized a wide difference in the respective spheres and destinies of man and woman. Man is, or should be, woman's protector and defender. The natural and proper timidity and delicacy which belongs to the female sex evidently unfits it for many of the occupations of civil life…. The harmony, not to say identity, of interest and views which belong, or should belong, to the family institution is repugnant to the idea of a woman adopting a distinct and independent career from that of her husband. So firmly fixed was this sentiment in the founders of the common law that it became a maxim of that system of jurisprudence that a woman had no legal existence separate from her husband…. The paramount destiny and mission of woman are to fulfill the noble and benign offices of wife and mother. This is the law of the Creator.

Justice Bradley concluded his opinion by arguing that it was completely appropriate for the legislature of Illinois to create occupational licensing restrictions based on conditions "founded on nature, reason, and experience" and that, "This fairly belongs to the police power of the State."

Discussion Questions

1. Were the sentiments regarding the proper roles of men and women expressed in this case only possessed by males, or did most females also share such sentiments back then?

2. Were such sentiments wicked? Misguided? Understandable? Appropriate for their day?

3. Are there any occupations today that are still better suited to men than to women? Navy Seal? Firefighter? Or are such stereotypes clearly sexist?

Many decades later, women once again went to the Supreme Court to argue a constitutional right to practice a chosen, but male-dominated, profession. By then, all hope of achieving victory by way of the Privileges or Immunity Clause of the Fourteenth Amendment was abandoned. (By then, this clause largely was interpreted to simply mean that a state could not discriminate by giving certain privileges to its own citizens while denying the same privileges to other American citizens who happened to reside in the state.) Not finding a path to victory in that body of law, women instead turned to another Fourteenth Amendment provision: the Equal Protection Clause (no state shall "deny to any person within its jurisdiction the equal protection of the laws"—in essence, states cannot irrationally discriminate based on race, gender, or any other irrelevant classification). By the 1970s it was this approach (helped no doubt by changing cultural values) that wound up succeeding.

The next case we will examine concludes our cases from the 1800s. It is the 1896 case that came up with the infamous "**separate but equal doctrine**" (i.e., it is acceptable to forcefully segregate the races in public facilities as long as each race is supposedly somehow given equal quality of accommodation). The case that follows was concerned about whites and blacks having to share the same railroad cars, but it wound up giving further legitimacy and cover for the next half-century to segregated (and nearly always inferior and underfunded) public schools, bathrooms, hotels, etc.

Plessy v. Ferguson
63 U.S. 537 (1896)

Homer Plessy was seven parts white and one part African American. He belonged to a group of citizens who opposed an 1890 Louisiana law that mandated that whites and "coloreds" ride in "separate but equal" railroad cars. The supposed purpose of this law was to maintain order and to ensure the comfort of passengers. A person who was one-eighth African American (like Plessy) was considered to be "colored" for purposes of the Louisiana law.

Plessy (and other members of his group who were opposed to the law) made it known to railroad authorities that he was planning to take a ride in one of the "white only" railroad cars. They tipped the authorities off in order to create a "test case" of sorts. Plessy bought his ticket and took his place in a railroad car reserved for the whites. He was ordered by railroad employees to vacate the car. When he refused, they had him arrested and jailed.

He was convicted under the statute and appealed to the Louisiana Supreme Court. The Louisiana Supreme Court upheld his conviction. He then appealed to the U.S. Supreme Court, who agreed to hear his case.

The issues became whether a law that required "separate but equal" public accommodations based on race violated either the **Thirteenth Amendment** (which abolished slavery or badges of slavery) or the **Fourteenth Amendment** (which in addition to mentioning privileges and immunities and requiring due process, requires all states to give people equal protection of law).

Writing for the majority (there was only one dissenter), Justice Brown dismissed the Thirteenth Amendment argument by maintaining that nobody was attempting to make a slave out of Homer Plessy. Slavery was a concept that required involuntary service for no pay and a state of perpetual bondage. The Louisiana law was not trying to turn Plessy into a slave. To rule otherwise "would be running the slavery argument into the ground.... A statute which implies merely a legal distinction between white and colored races ... has no tendency to ... reestablish a state of involuntary servitude." In other words, simply "refusing accommodations to colored people cannot be justly regarded as imposing any badge of slavery or servitude" upon that person.

The Fourteenth Amendment issue (equal protection) seemed to give the Court a little more trouble since it recognized that its purpose was to prevent states (especially those in the South) from persecuting the (then) newly freed slaves by passing onerous laws that would vastly curtail their rights by imposing various hardships. Nevertheless, Justice Brown did not believe that Louisiana's "separate but equal" law rose to the level of an equal protection violation. He wrote that,

> The object of the [Fourteenth A]mendment ... could not have been intended to abolish distinctions based upon color, or to enforce social, as distinguished from political, equality, or a commingling of the two races upon terms unsatisfactory to either. Laws permitting, and even requiring, their separation in places where they are liable to be brought into contact do not necessarily imply the inferiority of either race to the other, and have been generally, if not universally, recognized as within the competency of the state legislatures in the exercise of their police power. The most common instance of this is connected with the establishment of separate schools for white and colored children, which has been held to be a valid exercise of the legislative power.

Justice Brown went on to note that in addition to segregated public schools, laws forbidding intermarriage between whites and blacks also existed and have been "universally recognized as within the police power of the state." He went on to blame the victims by stating that if African Americans wind up feeling stamped with a badge of inferiority due to the forced separation of the races, "it is not by reason of anything found in the act, but solely because the colored race chooses to put that construction on it."

Justice Brown concluded by arguing that you cannot force people to socially accept one another by way of laws and compulsion. "If the two races are to meet upon terms of social equality, it must be the result of natural affinities, a mutual appreciation of each other's merits, and a voluntary consent of individuals."

As noted earlier, there was one dissenter to the majority's opinion, that of Justice Harlan. He wrote a dissent in support of Plessy's equal protection claims that simultaneously somehow managed to show both his progressive and racist attitudes in the very same paragraph. First, he showed the ugly side of his views, followed by a demonstration of rather more noble views when he wrote that,

> The white race deems itself to be the dominant race in this country. And so it is in prestige, in achievements in education, in wealth and in power. So, I doubt not, it will continue to be for all time if it remains true to its great heritage and holds fast to the principles of constitutional liberty. But, in view of the Constitution, in the eye of the law, there is in this country no superior, dominant, ruling class of citizens. There is no caste here. Our Constitution is color-blind, and knows nor tolerates classes among citizens. In respect to civil rights, all citizens are equal before the law. The humblest is the peer of the most powerful. The law regards man as man.

Demonstrating some accurate prophetic foresight, Justice Harlan predicted that the majority's opinion would someday "prove to be quite as pernicious as the decision made by this tribunal in the *Dred Scot Case*." He was proven to be right, but it took some time.

Discussion Questions

1. Why was the Supreme Court clearly wrong when it said that a "separate but equal" philosophy does not imply the inferiority of any race?

2. What do you think of the Supreme Court's assertion that if a racial minority saw "separate but equal" as offensive, it must be due to their own inferiority complex?

3. Why was it doubtful that the United States ever had public accommodations of equally good quality when we had the "separate but equal" policy in effect?

The "separate but equal" doctrine upheld in the *Plessy* decision was eventually overturned 58 long years later in the famous school desegregation case of *Brown v. Board of Education.* By then, it became woefully apparent that there was no such thing as equality of accommodations when the races were segregated by legal mandate. White schools received much more money than did black schools. Black restrooms were vastly inferior to white restrooms, and so on. The philosophy of "separate but equal" defended so "eloquently" by the majority opinion in *Plessy* created two Americas when it came to schools, restrooms, railroad cars, theaters, hotels, public housing, public parks, libraries, and institutions of all kinds. This history made a lie out of the *Plessy* majority's opinion that "separate but equal" could be anything other than a legal contradiction in terms.

We now leave the 1800s and move on to disturbing Supreme Court decisions of the twentieth century. This section will begin with the 1927 case of *Buck v. Bell*, a case that Adolph Hitler, the century's strongest advocate for "purifying" the human race, would have loved. In fact, Nazis prosecuted for war-time atrocities sometimes made reference to this case in defense of their eugenics. In reading this case, ask yourself if it would give some constitutional cover not just to the forced sterilization of the "feeble-minded," but to other "weak" people (career criminals, addicted people, those of lower I.Q., mentally ill people, etc.) as well.

Buck v. Bell
274 U.S. 200 (1927)

Carrie Buck was an eighteen-year-old, allegedly "feeble-minded" woman who had been committed to a Virginia "state colony" for the mentally infirm. Her mother apparently had also been perceived as being "feeble-minded," and had Carrie out of wedlock.

In 1924, the state of Virginia had passed a statute allowing for the forced sexual sterilization of patients of certain mental institutions (including the one where Buck resided) who had been rendered "insane" or "feeble-minded" due to hereditary factors. This operation could be performed upon the recommendation of the mental institution's superintendent, provided that a hearing was first held in which it was verified that that the forced sterilization would be "in the best interests of the patient and of society."

After the evidentiary hearing took place, the institution's board of directors issued the order that Buck be sterilized. Buck and her guardian appealed this decision up through the Supreme Court of Appeals of Virginia, losing all the way. Finally, the case reached the U.S. Supreme Court.

The U.S. Supreme Court ruled 8–1 in favor of the decision to sterilize. Two issues were raised on appeal: (1) Would the forced sterilization violate Buck's due process rights, and (2) Would the forced sterilization violate Buck's right to equal protection?

The famous Justice Oliver Wendell Holmes delivered the opinion for the eight justices in the majority (the sole dissenter wrote no opinion explaining his vote). Justice Holmes first addressed the "due process" argument advanced by Buck. He first noted that the decision to sterilize was only granted after a careful review had been made. But Buck's argument was not based on lack of procedures given her, but rather on the substance of the matter itself: it was her argument that "in no circumstances could such an order be justified" (no matter how much legal process was given to her). She apparently was arguing that the Due Process Clause of the Fourteenth Amendment, when it provides that neither life, liberty, nor property can be taken without due process of law, also "extends to all those limbs and faculties by which life is enjoyed" including the "right of bodily integrity." Justice Holmes agreed that due process would cover such things, however, he felt that "we cannot say as a matter of law that the grounds [for the forced sterilization] do not exist." In ruling the best interest of society indeed supported the sterilization, Holmes noted that,

> We have seen more than once that the public welfare may call upon the best citizens for their lives. It would be strange if it could not call upon those who already sap the strength of the State for these lesser sacrifices ... in order to prevent our being swamped with incompetence. It is better for all the world, if instead of waiting to execute degenerate offspring for crime, or to let them starve for their imbecility, society can prevent those who are manifestly unfit from continuing their kind. The principle that sustains compulsory vaccination is broad enough to cover cutting the Fallopian tubes. Three generations of imbeciles are enough.

Having finished addressing the due process argument, Holmes moved on to discuss Buck's equal protection concerns. He agreed with her that the law, as drafted, only put those who were institutionalized at risk of sterilization, while leaving undisturbed that huge number of people who were "insane" or "feeble-minded" but who lived outside of institutions. Nevertheless, he concluded that the state's resources were limited in addressing the goal of reducing the problem of hereditary mental deficiencies and that "the law does all that is needed when it does all that it can."

Discussion Questions

1. How difficult would it be for society to draw a proper line distinguishing "insane" people who should be sterilized vs. the merely "mentally ill" who should be left alone?

2. What percentage of the American public could be classified today as suffering from some form of serious mental illness? What percentage of Americans would you classify as feeble-minded?

3. Would you feel comfortable having elite judges and scientific experts classify people as too "insane" or too "stupid" to have children?

Justice Holmes' line cited a few paragraphs above, that "three generations of imbeciles are enough," became the most memorable line from this opinion. The concept of **eugenics** (the science of improving the human race through selective mating) had gained a lot of popularity in the U.S. during this era. The decision in *Buck* no doubt gave further legitimacy to the movement. However, eugenics fell into disfavor in mid-century America when people here witnessed its philosophy being strongly embraced by the Nazis. It was used by Hitler to justify mass sterilizations of undesirables getting in his way of creating a "master race." In fact, it was during World War II, specifically in 1942, that the U.S. Supreme Court (in the case of *Skinner v. Oklahoma*) firmly distanced itself from its holding in *Buck*.

While eugenics and sterilizations lost favor since the rulings in these previous two cases, a growing body of literature in biosocial criminology has begun exploring whether criminal traits and behaviors can be inherited. The literature is unanimous in arguing that there is no such thing as a "crime gene"; however, criminal tendencies such as antisocial behavior, violence, and aggression may be heritable (i.e., handed down from generation to generation). Given that this literature argues for the need to look at genetic as well as environmental indicators of criminality, many novices pause because of their fear that this growing body of work harkens back to antiquated ideas about eugenics. On the contrary, this literature argues that we need to explore both nature and nurture in explaining criminal propensities. For those of you interested in these types of studies, see the work of DeLisi, Caspi, Moffitt, Wright, Beaver, or Vaughn (all prominent scholars in biosocial criminology).

The next case we are to consider involves forcing school children against their will to say the Pledge of Allegiance, even when it violates their religion and family teaching to do so. Though the Court held 8 to 1 in favor of the school district, it amazingly changed its mind just three short years later in a similar case when it completely reversed its opinion.

Minersville School District v. Gobitis
310 U.S. 586 (1940)

The Gobitis children, aged twelve and ten, were expelled from their public school in Pennsylvania for refusing to salute the flag and recite the Pledge of Allegiance. Their refusals were based on the fact that they and their parents were Jehovah's Witnesses, and as such, they believed that saluting the flag and reciting the Pledge were forms of idolatry that interfered with their undivided loyalties to God. Nevertheless, the school district had a policy requiring that students participate in these secular rituals and provided for discipline (including expulsion) if they did not. After his children had been expelled from school, Mr. Gobitis filed a lawsuit asking the courts to require readmission of his children to the public schools so that he would not be forced to pay private school tuition. This case wound its way to the Supreme Court.

Writing for the 8-to-1 majority, Justice Frankfurter opined that this was a tough decision to have to make. He agreed that forcing someone, including a child, to violate religious beliefs is ordinarily something the government should never do. However, there were exceptions to every rule. Here, he said, were two competing values: that of the interest of the government to promote "national unity" vs. the religious concerns of the students and their family. A balancing test would have to be employed in which the two competing interests would be weighed.

On balance, it was held that the need for national unity outweighed the religious interests of the children. The Court reasoned, "We are dealing with an interest inferior to none in the hierarchy of legal values. National unity is the basis of national security." The Court went on to say, "The ultimate foundation of a free society is the binding tie of cohesive sentiment.... We live by symbols. The flag is a symbol of our national unity, transcending all internal differences, however large."

The Court also expressed its fear that if schools allowed dissidents to refuse to recite the Pledge of Allegiance, other impressionable young children might get the idea that this was acceptable and join in with the refusal. At least this was a legitimate concern of the school district, and the Court did not feel competent to second-guess the school board when it came to issues of child psychology and pedagogy. To hold otherwise "would in effect make us the school board for the country. That authority has not been given to the Court, nor should we assume it."

In any event, the Court concluded that forcing these two children to participate in secular flag rituals would not do all that much harm anyway. Parental influence and teachings on matters of religion would always weigh more heavily on the minds of children than would any "secular" ceremonies in which the school might compel students to participate.

Justice Stone was the sole dissenter in this case. He agreed that the government might, at times, suppress religious practices that are dangerous to public safety, order, or morals. "But it is a long step ... that government may, as a supposed educational measure and as a means of disciplining the young, compel public affirmations which violate their religious conscience."

Discussion Questions

1. If fostering "national unity" was the goal, in what way was compelling people to say the Pledge of Allegiance against their will probably counter-productive to that goal?

2. How would you respond to the Supreme Court's concern that if all children were not required to recite the Pledge, then other children might get the idea that it is acceptable for them to abstain as well?

The *Minersville School District* case above was overturned by the U.S. Supreme Court just three years later in the case of *West Virginia State Board of Education v. Barnette*, 319 U.S. 624 (1943). Once again, the facts involved Jehovah's Witness school children who were disciplined for refusing to cite the Pledge of Allegiance. This time, the Supreme Court ruled in favor of the Jehovah's Witnesses (in effect, reversing itself). During the three years between the two decisions, America had entered World War II, and there were some new justices on the Court.

Writing for the majority, Justice Jackson, in the slightly more recent *Barnette* case, wrote his now-famous lines:

> If there is any fixed star in our constitutional constellation, it is that no official, high or petty, can prescribe what shall be orthodox in politics, nationalism, or other matters of opinion or force citizens to confess by word or act their faith therein.

The Court concluded by comparing the mandatory saluting of the flag to similar requirements in Nazi Germany and stressed that public schools should not "strangle the free mind at its source."

Now that we are talking about World War II-era cases, we would be remiss if we did not consider the infamous Japanese American internment case of 1944. It seems that war can bring out the best and worst in our society. Emotions can run high.

Korematsu v. United States
323 U.S. 214 (1944)

Fred Toyosaburo Korematsu, a U.S. citizen whose parents were born in Japan, was himself born and raised in the United States. He was residing in California during World War II when President Roosevelt issued an executive order empowering military authorities to establish zones within the United States in which aliens and Americans of Japanese descent could be excluded from living due to national security concerns. The commanding general of the U.S. Army's Western Command designated the West Coast as one such zone. The fear was that people of Japanese heritage on the West Coast might be in a position to engage in acts of espionage or sabotage should the Japanese seek to invade. It should be noted that Korematsu's personal loyalty to the United States was never directly contested. It should also be noted that the executive order that targeted aliens and Americans of Japanese descent did not also target Americans of German or Italian descent, even though the United States was at war with Germany and Italy, as well as Japan.

Korematsu was ordered to leave his residence and be reassigned to a Japanese American **internment camp** (a sort of non-punitive detention facility). Korematsu ignored the order to leave and continued to reside in his California home. He was subsequently convicted of a federal law that made it a misdemeanor (punishable by up to one year of imprisonment) to knowingly enter or remain in any military zone affected by such an order. He appealed his conviction to the U.S. Court of Appeals, but his conviction was affirmed. He then appealed to the U.S. Supreme Court.

The issue before the Supreme Court was whether or not this presidential order (backed by Congress as well) exceeded the government's war powers when it restricted the rights of Japanese Americans to live where they wished. In a 6–3 decision, the Supreme Court sided with the government and ruled that the order was constitutional.

Writing for the majority, Justice Black held that "we are unable to conclude that it was beyond the war power of Congress and the Executive to exclude those of Japanese ancestry from the West Coast war area at the time they did" in that "exclusion from a threatened area has a definite and close relationship to the prevention of espionage and sabotage." The Court admitted that "all legal restrictions which curtail the civil rights of a single racial group are immediately suspect." But it also noted, "That is not to say that all such restrictions are unconstitutional. It is to say that courts must subject them to the most rigid scrutiny." Even after subjecting the race-based executive order to its utmost "rigid scrutiny," the Court still favored the government when it went on to say that:

> we cannot reject as unfounded the judgment of the military authorities and of Congress that there were disloyal members of that population, whose number and strength could not be precisely and quickly ascertained. We cannot say that the war-making branches of the Government did not have ground for believing that in a critical hour such persons could not readily be isolated and separately dealt with, and constituted a menace to the national defense and safety which demanded that prompt and adequate measures be taken to guard against it.

The Court upheld the exclusion order even though it was "not unmindful of the hardships imposed by it upon a large group of American citizens. But hardships are part of war.... Citizenship has its responsibilities as well as its privileges, and in time of war the burden is always heavier." In addition, it opined that since the West Coast was so dangerously "threatened by hostile forces" that "the power to protect must be commensurate with the threatened danger." The justices also noted that even though many, if not most, Japanese Americans no doubt remain loyal to the United States, Japanese Americans nevertheless posed a higher risk than Americans of other nationalities. "That there were members of the group who retained loyalties to Japan has been confirmed by investigations made subsequent to the exclusion. Approximately five thousand American citizens of Japanese ancestry refused to swear unqualified allegiance to the United States and to renounce allegiance to the Japanese Emperor, and several thousand evacuees requested expatriation to Japan." Since there is no way to ascertain quickly who is loyal and who is not, the order was a constitutionally sound war power.

In his concurring opinion, Justice Frankfurter wrote that this order excluding Japanese Americans from certain regions of the country had to be considered in the "context of war." He suggested that both the Supreme Court and the military have different types of constitutional duties to perform during war and that military orders that might be "lawless" in peacetime could make sense in the context of war.

Justices Roberts, Murphy, and Jackson all filed separate dissenting opinions. Justice Roberts wrote that Korematsu was denied due process of law in being forced to "submit to illegal imprisonment." Justice Murphy wrote, "Being an obvious racial discrimination, the order deprives all those within its scope of the equal protection of the laws as guaranteed by the Fifth Amendment.... In excommunicating them without benefit of hearings, this order also deprives them of all their constitutional right to procedural due process ... mainly upon questionable racial and sociological grounds.... Under our system of law individual guilt is the sole basis for deprivation of rights." Finally, Justice Jackson, in his own dissent, wrote, "Now, if any fundamental assumption underlies our system, it is that guilt is personal and not inheritable.... But here is an attempt to make an otherwise innocent act a crime merely because this prisoner is the son of parents as to whom he had no choice, and belongs to a race from which there is no way to resign."

It should be noted that in the 2018 case of *Trump v. Hawaii* all nine justices of the Supreme Court repudiated the *Korematsu* precedent. The majority wrote, "*Korematsu* was gravely wrong the day it was decided, has been overruled in the court of history, and—to be clear—has no place in law under the Constitution." The dissenters, while worried the majority was making the same mistake regarding the so-called "Muslim Ban" advanced by the Trump Administration, agreed "[t]his formal repudiation of a shameful precedent is laudable and long overdue."

Discussion Questions

1. Why do you suppose the Supreme Court saw Japanese Americans so vastly differently than German Americans during World War II? Was this distinction fair?

2. What do you suppose that Justice Murphy (in his dissent) meant when he said that placing Japanese Americans in internment camps was like "excommunicating them"?

3. What lesson can we learn from this episode with regards to how we might fail to properly protect constitutional rights during future periods of extreme national stress?

Our chapter concludes with a case from 1986. It deals with the criminalization of gay sex (not gay marriage, but gay sex). This Supreme Court case was overturned by the same court just a mere decade and a half after it was decided in the famous case of *Lawrence v. Texas*.

Bowers v. Hardwick
478 U.S. 186 (1986)

After Michael Hardwick failed to appear for court to answer for a public drinking charge, a warrant was issued for his arrest. A few days later, police officers went to his home to serve the warrant and were invited in by Hardwick's roommate, who had been sleeping on the couch. After lawfully entering the home, the officers were told by Hardwick's roommate that Hardwick was in a back bedroom. Officers walked to the bedroom and saw through the open bedroom door that Hardwick was having sex with another man. Hardwick was arrested for violating Georgia's statute prohibiting "sodomy," (basically, the legislature's term at the time for gay sex).

The prosecutor assigned to the case wound up dropping the charges, but Hardwick was not satisfied and went on to sue the state of Georgia (specifically Bowers, its attorney general) in an effort to obtain a court ruling declaring Georgia's sodomy statute to be unconstitutional. Hardwick's position was that as a practicing homosexual, he was at risk of being arrested at any moment as long as the "sodomy" statute remained on the books undisturbed.

Hardwick lost his case in the U.S. District Court, but won it on appeal to the U.S. Court of Appeals. Georgia then petitioned the U.S. Supreme Court that agreed to hear the matter. The issue in the case, according to Justice White writing for the 5–4 majority, was "whether the Federal Constitution confers a fundamental right upon homosexuals to engage in sodomy" and thus any state laws to the contrary must be struck down. The Court ruled that the U.S. Constitution guaranteed no such right.

Of course, the U.S. Constitution does not even bring up the specific subject of homosexuals or their rights. Justice White, however, said that this omission, in and of itself, would not pose an insurmountable barrier to finding a constitutional right to gay sex. He noted that the Court in the past had many times found "fundamental liberties" not specifically mentioned in the Constitution that would find protection under the Fourteenth Amendment's guarantee of "due process." The Fourteenth Amendment states that before a state could take away someone's "life, liberty, or property," it must first provide "due process of law." The list of what constitutes "liberty" is left for the courts to decide. It is conceivable that gay sex is part of liberty. Furthermore, some liberties, in the Court's view as outlined in many past decisions, can be deemed to be so huge that they constitute not just a liberty, but a "fundamental liberty." (A **fundamental liberty** is one that is so basic that no amount of procedure could take it away. In other words, despite the Fourteenth Amendment's literal reading that seems to suggest that any liberty can be taken if enough due process is given, some human freedoms are so important that they can never be taken away, no matter how many hearings or other legal process is provided. This is now known as the **substantive due process doctrine**.) So, the question became whether or not gay sex is one of the "fundamental liberties" that essentially cannot be taken away.

In answering this question, Justice White identified the Court's omnipresent worry in this area of "fundamental rights" jurisprudence that constitutional interpretation "involves much more than the imposition of the Justices' own choice of value." Otherwise, the public would lose respect and confidence in the Court's decisions, seeing them as mere power plays. So, the Court in the past had always followed one of **two "fundamental rights" determination tests**: The first test asked whether the liberty in question was one of those rights "implicit in the concept of ordered liberty such that neither liberty nor justice would exist if they were sacrificed." The other test asked whether the right was one of "those liberties that are deeply rooted in the Nation's history and tradition."

Justice White wrote, "it is obvious to us that neither of these formulations would extend a fundamental right to homosexuals to engage in acts of consensual sodomy." This was because "proscriptions against that conduct have ancient roots.... Sodomy was a criminal offense at common law, and was forbidden by the laws of the original 13 States.... In fact, until 1961 all 50 States outlawed sodomy, and today, 24 States and the District Columbia" continue to do so. Given all of this, "to claim that a right to engage in such conduct is 'deeply rooted in this Nation's history and tradition' or 'implicit in the concept of ordered liberty' is, at best, facetious."

Justice White noted that Hardwick's attorneys argued that the fact that the sexual actions had taken place in one's home should make a difference. After all, they said, "If the First Amendment means anything, it means that the State has no business telling a man, sitting alone in his house, what books he may read or what films he may watch" (trying to build a case for privacy by citing language from the *Stanley* case). But Justice White rejected such an argument by noting that though "*Stanley* did protect conduct that would not have been protected outside the home" it did not stand for the proposition that all crimes are protected merely because they occur at home. Otherwise, "Victimless crimes, such as the possession and use of illegal drugs," would escape punishment simply by being performed in the home.

As to Hardwick's assertion that sex between two consenting adults should be given some sort of fundamental privacy protection, the Court expressed concern about how difficult it would be "to limit the claimed right to homosexual conduct while leaving exposed to prosecution adultery, incest, and other sexual crimes.... We are not willing to start down that road."

Hardwick had argued that even if gay sex between consenting adults in the home was not deemed to be a "fundamental liberty," it still nevertheless was a "liberty" at some level, and a state still had to use a "rational basis test" for even this **non-fundamental liberty** to be denied. Justice White agreed that this was the current state of Supreme Court jurisprudence. However, Justice White did find a "rational basis" for the Georgia sodomy statute. He disagreed with Hardwick's argument that religious or private morality could not be the foundation for a "rational basis" finding under secular law. Rather, he wrote, "The law ... is constantly based on notions of morality, and if all laws representing essentially moral choices are to be invalidated under the Due Process Clause, the courts will be very busy indeed."

In a concurring opinion, Justice Burger agreed with the majority's holding, but wanted to give his angle on things. He opined, "To hold that the act of homosexual sodomy is somehow protected as a fundamental right would be to cast aside millennia of moral teaching."

Four justices dissented from the ruling. Justice Blackman, in his dissent, wrote that the majority of justices displayed an "almost obsessive focus on homosexual activity." He further opined, "only the most willful blindness could obscure the fact that sexual intimacy is a sensitive, key relationship of human existence, central to family life, community welfare, and the development of human personality" (quoting from a former Supreme Court decision in another matter). Justice Stevens, in a separate written dissent, wrote, "[T]he fact that the governing majority in a State has traditionally viewed a particular practice as immoral is not a sufficient reason for upholding a law prohibiting the practice; neither history nor tradition could save a law prohibiting miscegenation [marriage between two people of different races] from constitutional attack." He also thought it was very insightful that even the prosecutor in this very case had no interest in pressing criminal charges despite strong evidence of "guilt" and that indeed the law had remained unenforced for decades.

Hardwick v. Bowers was overturned just 17 years later in the 2003 case of *Lawrence v. Texas* (539 U.S. 558). In reaching its decision, the Court wrote that reliance in the former case on history and tradition was misplaced because of the "emerging awareness" in the past half-century that private sex between consenting adults was purely the private business of those consenting. It went on to also note that the European High Court had recognized the right to gay sex and had struck down laws to the contrary. It further noted that even though laws criminalizing gay sex could still be found in the statute books of some states, such laws were almost never enforced. Given these points, it was apparent to the Court that *Bowers* had been "wrongfully decided" and that gay sex was indeed part of privacy that in turn is part of fundamental liberty. (In his dissent in *Lawrence*, Justice Scalia expressed his concern that this decision recognizing gay sex as a fundamental right must inevitably lead to the Court's ultimate recognition of a constitutional right to gay marriage, despite protestations to the contrary. In fact, in later years, gay marriage supporters ironically pointed to their adversary Scalia's reasoning within his dissent in *Lawrence* as "support" for their gay marriage advocacy.)

Discussion Questions

1. Do you think that a person can believe that gay sex is wrong for religious or other personal reasons while simultaneously believing that there is a constitutional right to engage in it if someone wants to do so?

2. In your opinion, was the Supreme Court correct in 2015 when it ruled (in the case of *Obergefell v. Hodges*) that there is there a fundamental right not only to gay sex but also to gay marriage?

3. Going forward, how do you think that courts should go about identifying what constitutes a "fundamental right" when the right is not specifically mentioned in the Constitution? Do the old tests for determining what constitutes a "fundamental right" still work?

This completes our chapter on "botched justice." What very late twentieth century or early twenty first century cases, if any, will eventually be considered by future Americans to clearly constitute "botched justice"? We will have to wait and see. Do you have some ideas already? Which decided cases, if any, are still controversial and might one day be overturned?

This chapter also completes our book. Despite some rogue cases of "botched justice," the U.S. Constitution (particularly in its first ten amendments, plus its fourteenth) seems to survive in the American psyche as a solid repository of criminal justice ethics.

Chapter Key Terms

Conquest doctrine
Diversity jurisdiction
Animus
Slaves of the state
Hands off doctrine
Civilly dead
Separate but equal doctrine
Thirteenth Amendment
Fourteenth Amendment

Eugenics
Internment camp
Fundamental liberty
Substantive due process doctrine
Two "fundamental rights" determination tests
Non-fundamental liberty

Index